Maxime Ballesteros

Les Absents

HATJE CANTZ

SANG BLEU

EDITOR/ÉDITRICE
Nadine Barth

EXECUTIVE PRODUCTION/
PRODUCTION ÉXÉCUTIVE
Sang Bleu Publishing, London

ART DIRECTION/DIRECTION ARTISTIQUE
B.A.M., London

TYPEFACE/CARACTÈRES
Suisse Works, NewParis Skyline
by Swiss Typefaces

PRODUCTION/FABRICATION
Heidrun Zimmermann, Hatje Cantz

PAPER/PAPIER
Profisilk 150 g/qm, MultiOffset 140 g/qm

BINDING/FAÇONNAGE
Conzella Verlagsbuchbinderei,
Urban Meister GmbH,
Aschheim-Dornach bei München

PRINTED BY/IMPRIMÉ PAR
F&W Druck- und Mediencenter GmbH,
Kienberg

PUBLISHED BY/PUBLIÉ PAR
Hatje Cantz Verlag GmbH
Mommsenstraße 27
10629 Berlin
Germany
Tel. +49 30 3464678-00
Fax +49 30 3464678-29
www.hatjecantz.com

A Ganske Publishing Group Company
Une entreprise du groupe d'édition Ganske

This book was published in collaboaration
with Sang Bleu Publishing,
29b Dalston Lane, London E8 3DF
United Kingdom
info@sangbleu.com
www.sangbleu.com

Hatje Cantz books are available internationally
at selected bookstores. For more information
about our distribution partners, please visit
our website at *www.hatjecantz.com*

Les livres publiés par Hatje Cantz sont
disponibles dans le monde entier dans
les bonnes librairies. Pour tous les
renseignements plus généraux, visitez
notre site internet *www.hatjecantz.com*

ISBN: 978-3-7757-4356-3
Printed in Germany

CAROLINE GAIMARI

Maxime is someone who lives to take pictures—which would be a worrying wager if he wasn't so good at it. His pictures underline the existence of subjective reality. We could be in the same place, at what I would describe as a "boring" party, and days later, when the proof of the party had adequately sat bathed in dye couplers and rehalogenising bleach, I would be confronted with the possibility of a somewhat parallel universe: there was another party happening in that same exact place and time. We had in fact been together in a place of unprecedented sexual freedom and earthly delight, I just hadn't had the eyes (or the will) to see the beauty in it at the time. Maxime has the gift of bringing out in people a love of the moment that has been cast aside in our modern age. The photos that he takes aren't in the realm of slapstick: the instant, easy gratification of a social media cookie reward. Maxime is a hunter, locked and loaded, waiting—hidden in plain sight—for the exact moment to take the shot, when the aim is precise, and his subject is blissfully unaware of his presence.

And despite being mostly hidden, Maxime intimately connects with his subjects. This, of course, is not really "news"—he is a photographer, and intimate connection with one's subject is arguably the most important tool in that trade. The specificity of Maxime's connection, however, is that his subject may be, for example, a pair of heels, the bearer of whom being most often completely unaware of the intimate connection happening in her (or his) southern hemisphere. It's a sort of futuristic virtual reality, where objects and places express their feelings and emotions through Maxime's lens.

And to be one of his human subjects—what a lucky place to play! All of these flexible daredevils are so coolly sexually confident! And the young men so brazenly, innocently nude. He is not a voyeur, this is reportage of youthful sexual empowerment and ownership. He proves with ease that it's not just the eyes that are the window to the soul; pairs of crossed legs find themselves in conversation and arched torsos express an unprecedented language of the body.

In Maxime's world, the esoteric comes across as downright banal, and the banal is made striking. Quirkiness is made beautiful, nudity is made commonplace. Not only could we wish to experience the same debaucherous festivities as Maxime, what a delight it must be just to walk down the street seeing through his eyes!

JOHN ISAACS

there is also a nomadic non place, a homeless fugitive which mirrors the other, a fleeting movement in which the unperceived can find its breath, there is magic, alchemy, vibrating forms alive to the possible, the impossible, pissing against the wall, the wind, howling, crying, laughing, flying, stumbling, stripping bare that which shame dictates is nude, stunting the feeble growth hormone of limbs destined to climb yet withered in the daylight vampire curse of spent big mac wrappers, tossing coins into the broken sewer, walking with bears, with angels, with comets, to swim once more in the pool of narcissus, to rescue time from the twilight of an untrustworthy memory, for this is the moment worlds collide, and the flying sparks of this collision are life, are the only moments, and as such the only tools we have against death, are the only way we elevate ourselves beyond the democratically elected funeral parlor of the everyday

THANK YOU

I would like to thank with all my heart all of the people featured in this book. The real ones as well as the fictional. And: Jen Gilpin, Maxime Büchi, Holger Liebs & Nadine Barth, the B.A.M. team, the Sang Bleu team, Caroline Gaimari, John Isaacs, Olivier Zahm, Jörg Koch, Johann König, Ricarda Messner, Camille Abbate, Marylène Ballesteros, Fred and Fred, Jon, Flore & Benjo, Jet Foto.
Maxime Ballesteros

FOR J.

Maybe it's a book about fear.
Fear of death and its contrary. Fear of
desire. Fear of love.
Fear
of the truth. Of reality.
A primal fear, almost ancestral. Which was born with your first breath,
and will only leave you, finally, at your last.

But we don't do books about fear. So it should be about something else.
Is it not for your vertigo, that you strive to climb trees, buildings, cranes or rocks;
only to lean over once too far from the ground,
and contemplate at the void,
melting under your feet?

POUR J.

Peut-être est-ce un livre sur la peur. La peur de la mort
et son contraire. La peur du désir. La peur de l'amour. La peur de la vérité. De la réalité.
Une peur primaire, presque ancestral. Qui vivrait depuis ton premier souffle.
Et qui ne te quitterait,
enfin, qu'a ton dernier.

Mais on ne fait de livre sur la peur. Alors ça devrait être autre chose.
N'est-ce pas justement depuis que tu as le vertige, que tu t'efforces à grimper
arbres,
immeubles, grues ou roches; seulement pour pourvoir,
un fois trop loin du sol, te pencher
et bien regarder le vide,
Se défaire sous tes pieds?

009 — 046

Battles

2005 The worst was to come but
obviously, no one suspected it
the barbecue had to be taken care of.

2005 Le pire était à venir mais
évidemment personne de s'en doutait,
il fallait bien s'occuper du barbecue.

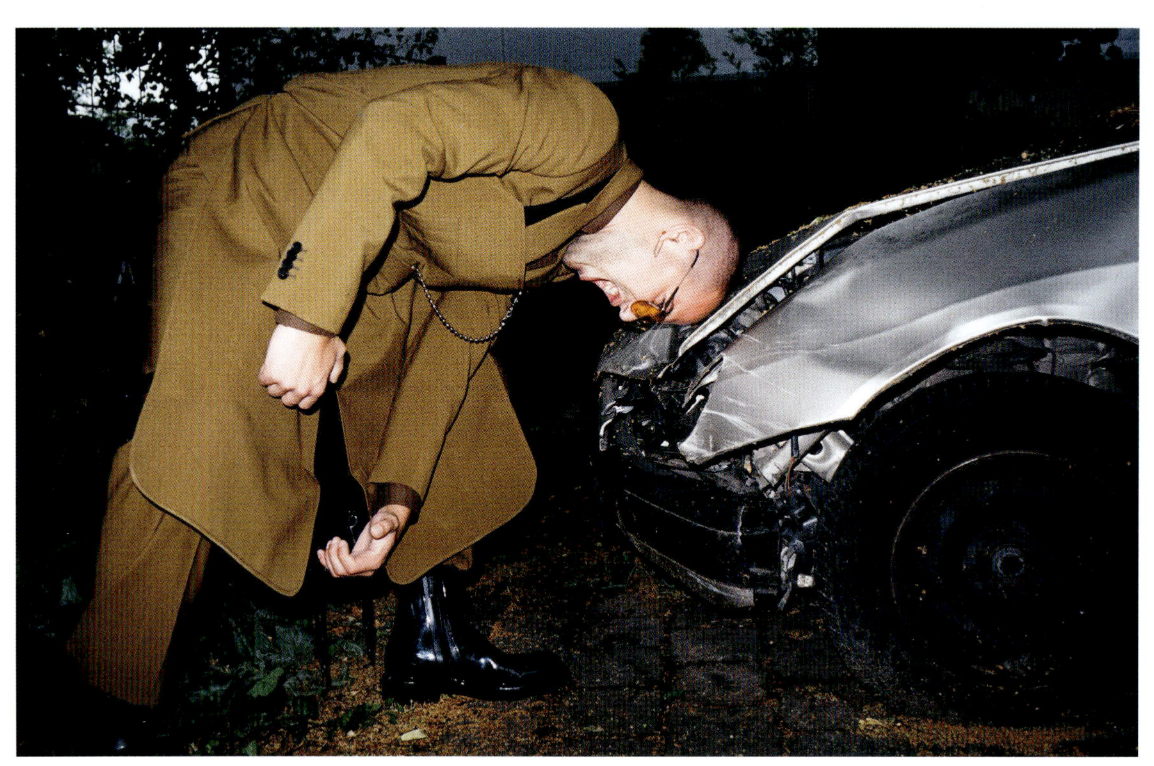

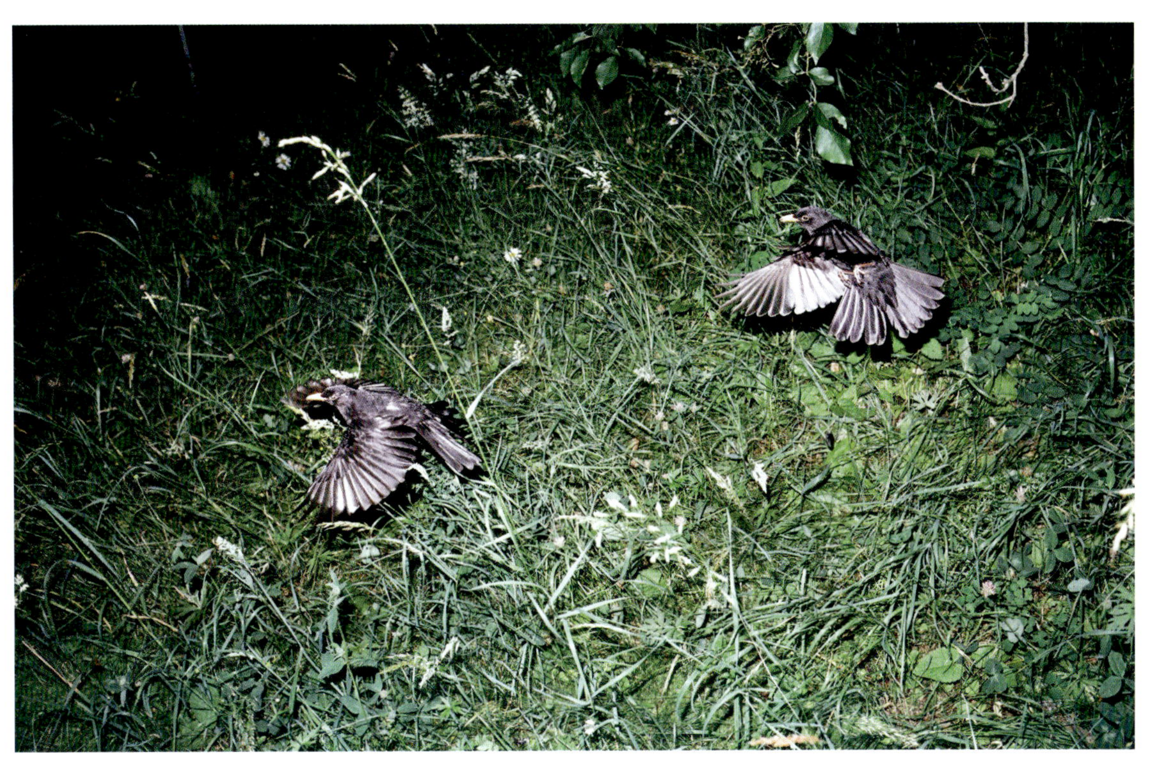

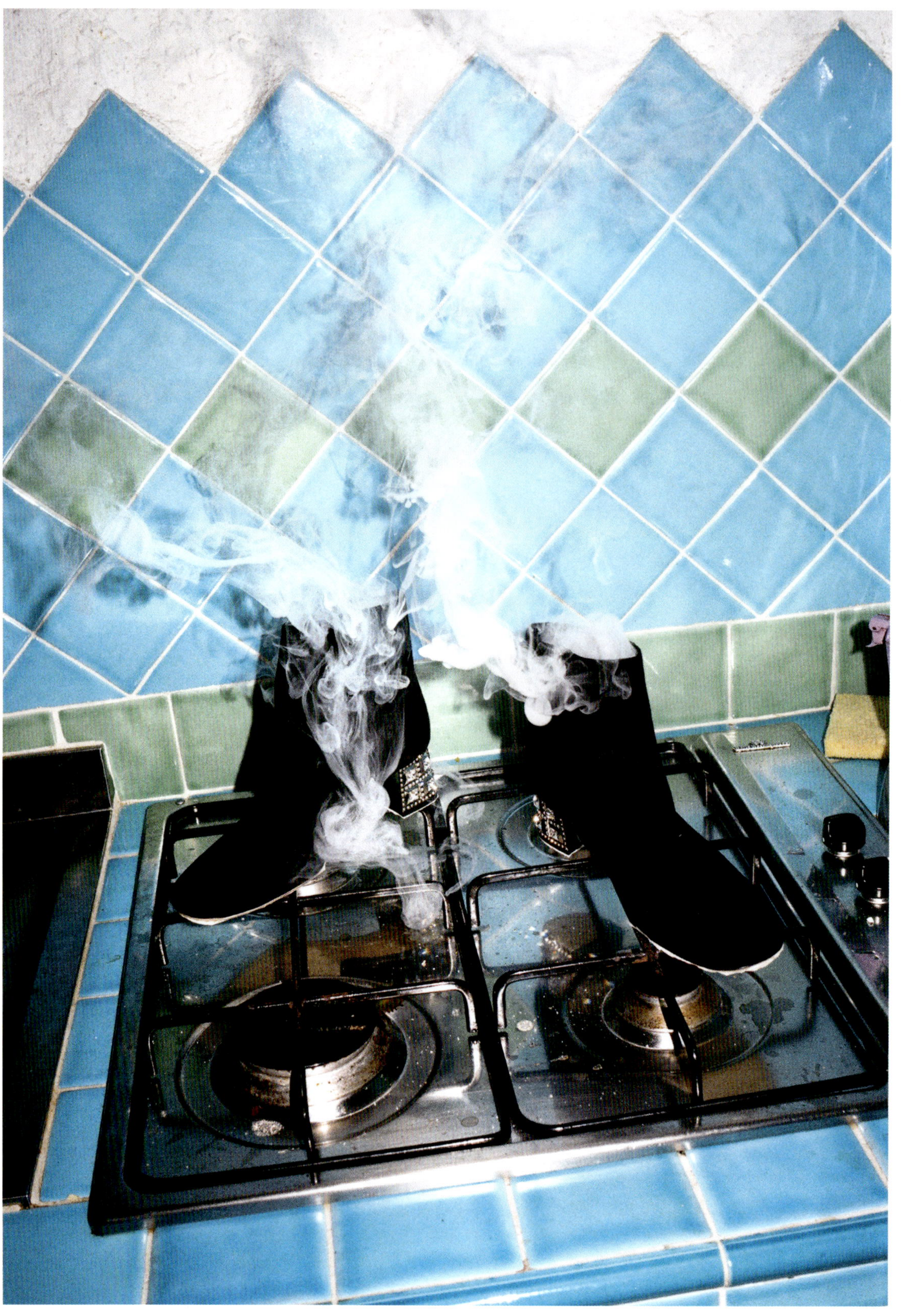

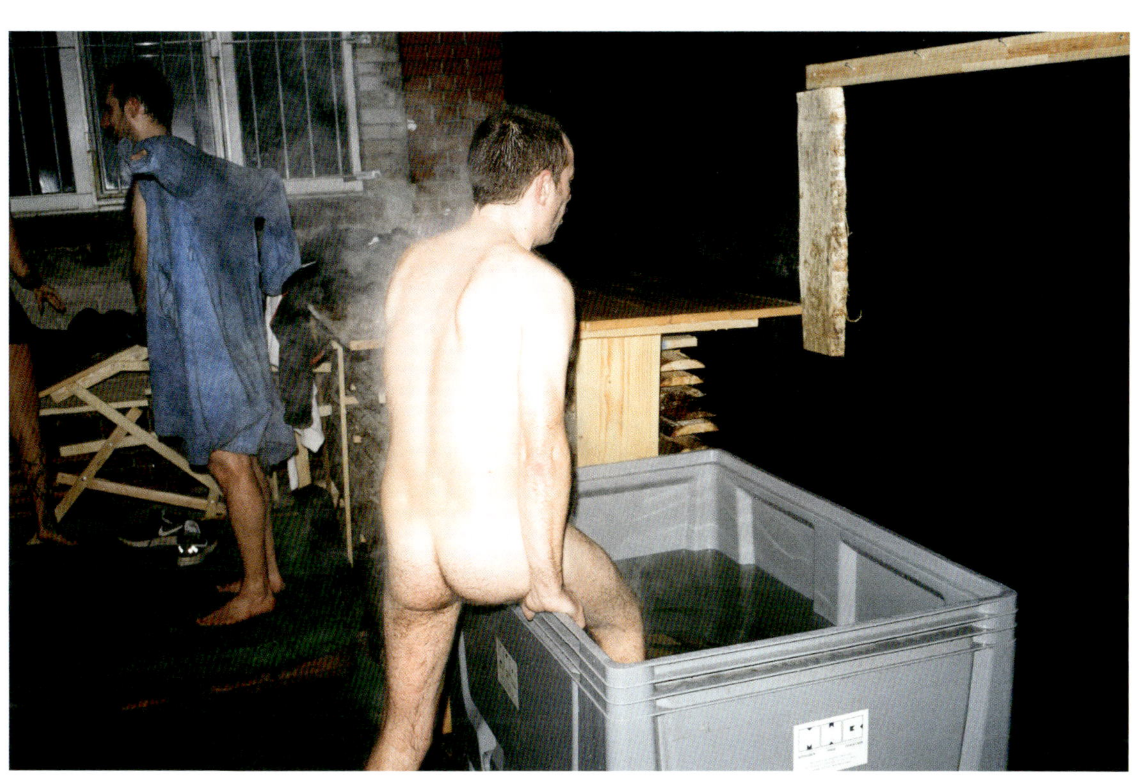

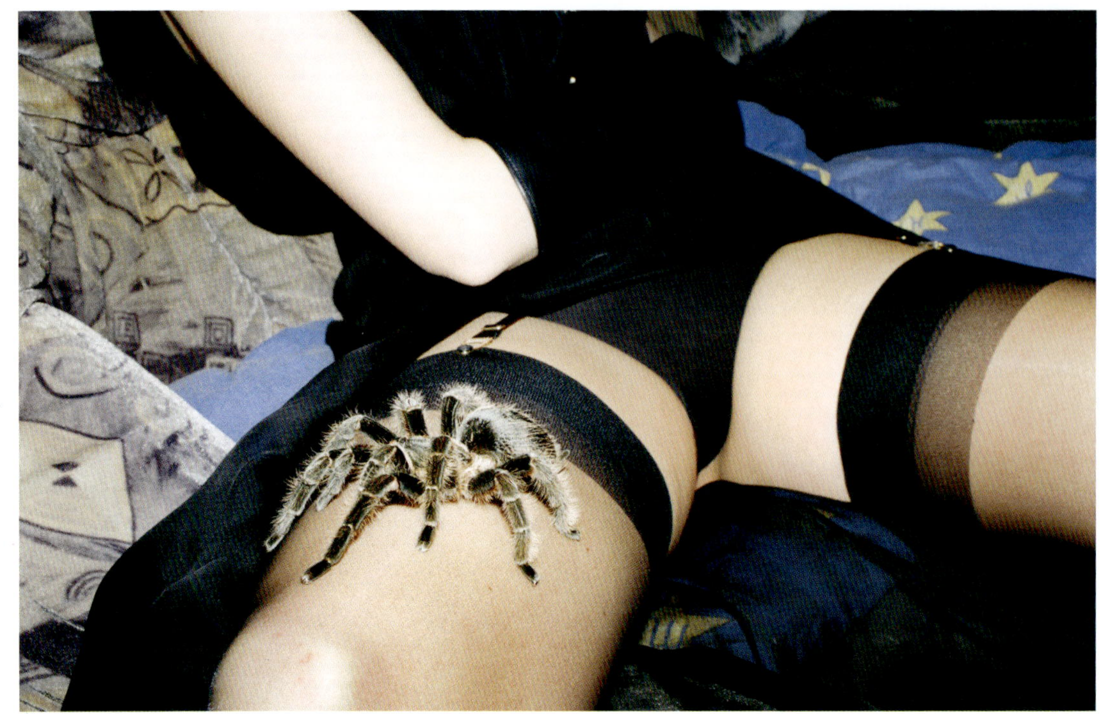

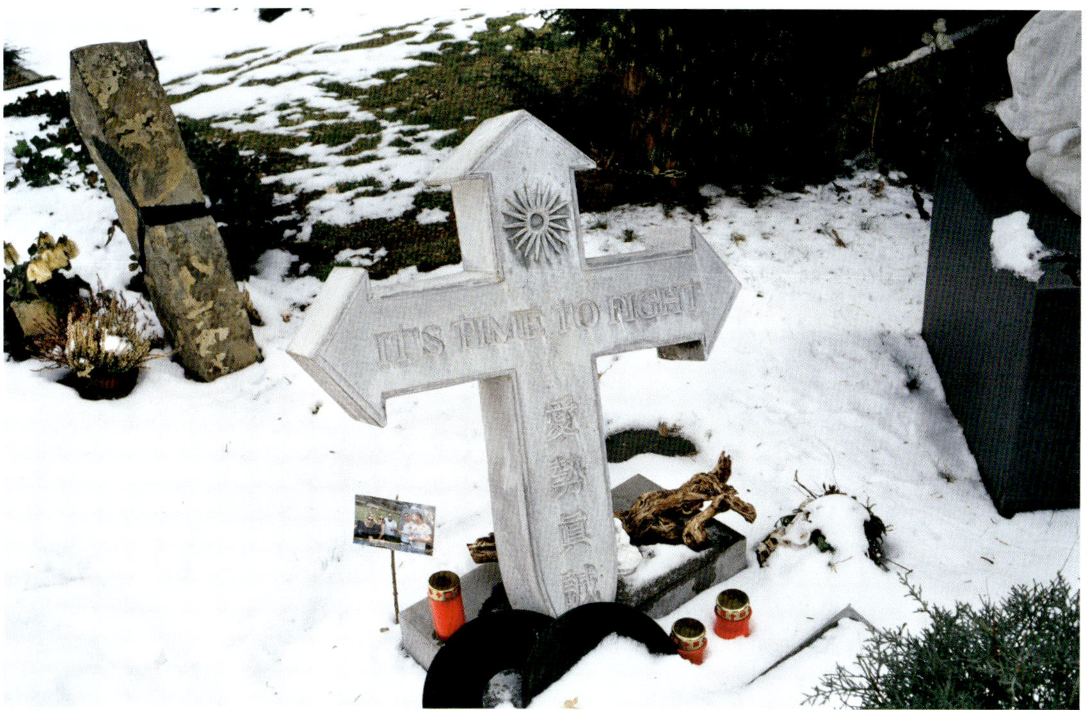

2004 You will never get better.
You will never be okay.
The happiest days and nights inevitably preface the saddest. You swell with happiness, and the next day feel like you've been pierced in the belly.
Nothing splashes. It pours slowly on you.
Why are you so vulnerable?
You will not get better because you lose yourself at every turn. You will not get better because you expect nothing. You expect nothing from life. And your absolute lack of ambition has already buried you alive. You are awfully short of endurance.
You wander quietly in the incredible mess that serves as your head, and apartment.
You know your internal clock by heart.
You should make a schedule for your depressions.
So you might manage the rest of your time better.

2004 Tu n'iras jamais mieux.
Tu n'iras jamais bien.
Les jours et les nuits les plus heureuses annoncent inévitablement les plus tristes.
Tu te gonfles de bonheur, et le lendemain tu es comme percé au ventre.
Rien ne gicle. Ça coule lentement sur toi.
Pourquoi es-tu si vulnérable?
Tu n'iras pas mieux car tu te perds à tous les étages. Tu n'iras pas mieux car tu n'attends rien. Tu n'attends rien de la vie. Et ton manque absolu d'ambition t'a déjà enterré vivant. Tu manques cruellement d'endurance.
Tu erres doucement dans l'incroyable bordel qui te sert de tête, et d'appartement.
Tu connais ton horloge interne par cœur.
Tu pourrais faire un planning de tes dépressions.
Ainsi tu utiliserais peut-être un peu mieux le reste de ton temps.

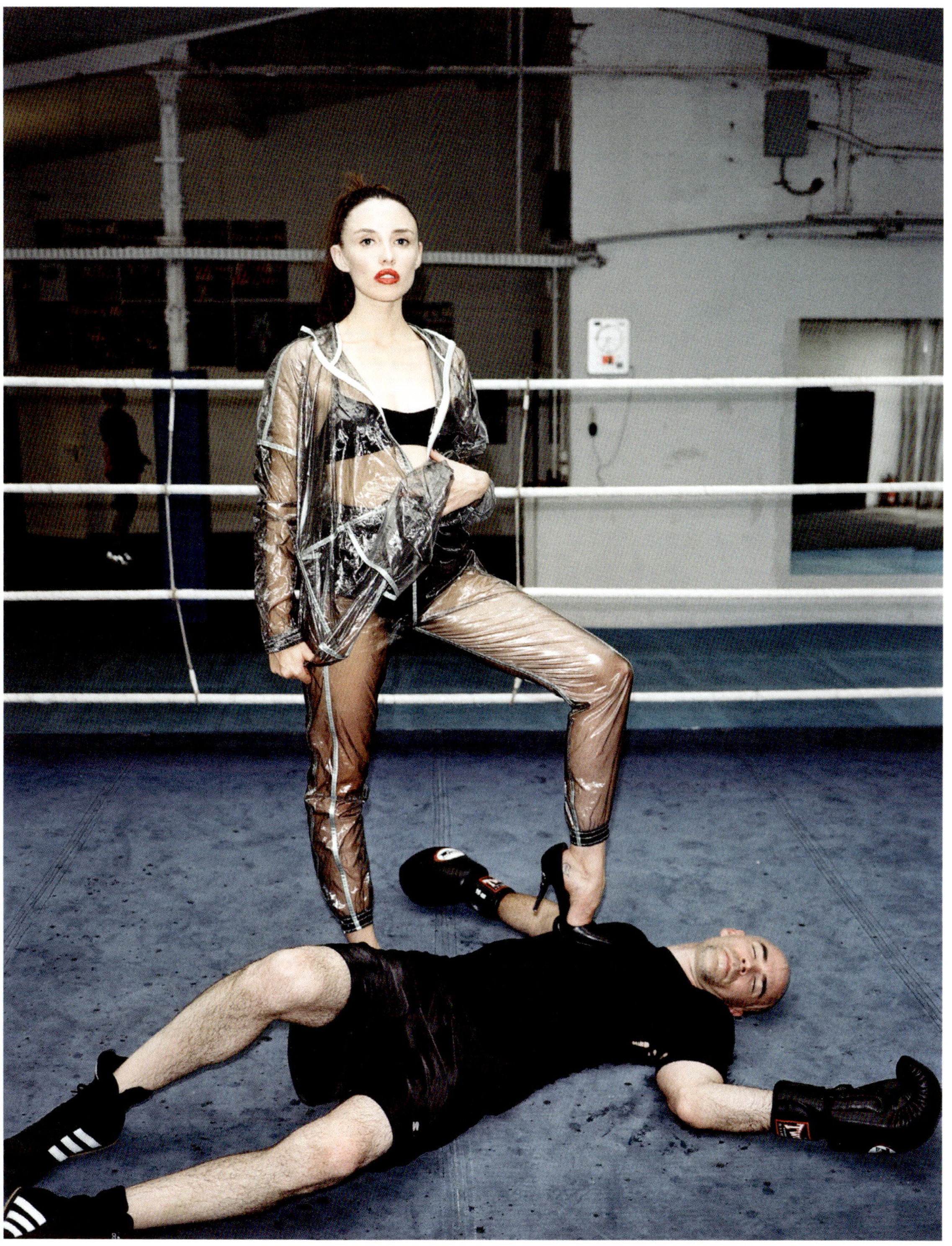

love at first sight, Berlin, 2016

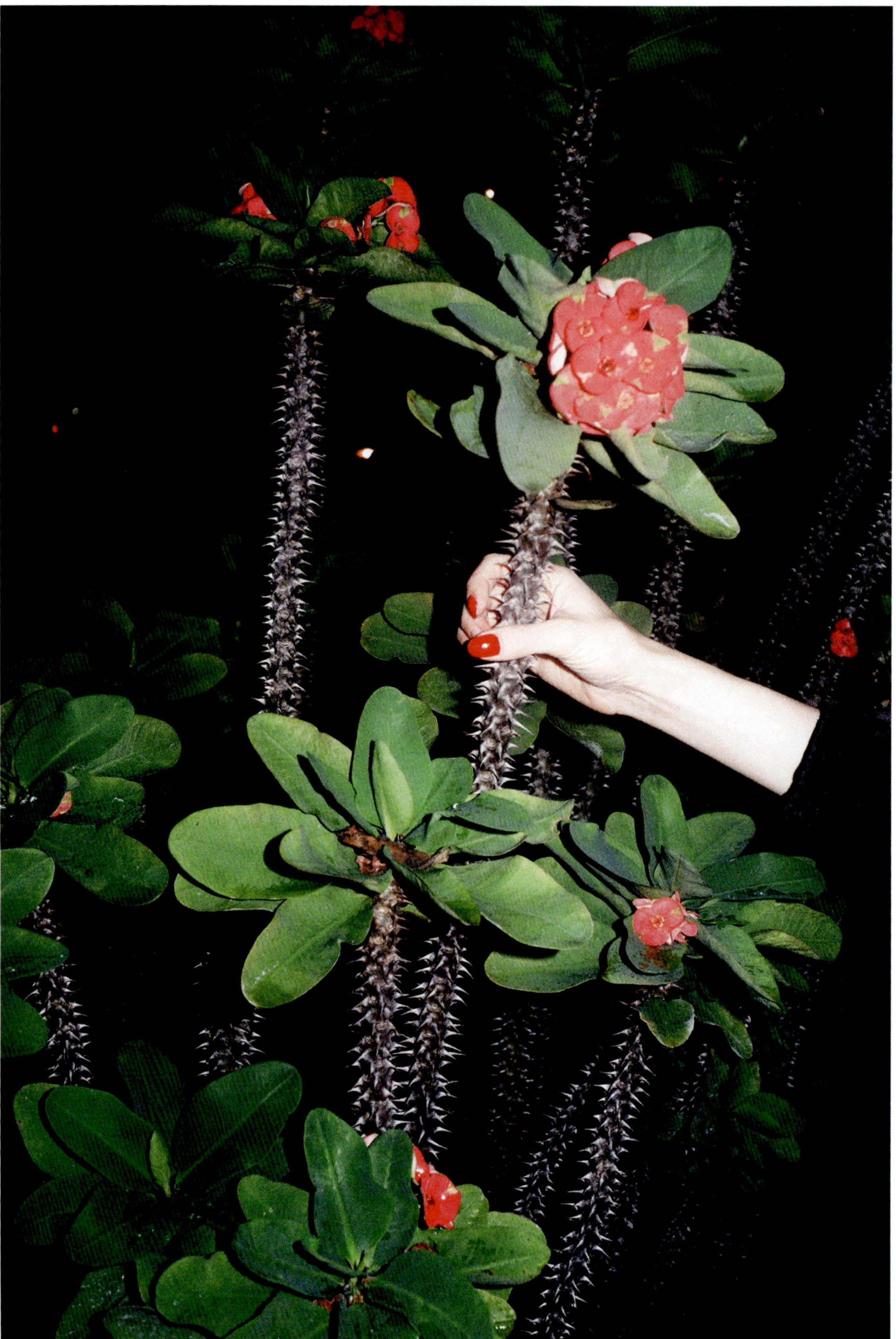

2016 I've never been to Miami, Florida.
It seems gigantic, but I would only be introduced to a tiny portion of it.
Walking up and down Mid and South Beach,
crossing the bay to Wynwood or Downtown.
The buses and sidewalks seem empty, and the streets full
of pick-up trucks in a rush and Lamborghinis slowing down.
The smell of gasoline in the heat fights against
the salty breeze of the ocean.
The air-conditioned world of the inside contrasts amazingly with the reality of the outside.
The luxurious hotels stand still in the heat, the rain and the strongest wind.
We can look at the waves raging on the beach from a balcony with a glass of exquisite
whisky, forgetting about the sounds of the V12 purring in circles behind, on Collins Ave.
We take an elevator down below, scrub our eyes from the sand kicking
in our faces, bewitched by the warmth and suddenly sublime taste of the
wind, a paper bag from the liquor store in my hands.
I'm amazed by the the surrealism of the multicolor papier-mâché like
architecture, that stands so high, and somehow so still on the grey asphalt.
So much that one could easily forget about the oil spills on the
tar, invisible from the beachfront terrace of a 37th floor.
It almost feels like parallel worlds that would have been shaken up
and forced into a little glass soda bottle.
At dusk, as if cooling down with the humid air, the streets would start smiling,
the aggressive and incessant honks be replaced by a melody of high heels clicking
and bypassers' conversations, punctuated with laughter transported by the wind.
The artificial lights would cover up the cracks of the not-so-old facades,
and the eyes would adapt to the moonlight brushing the beach.

Running from black-tie parties to dive bars, to a psychedelic tour bus to empty wooden
cabins on the beach, we try to inhale as much smells as a sleepless night will allow us.
And I fall asleep with a smile, under a light blanket.
It's freezing and I don't know how to stop the air conditioning,
but I wrap myself in the warm feeling that those we shared our
night with have left inside of me.

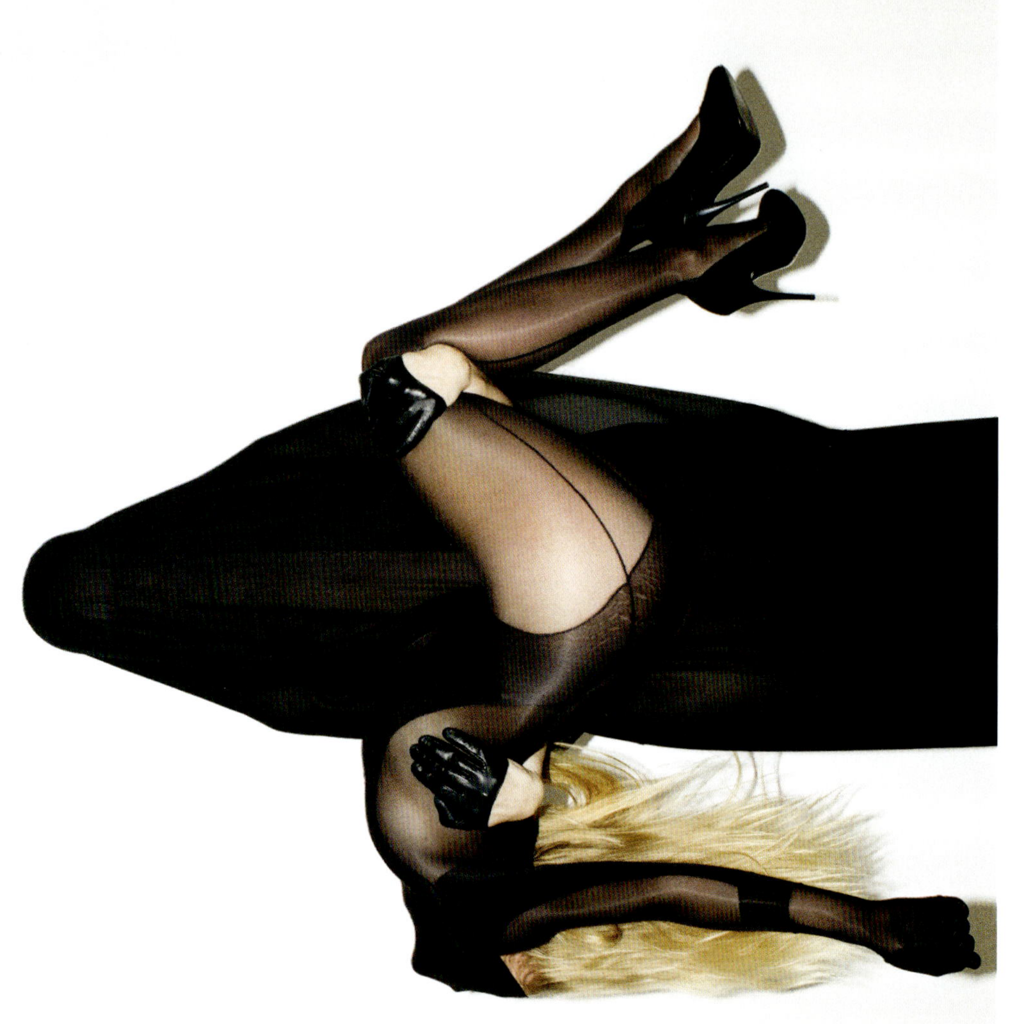

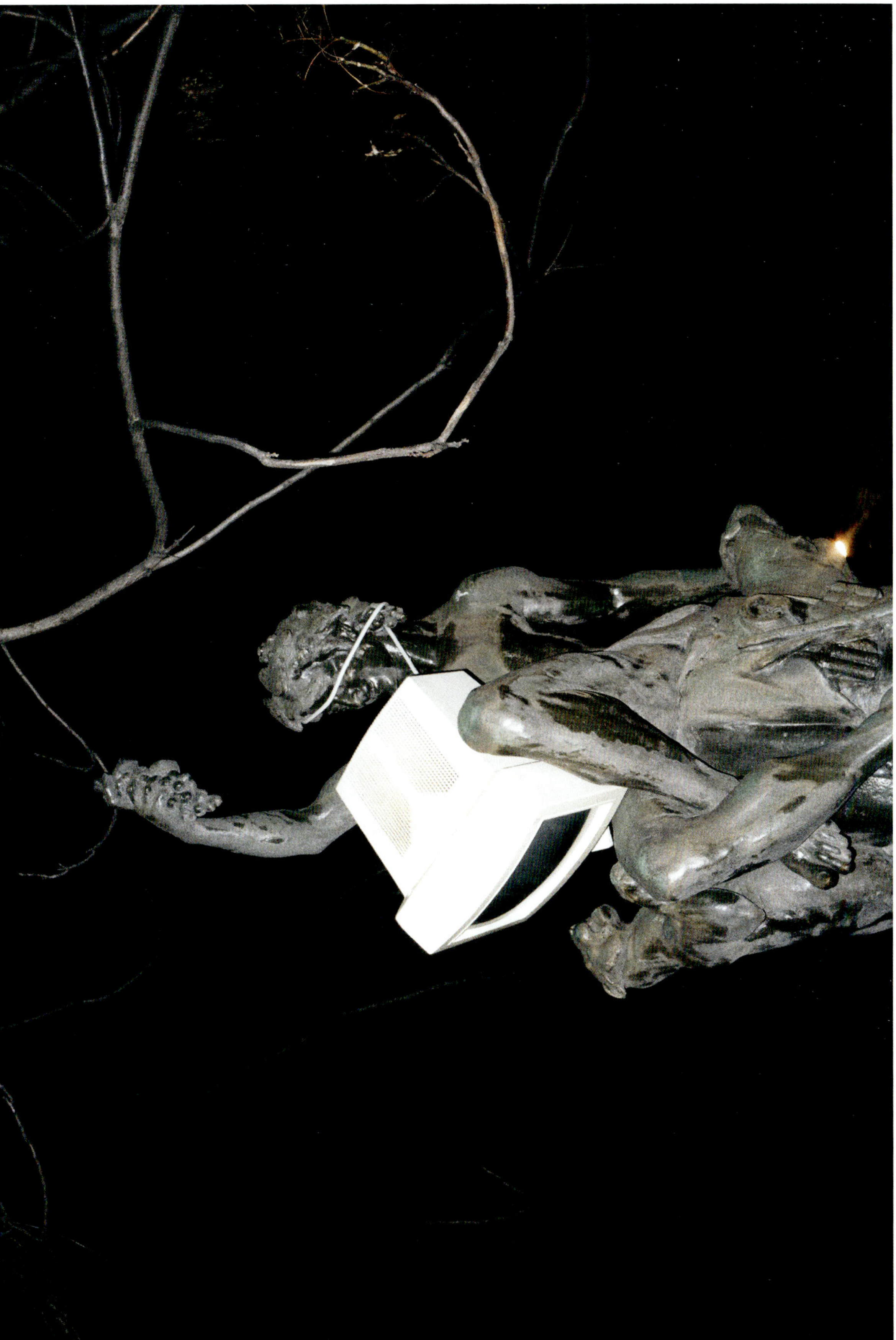

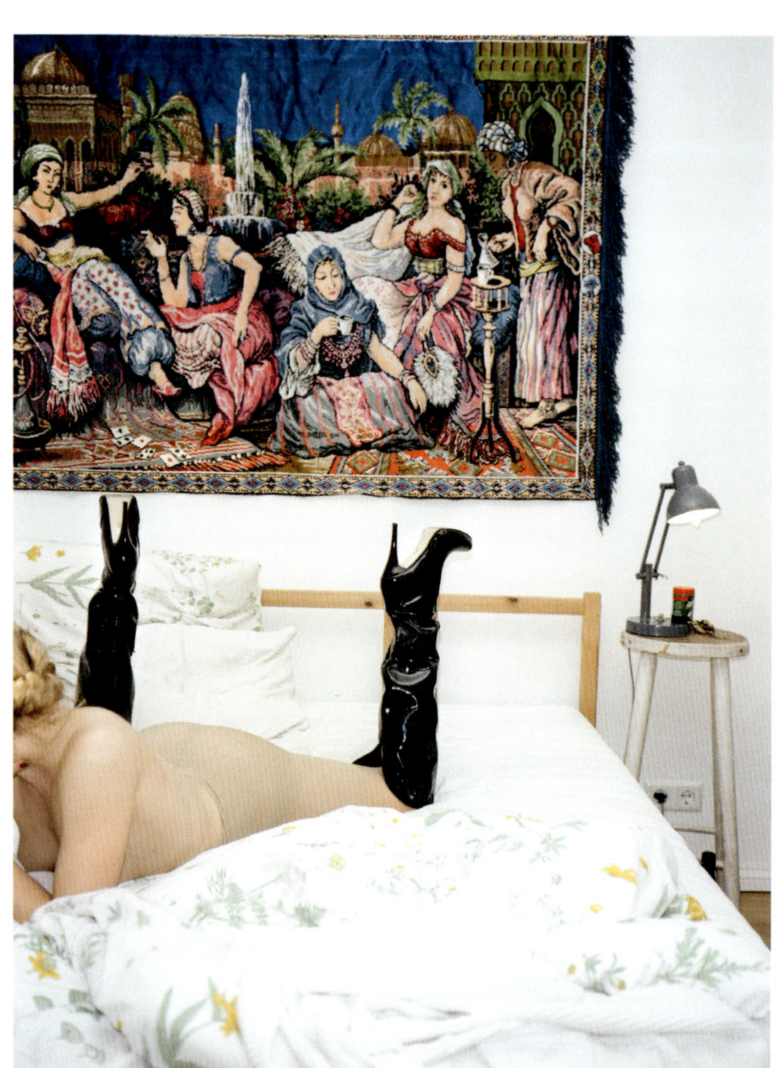

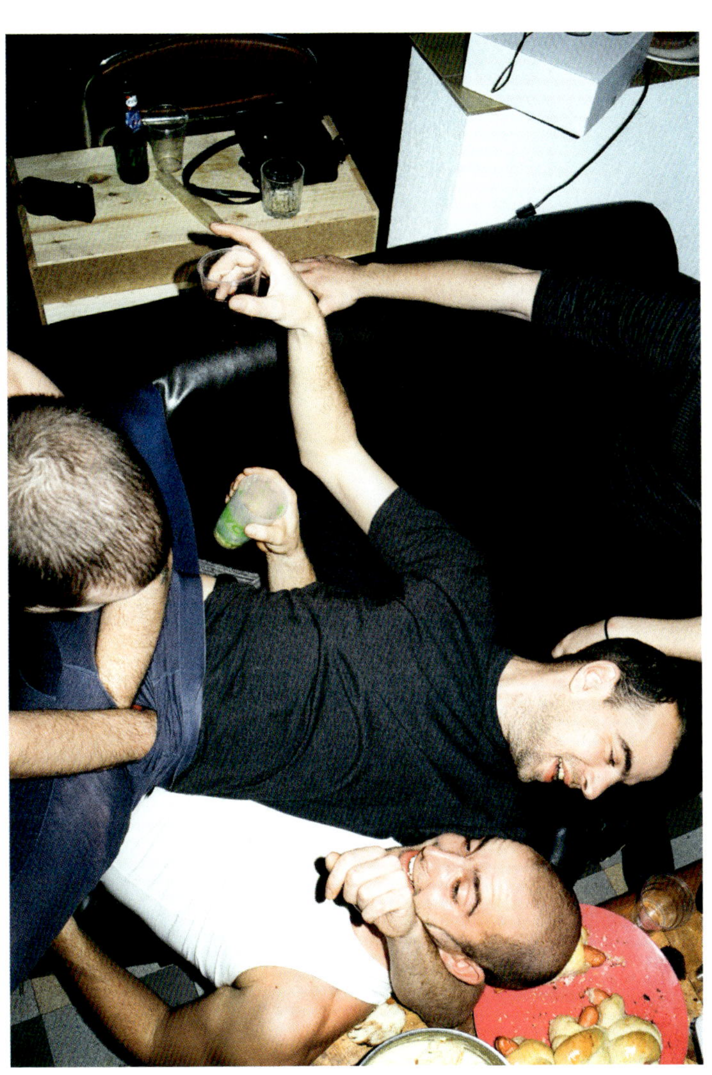

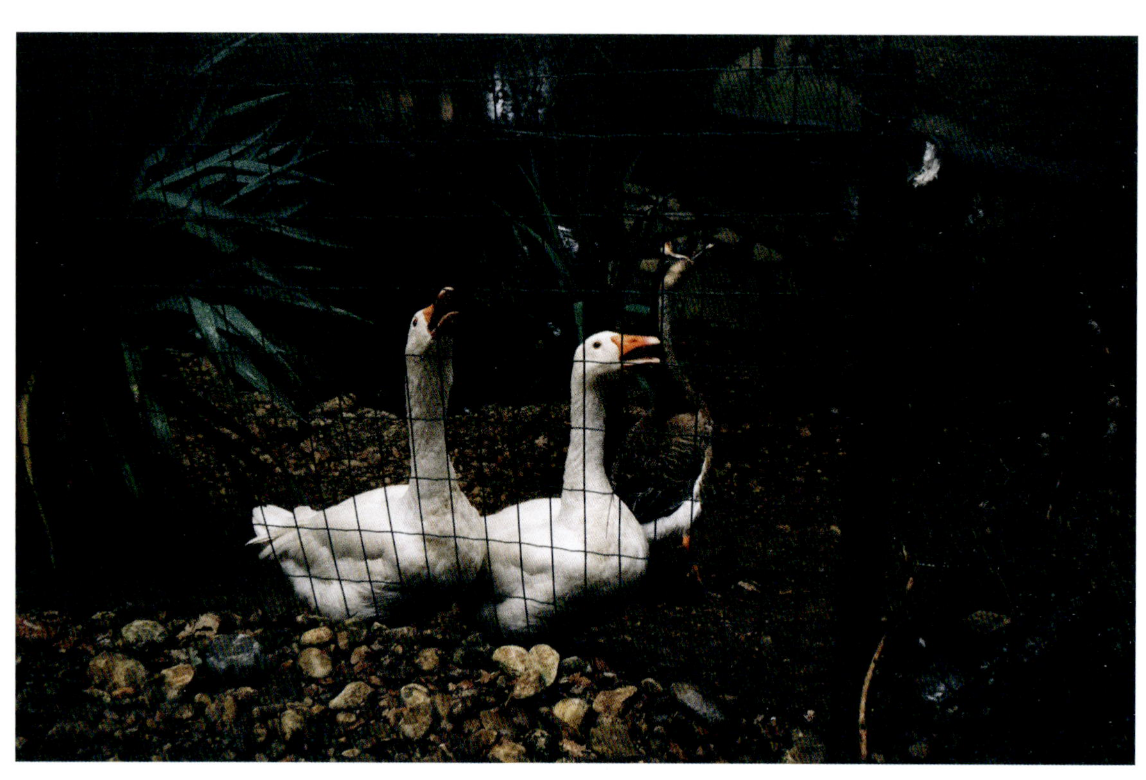

opera, Haute Provence, 2016

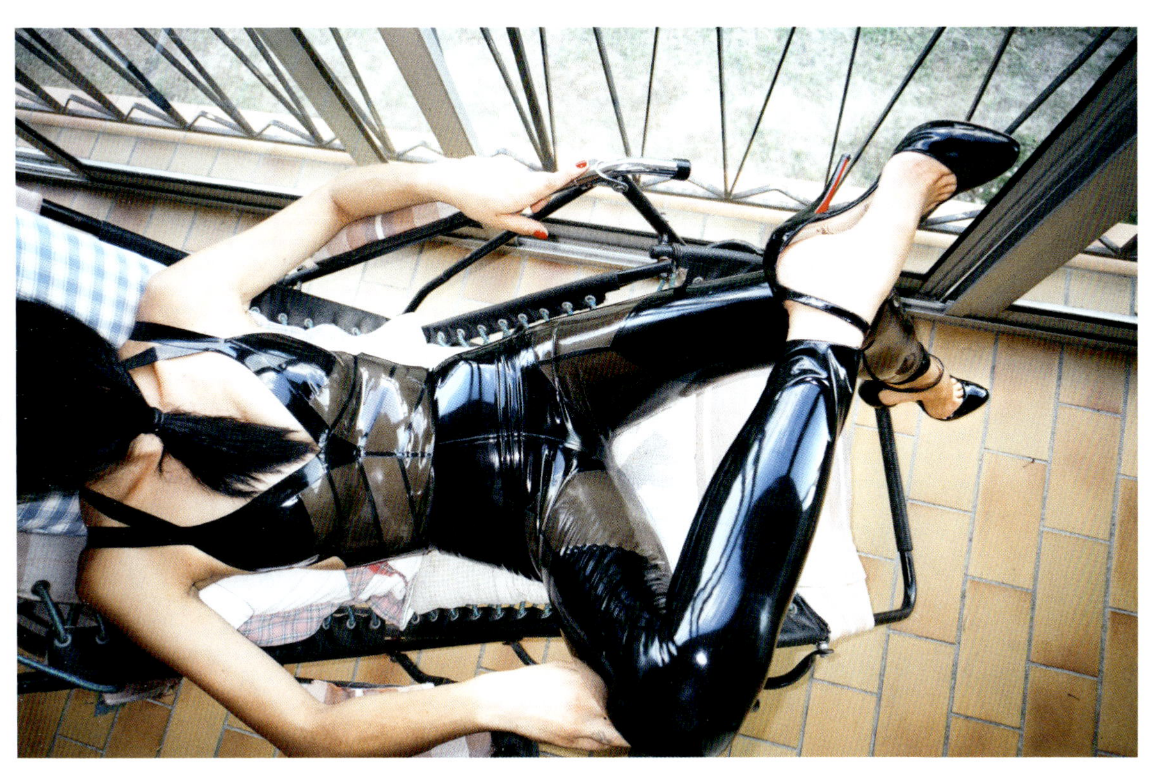

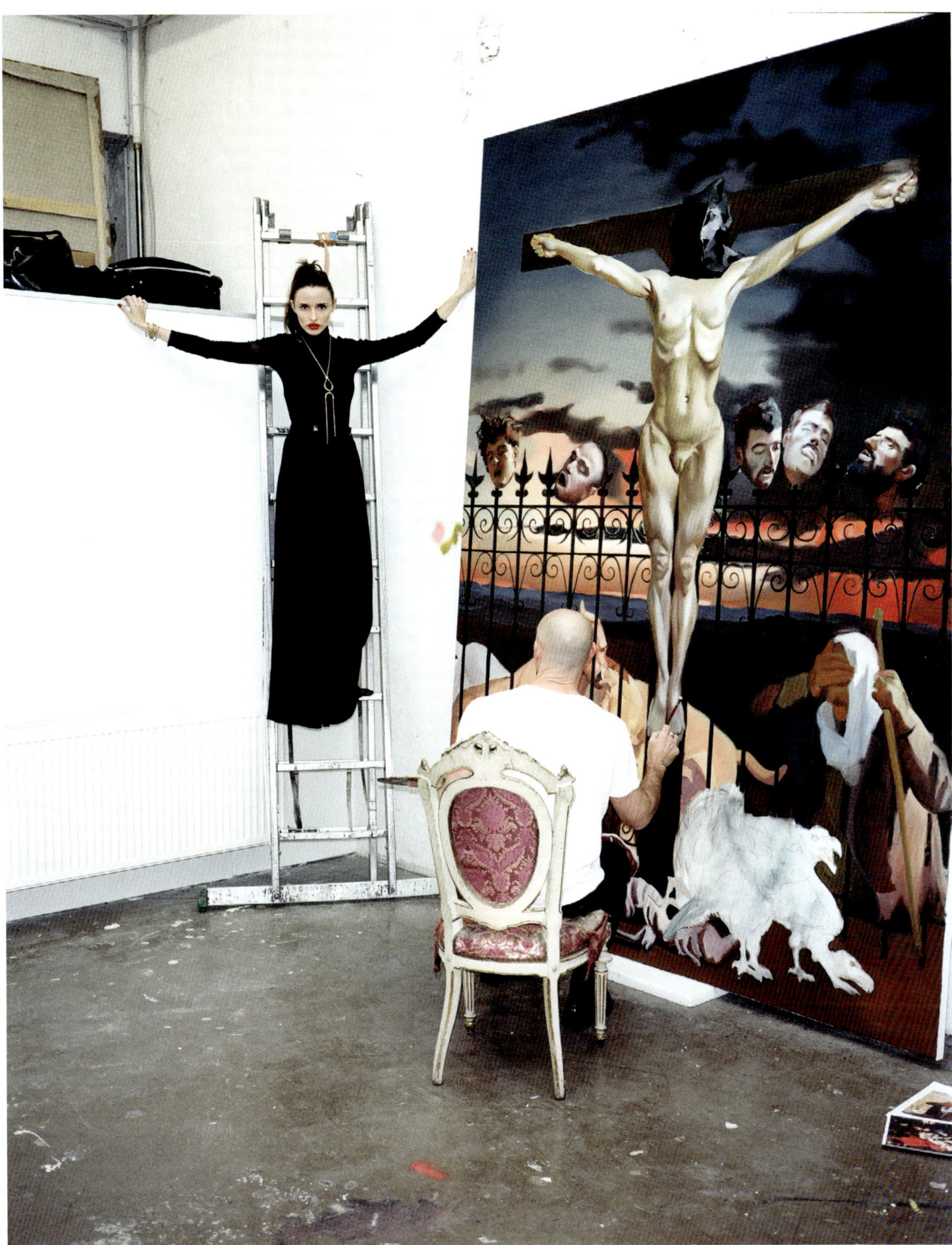

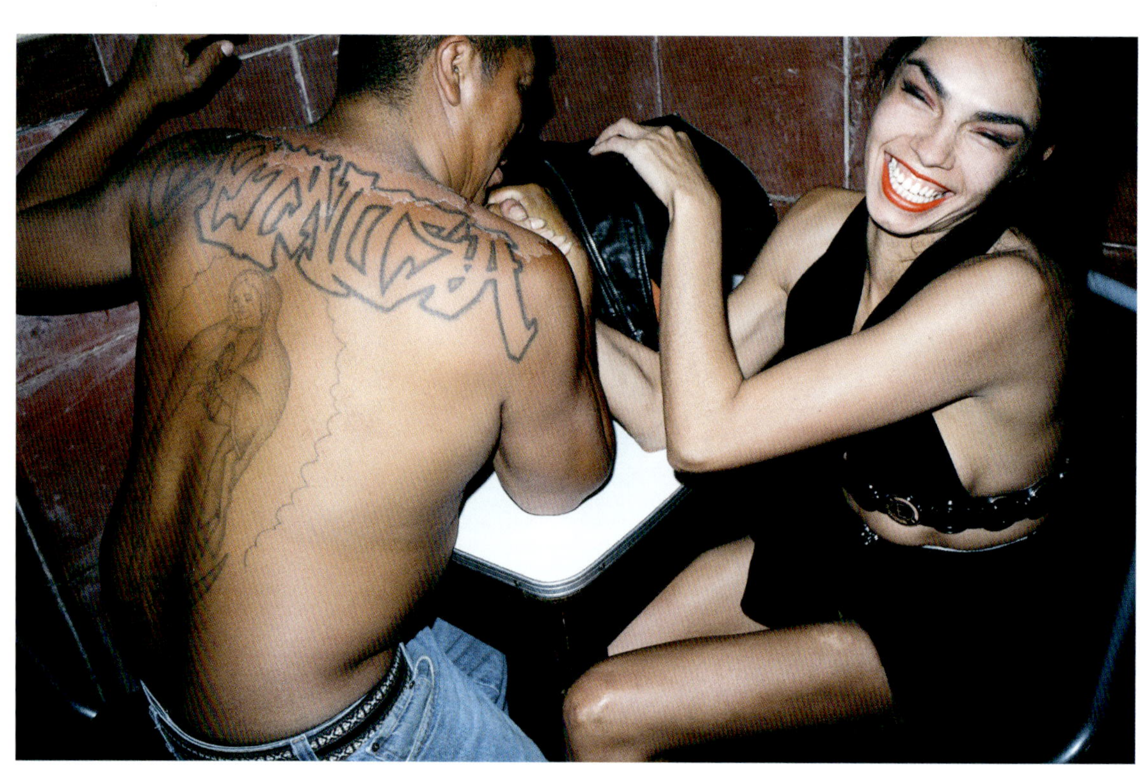

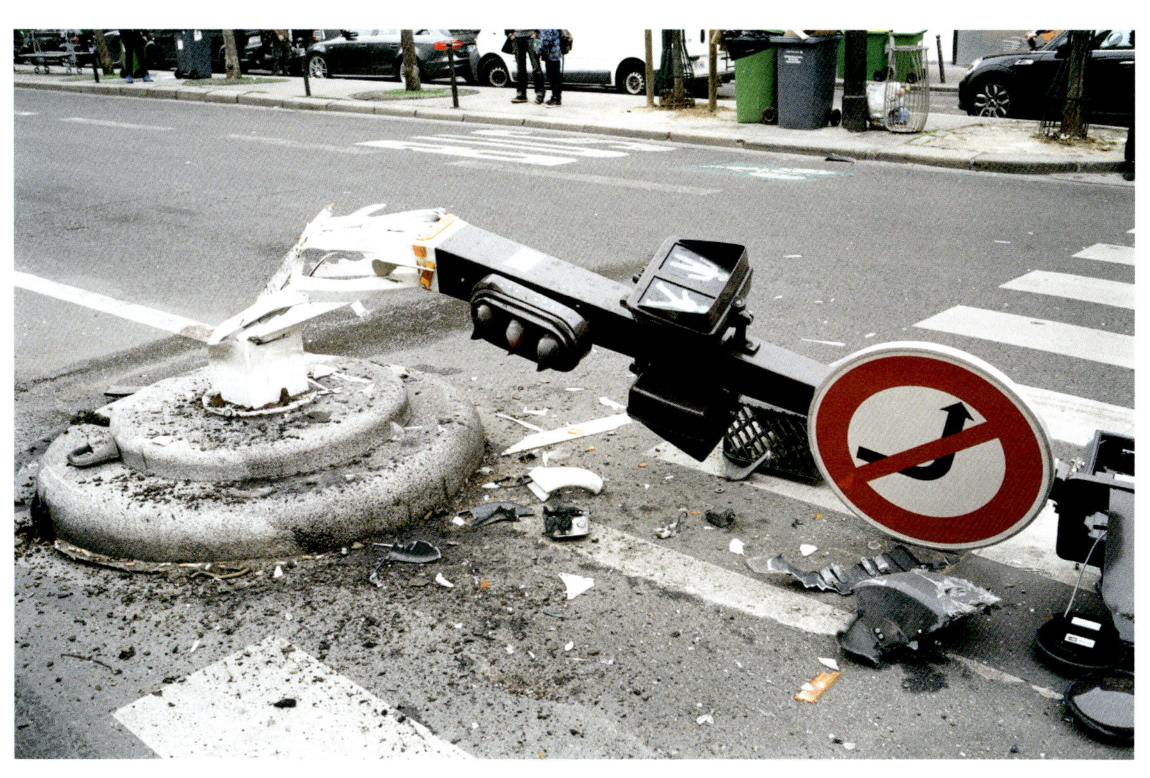

wrong turn, Paris, 2015

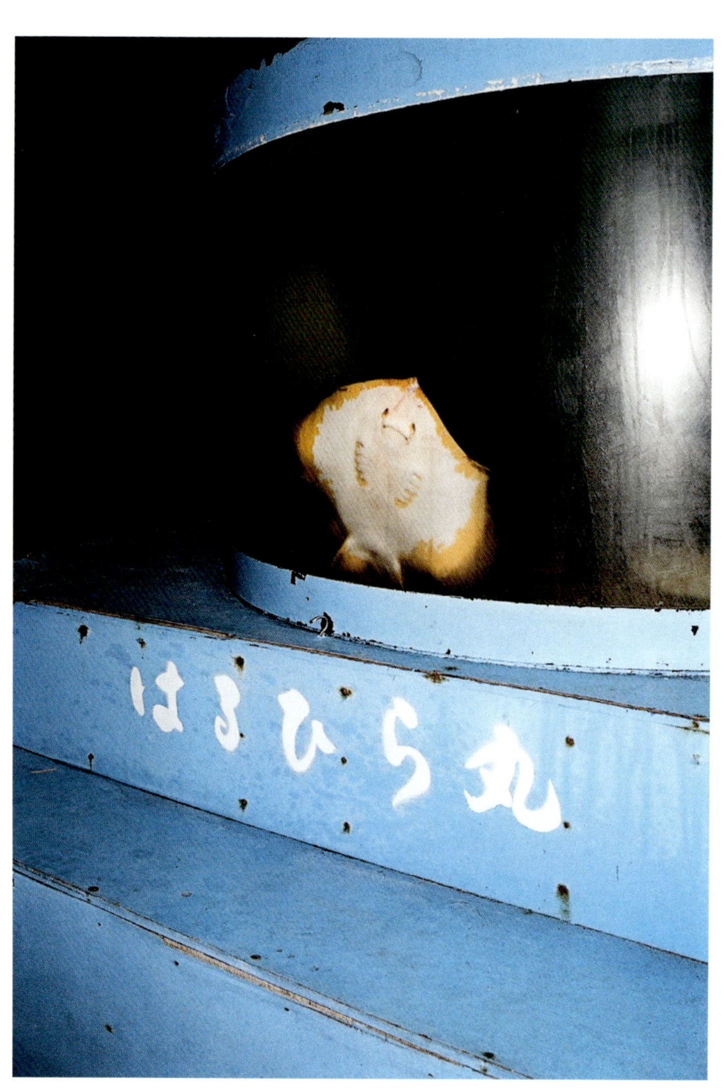
はるひら丸

TU M'AS FRAPPÉE
JTE RETROUVERAI!

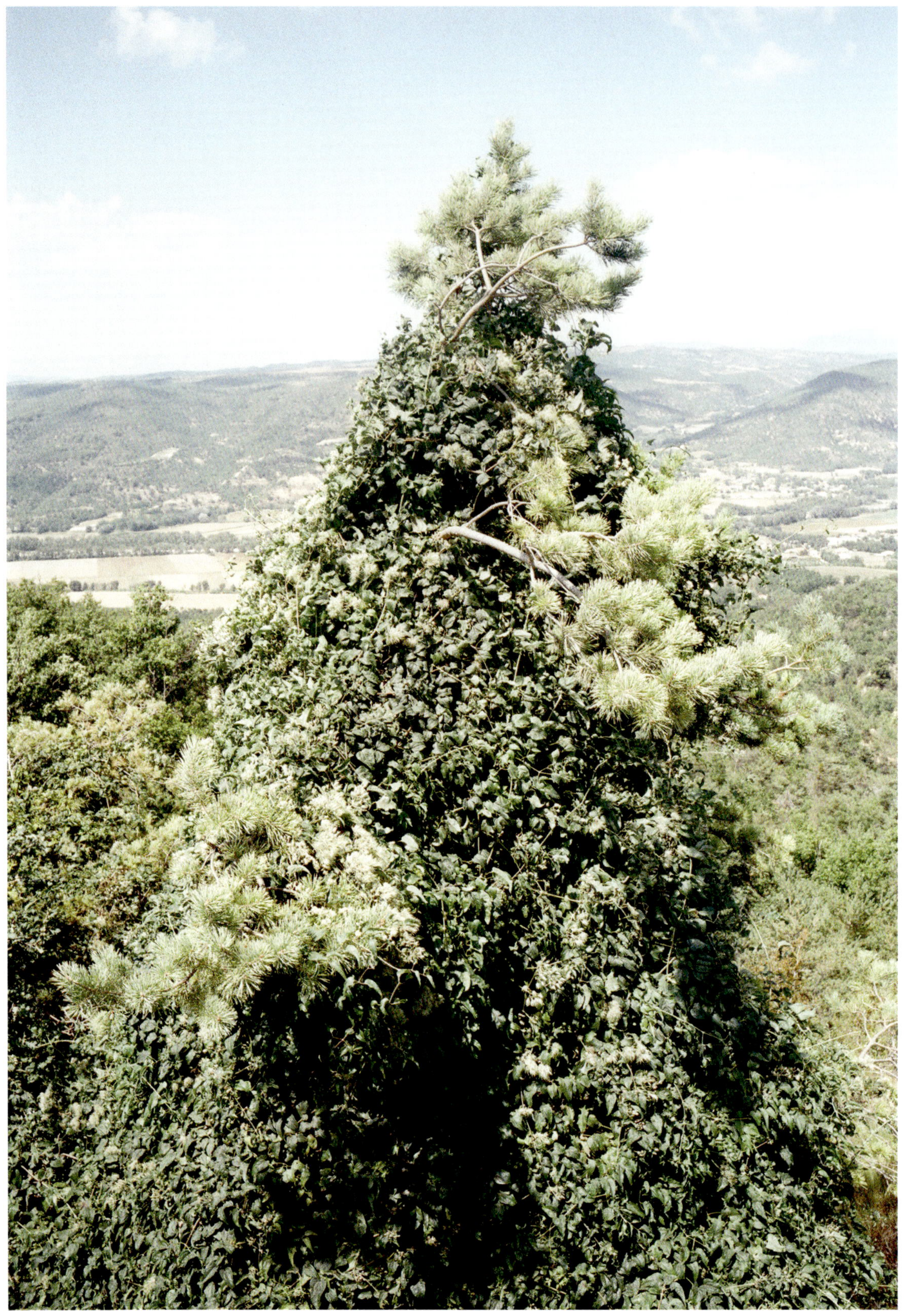

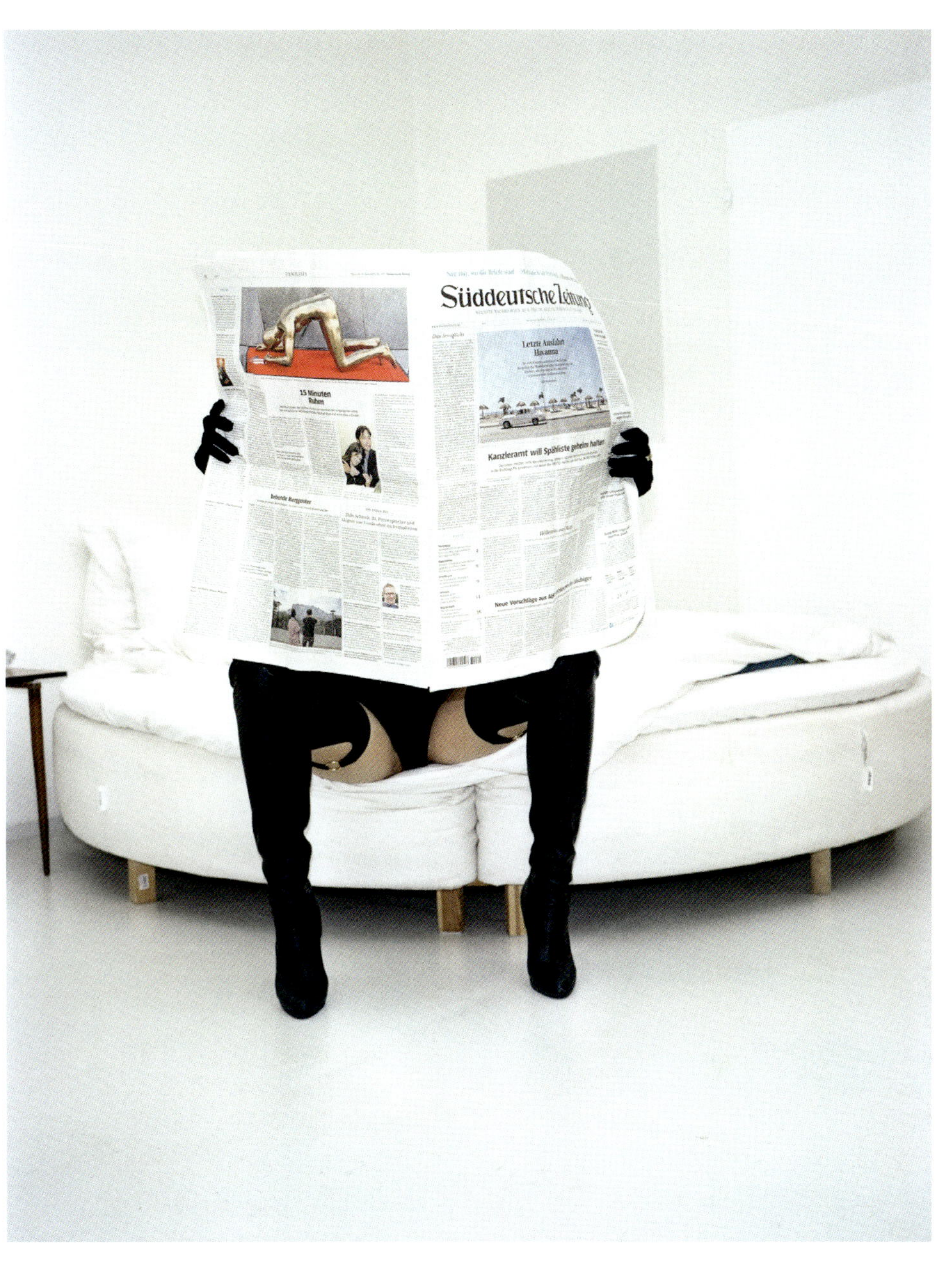
Süddeutsche Zeitung
15 Minuten Ruhm
Letzte Ausfahrt Havanna
Kanzleramt will Spähliste geheim halten

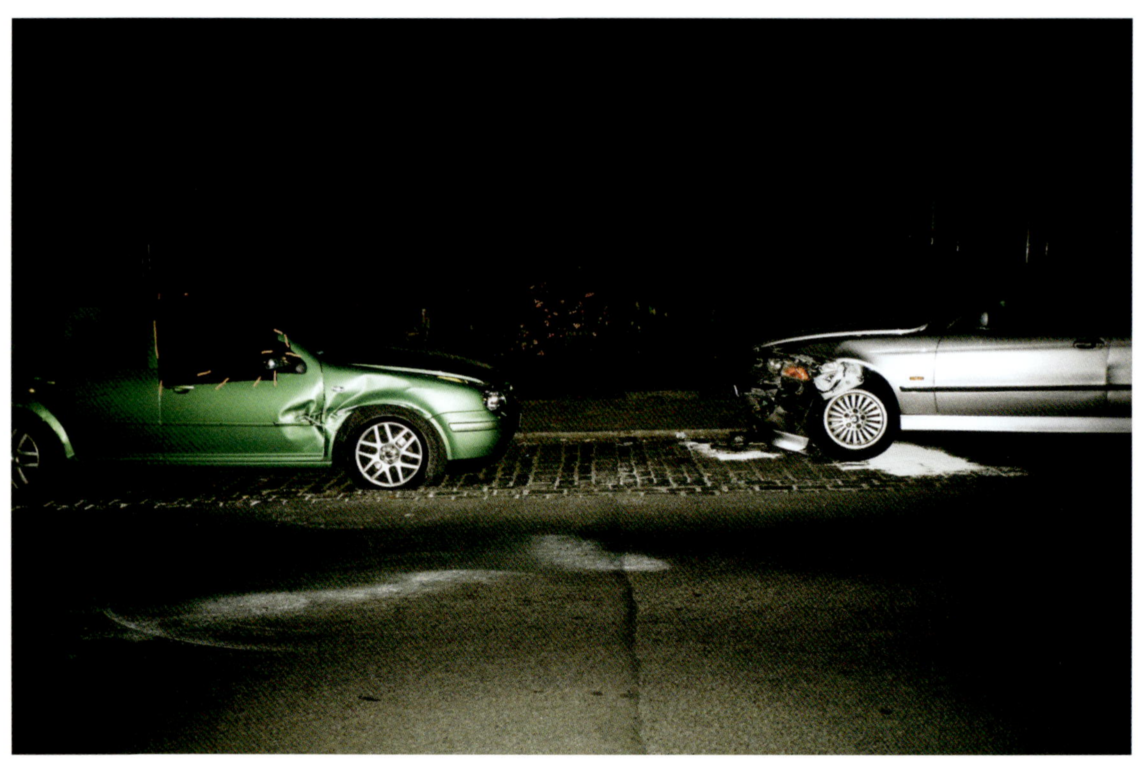

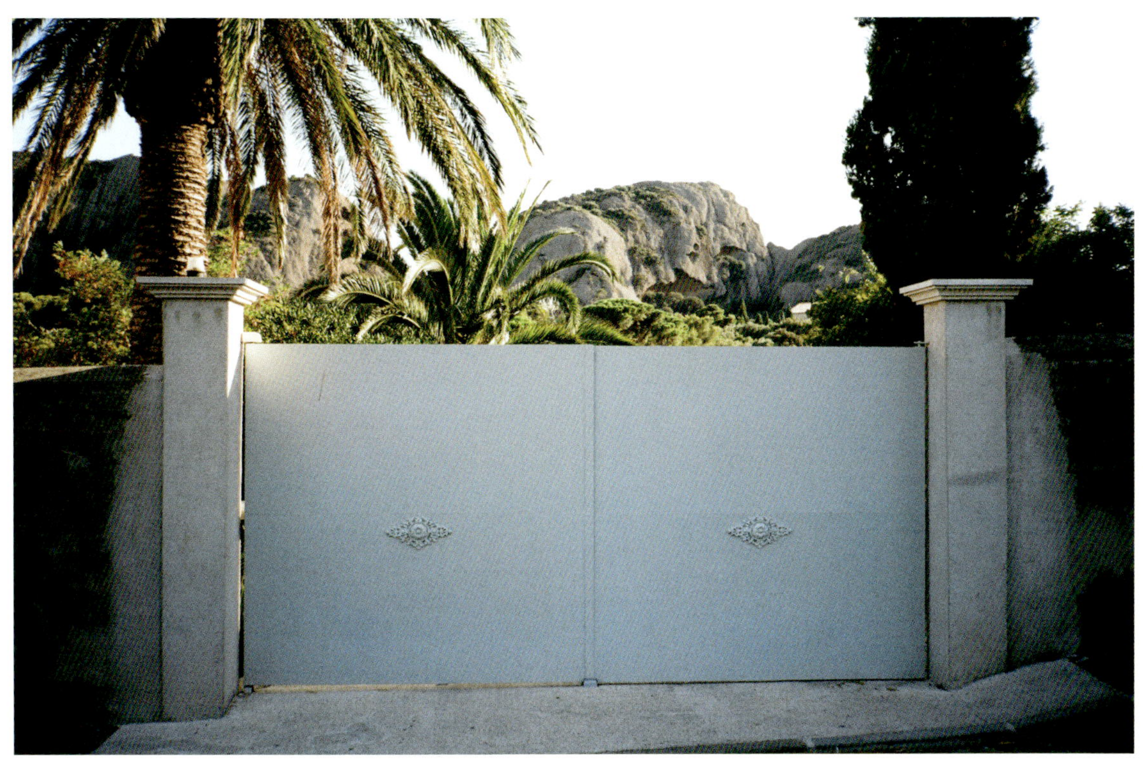

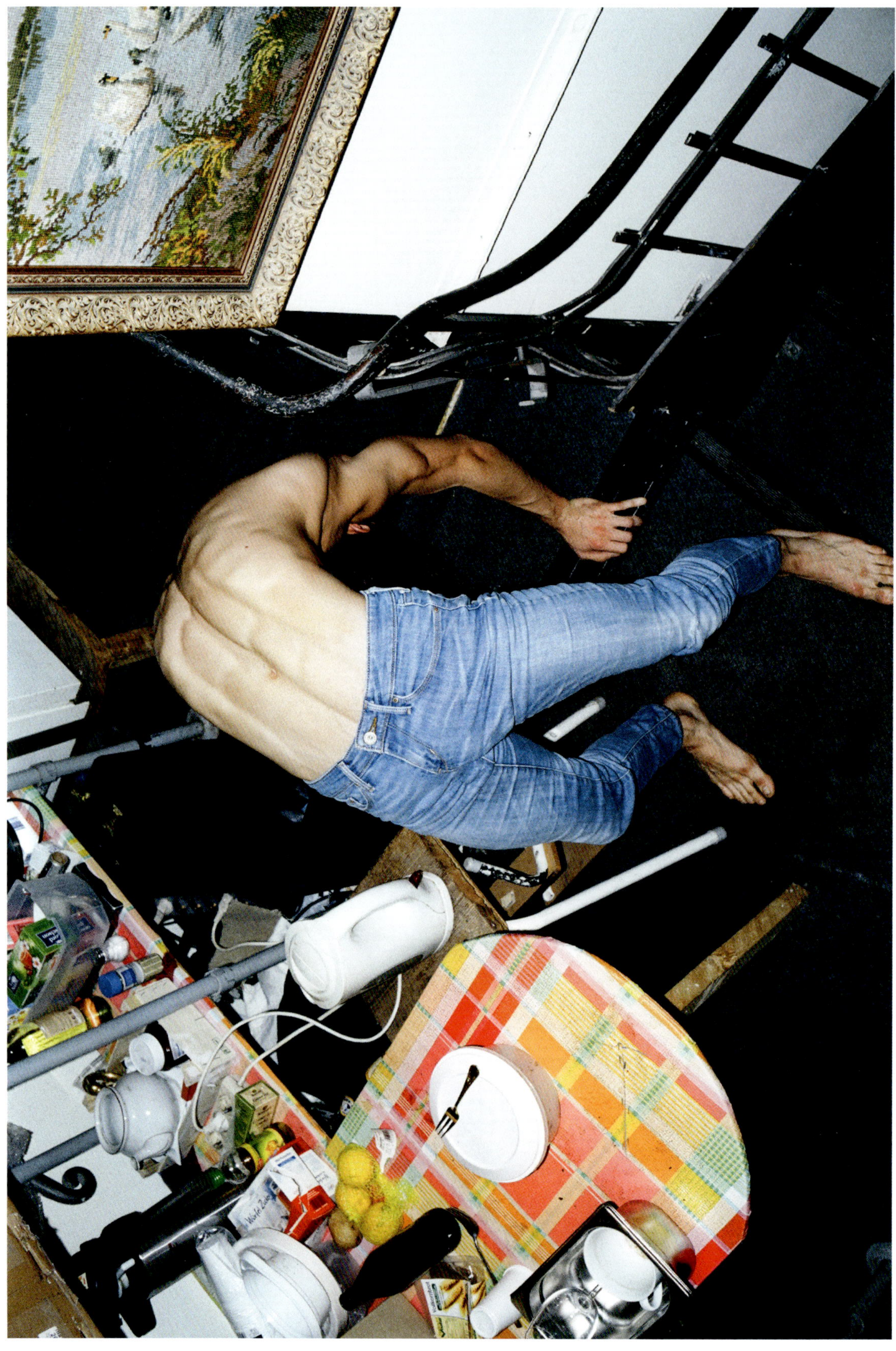

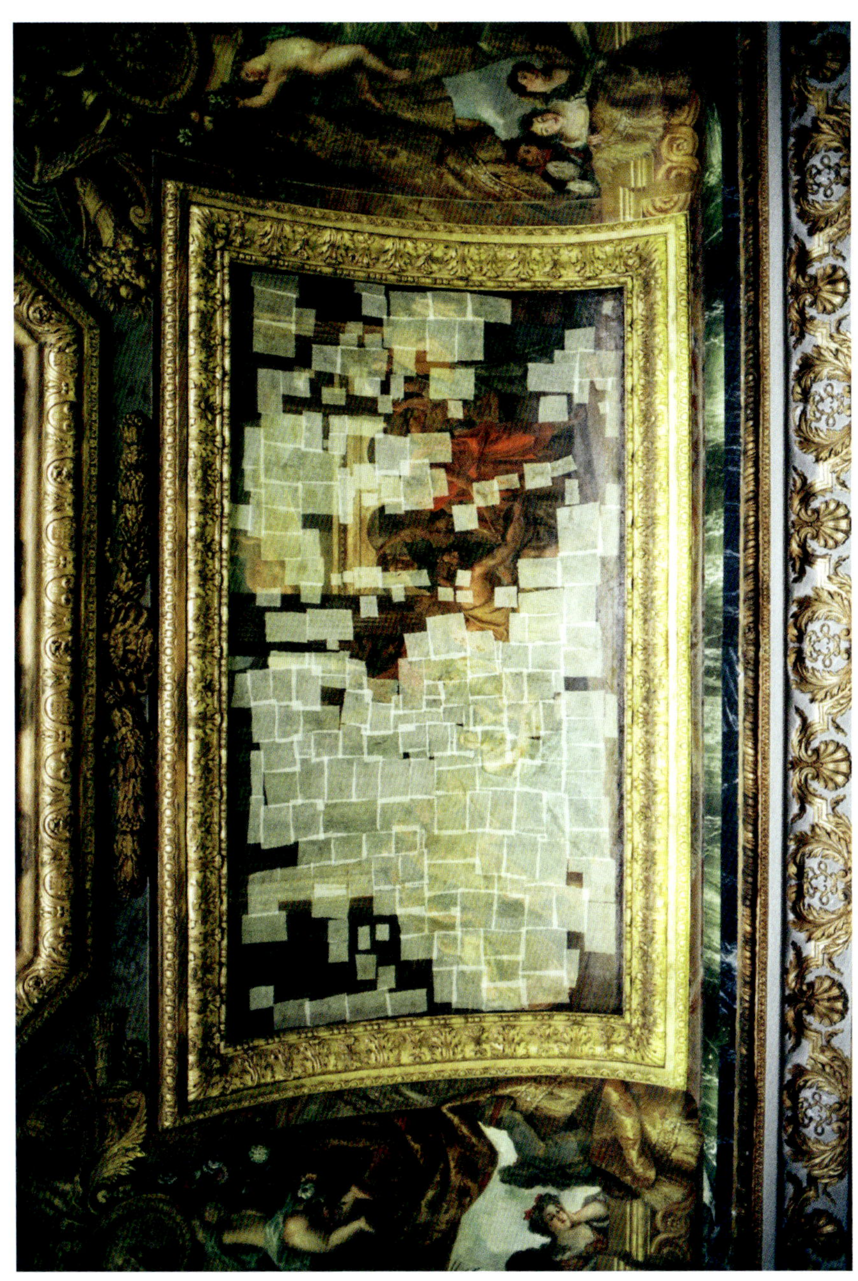

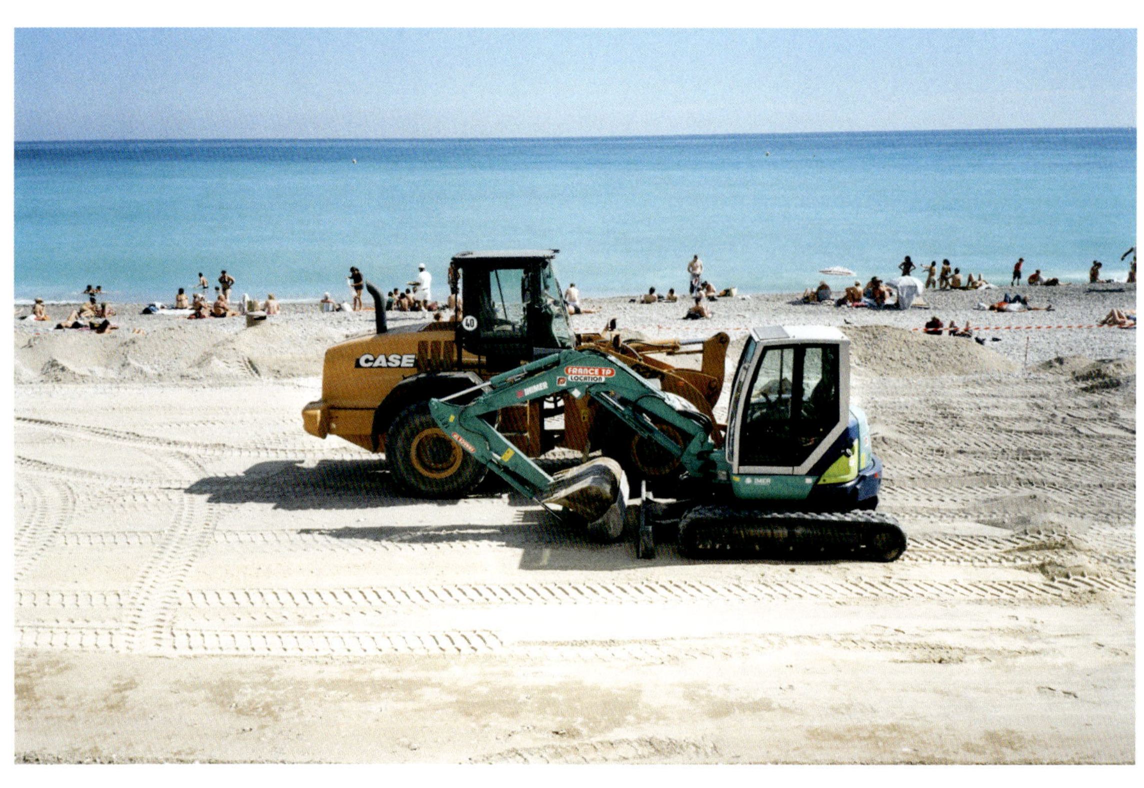
CASE
40
FRANCE TP
LOCATION
IHIMER

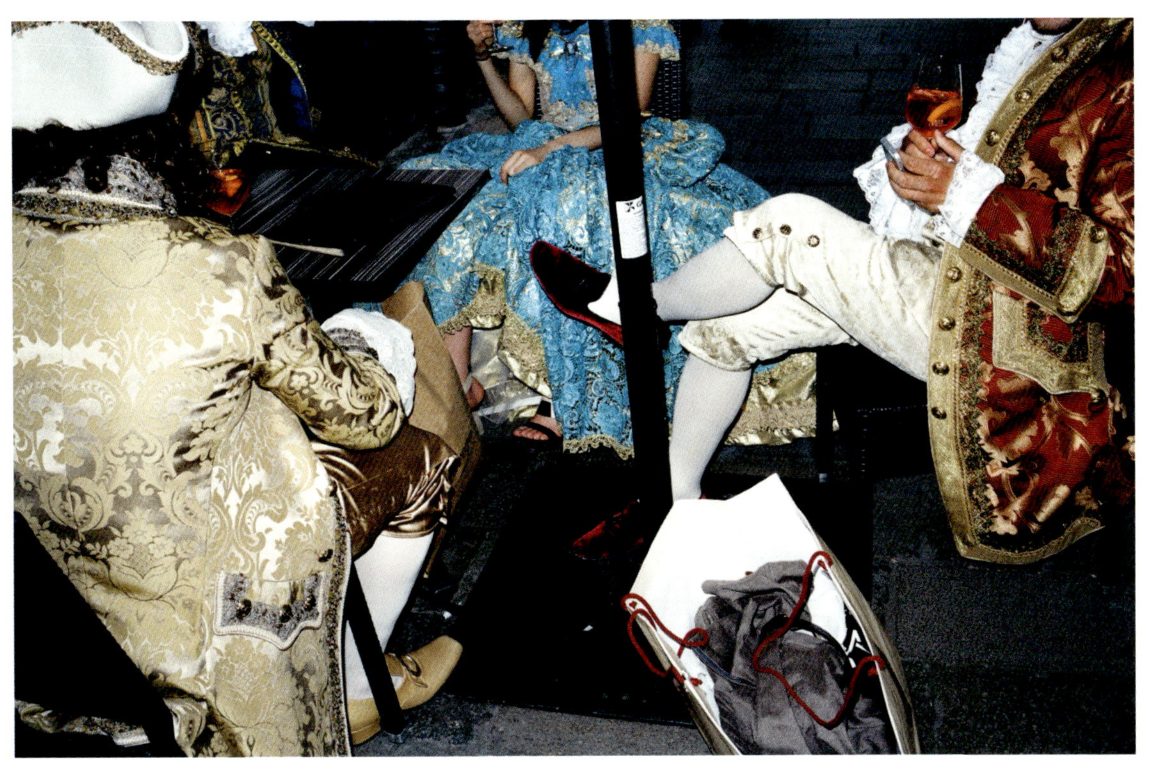

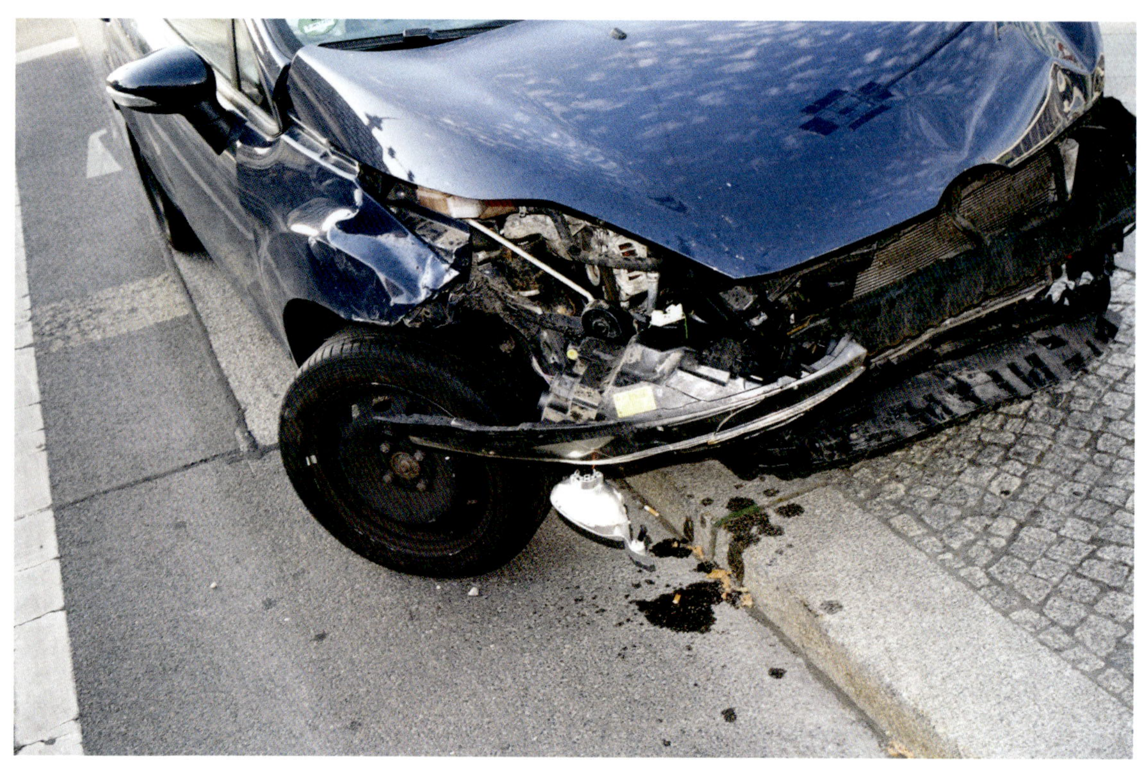

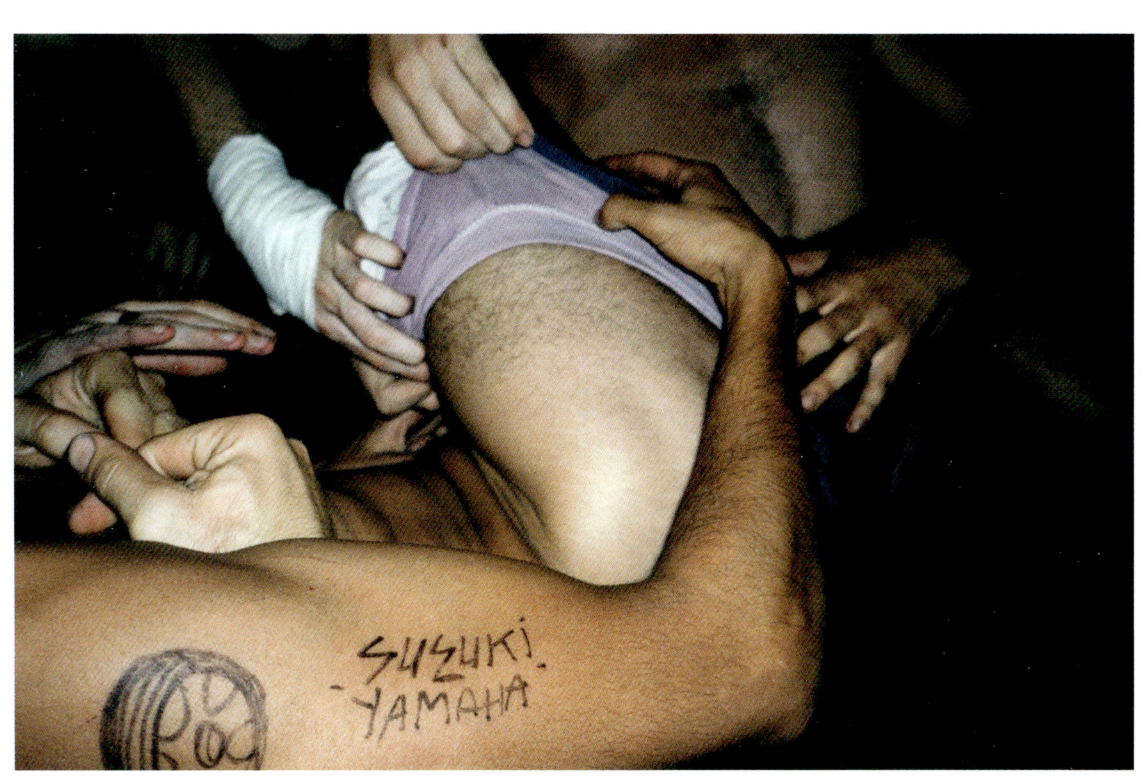
SUZUKI
YAMAHA

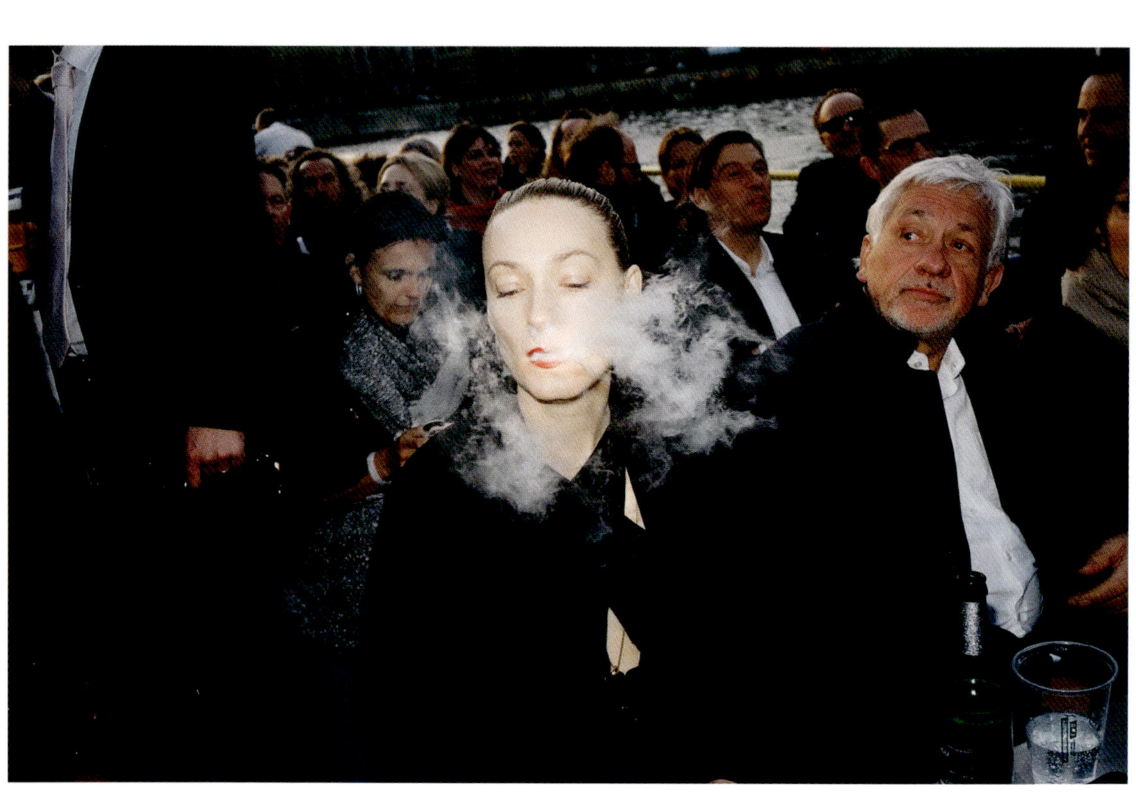

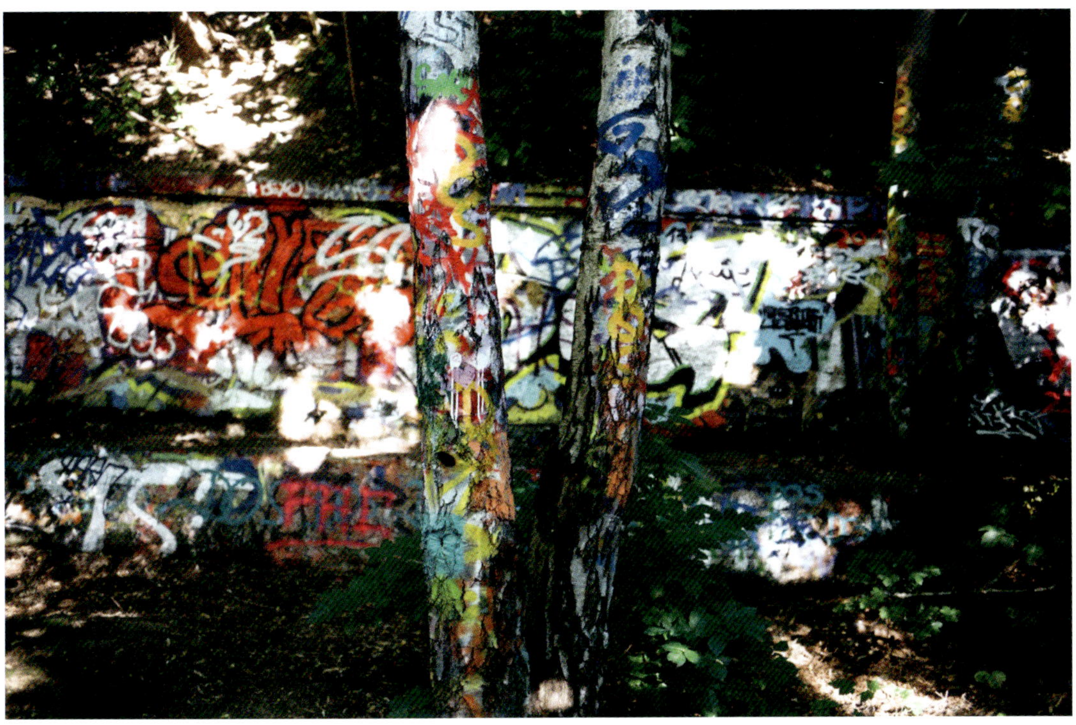

2016 A lion in a cage, you are like a fucking lion in a cage.
Much less imposing, less blond, and with shorter hair.
Cropped nails.
The cage is right here.
Flexible.
You can poke your big paws through the bars. Sense the outside goings-on.
Observe. Assimilate.
You go around in circles and seethe.
Sometimes you're fine there.
Sometimes.
The irony is that behind you, the door is wide open.
But you persist to stare ahead without advancing a step.

2016 Un lion en cage, tu es un putain de lion en cage.
Beaucoup moins imposant, moins blond, et les cheveux plus courts.
Les ongles ras.
La cage est bien là.
Flexible.
Tu peux passer tes grosses pattes à travers les
barreaux. Sentir ce qu'il se passe dehors.
Observer. Assimiler.
Tu tournes en rond et tu bouillonnes.
Parfois tu y es bien.
Parfois.
L'ironie est que derrière toi, la porte est grande ouverte.
Mais tu t'entête à regarder devant sans avancer d'un pas.

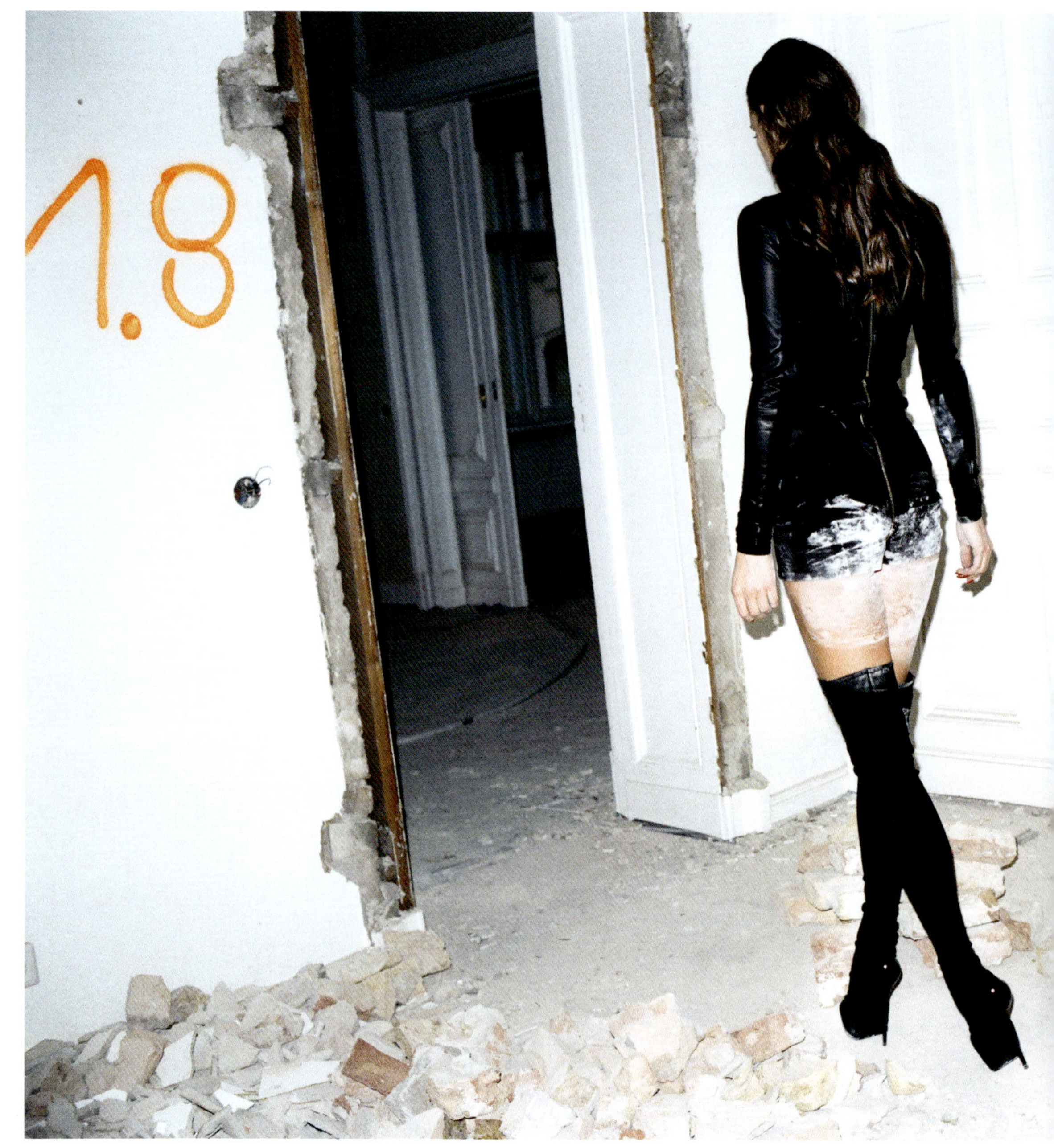
1.8

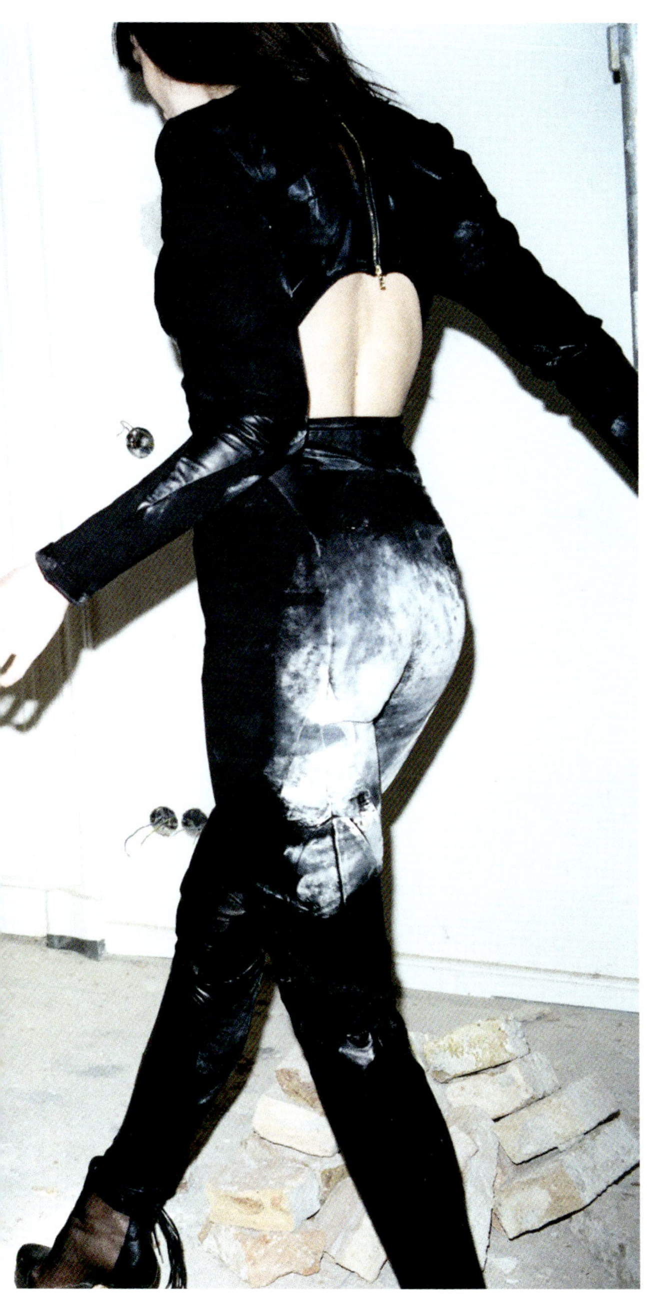

047 — 082

The 3000 days before

On the road

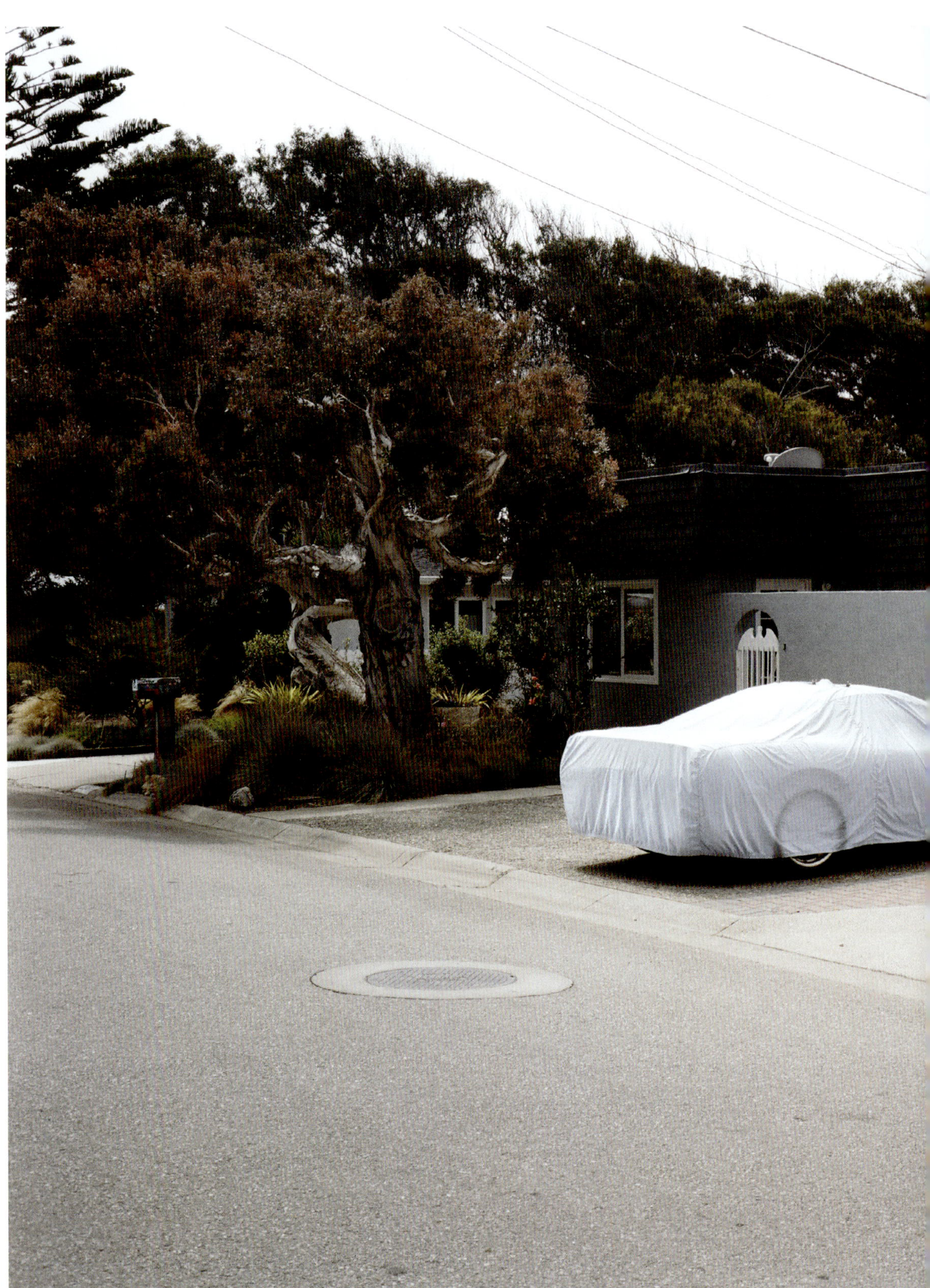

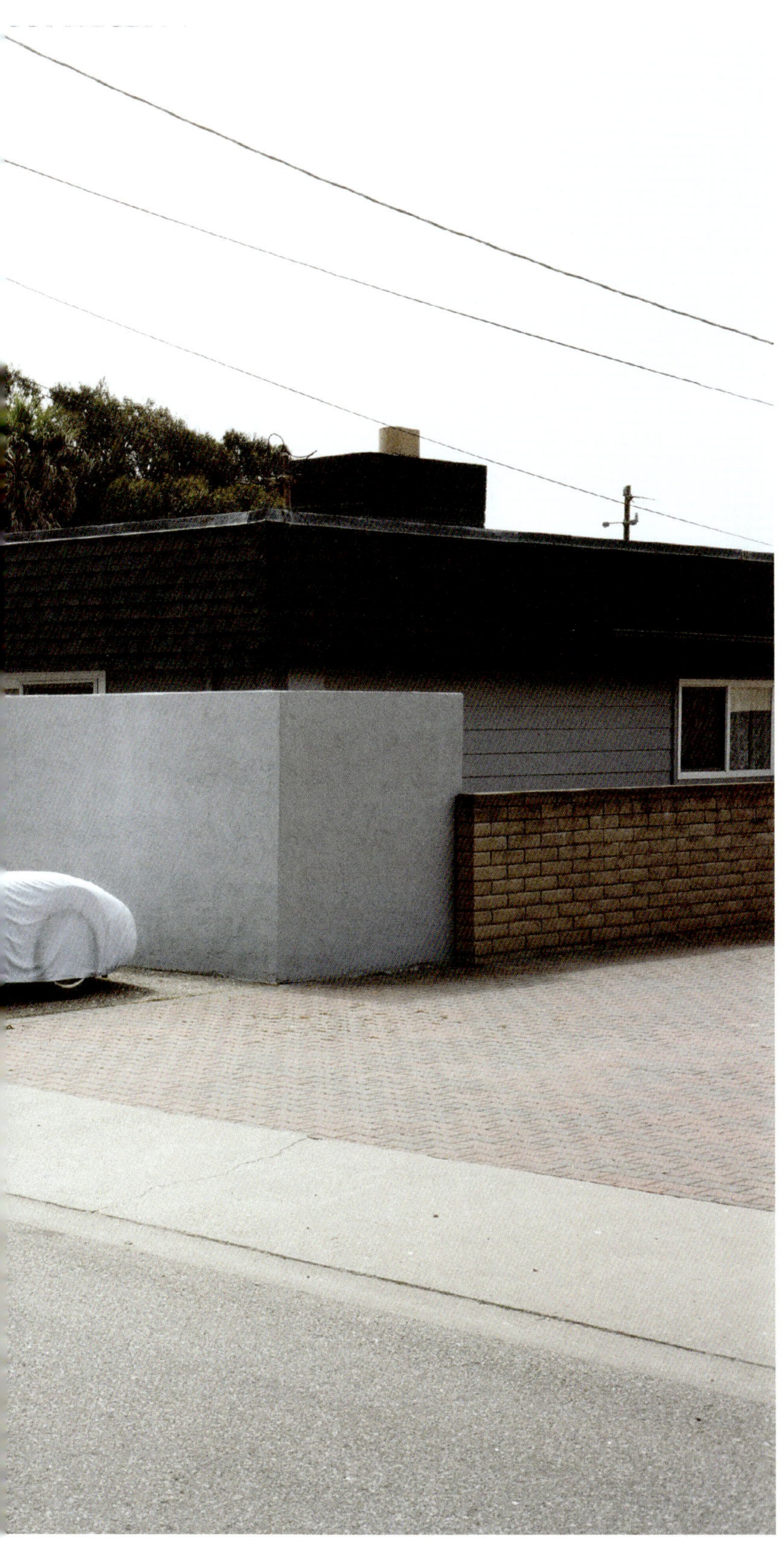

the house of fun, Morro Bay, 2012

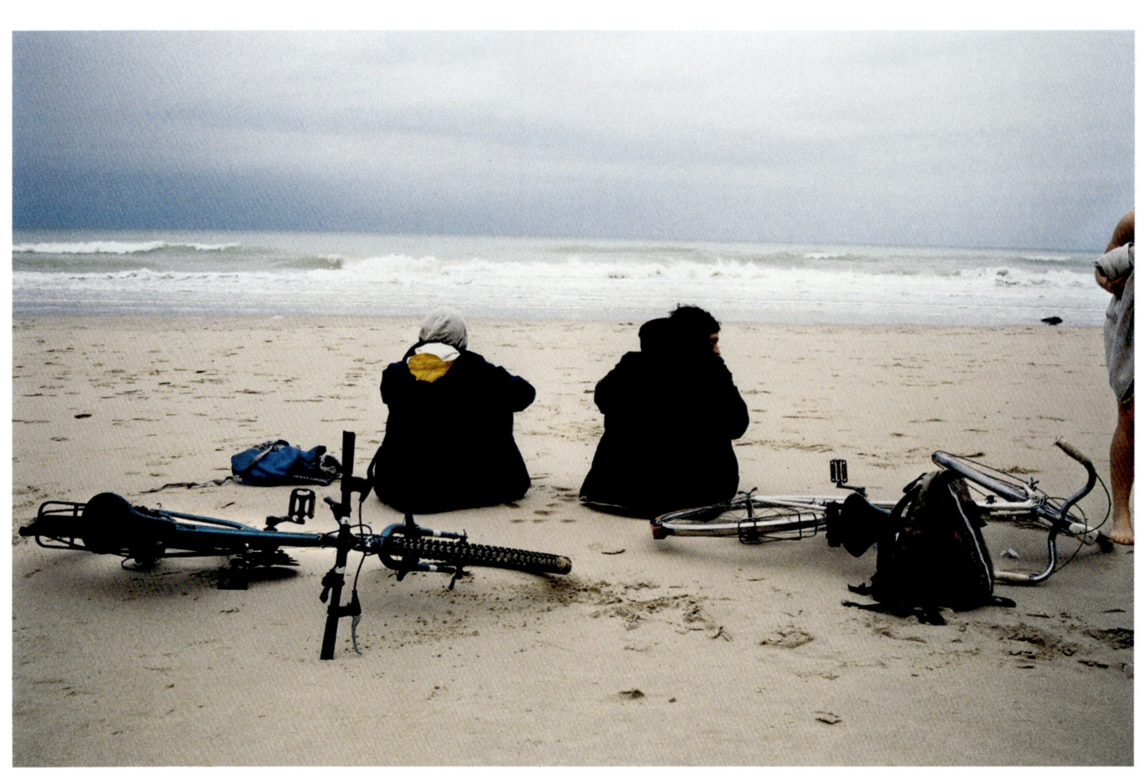

en attendant la marée, Varengeville-sur-Mer, 2012

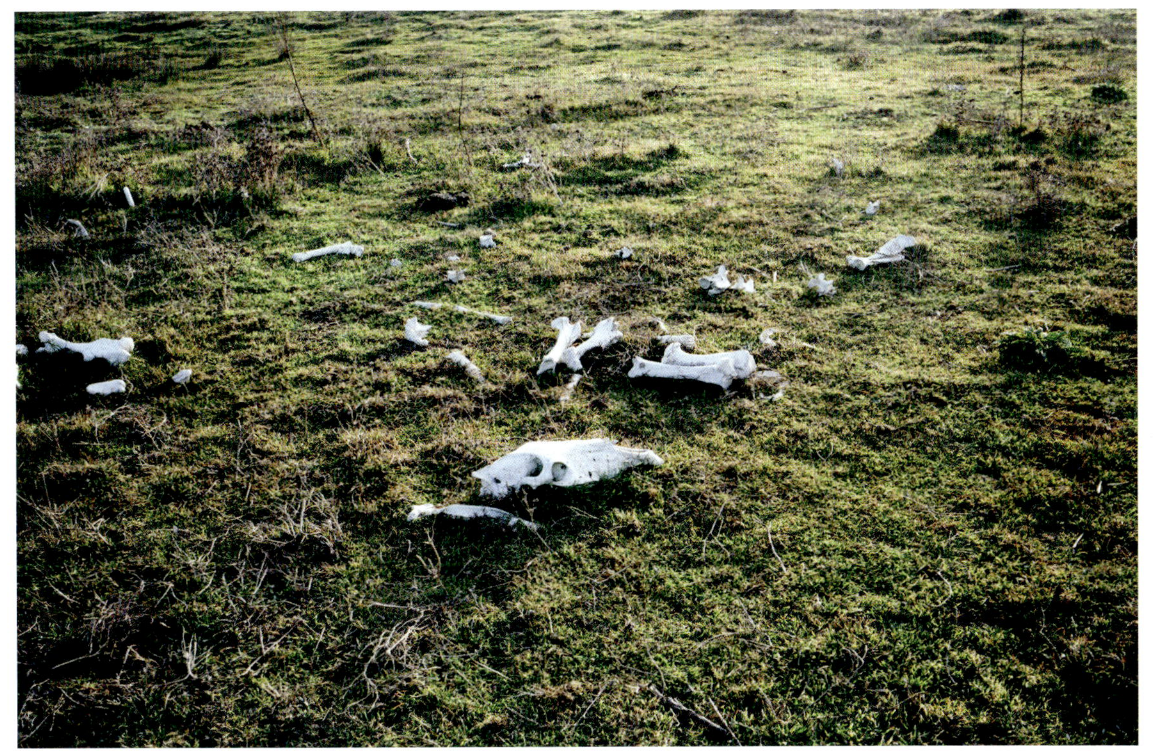

2006 If the storm had not
ravaged the forest,
they would have gone picnicking this afternoon.

2006 Si la tempête n'avait pas
ravagé la forêt,
ils seraient bien allé pique-niquer cet après-midi.

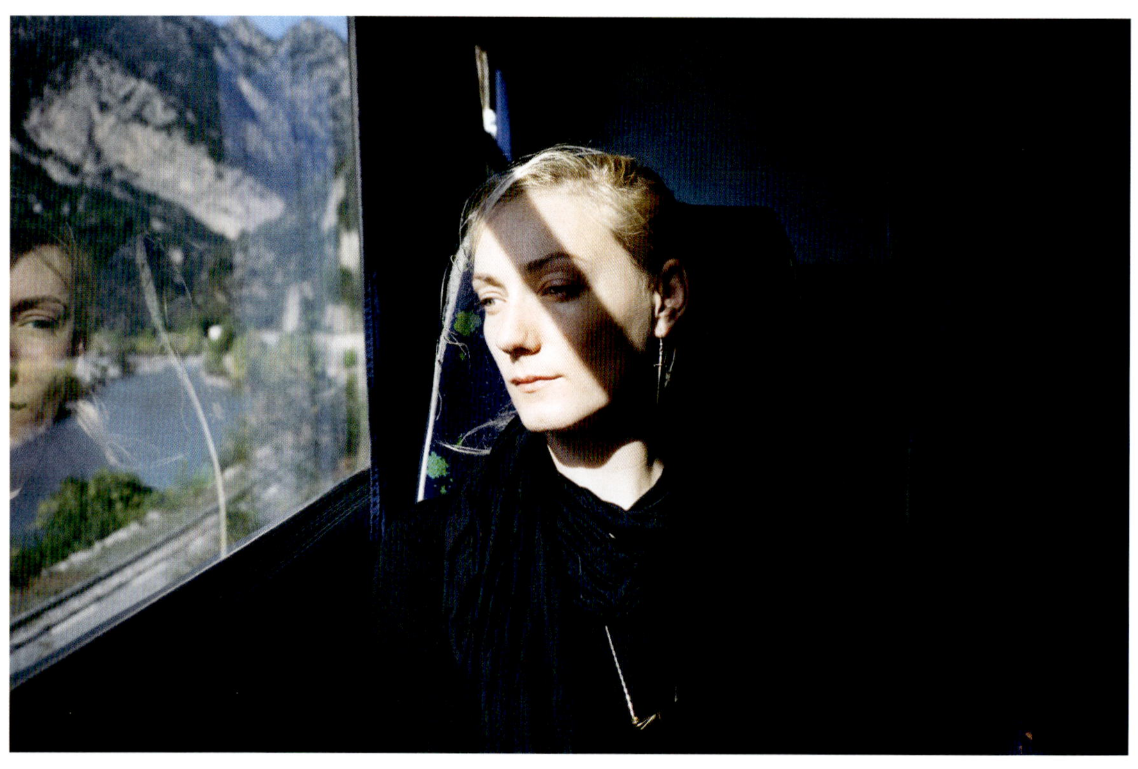

Jen as her own sundial, stopping time on the train, Provence, 2010

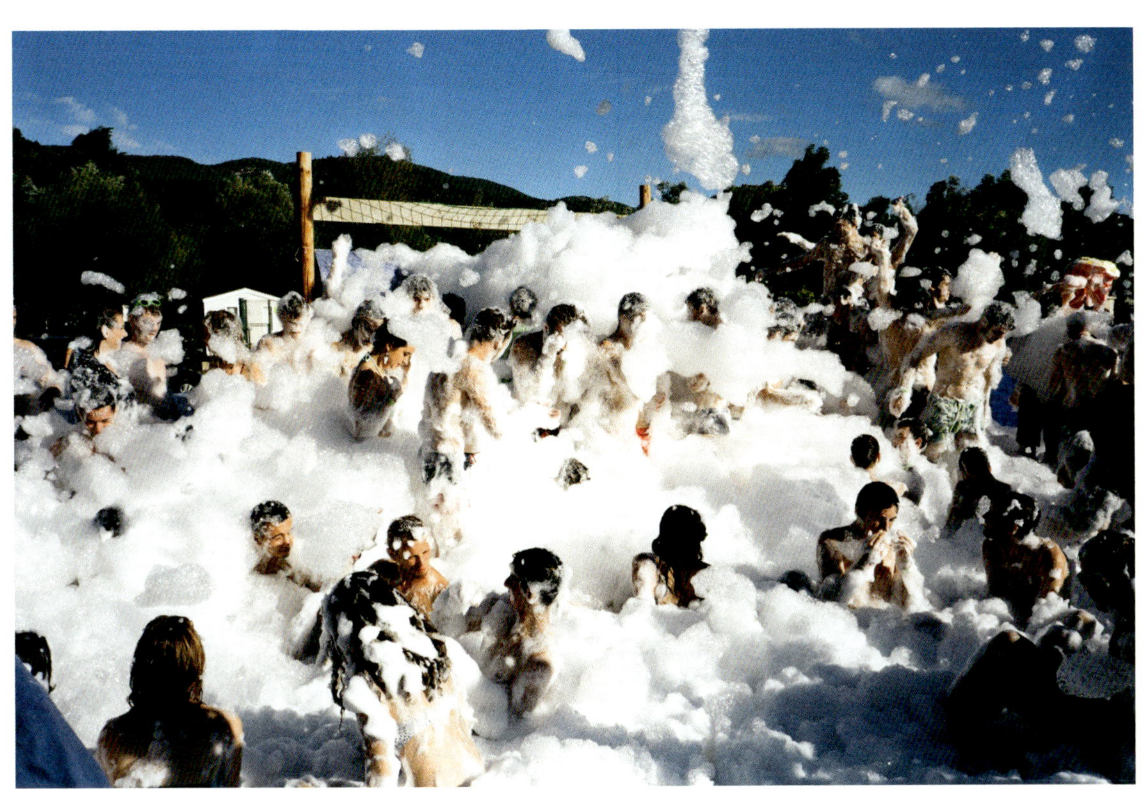

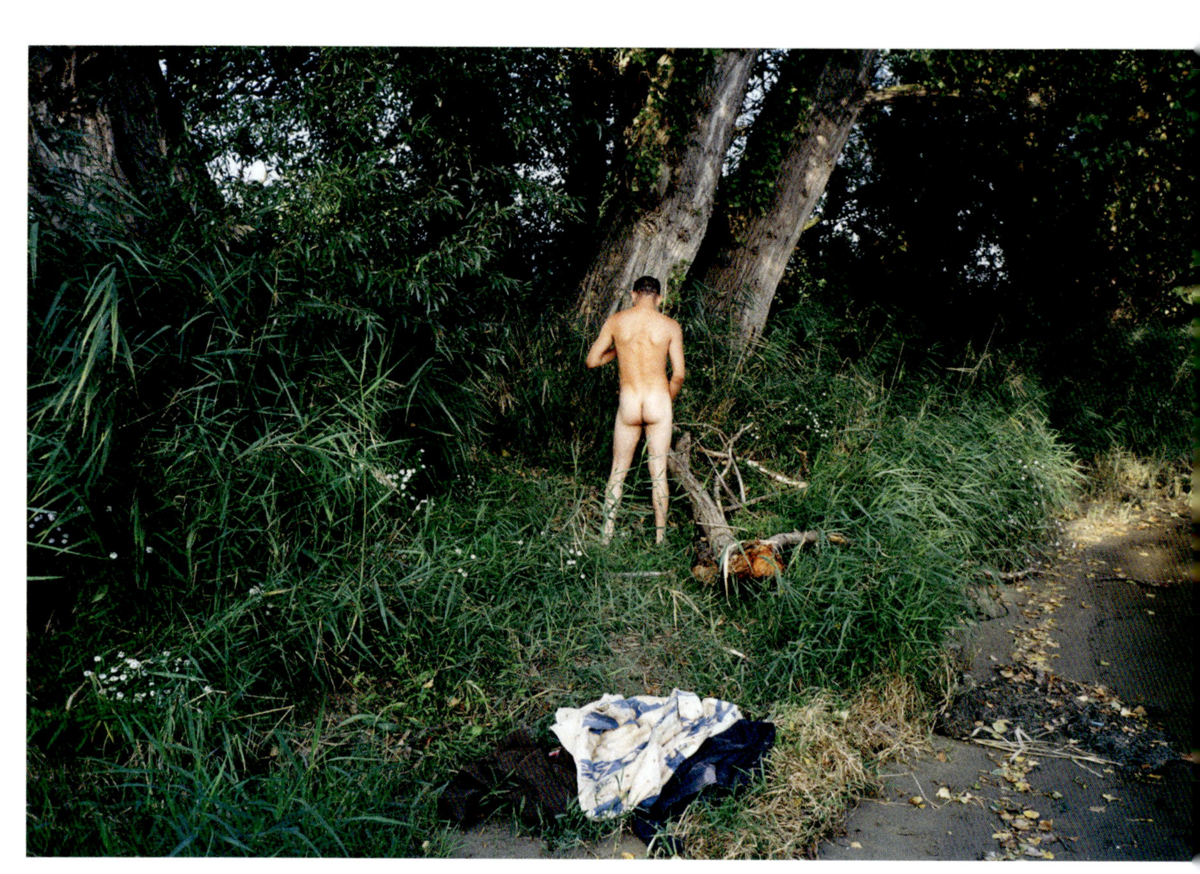

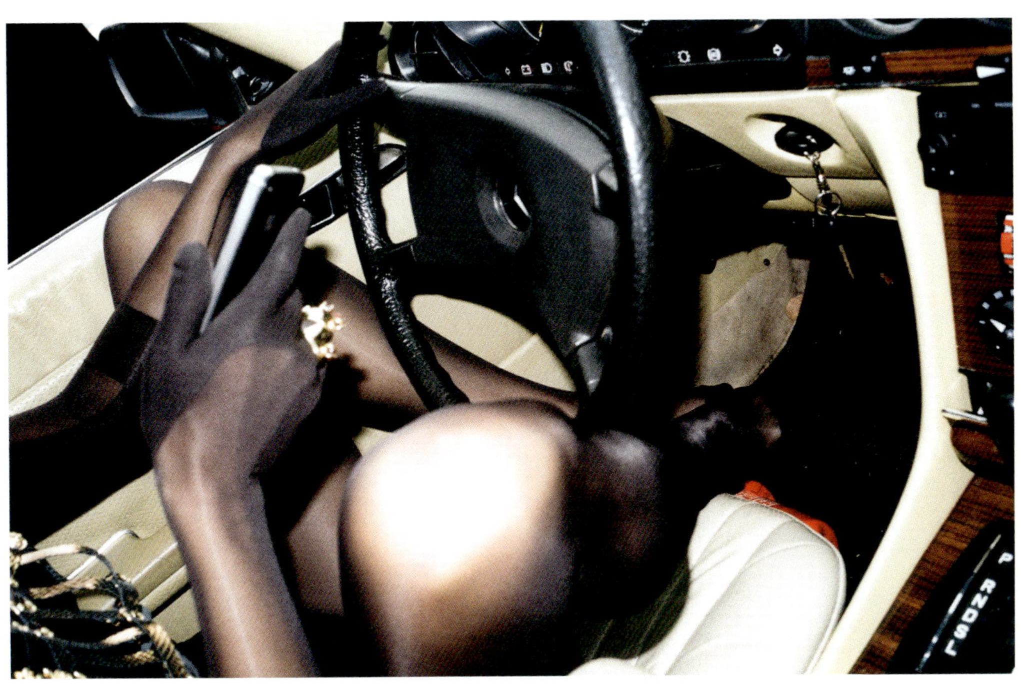

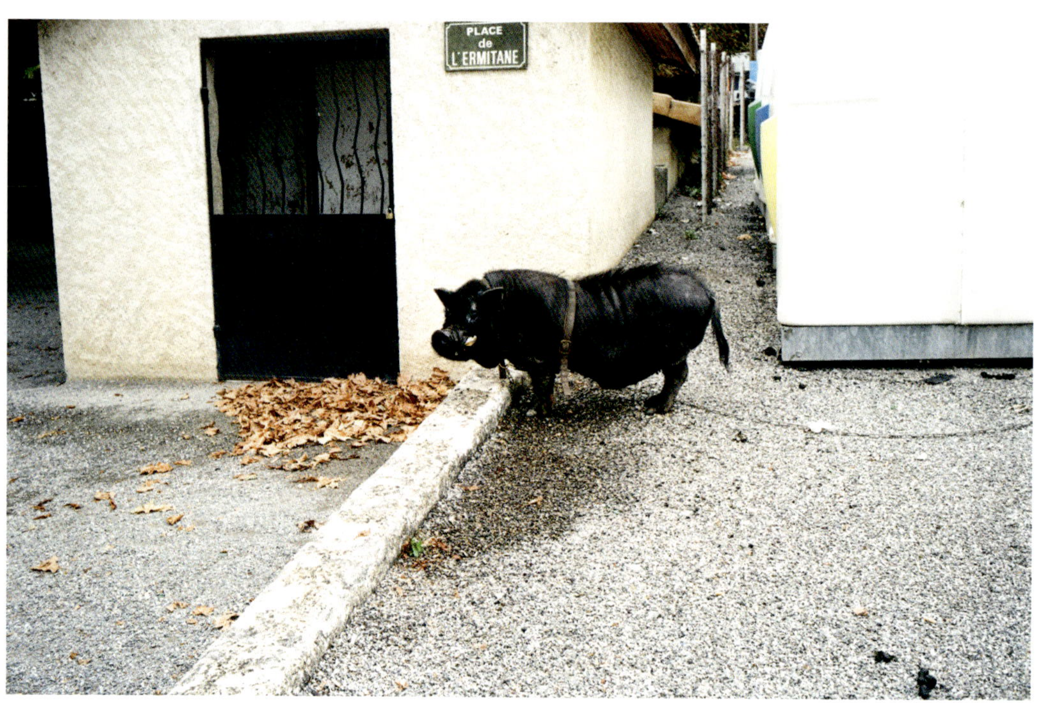
PLACE
de
L'ERMITANE

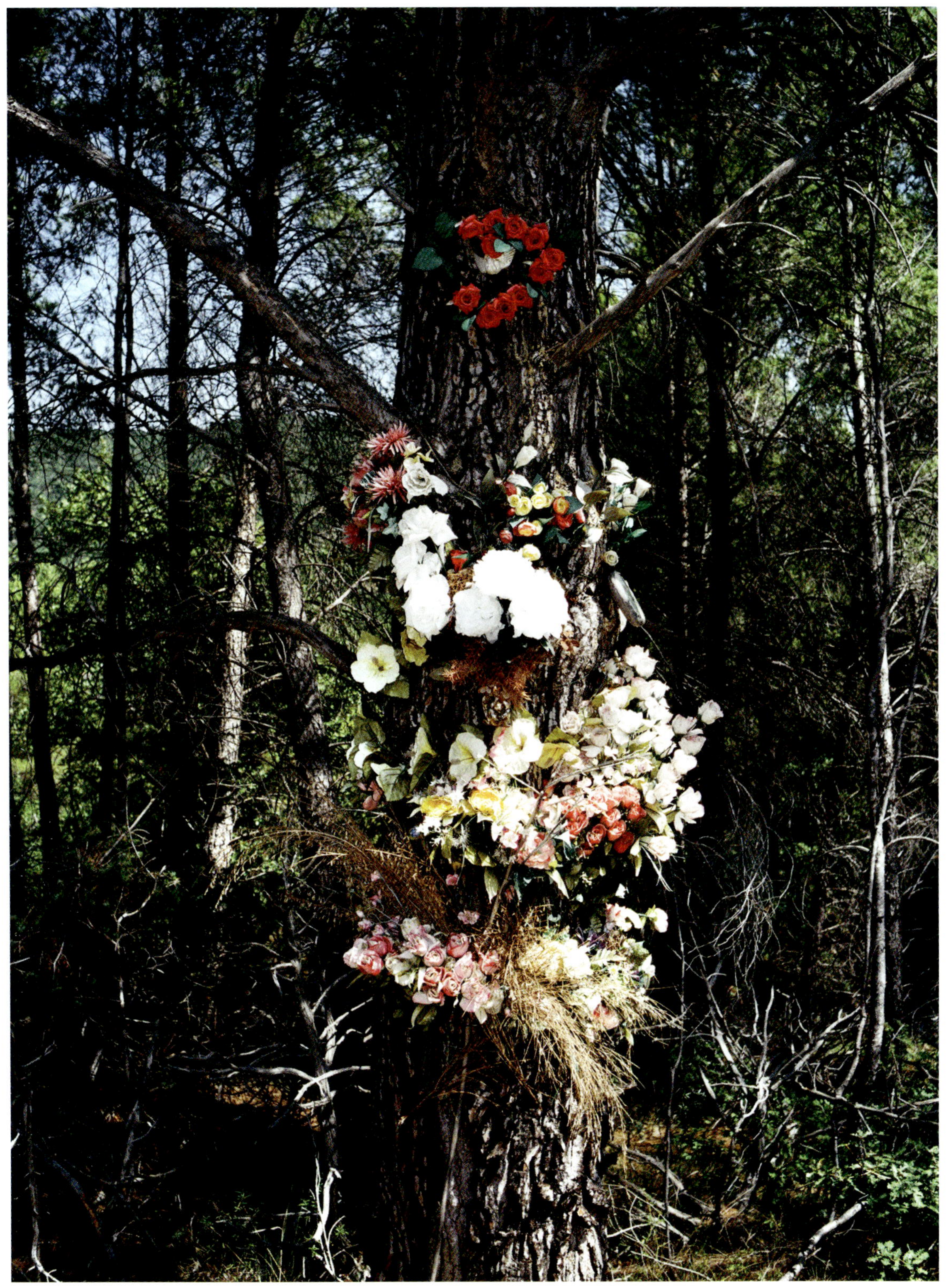

birth of a tree, 2011

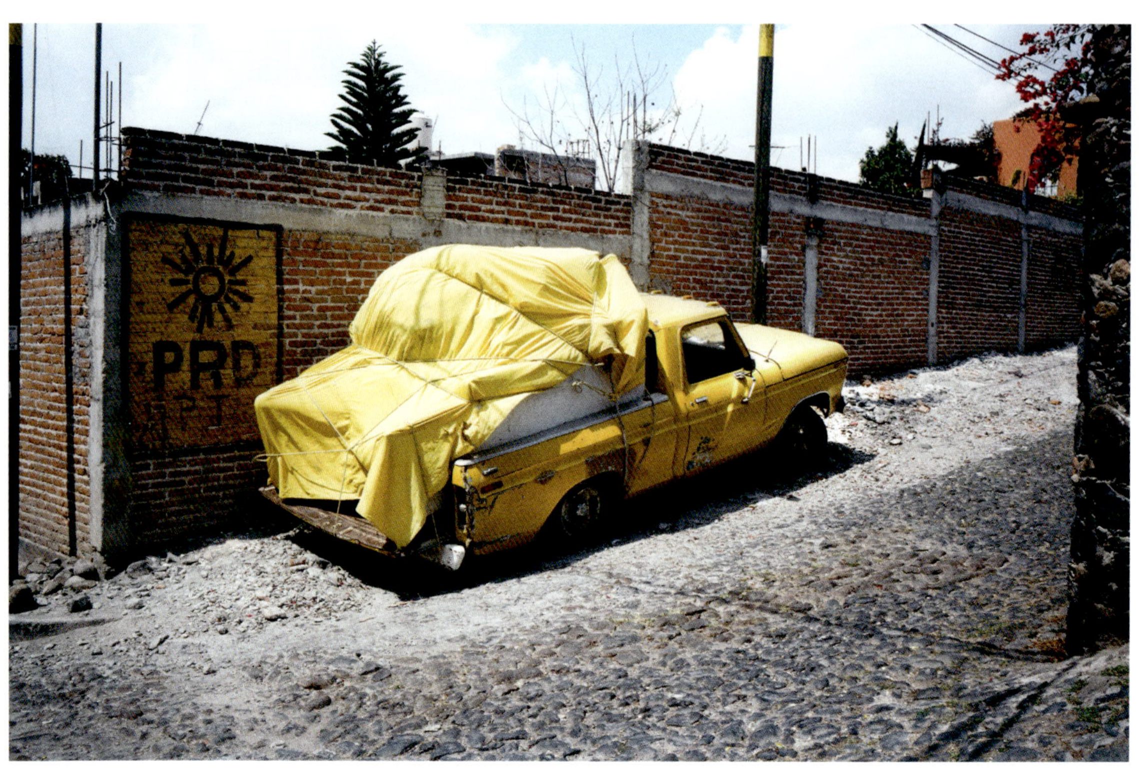
PRD

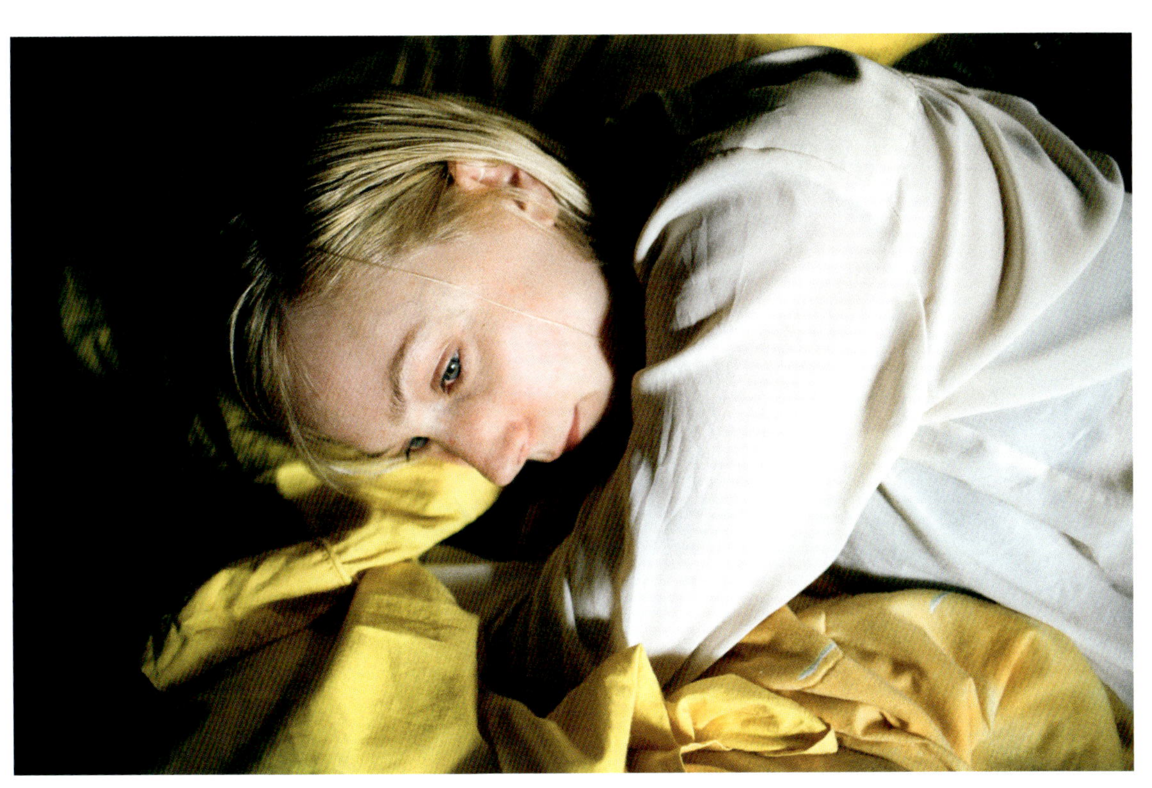

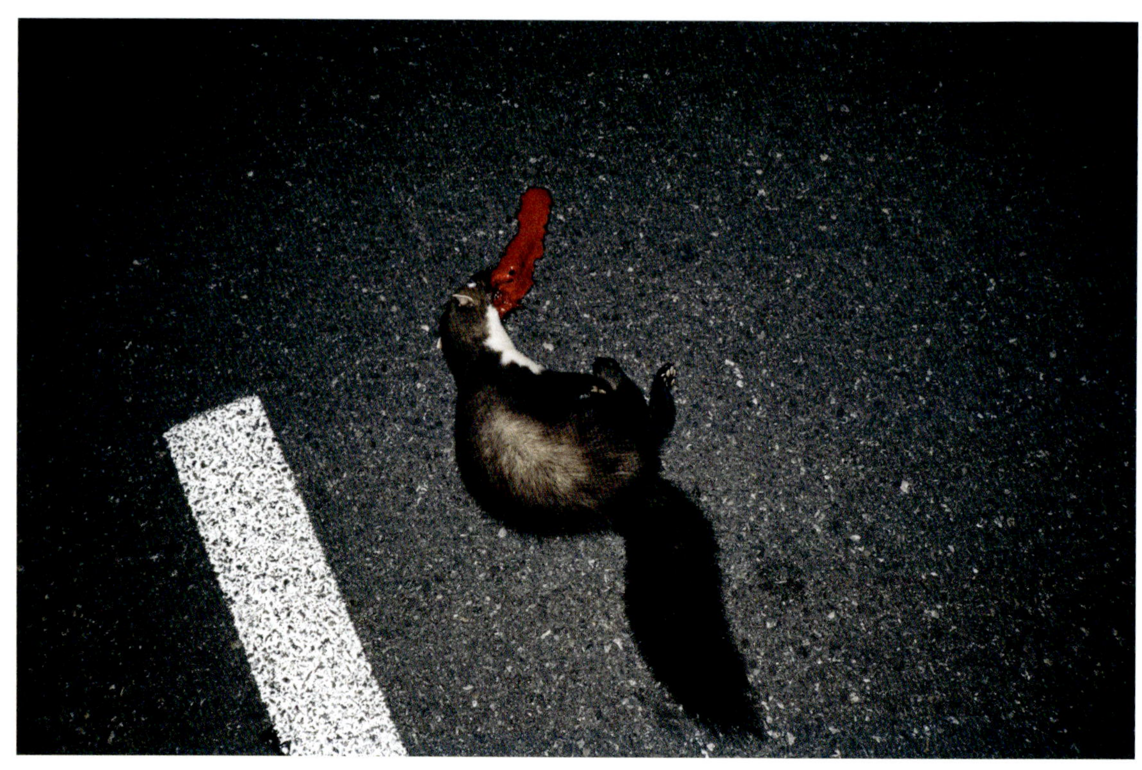

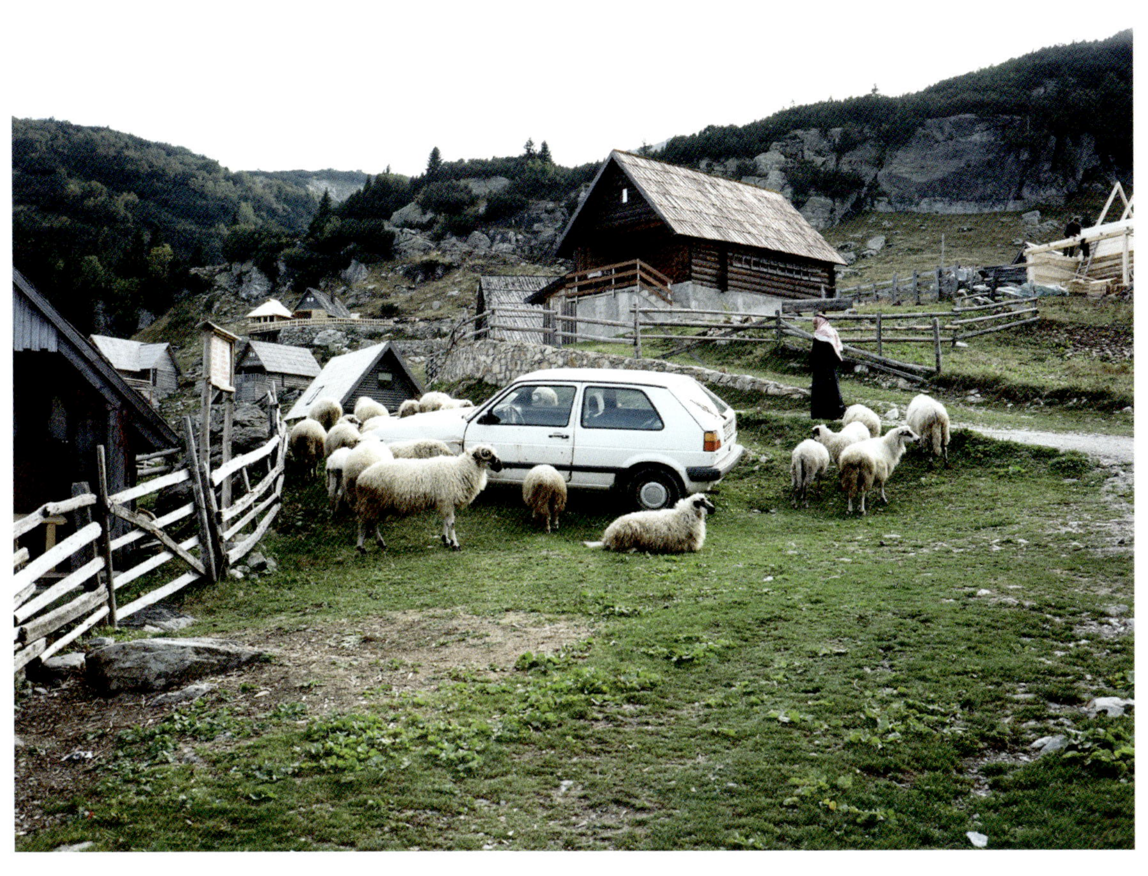

drive-in, Prokoško, 2015

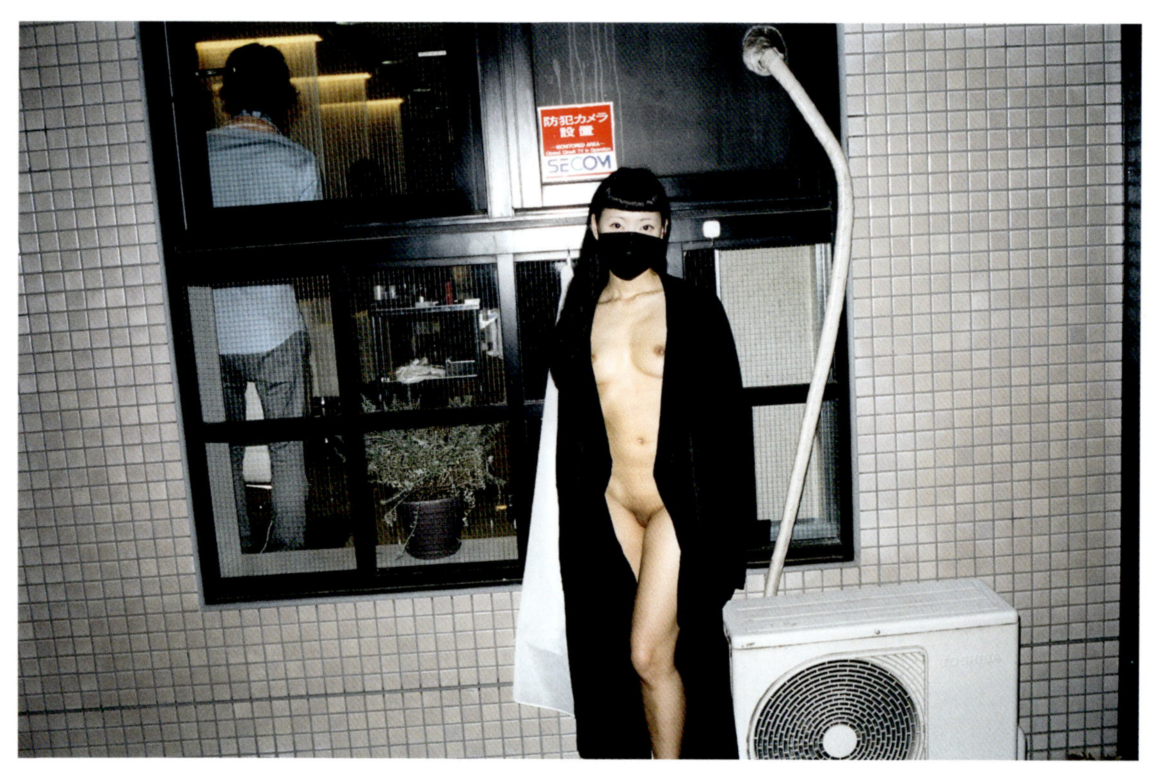

armor, Tokyo, 2014

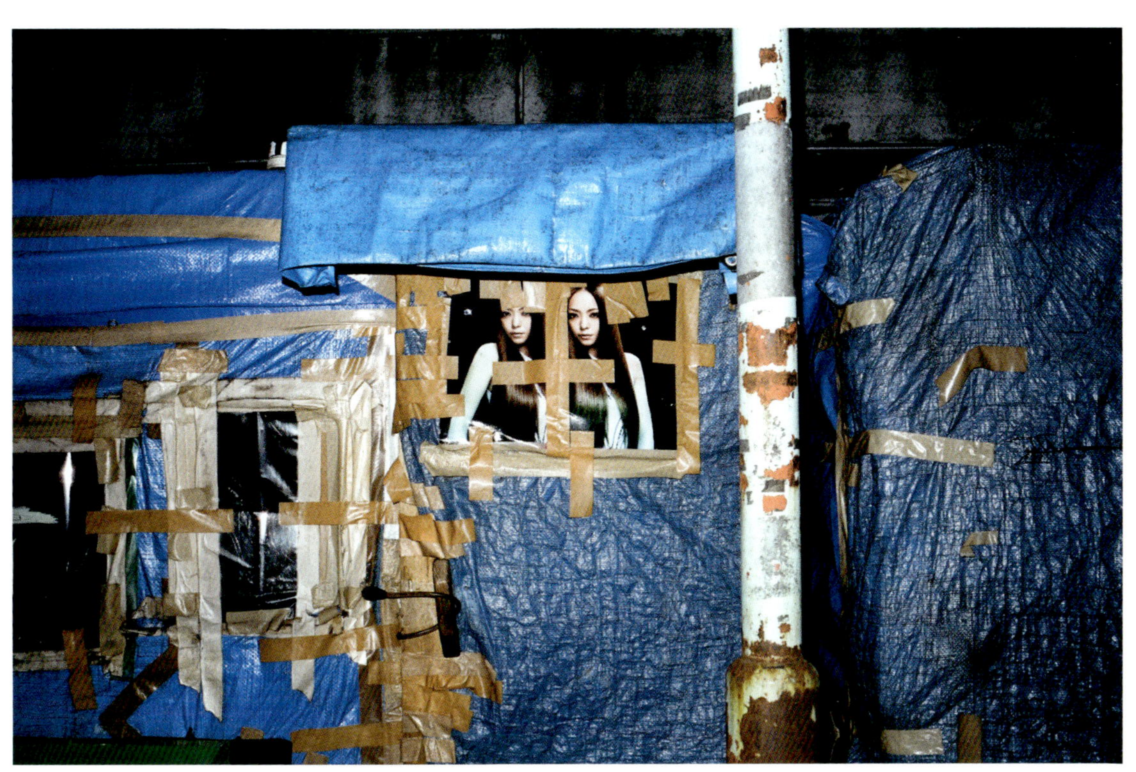

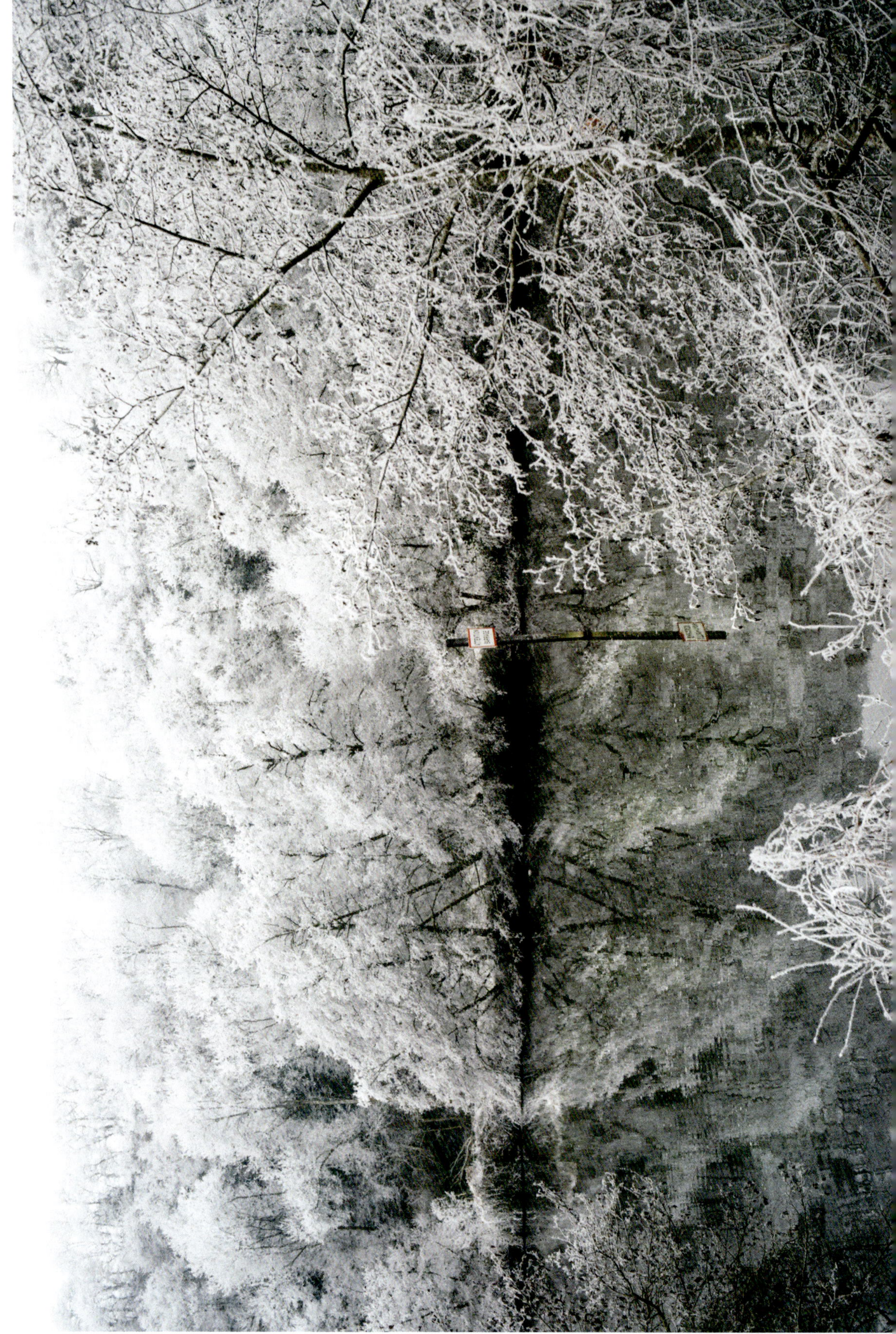

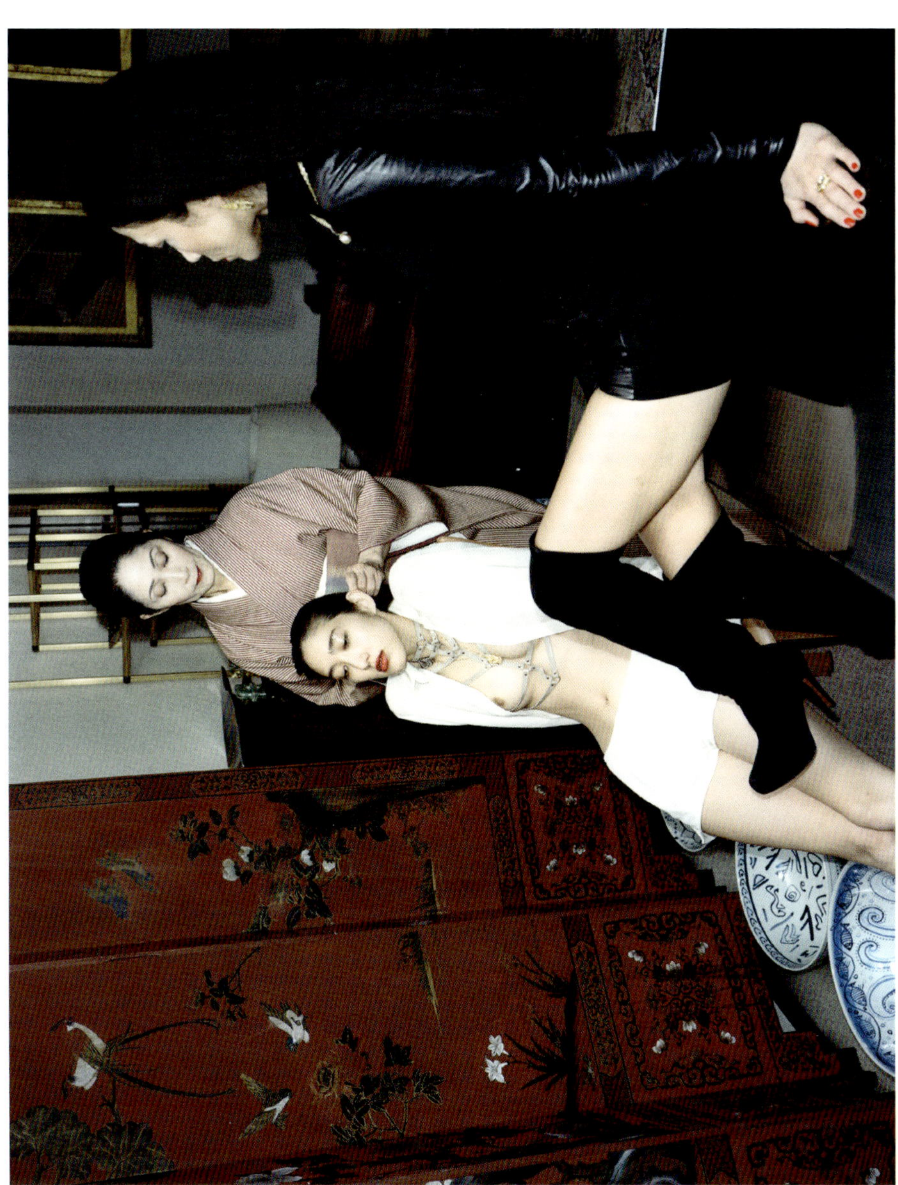

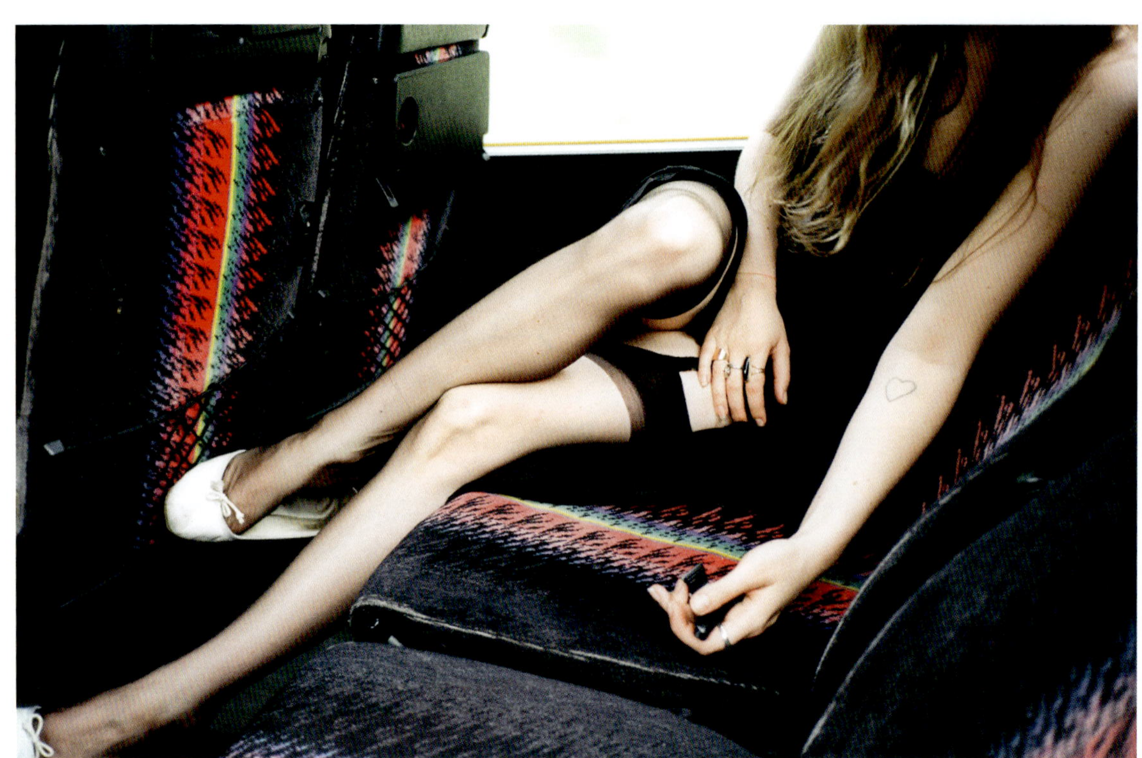

2006 What was really
erotic, was black stockings
plus time.

2006 Ce qui était vraiment
érotique, c'était les chaussettes noires,
plus le temps.

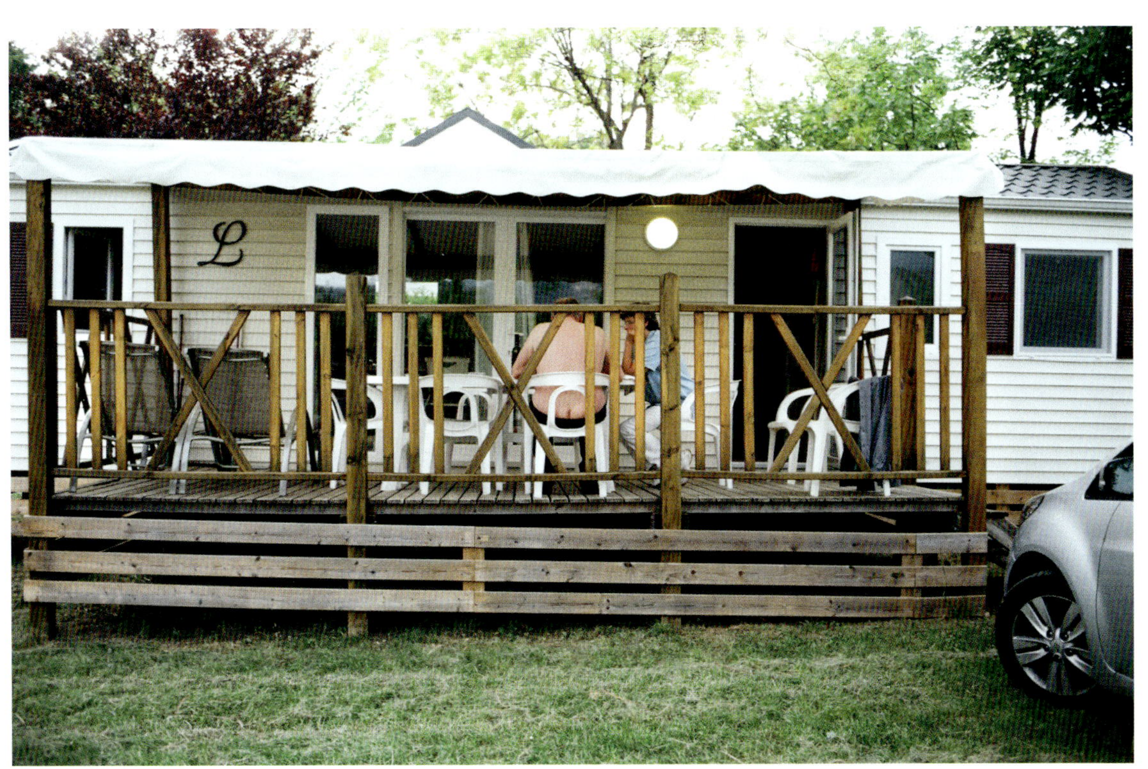
L

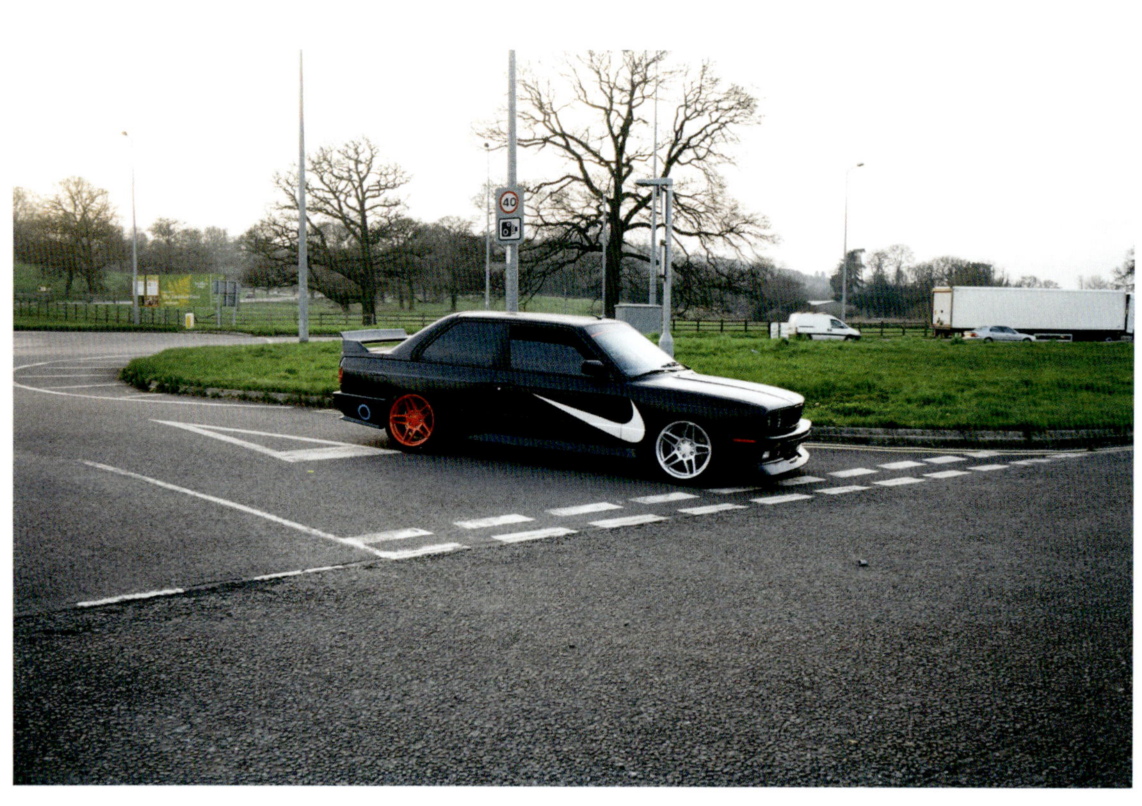
40

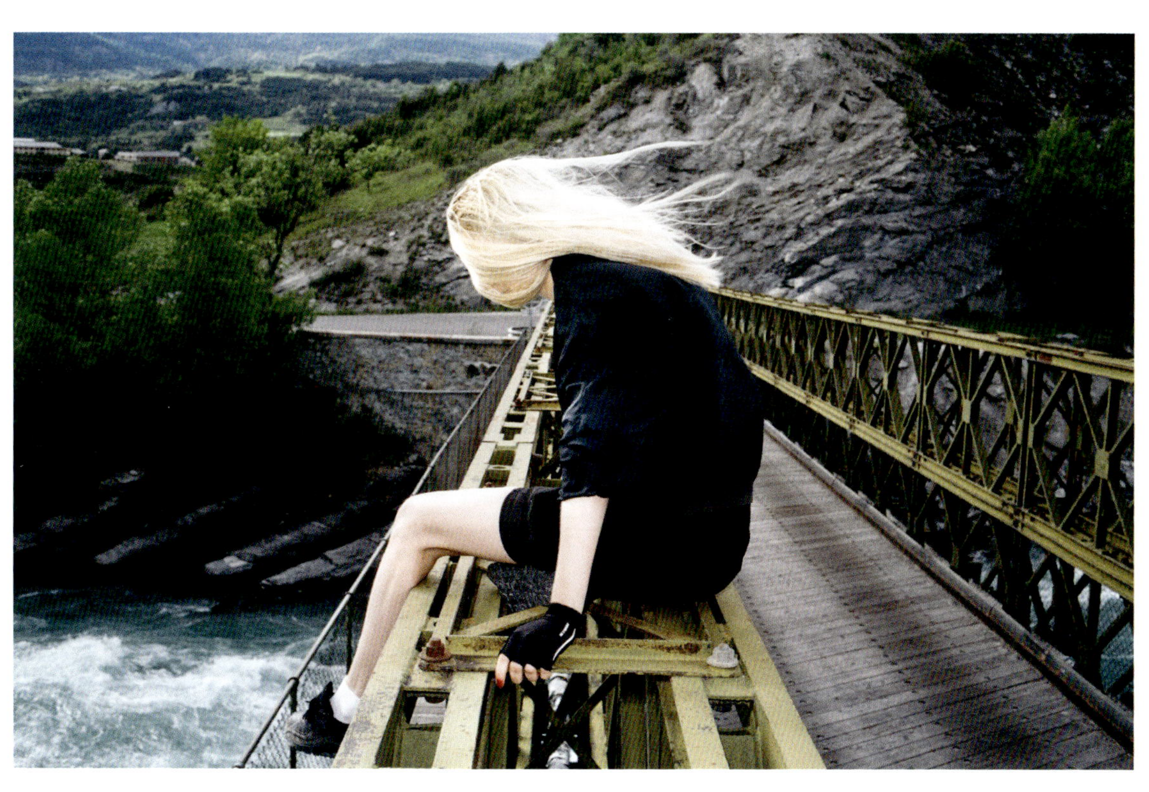

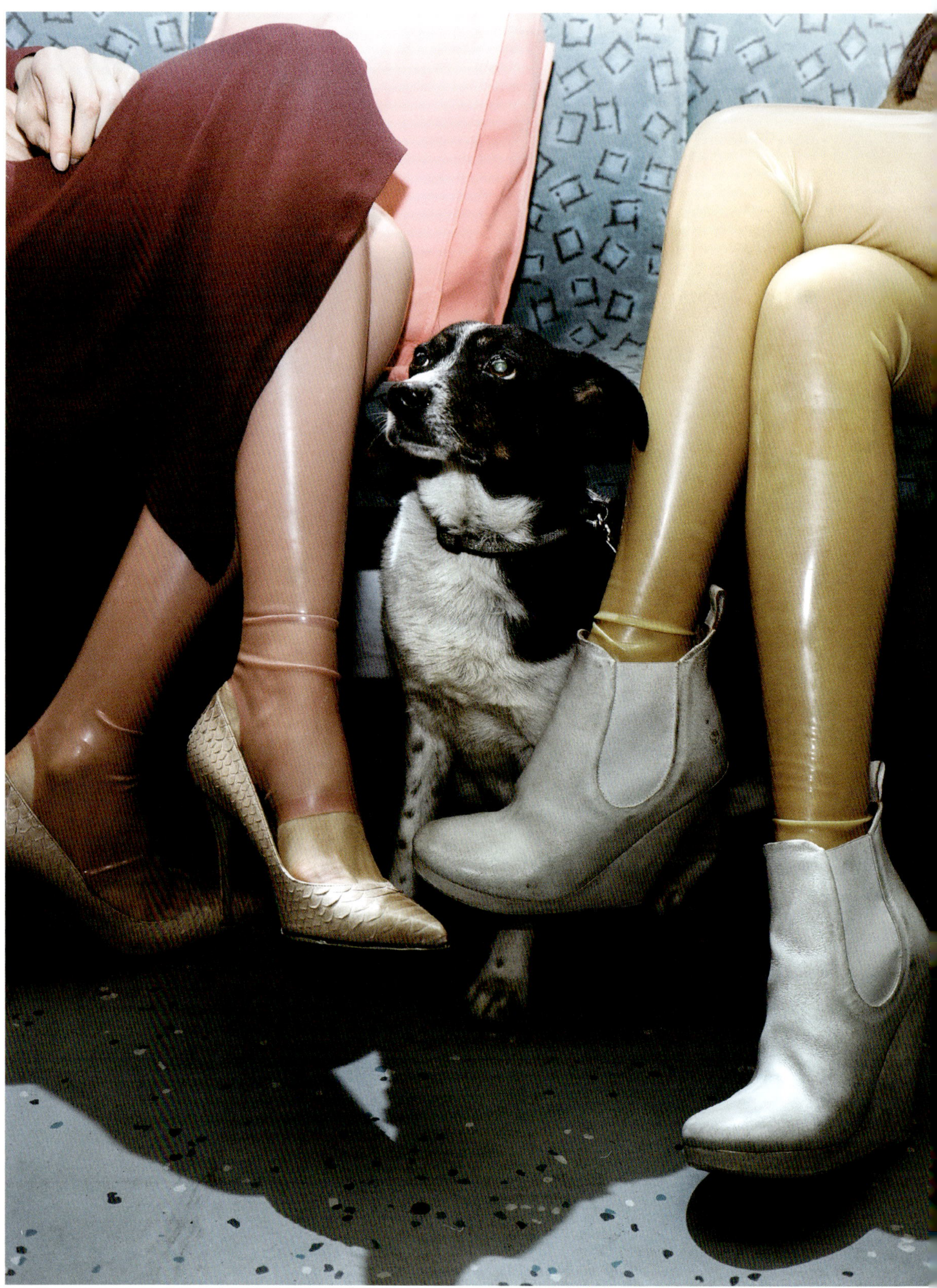

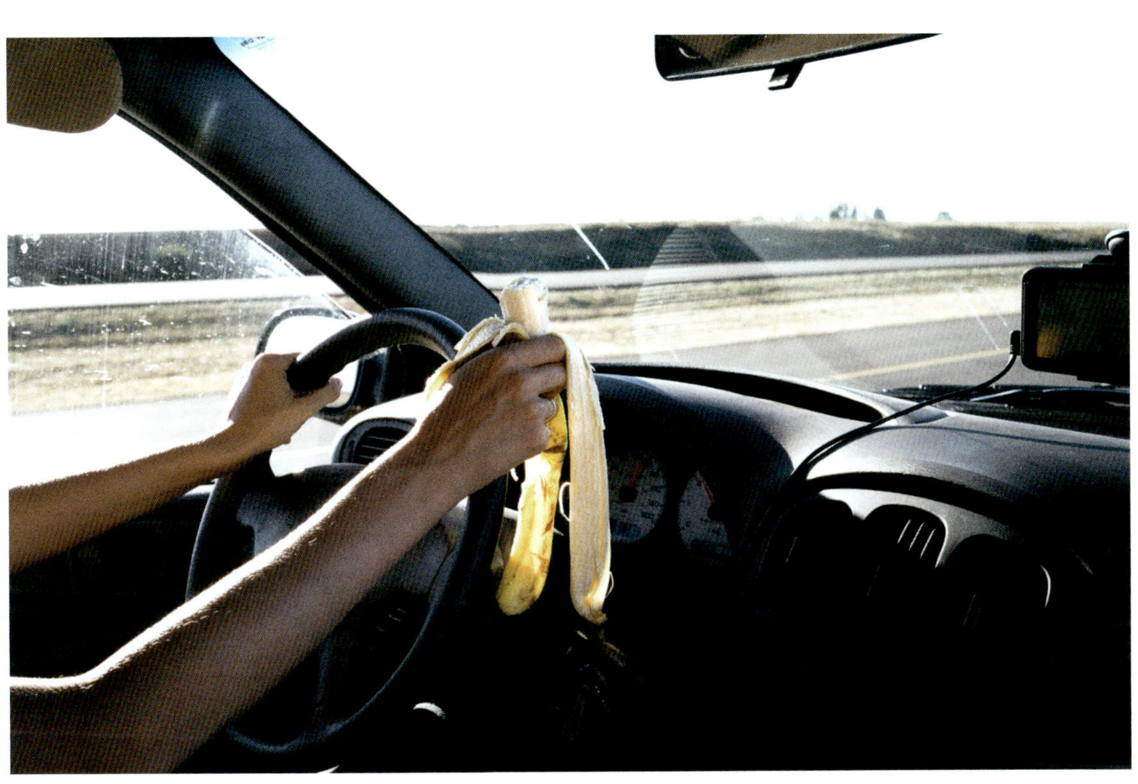

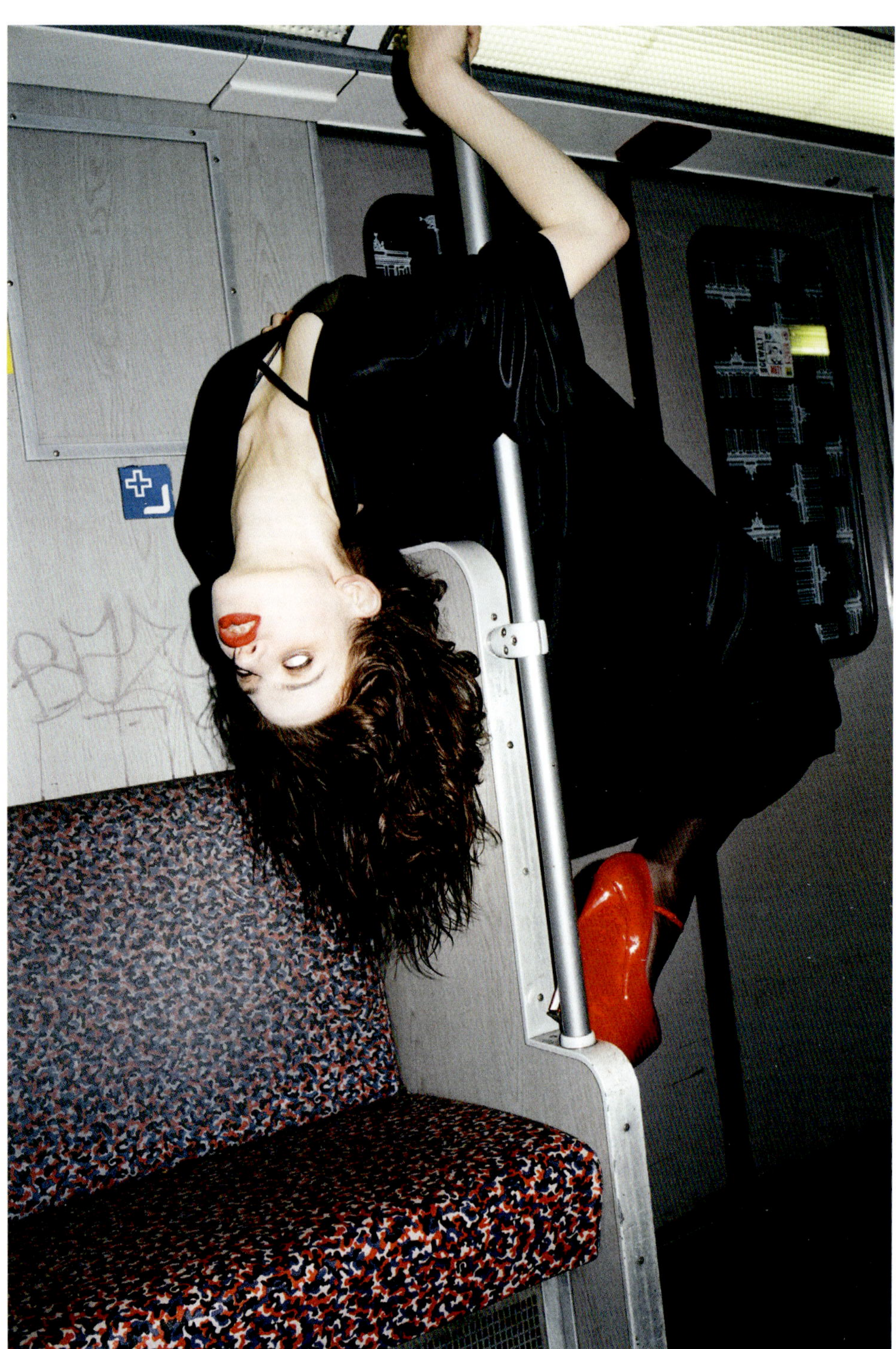

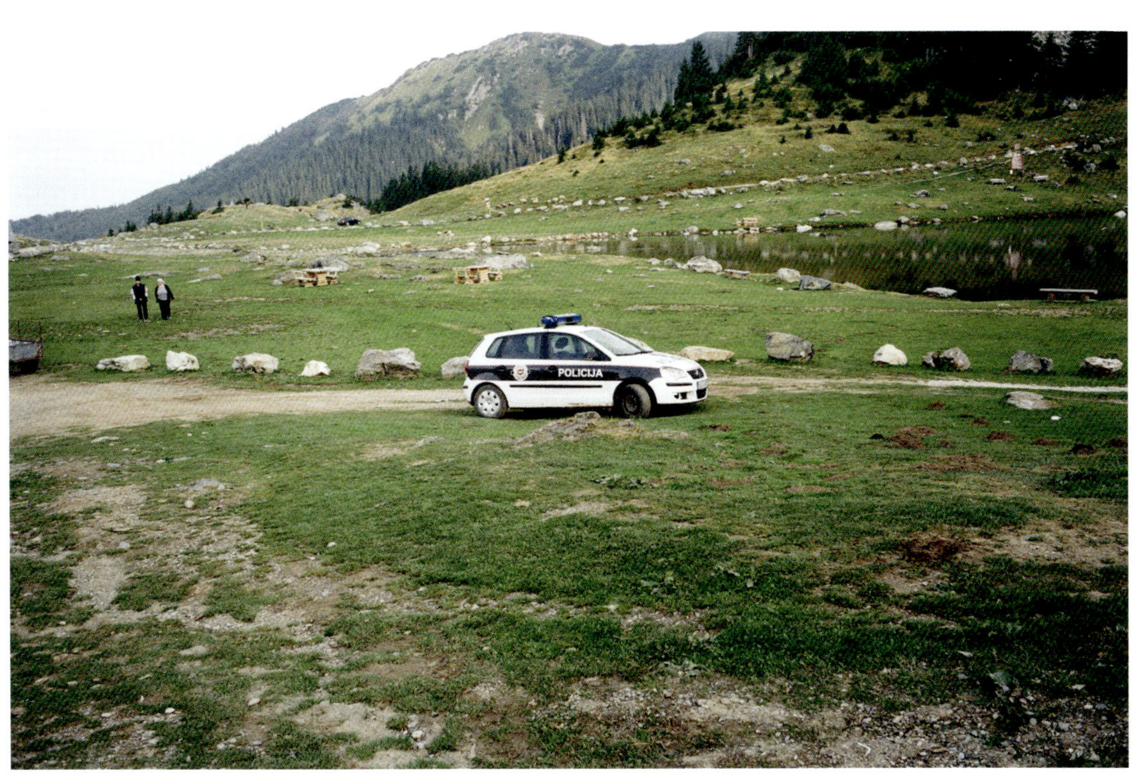
POLICIJA

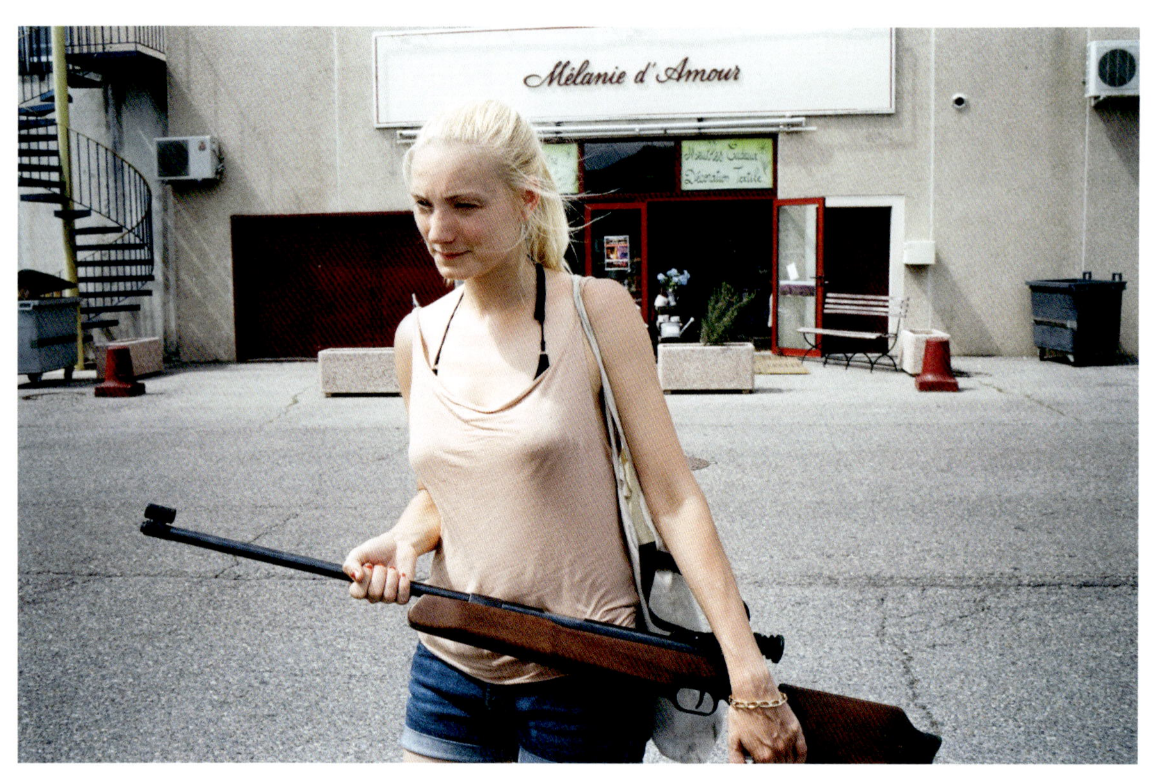

Jen killing time, Digne, 2011

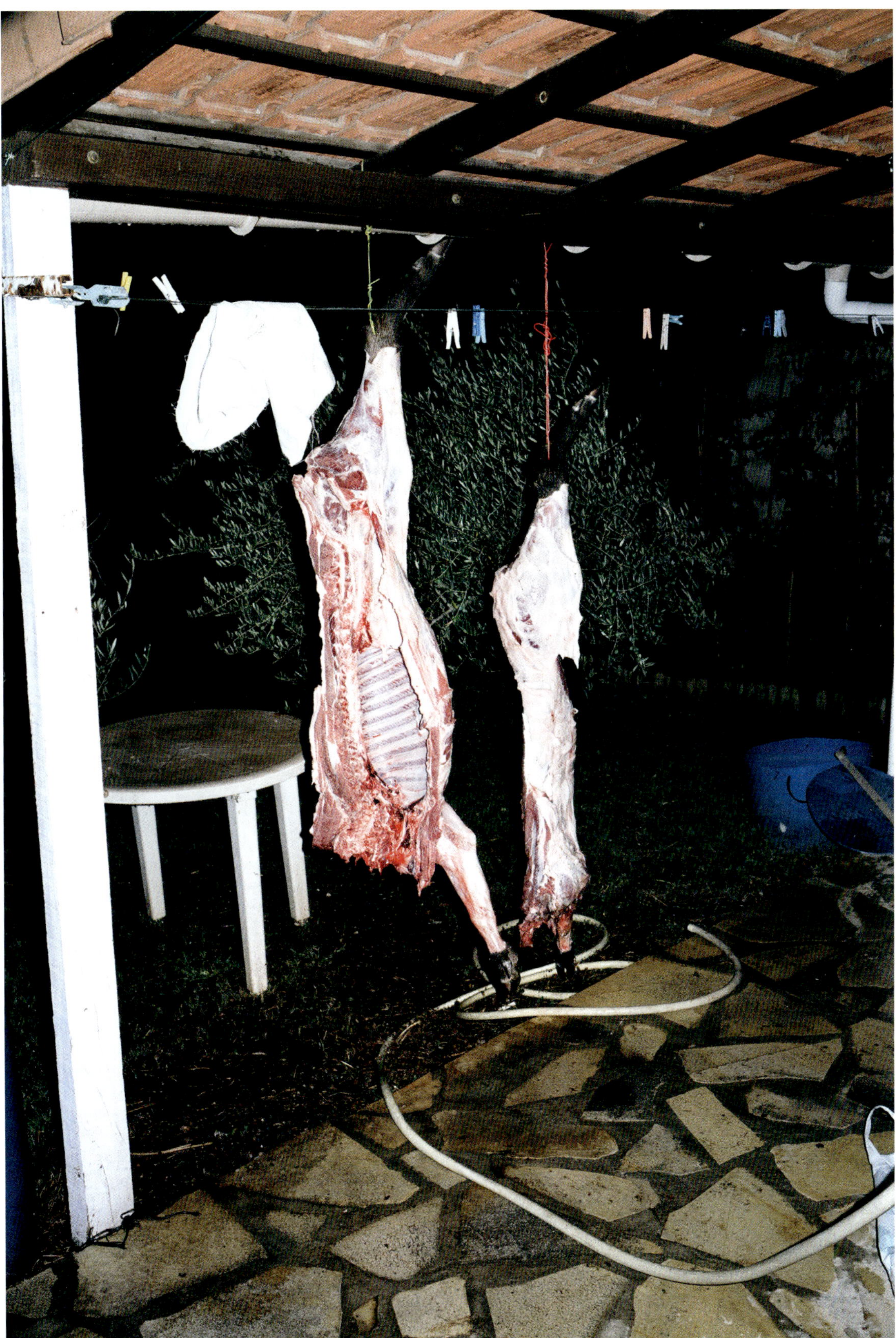

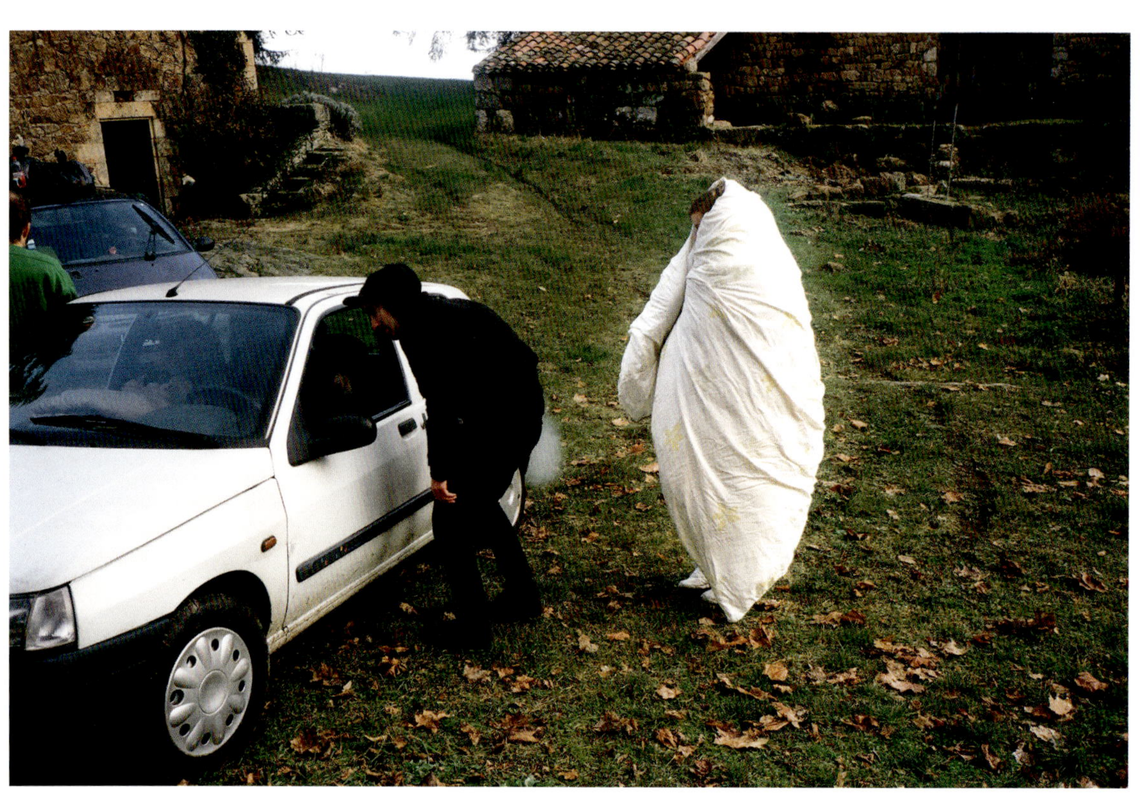

2007 The possessions of an old man, apparently dead, are scattered on the sidewalk and into the garbage bins. Letters, photos, bills, syringes and other medical equipment. Personal effects. You pick up many photo slides, an album, numerous letters. You put them under your car, it's dark and it's raining. You panic. You feel that A., sleeping beside you on an old mattress you keep in the back, has a strange attitude. You look at the lights through the black tinted glass for a while. You don't want to touch these things anymore. But you still keep them.

You discover that the city is beautiful at night. You walk together for a long time. You are in the chic neighborhoods, there is no one but you in the streets.

In the park near the Eiffel Tower, it begins to rain again and in the cabin where you shelter, A. cries for the first time.

2007 Les affaires d'un vieil homme apparemment mort sont répandues sur le trottoir et les poubelles. Correspondance, photos, factures, seringues et autre appareillage médical. Effets personnels. Tu récupères beaucoup de diapositives, un album photo, de nombreuses lettres. Puis tu les mets sous ta voiture, et il fait nuit et il pleut. Tu paniques. Tu trouves que A., qui s'endort à coté de toi sur le vieux matelas que tu gardes à l'arrière, a une attitude étrange. Tu regardes un peu les lumières de la ville à travers les vitres teintées noires. Tu ne veux plus toucher à ses affaires-la. Mais tu les gardes.

Tu découvres que la ville est belle la nuit. Vous marchez longtemps. Vous êtes dans les quartiers chics il n'y a que vous dans les rues.

Dans le parc tout proche de la tour Eiffel, il se met à pleuvoir encore et dans la cabane où vous vous abritez, A. pleure pour la première fois.

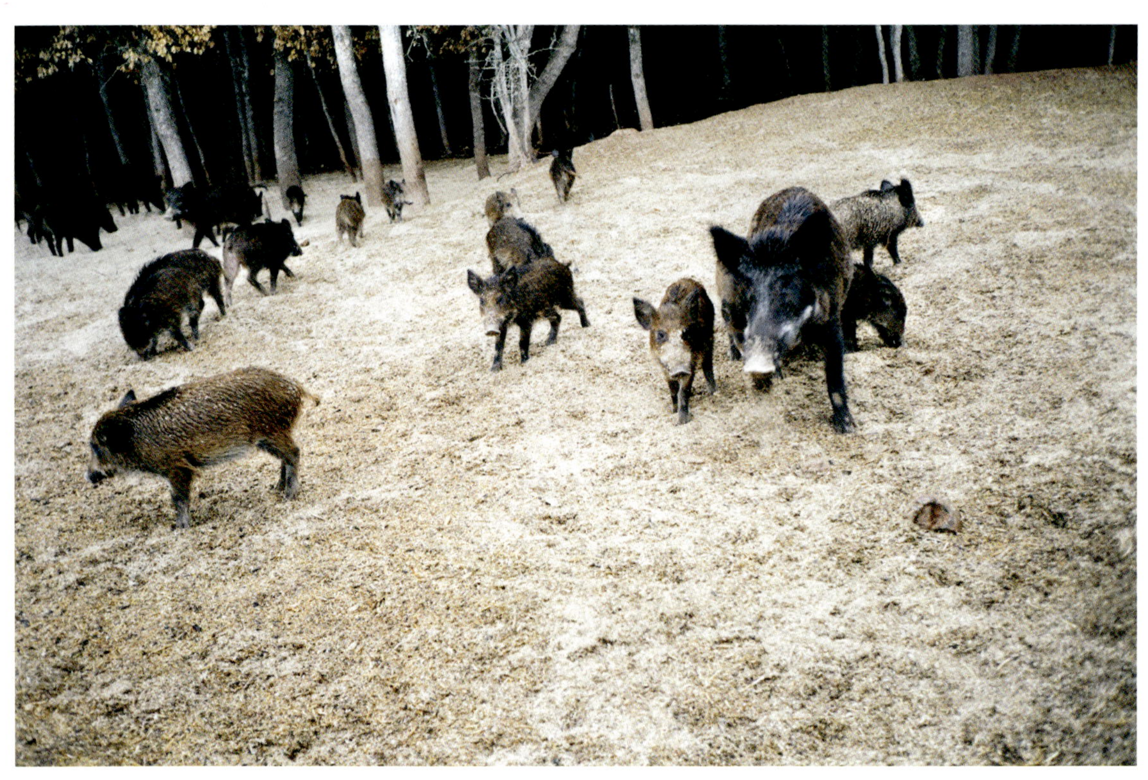

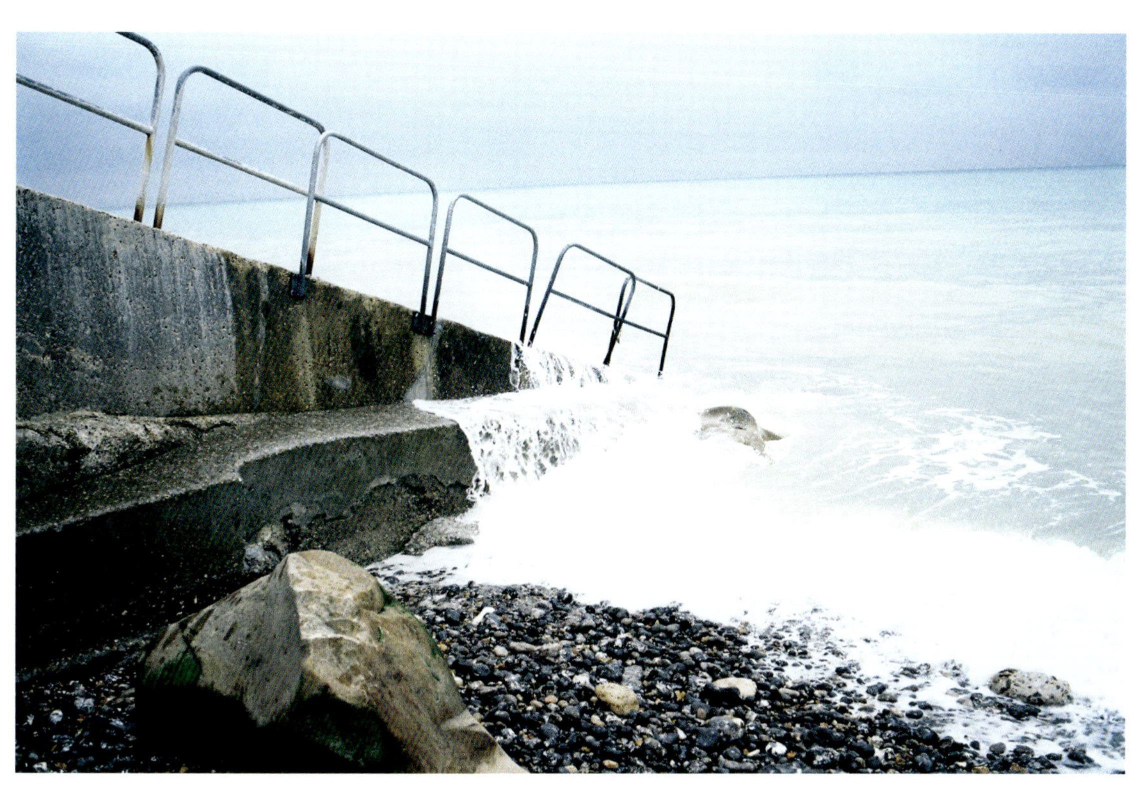

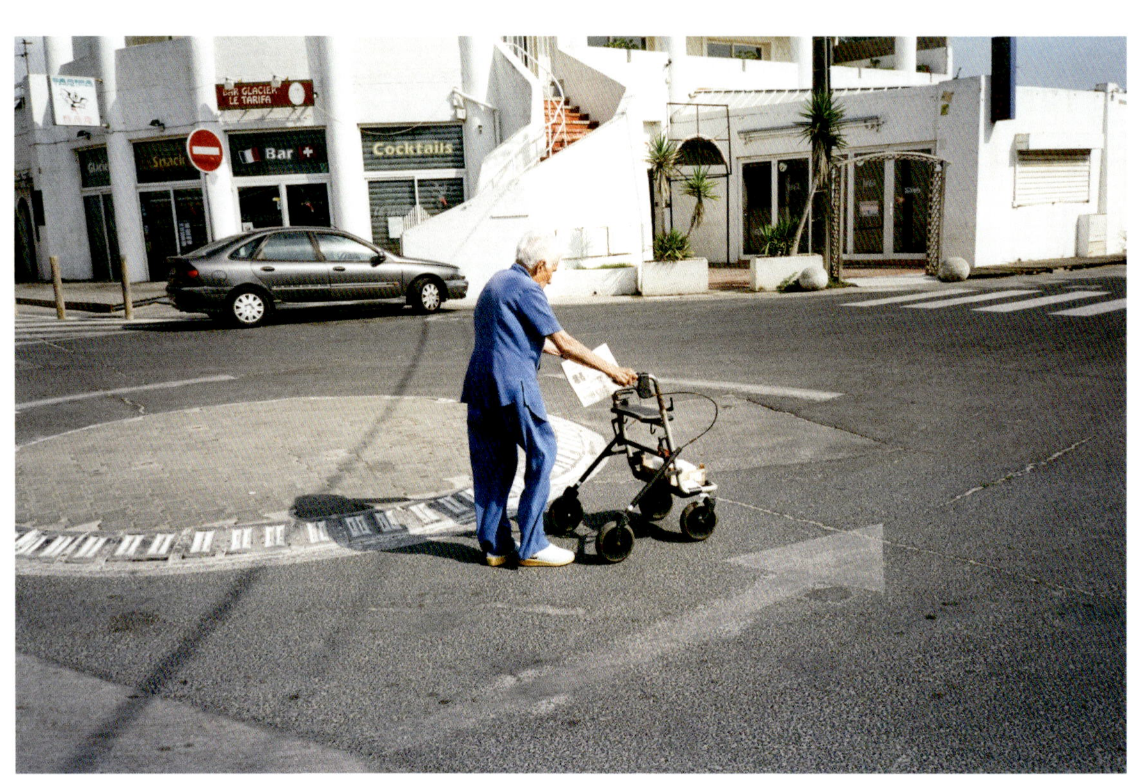
LE TARIFA
Snack
Bar
Cocktails

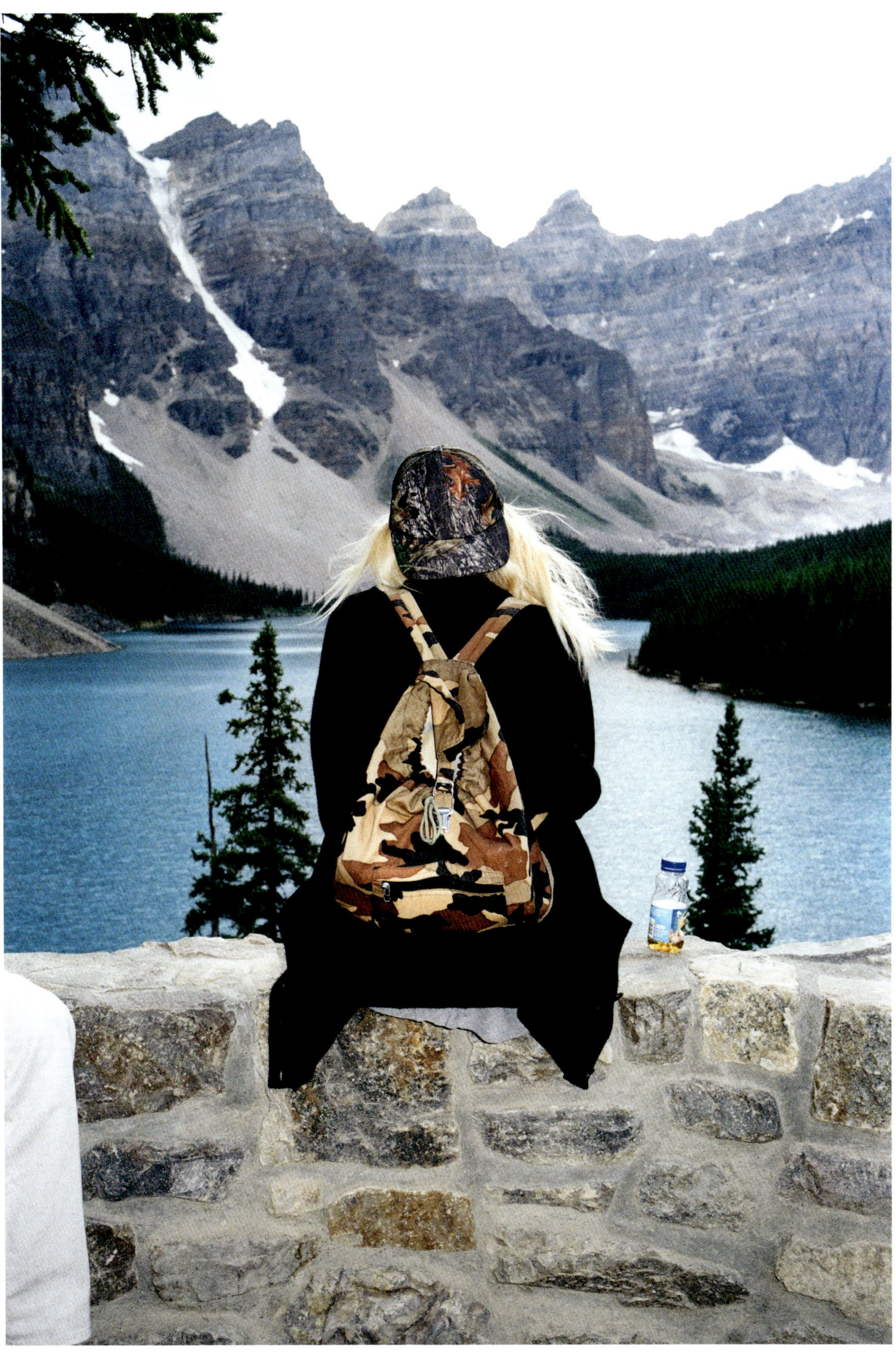

Des après-midi à la fenêtre

L'amour

2005

His heart
was so heavy that it
was falling on his balls,
causing a discrete erection.

2005

Son coeur
était si lourd qu'il
lui tombait sur les couilles,
provoquant une discrète érection.

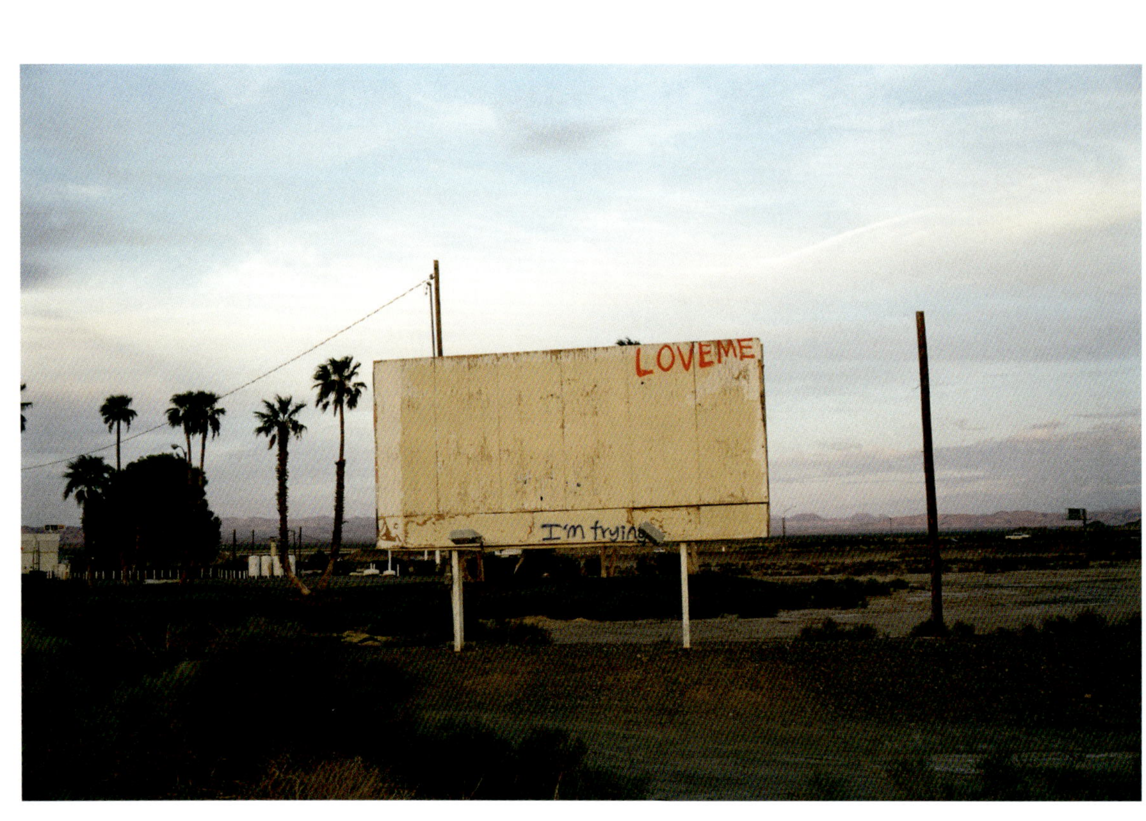
LOVEME
I'm trying

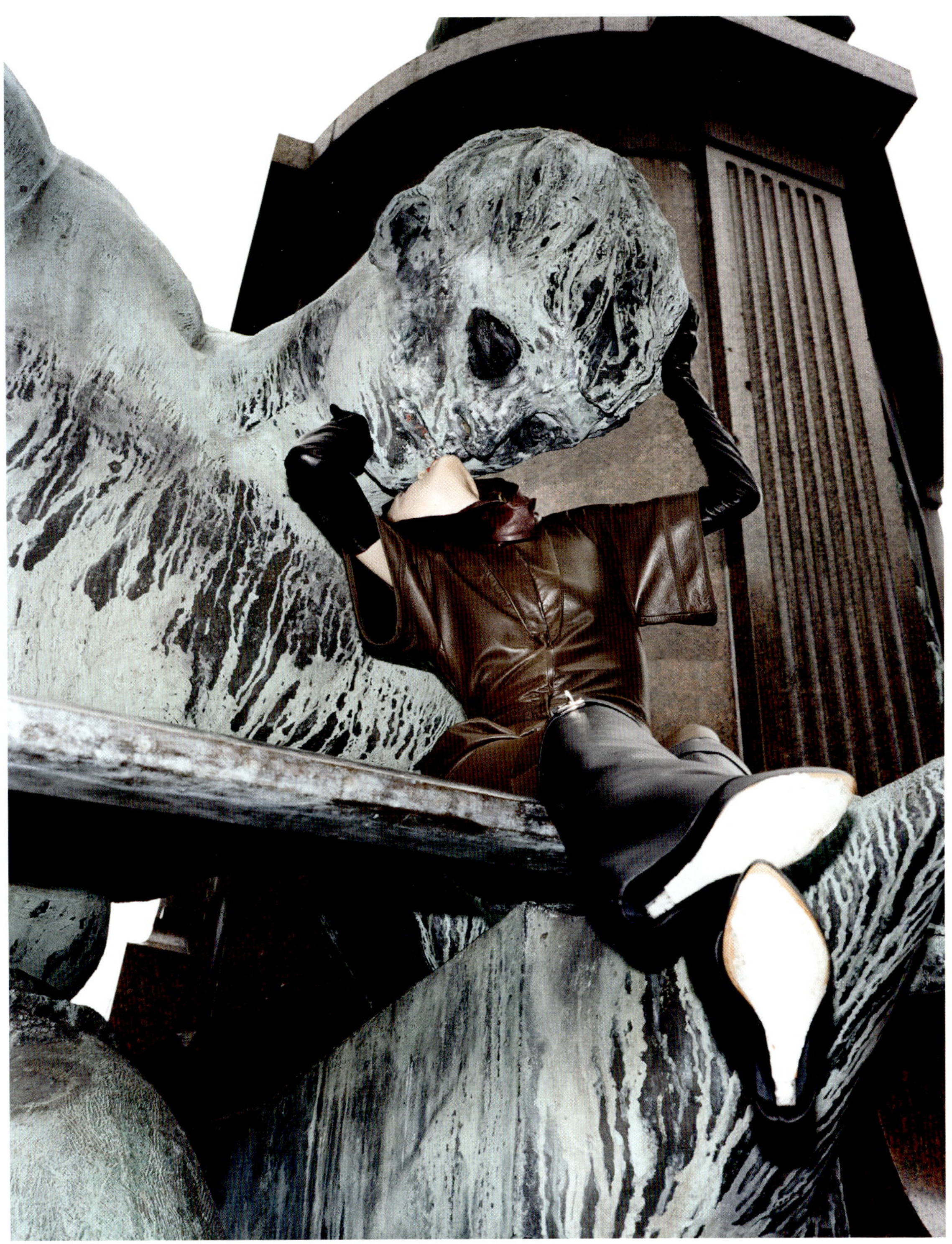

bronze's tenderness, Berlin, 2012

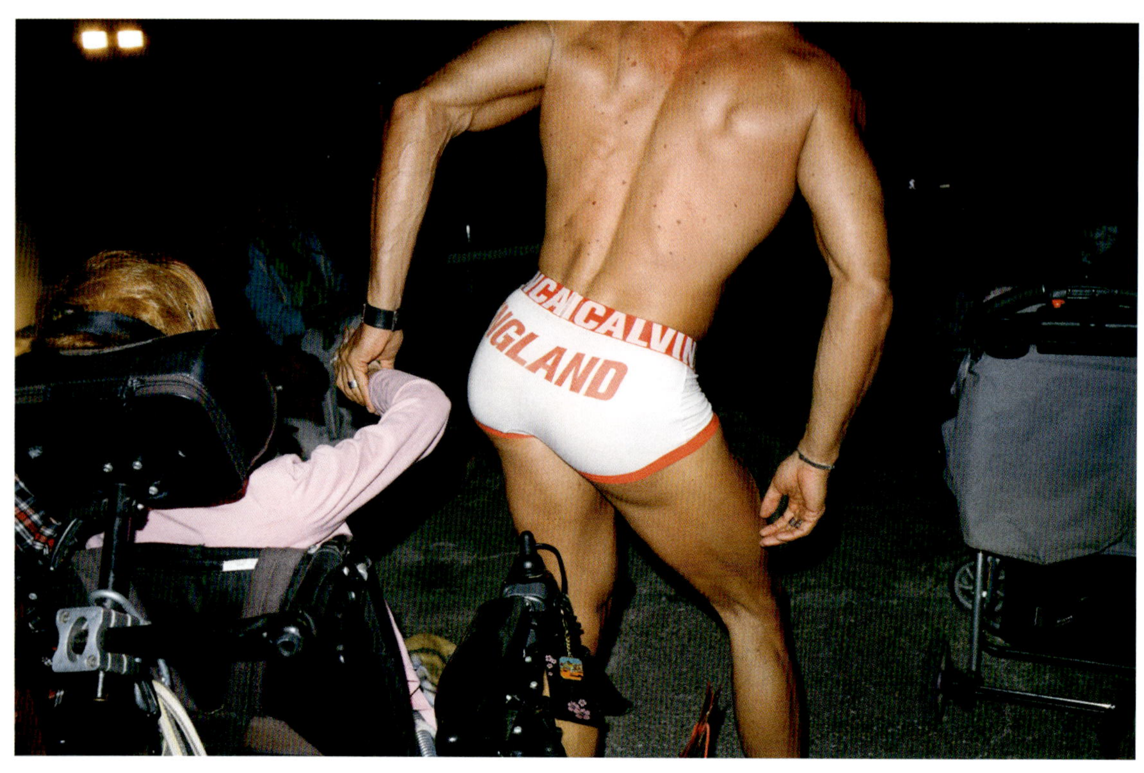
CALVIN

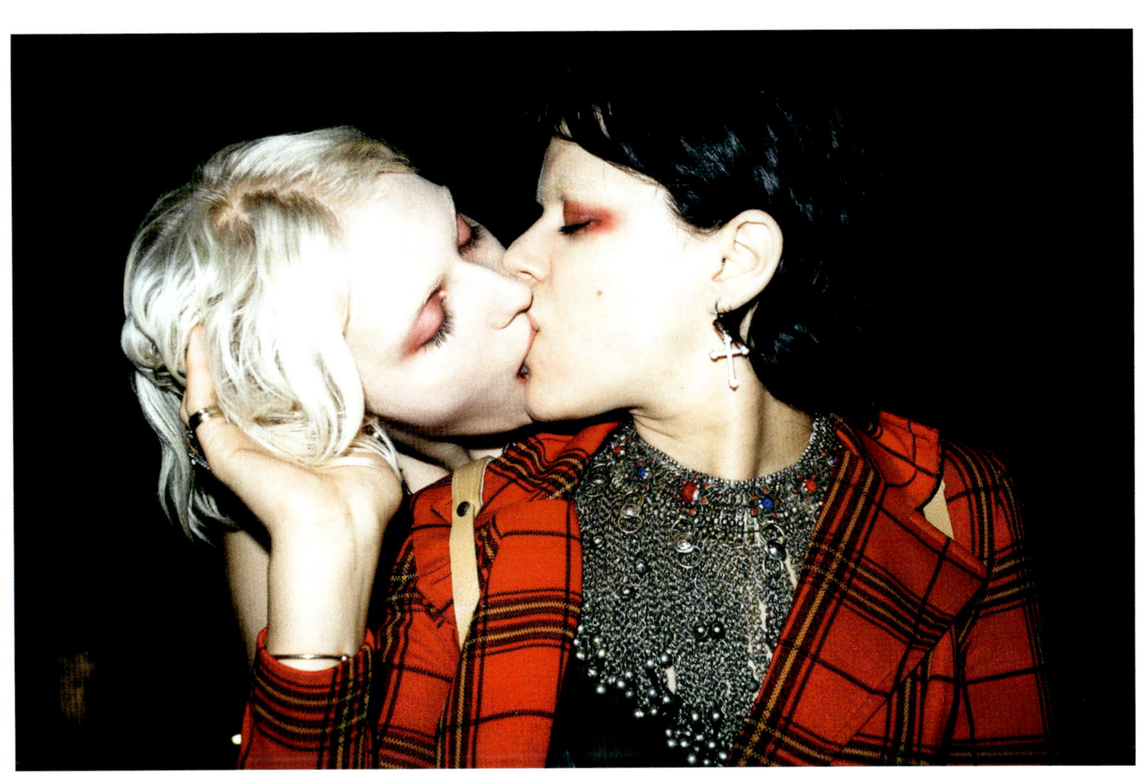

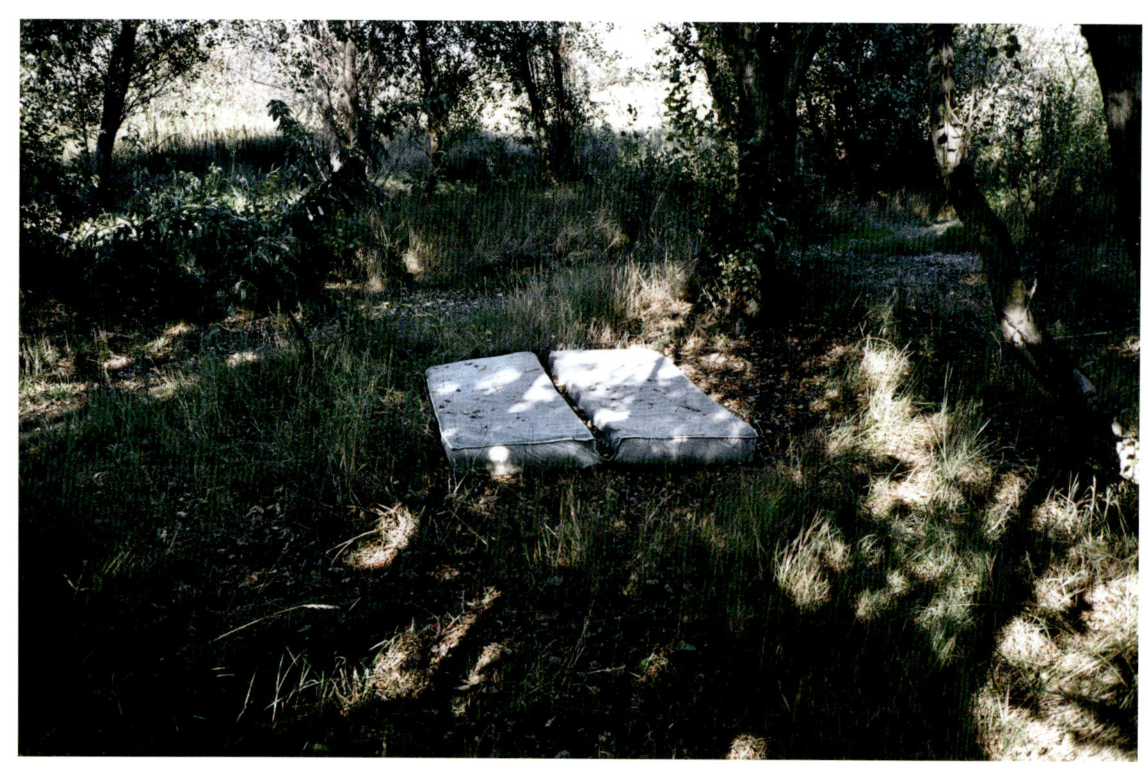

king size, Montpellier, 2010

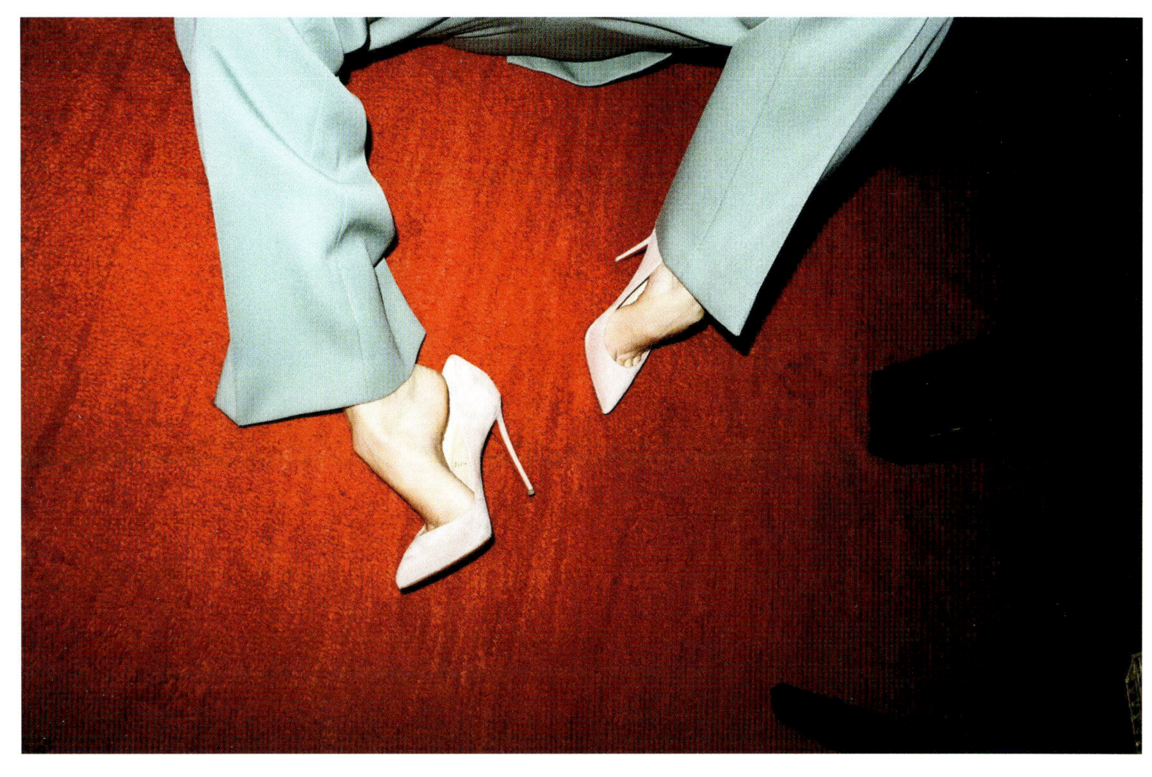

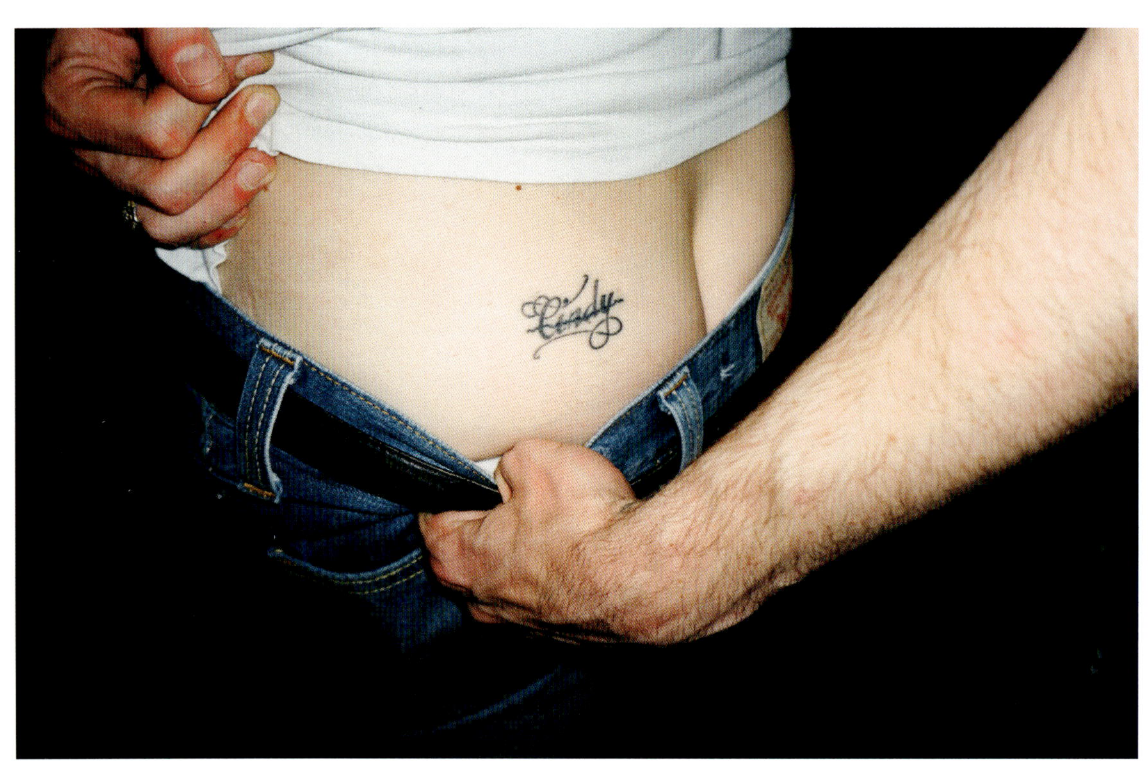
Cindy

2006 Finally it's sad to go home knowing that she will not come here anymore.
That she will not ring the bell at 5am to sleep with you.
That she will not surprise you by arriving at your
place in the middle of the day without warning.
She has returned to Brussels. At least you think so.
She returned your keys.
You don't really know how to contact her, but would you try if you knew?
Yes.
She didn't go back to Brussels.
You saw her tonight and she was in a car, and you on the street.
She is in your city. And you must accept it.
She will never come back home but she is still here.
You must forget. You must mourn for her.
You are not able. To mourn.
This situation would make you crazy if you were not so drunk.
And you wait, still, for her to knock on your door.
Again.
After a while, you don't wait anymore.
But
you can't
think about her
without a pang. You are incoherent. You scatter your love in memories.
You don't move on. You don't turn the page. Everything remains.
Fortunately you have a poor memory.
You have something like four or five goldfishes in your head, no more.

2006 Finalement c'est triste de rentrer à la maison et de savoir qu'elle n'arrivera plus.
Qu'elle ne sonnera plus à 5h le matin pour dormir avec toi.
Qu'elle ne te surprendra plus en plein après-midi à entrer sans rien dire.
Elle est repartit à Bruxelles. Enfin tu penses.
Elle t'a rendu tes clés.
Tu ne sais pas vraiment où la joindre mais si tu savais essaierais-tu seulement?
Oui.
Elle n'est pas retournée à Bruxelles.
Tu l'a croisée ce soir, elle était en voiture et toi dans la rue.
Elle est dans ta ville. Et tu dois l'accepter.
Elle ne reviendra plus chez toi mais elle est toujours là. Tu dois oublier.
Tu dois faire ton deuil d'elle.
Tu ne sais pas faire.
Le deuil de. Cette situation te rendrait fou si tu n'étais pas si saoul.
Et tu attends toujours, quand même qu'elle sonne à ta porte. Encore.
Plus tard,
tu n'attends
plus.
Mais
tu ne peux penser
à elle
sans un pincement. Tu es incohérent. Tu éparpilles ton amour dans des
souvenirs. Tu ne passes pas à autre chose. Tu ne tournes pas de page.
Tout reste là.
Heureusement tu as très peu de mémoire.
Tu as peut-être l'équivalent de quatre ou cinq poissons rouges dans le crâne, pas plus.

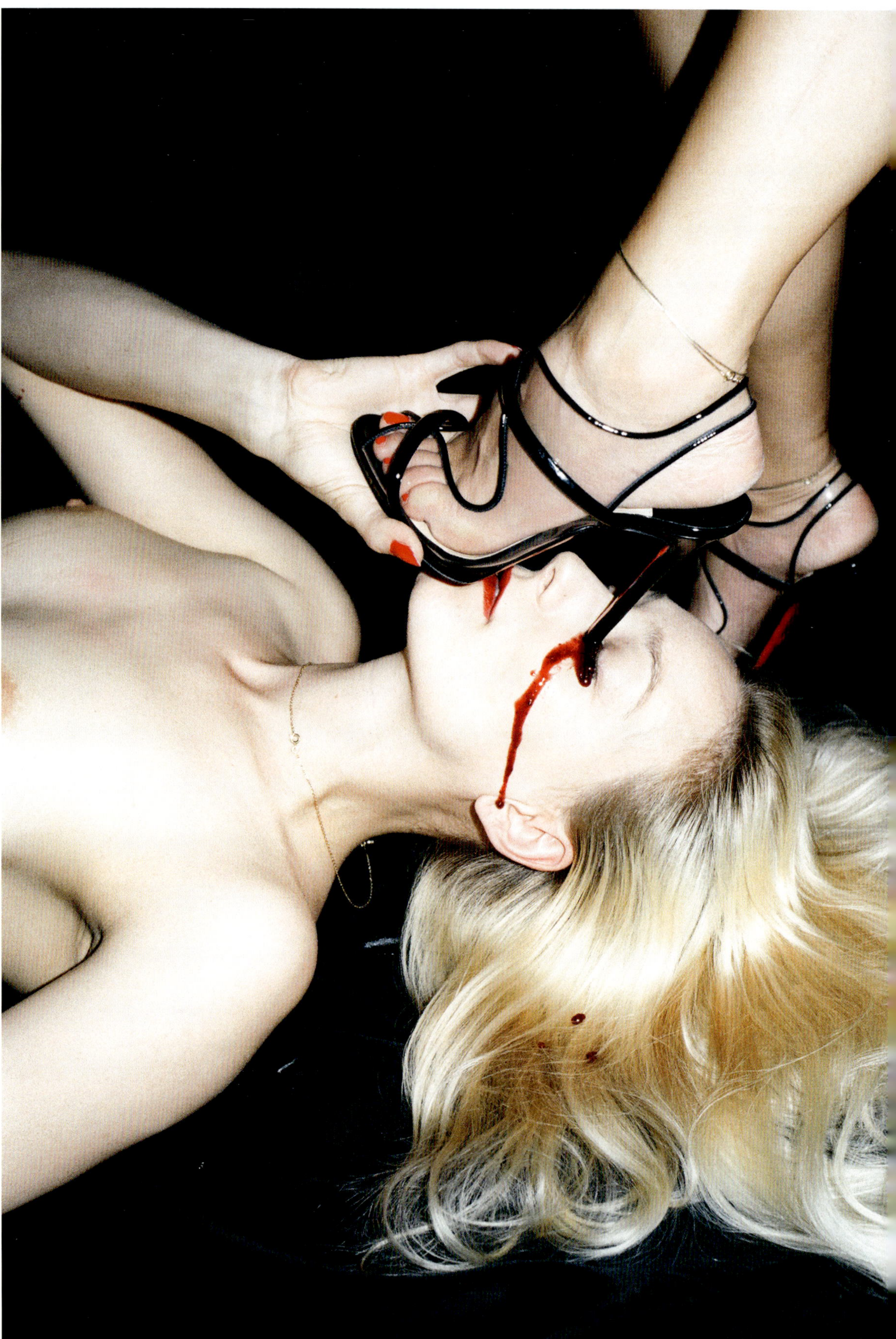

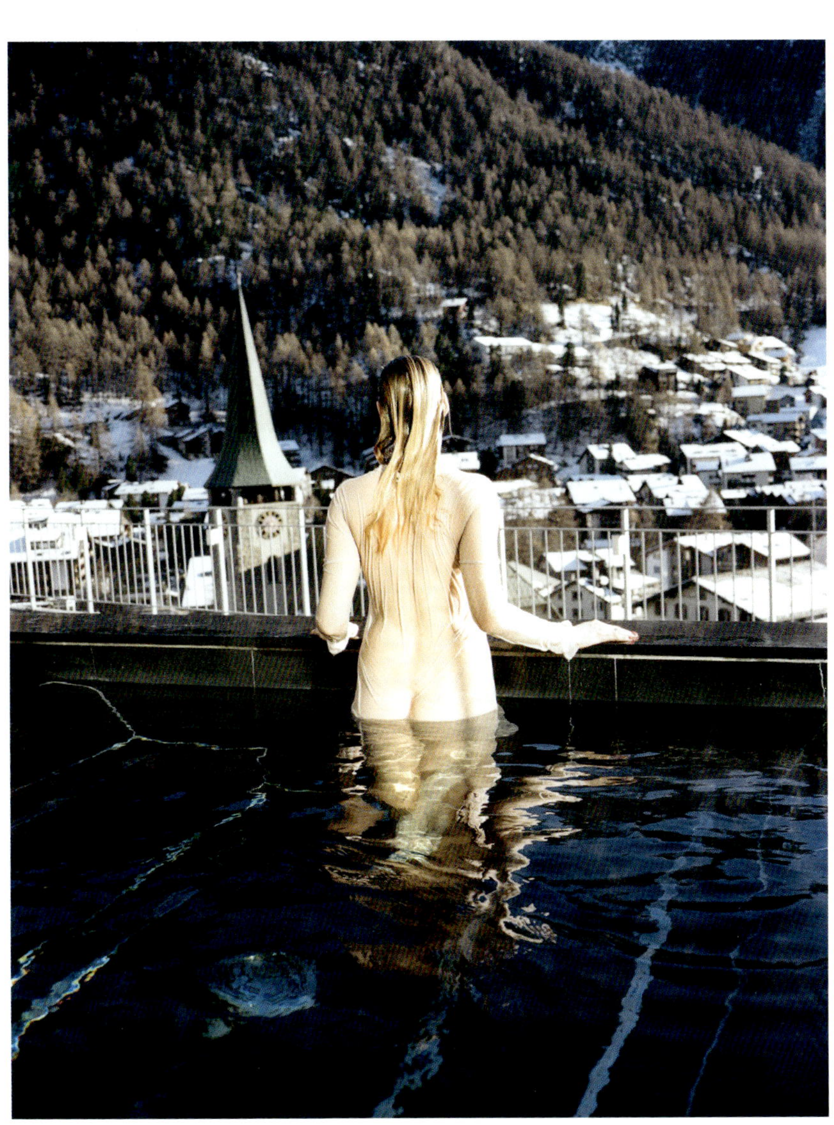

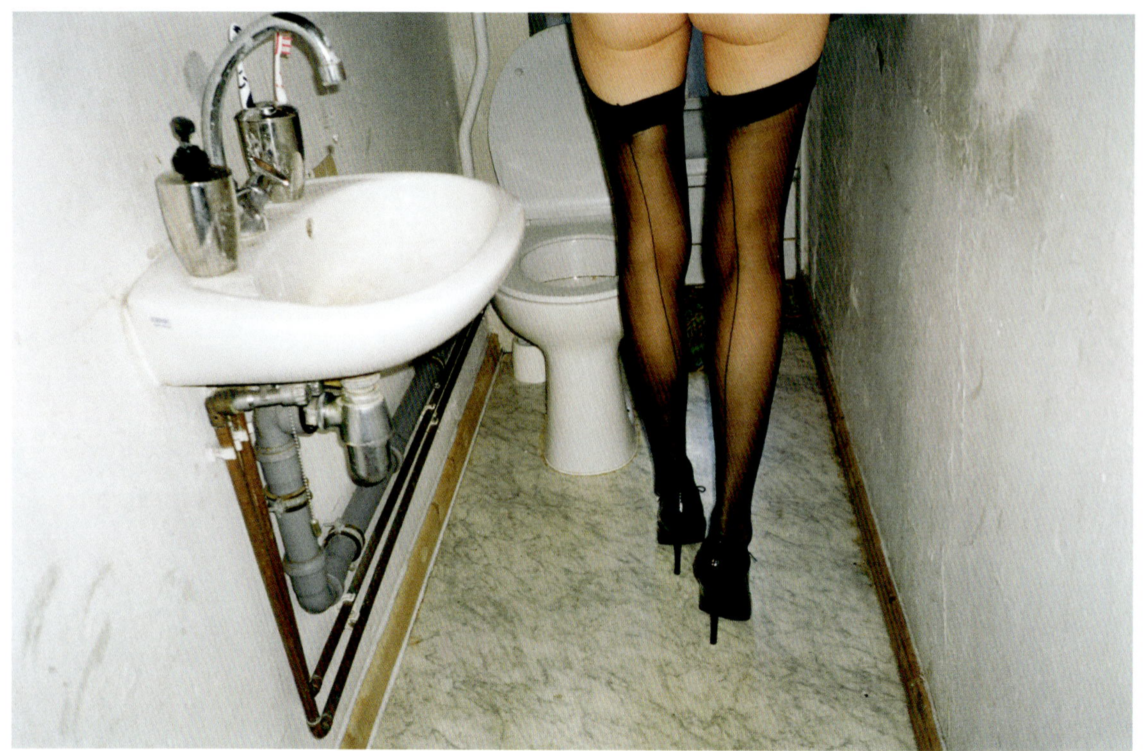

August 2015

Since that night we met 6 years ago, since this afternoon,
I woke up holding you in my arms in your tiny apartment,
realizing that you don't speak French anymore when you are sober,
and that you are so beautiful I don't know how it's gonna be possible to ever get out
of your bed, there hasn't been one single day I didn't feel like the luckiest person on earth.
I had no idea back then you'd change my life forever,
that we'd take each other on so many adventures,
and drink so much whisky together.
I love you so much I almost feel like I'd want to grow old just to spend more time with you.

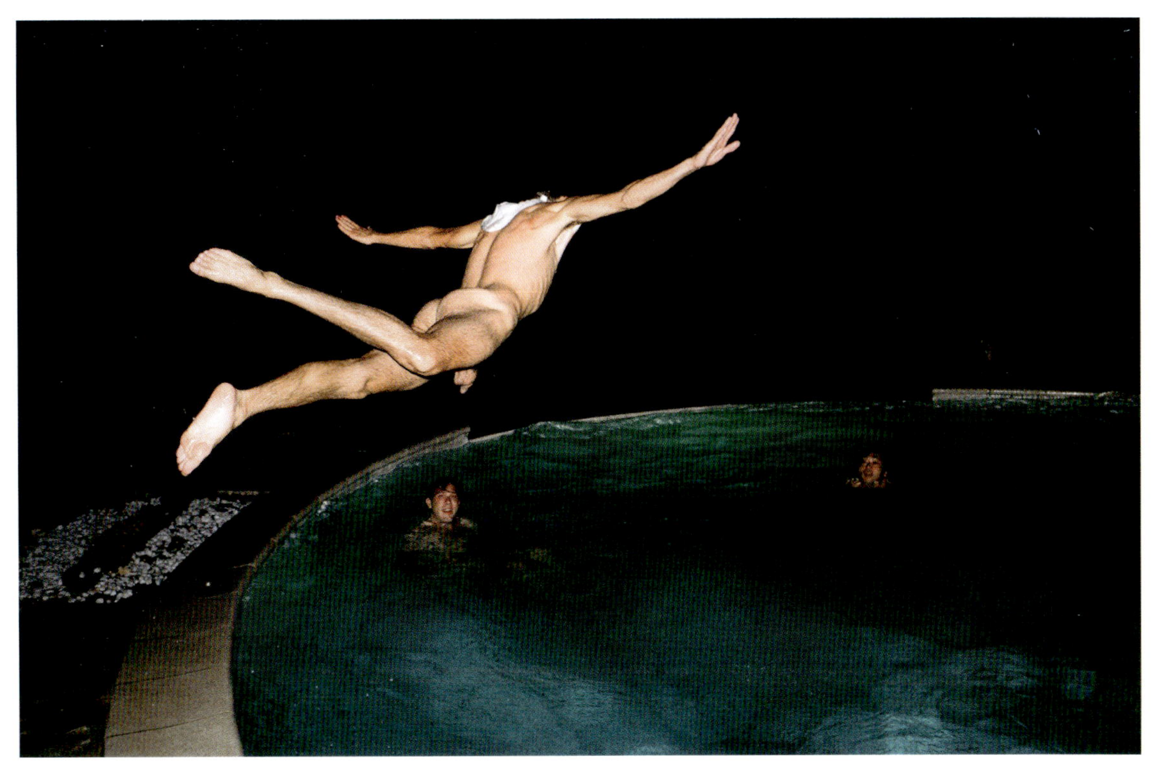

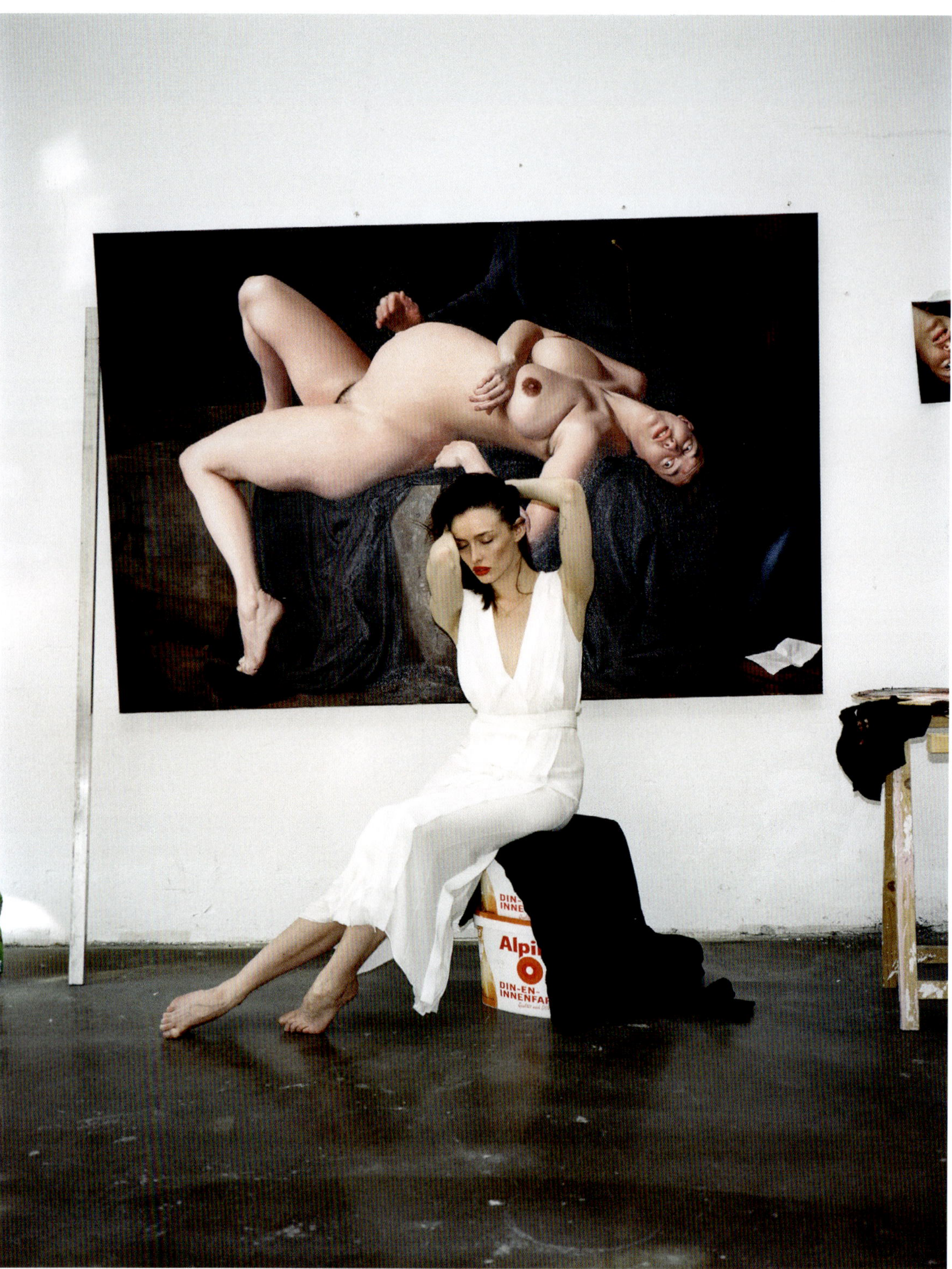

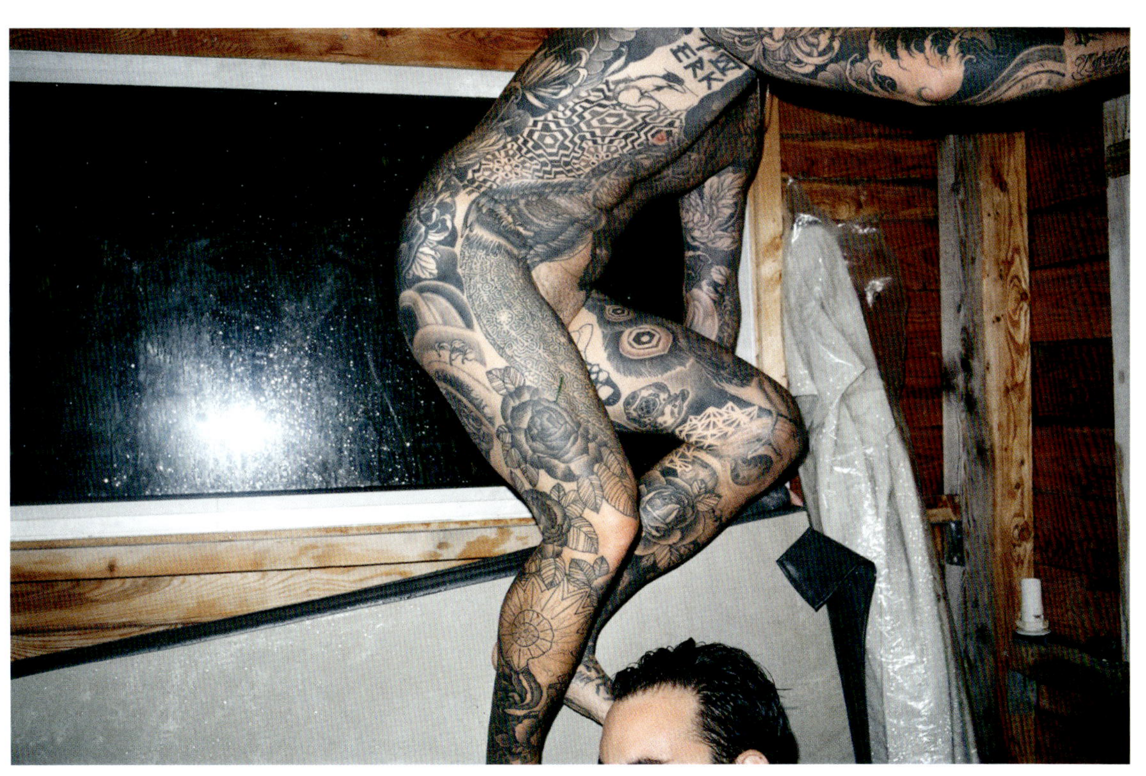

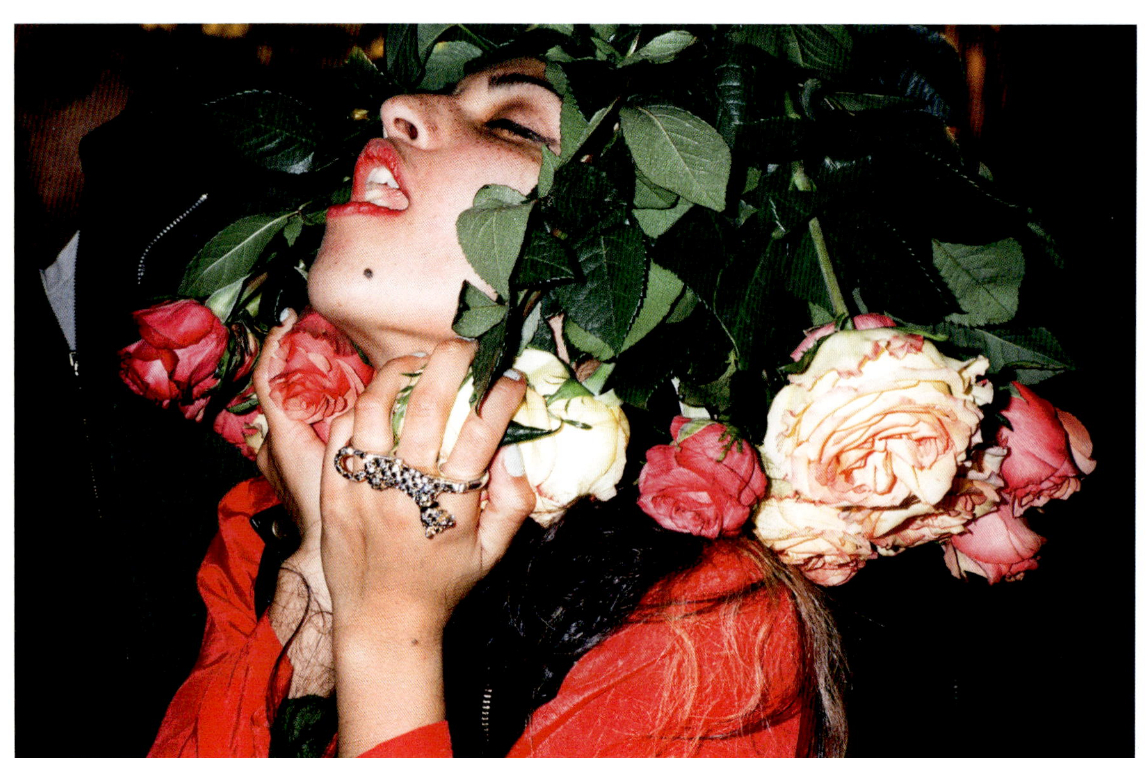

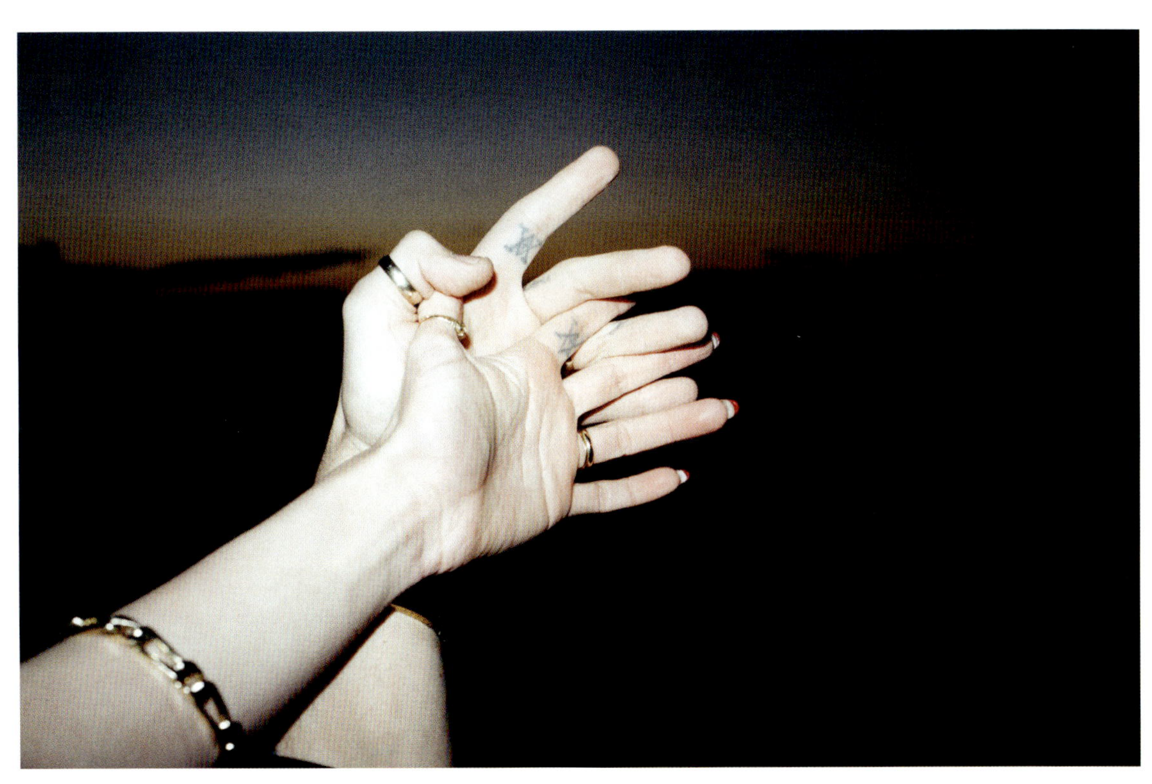

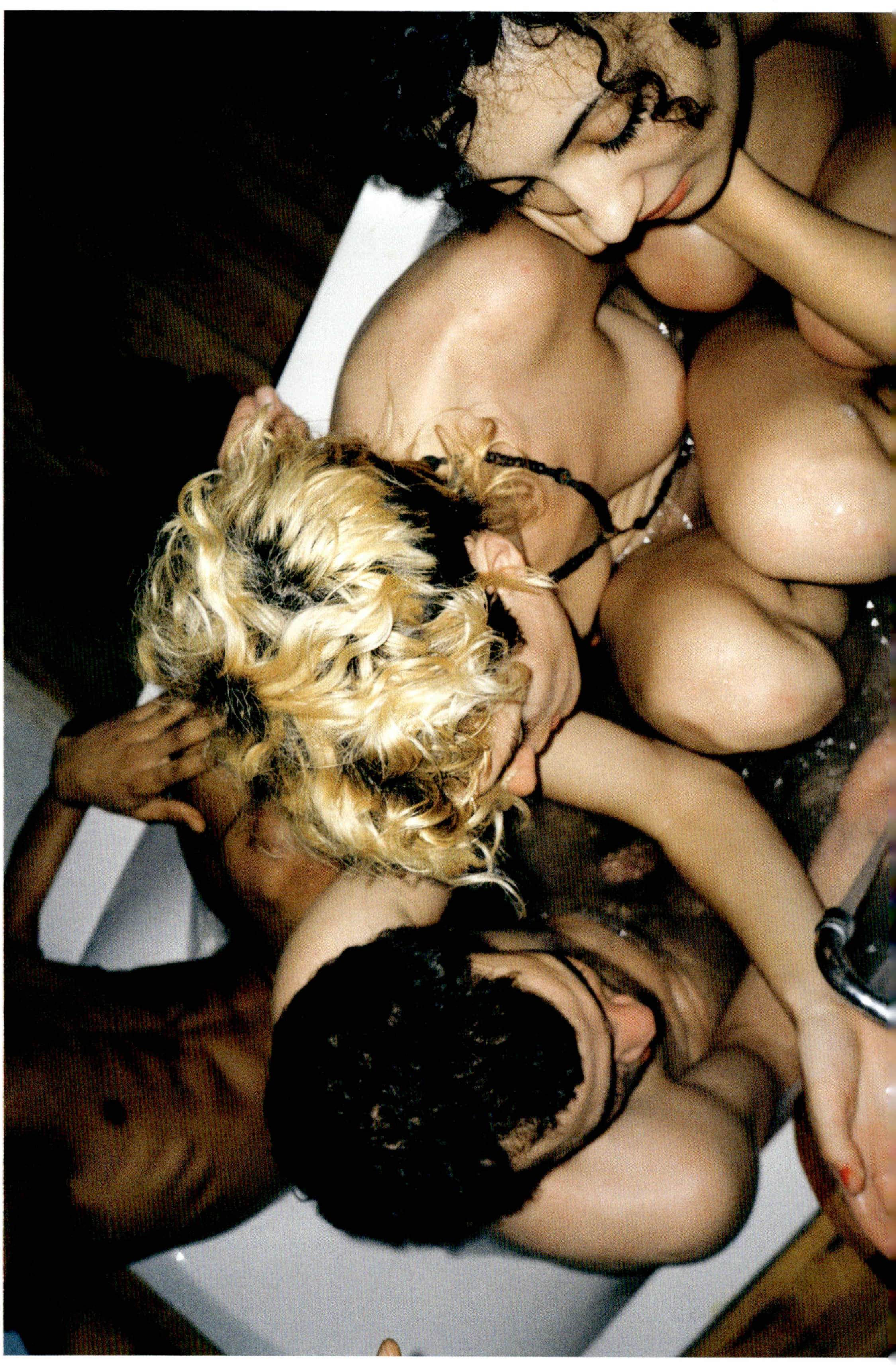

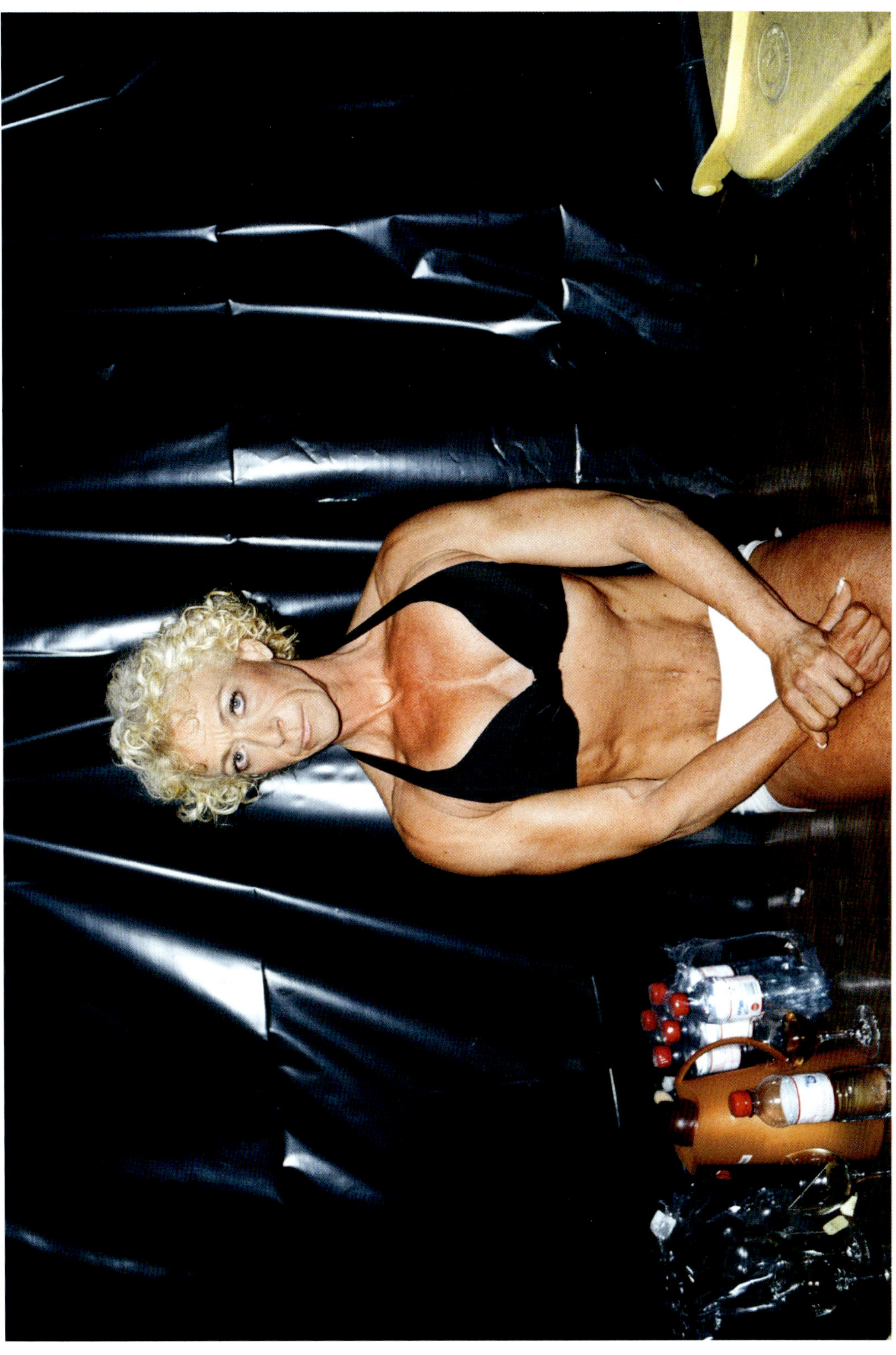

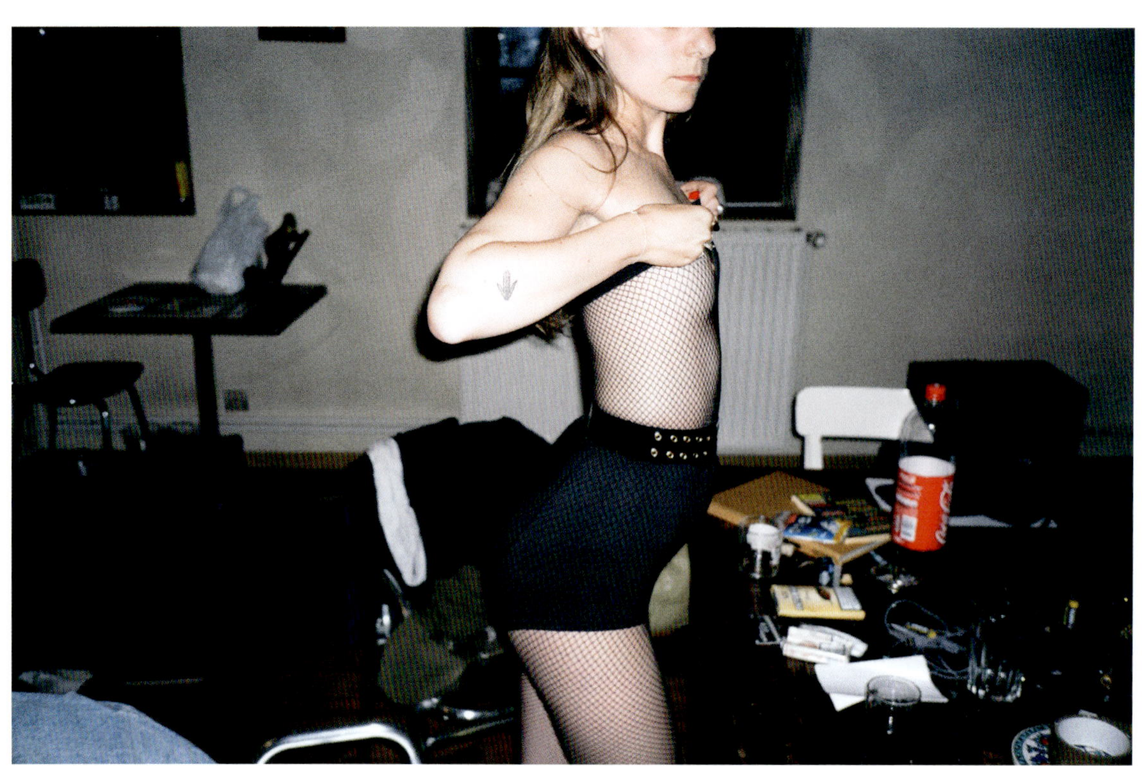

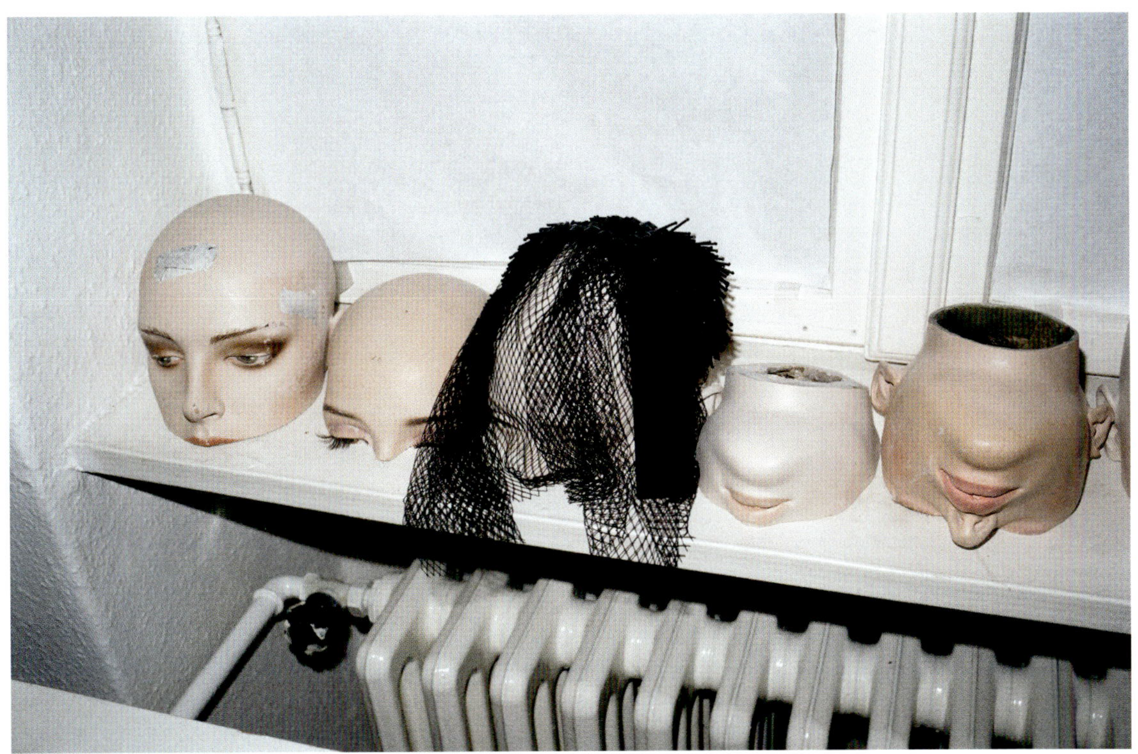

2005 It was in December that everything stopped.
I was on my way home when you called me that winter.
I was fine as I told you on the phone.
Less than an hour later you were dead.
Almost two years later and I still cannot believe it.
It took me a long time to understand that you made this choice out of love.
Today I have a hole in my gut that bears your name.
Today I love you.

2005 C'est en décembre que tout s'arrêta.
Je rentrais chez moi quand tu as appelé cet hiver.
J'allais bien comme je te l'ai répondu au téléphone.
Moins d'une heure plus tard tu seras mort.
Presque deux ans plus tard je n'en reviens toujours pas.
J'ai mis longtemps à comprendre que tu avais fait ce choix par amour.
Aujourd'hui j'ai un trou au ventre qui porte ton nom.
Aujourd'hui je t'aime.

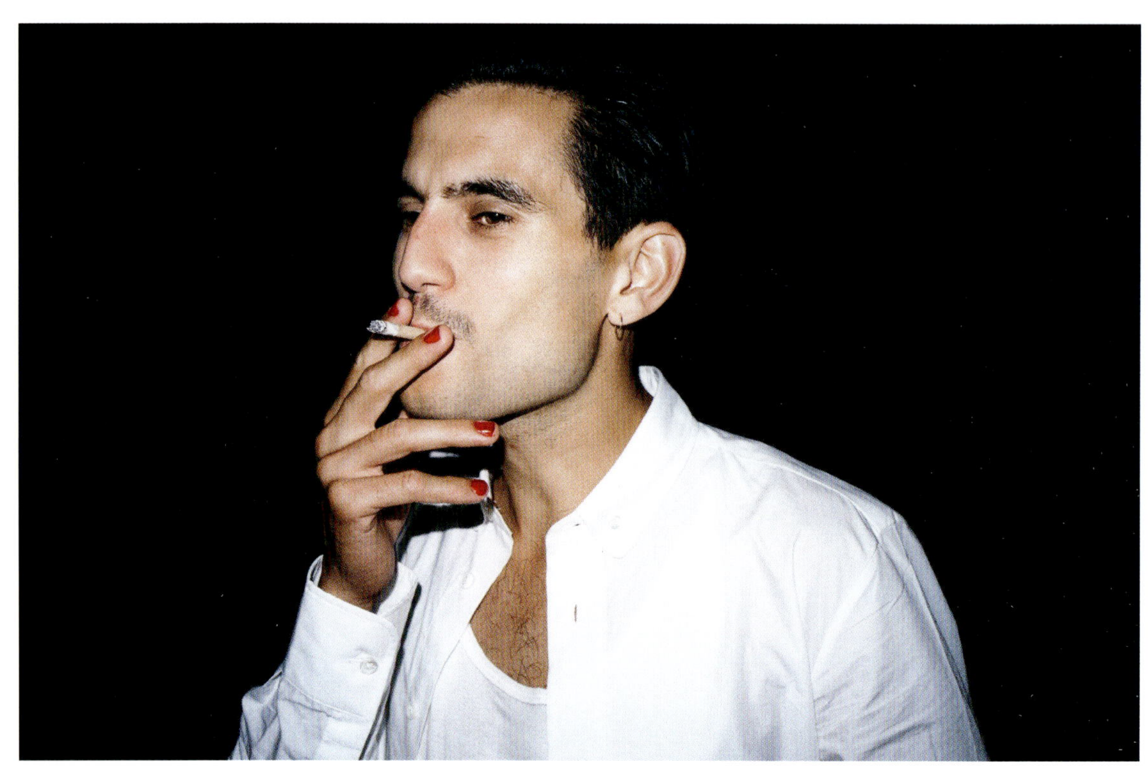

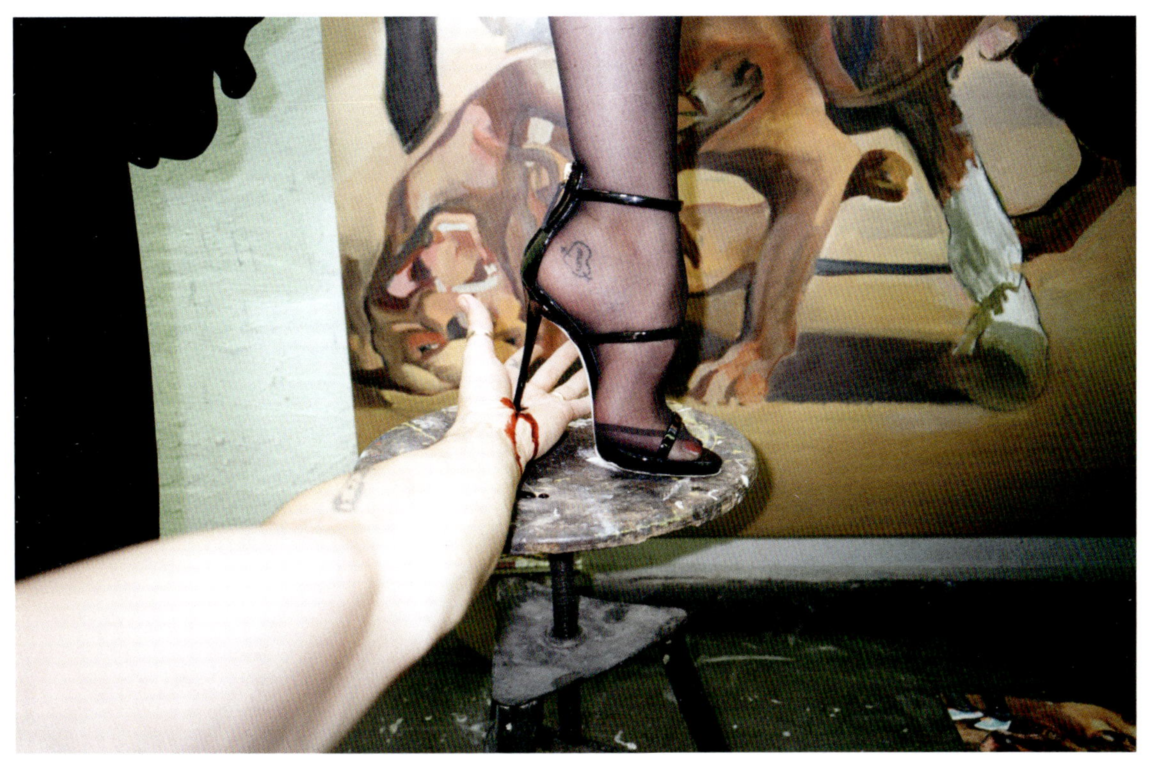

love letter, Berlin, 2016

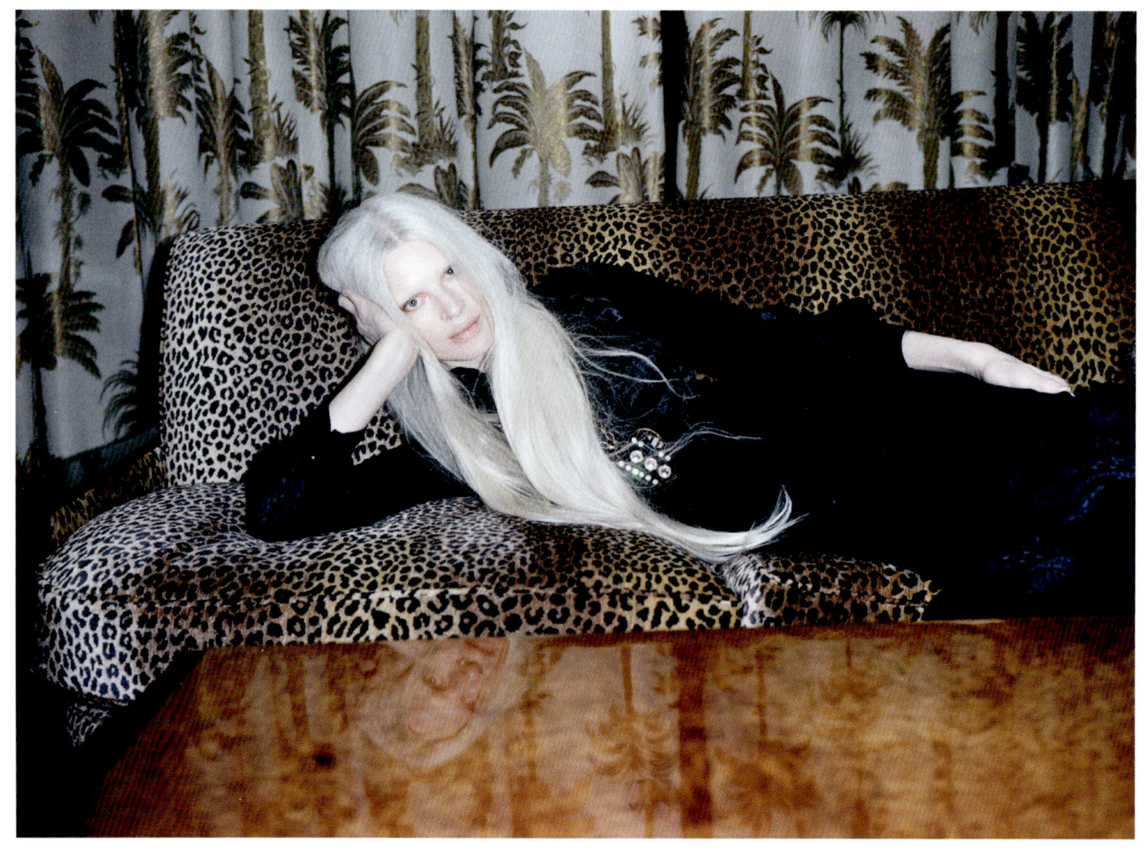

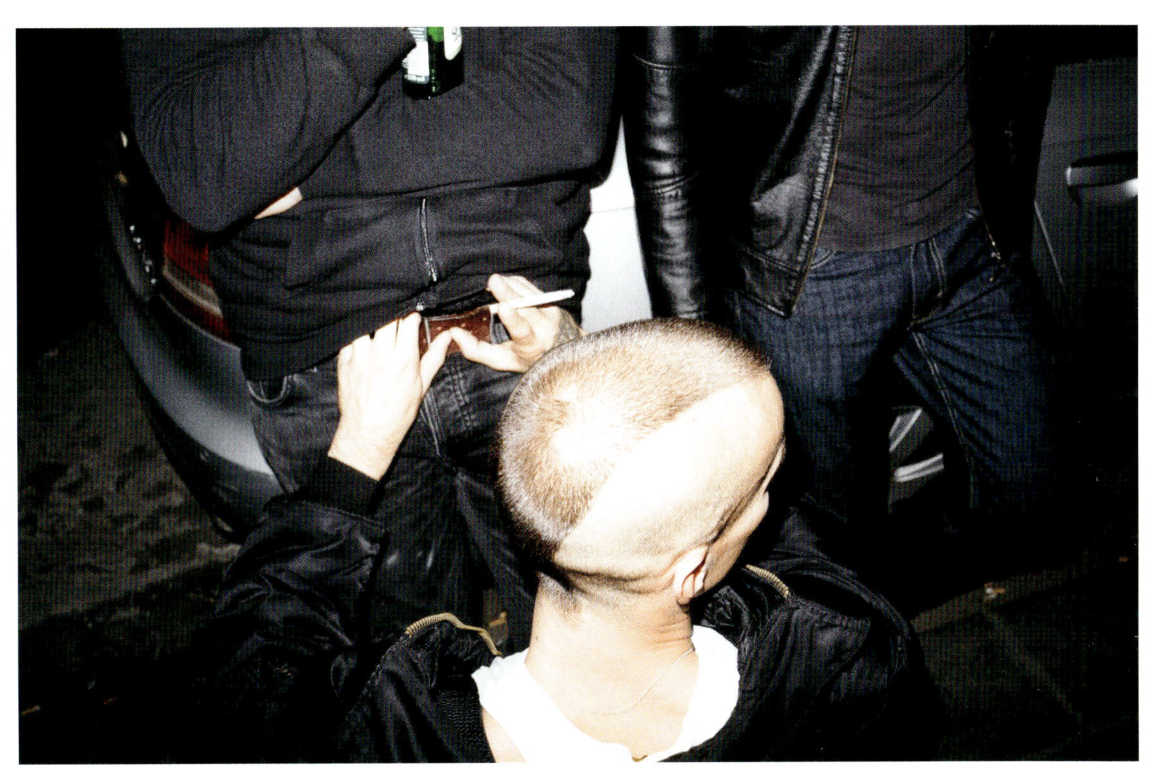

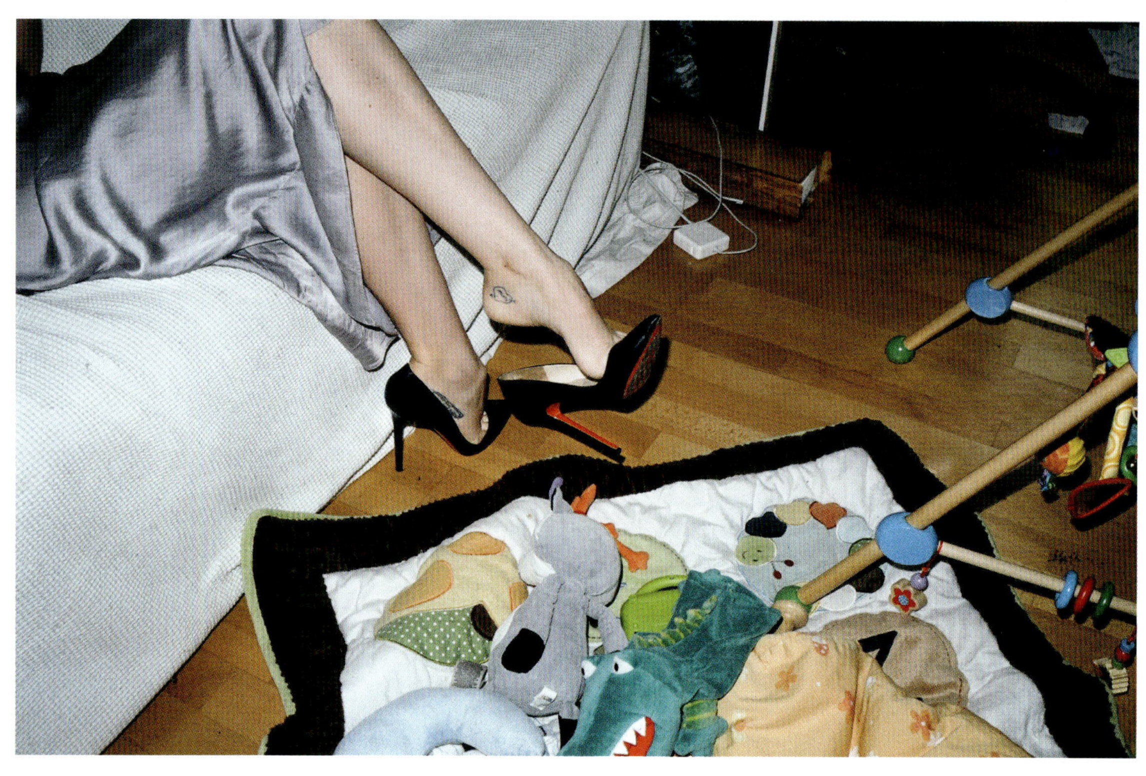

rattles, Berlin, 2013

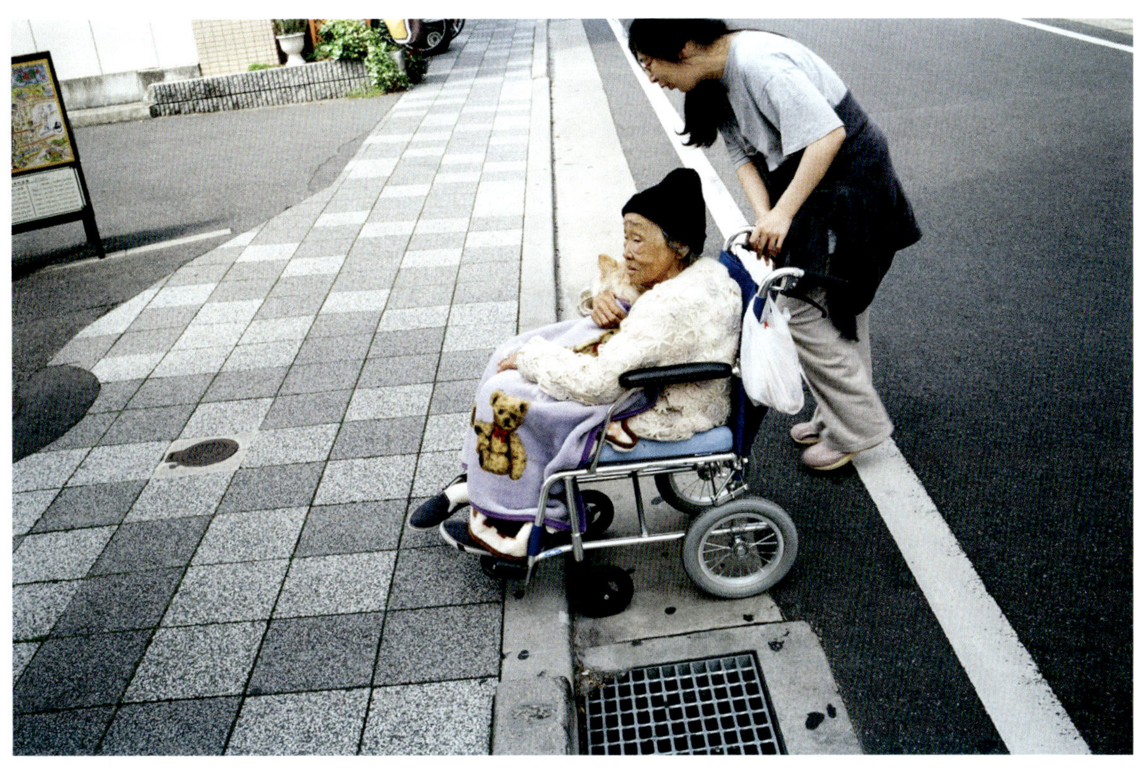

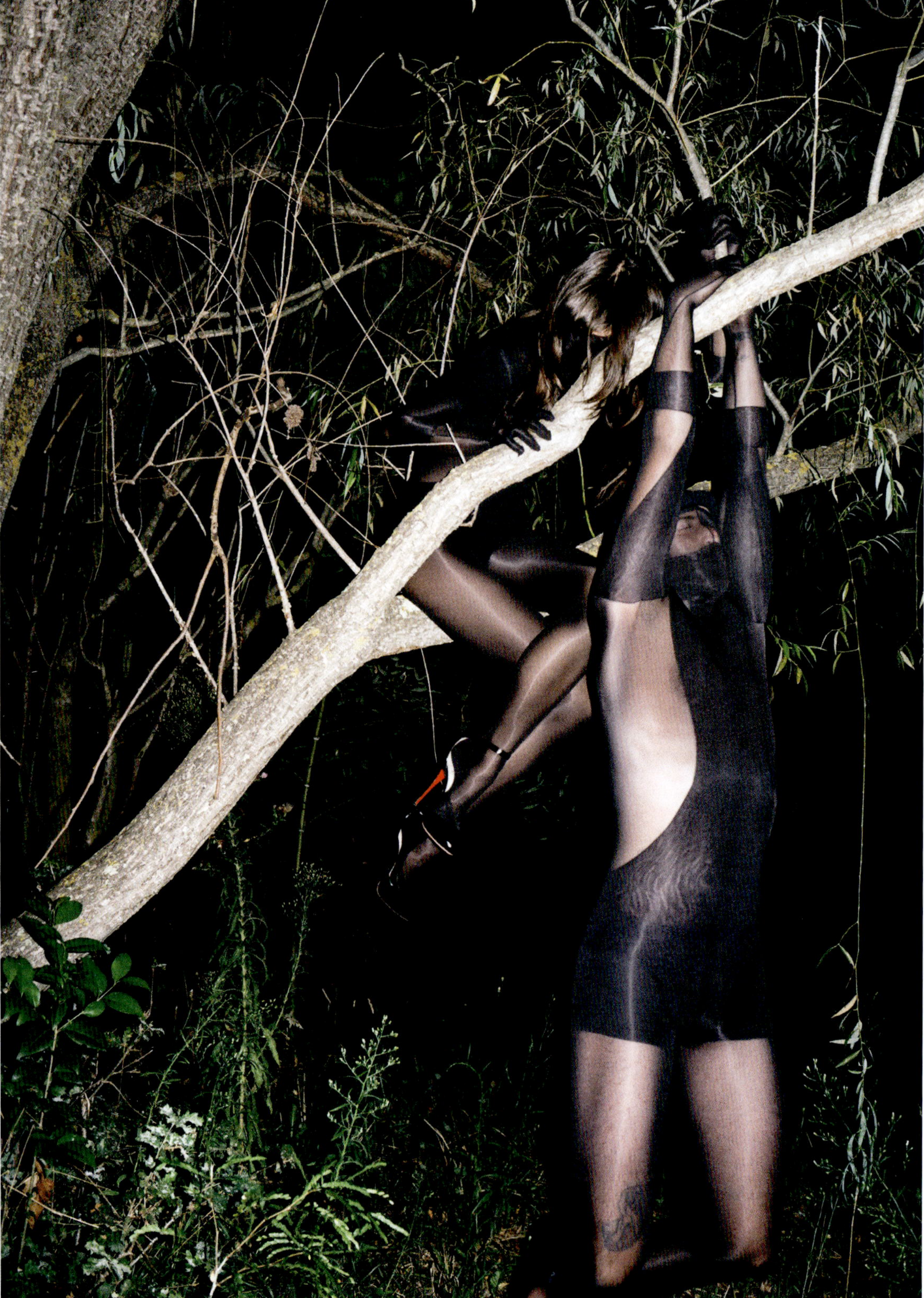

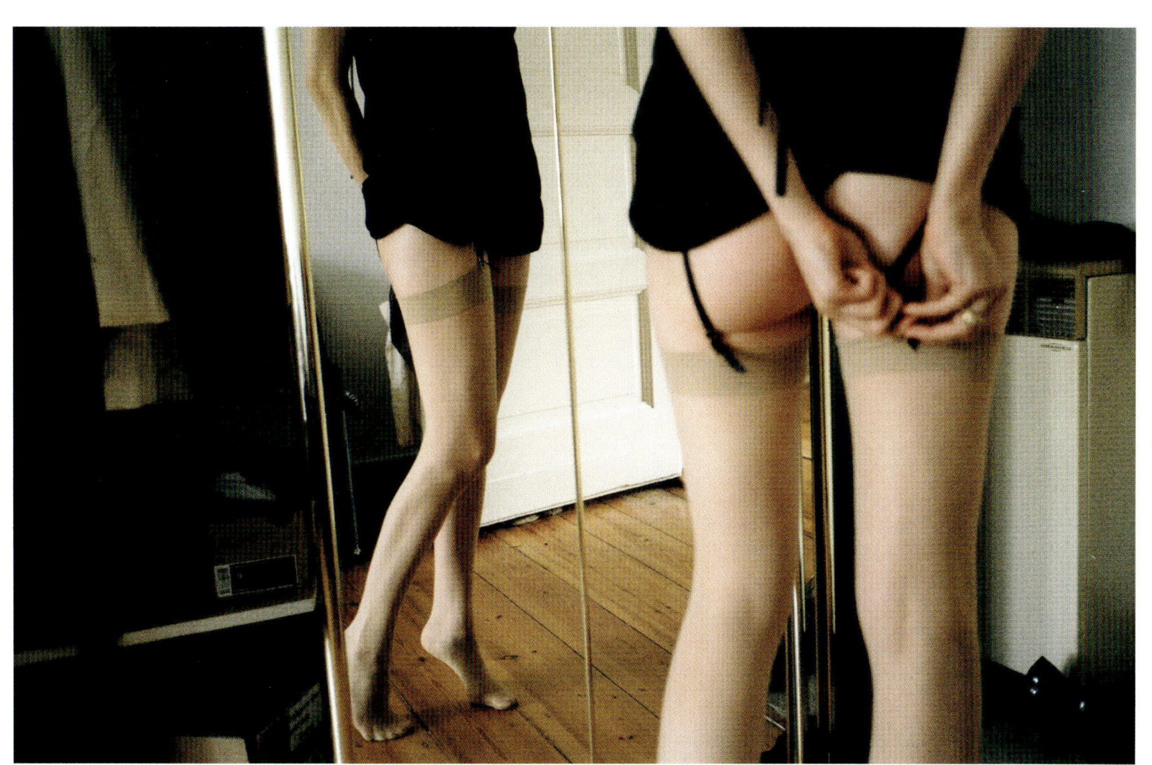

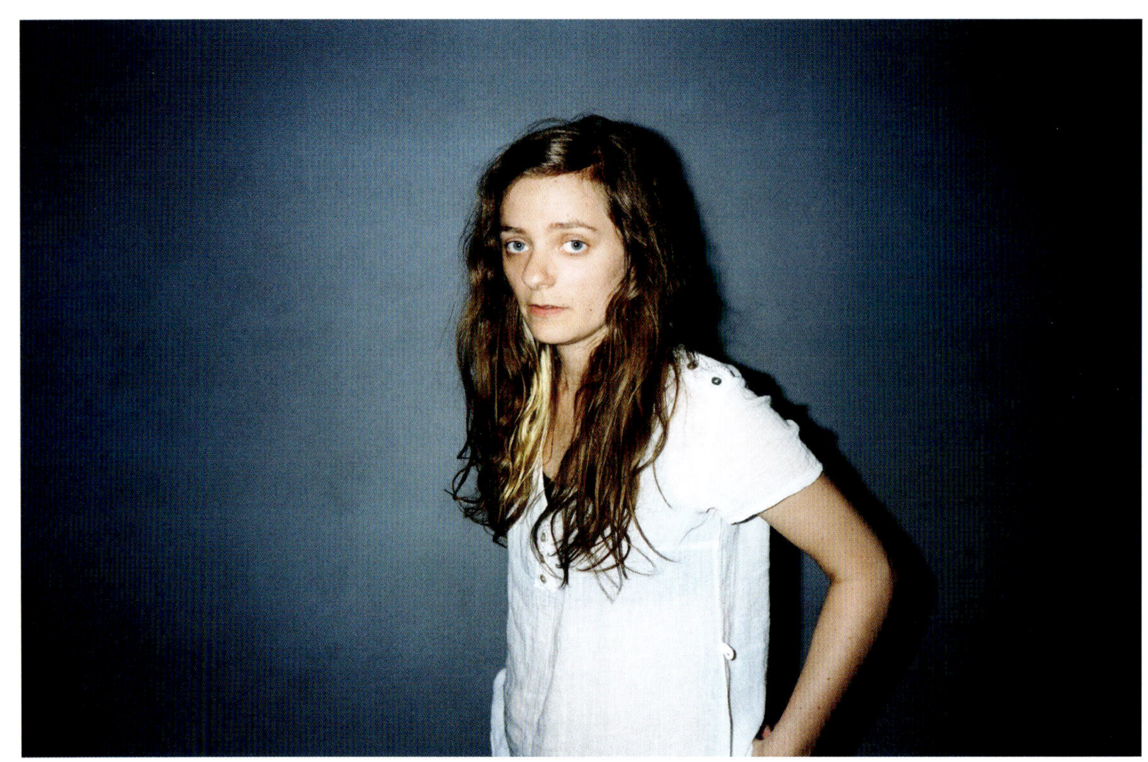

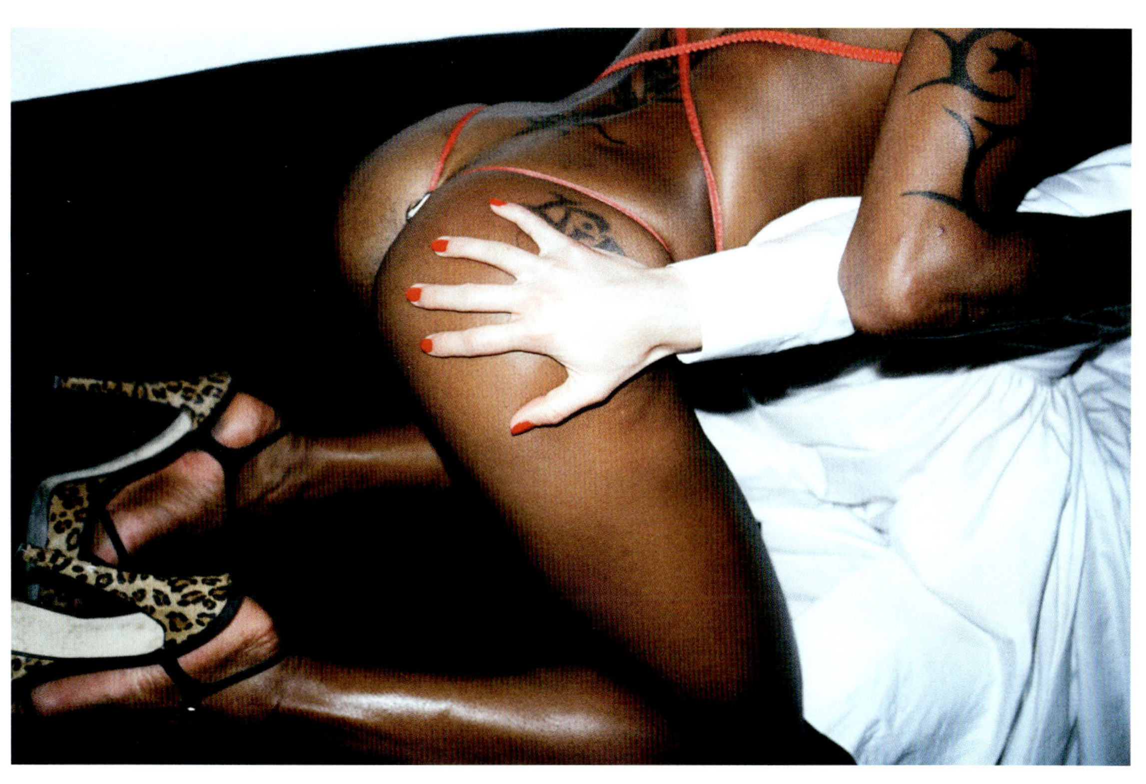

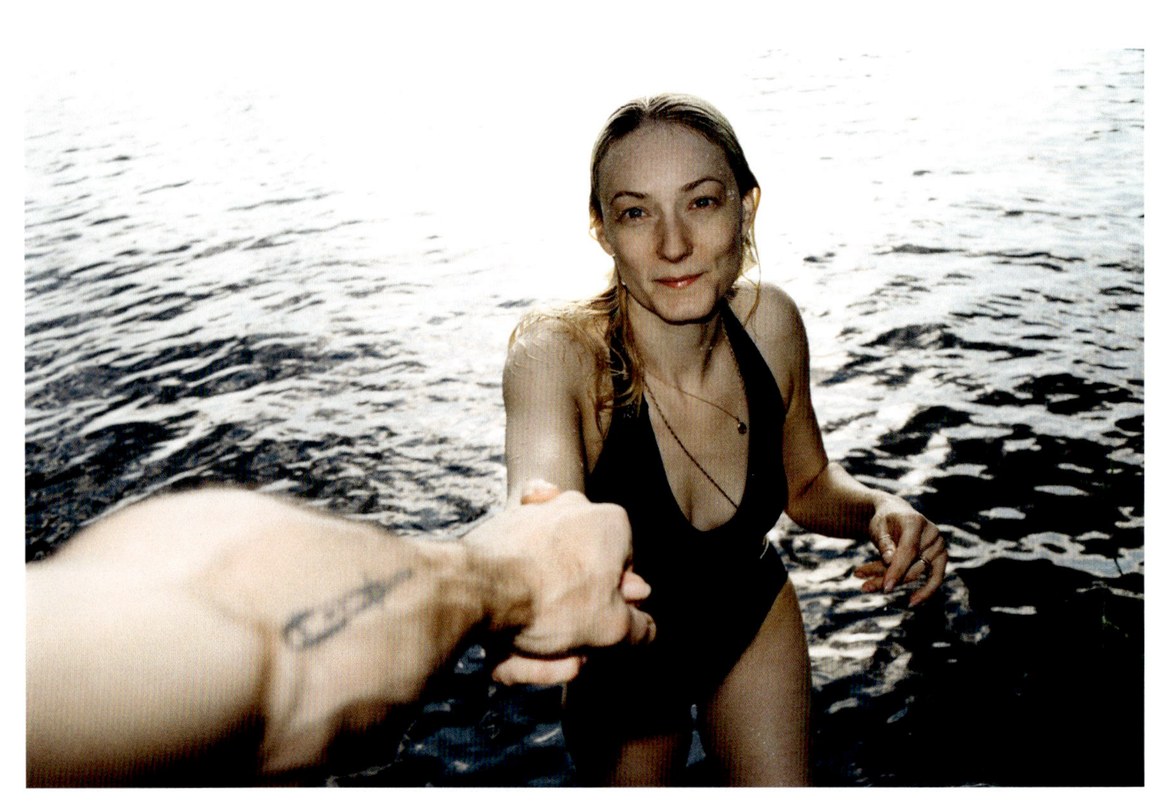

2017

(...)
Later,
you walk along the streets, aimlessly. One might think that you stroll,
but you do not stroll. You walk.
Aimlessly. You sit down on a wet bench to write down these words,
your butt freezing on the damp wood. Your bike at your side.
You don't know what your friends are doing.
You don't want to go home. Back to this apartment you used to share. Lying down on
that glacial bed with empty blankets. As close to the edge as possible.
So you keep walking.
Through the rain. The melting snow cracks under your feet.
You have never walked before. Too slow. Always at full speed
by bike or by car. Maybe time itself has slowed down.
In the park where you sit, feet in the mud, there is a sculpture. A writing desk,
a bit oversized, but not much.
And two chairs, one of which is deliberately turned over.
Lying on the ground. Under the rain.
You feel the same.
You feel the icy breeze taking your hand.
You imagine ghost arms tighten around your body, tenderly.
But you don't believe in ghosts. Or barely.
You are 32, and this is all too familiar to you.
(No more ink, the page is left blank)

2017

(...)
Plus tard,
tu marches le long des rues, sans but. Certains pourraient croire que tu flânes,
mais tu ne flânes pas. Tu marches.
Sans but.
Et pour écrire ces mots, tu t'assois sur un banc trempé,
le cul bien au frais sur le bois humide. Ton vélo à la main.
Tu ne sais pas ce que font tes amis.
Tu n'as pas envie de rentrer chez toi. Dans cette appartement que vous partagiez.
T'allonger dans ce lit glacé aux couvertures vides. Aussi près du bord que possible.
Alors tu continues à marcher.
Sous la pluie. La neige fondue qui craque sous tes pieds.
Avant, tu ne marchais jamais. Trop lent. Toujours à fond en vélo
ou en voiture. Peut-être le temps ralentit-il maintenant?
Dans le parc ou tu es assis, les pieds dans la boue, il y a une sculpture. Une table
d'écriture un peu surdimensionnée, mais pas trop. Avec deux chaises, dont une est
définitivement renversée. Allongée par terre. Sous la pluie.
Tu te sens pareil.
Et tu sens la brise glaciale te prendre par la main.
Tu imagines des bras fantômes se serrer autour de ton corps, tendrement.
Mais tu ne crois même pas aux fantômes. Ou à peine.
Tu as trente-deux ans, et tout ça ne t'est que trop familier.
(Plus d'encre, la page est laissée blanche)

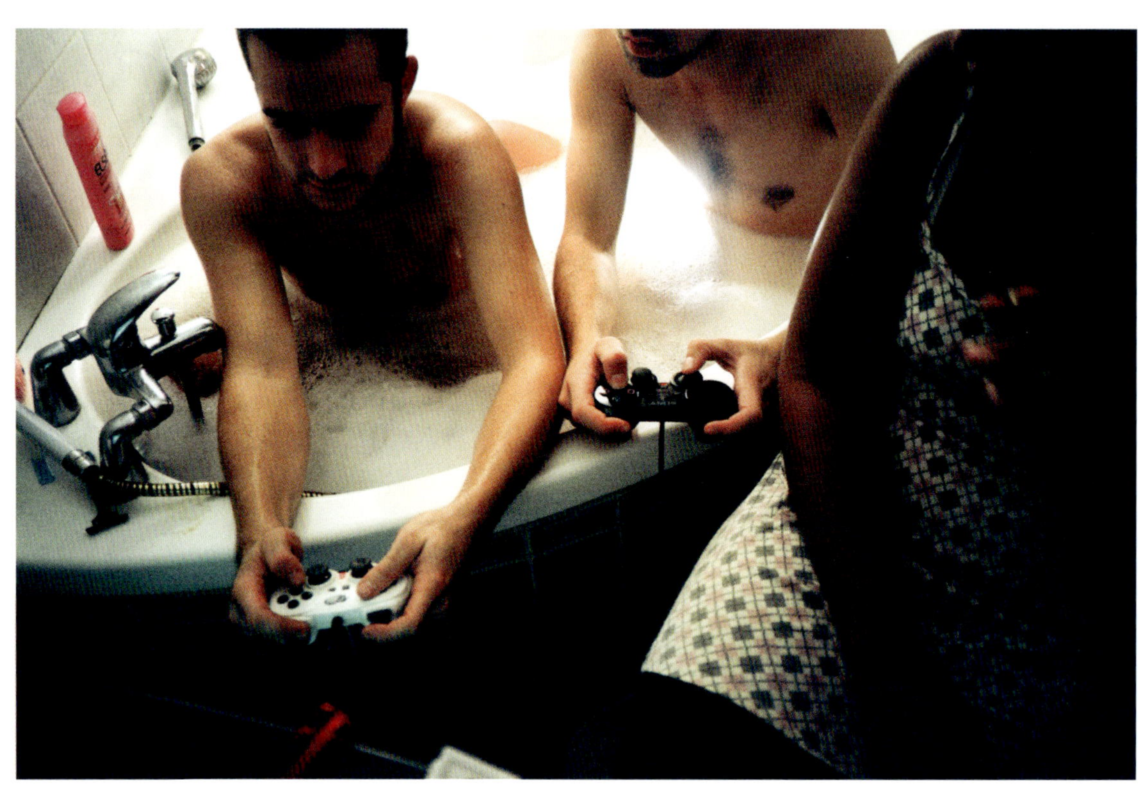

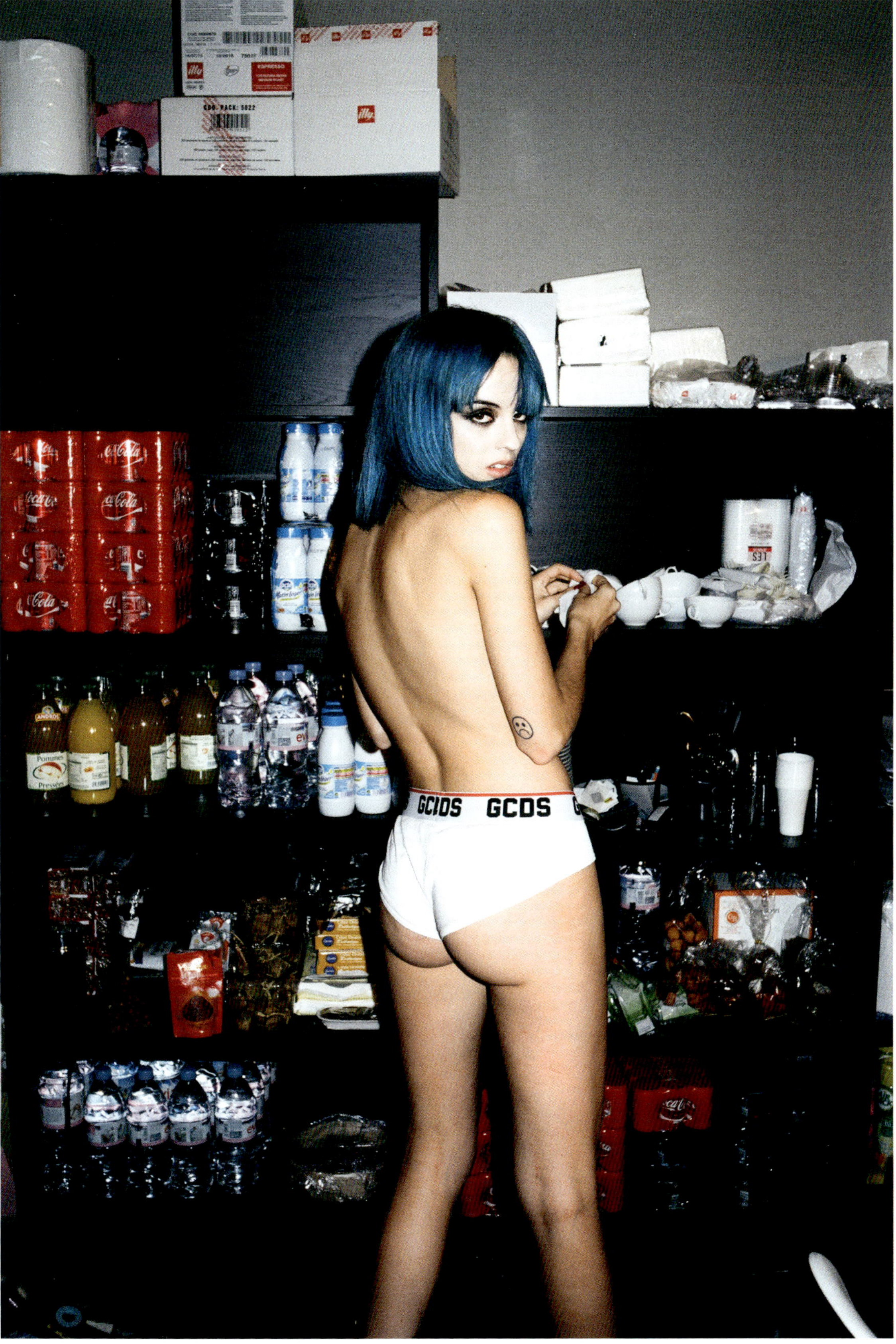
GCDS GCDS

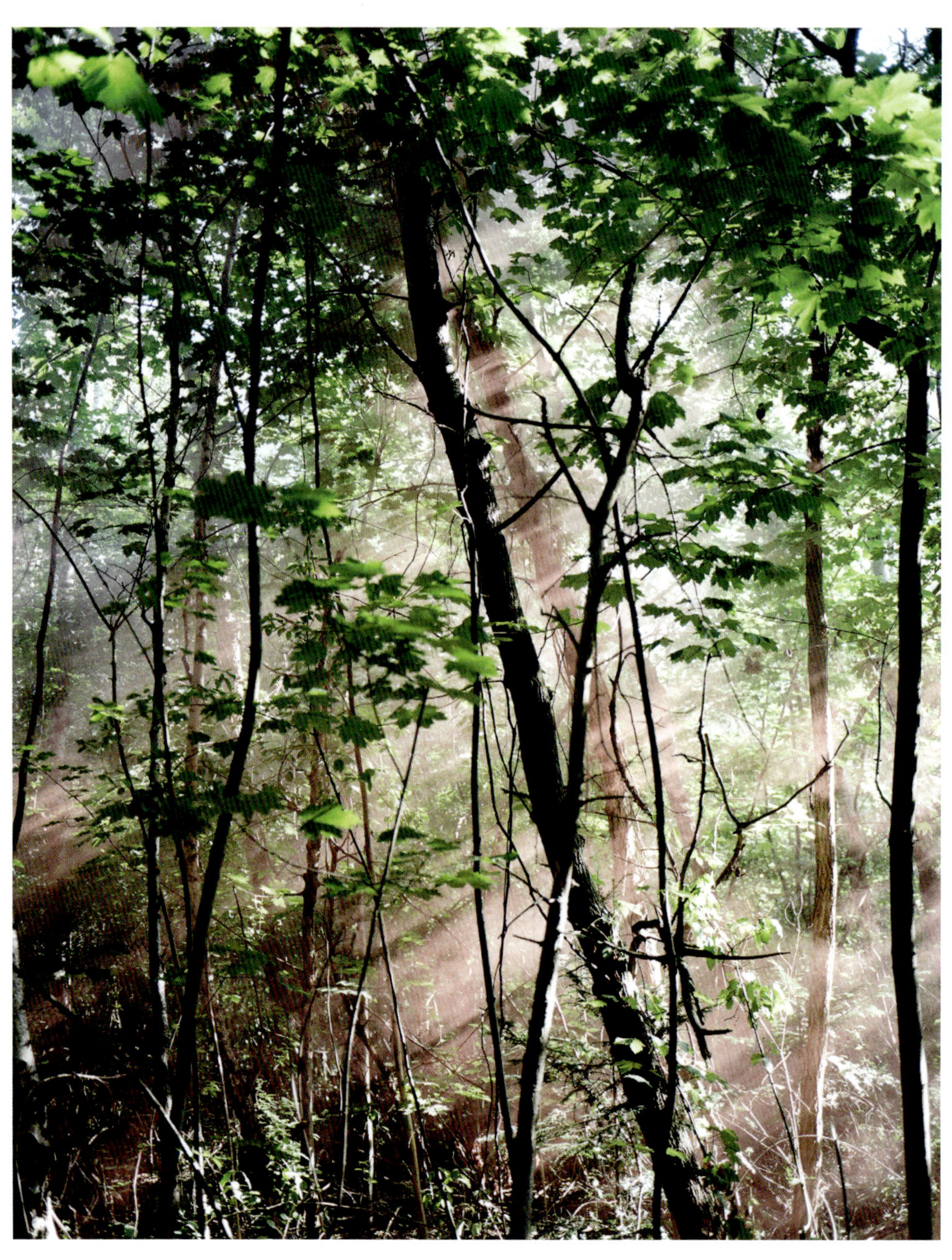

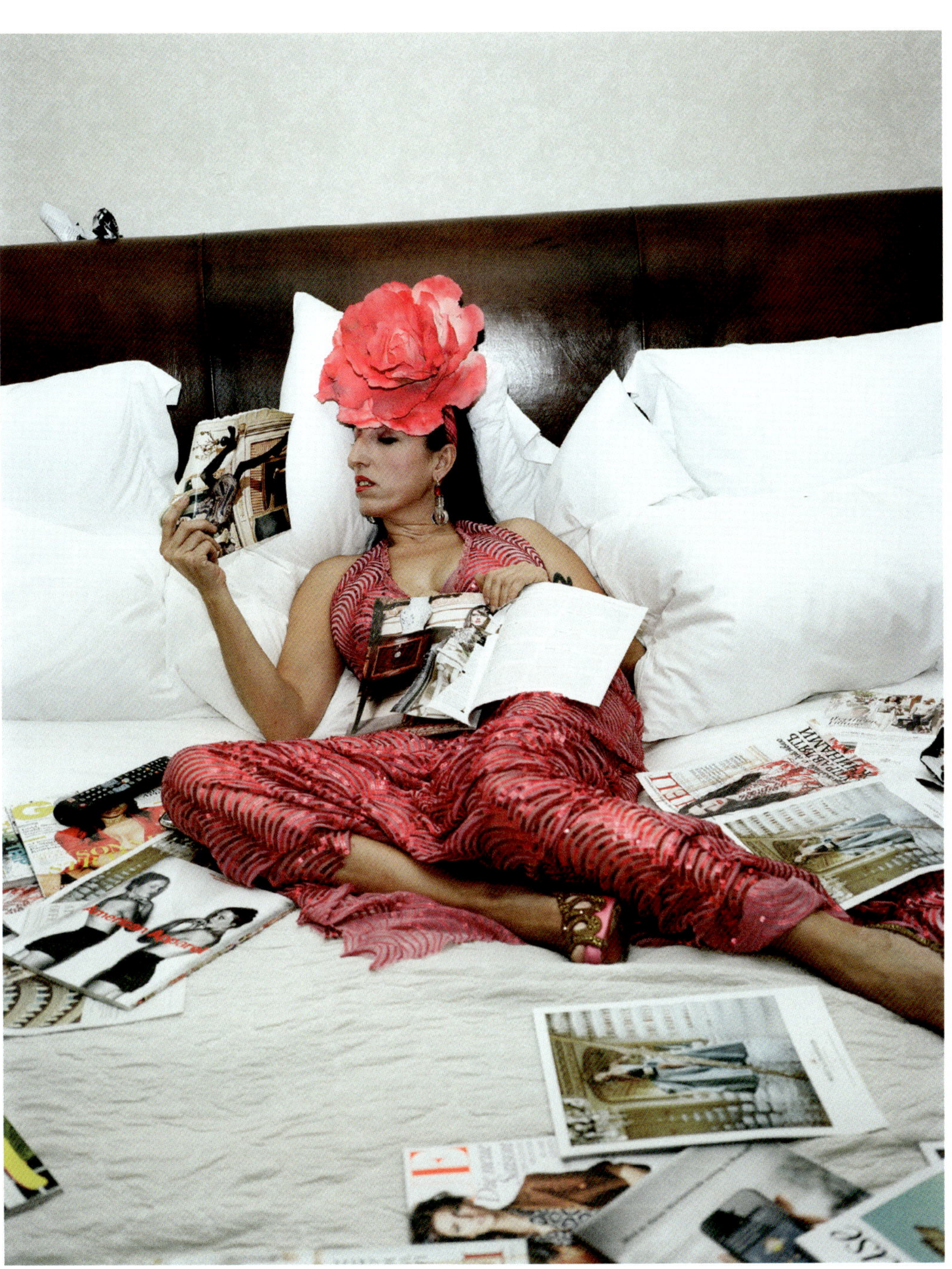
American Apparel

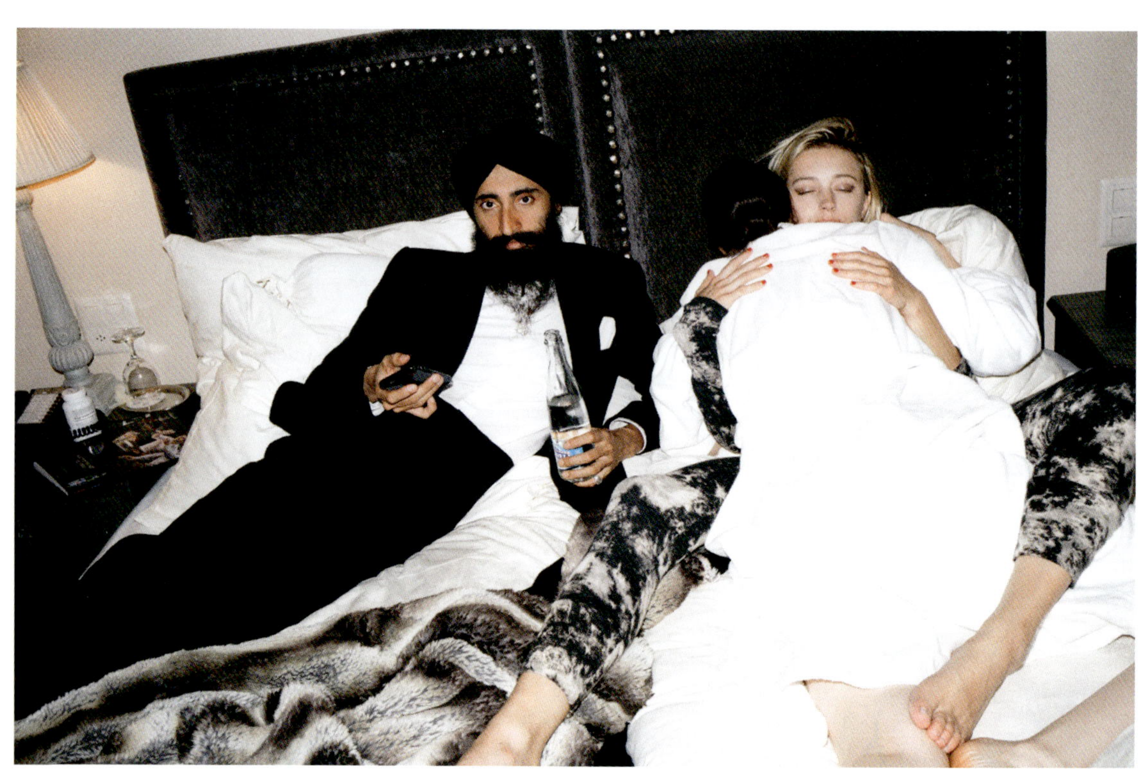

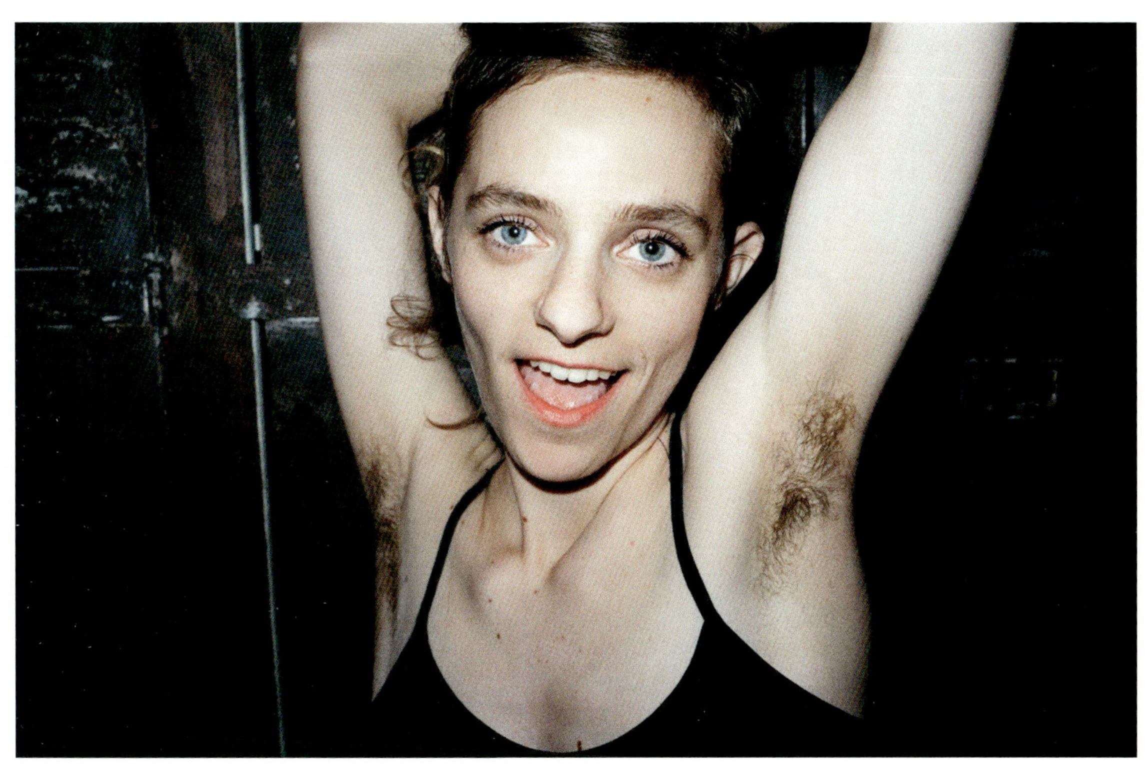

123 — 152

Marble bench

Solitudes

2006 He could not imagine anything more
unbearable than to continue living here
yet he was striving
never to leave his room again.

2006 Il n'envisageait rien de plus
insupportable que de continuer à vivre ici,
mais il s'efforçait malgré tout
de ne plus quitter sa chambre.

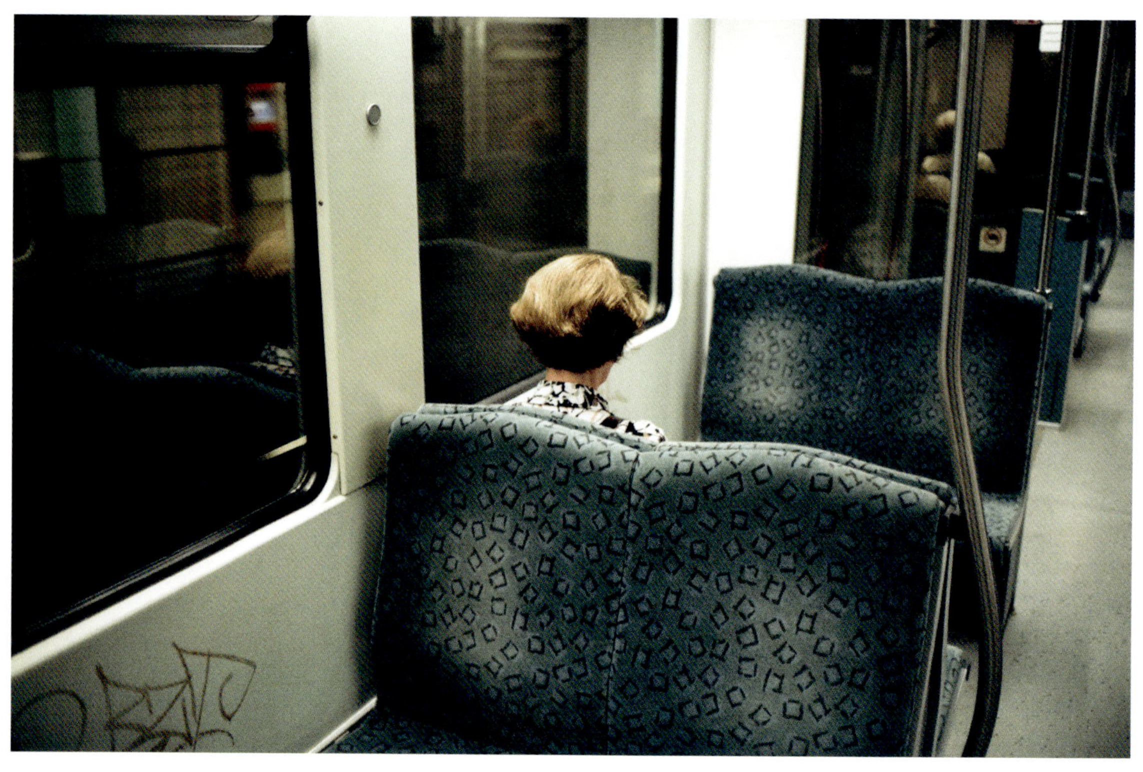

les absents, Berlin, 2014

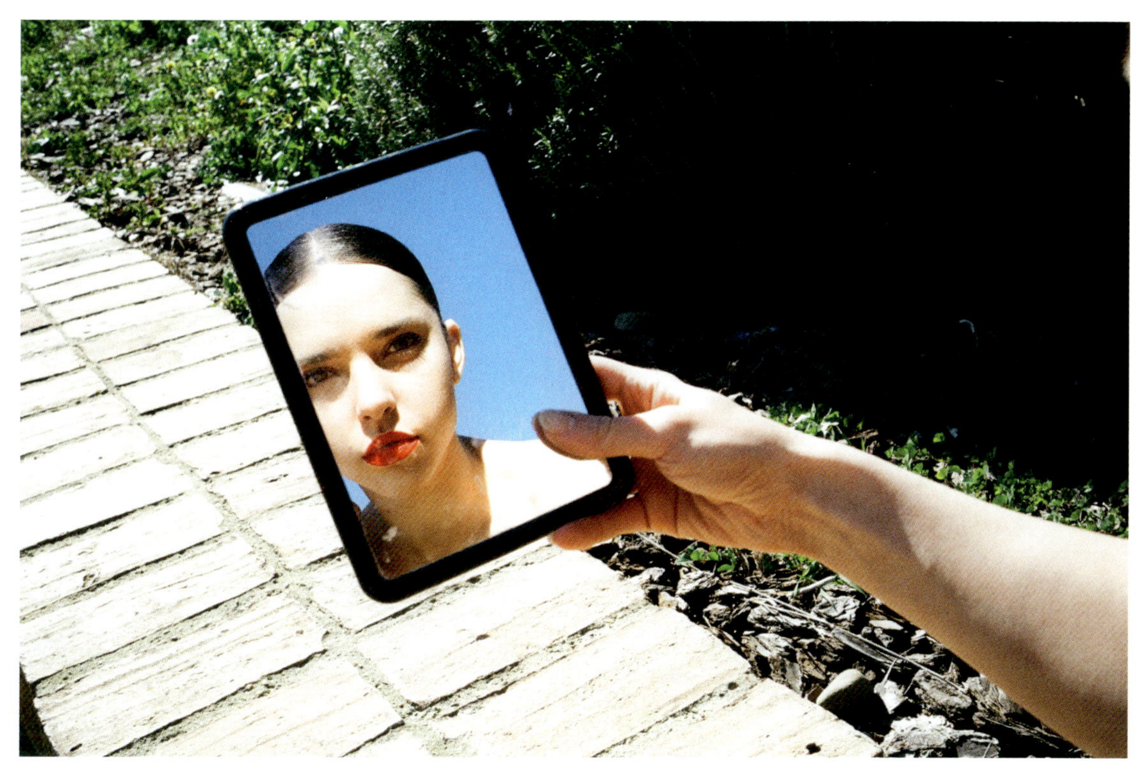

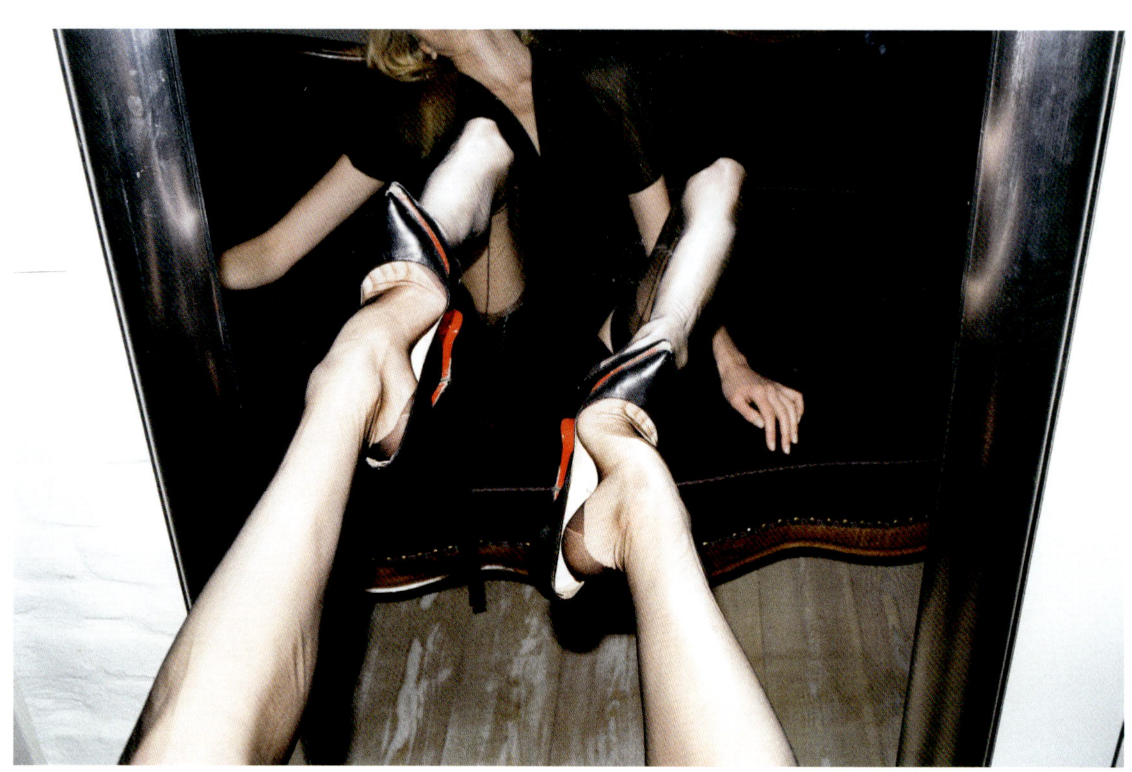

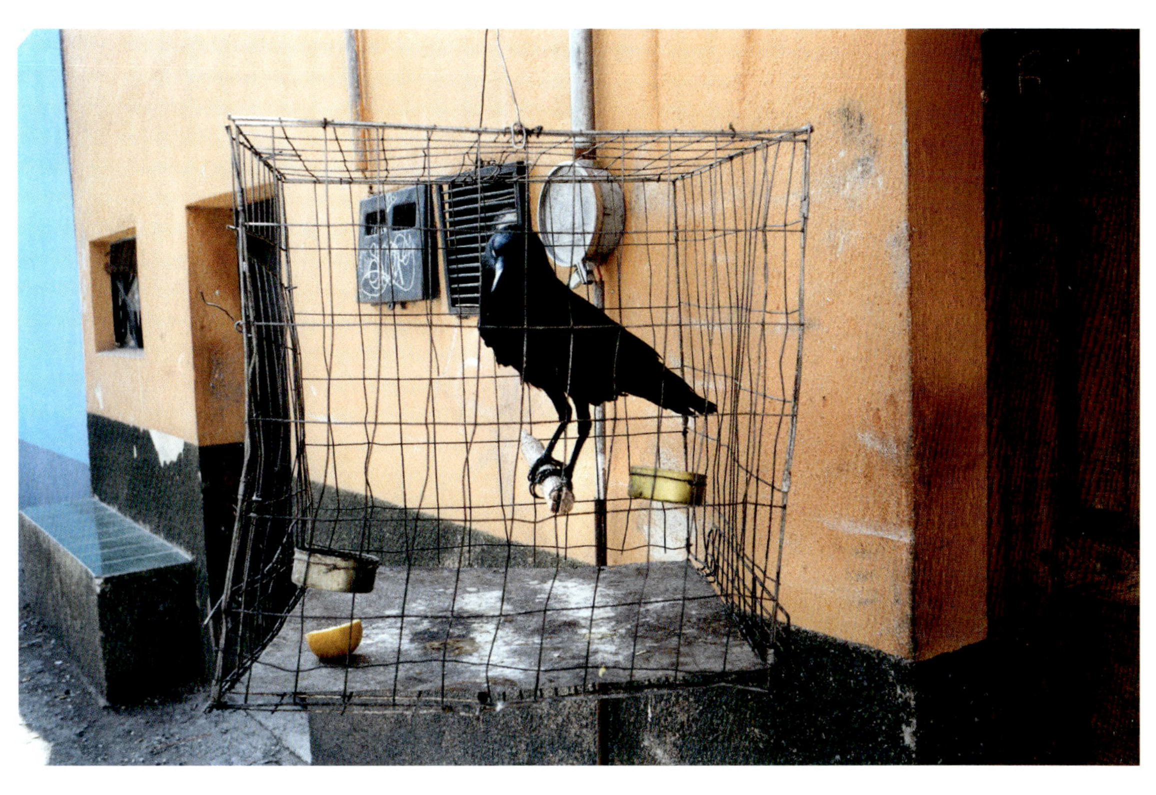

the triumph of vanity, Mexico, 2016

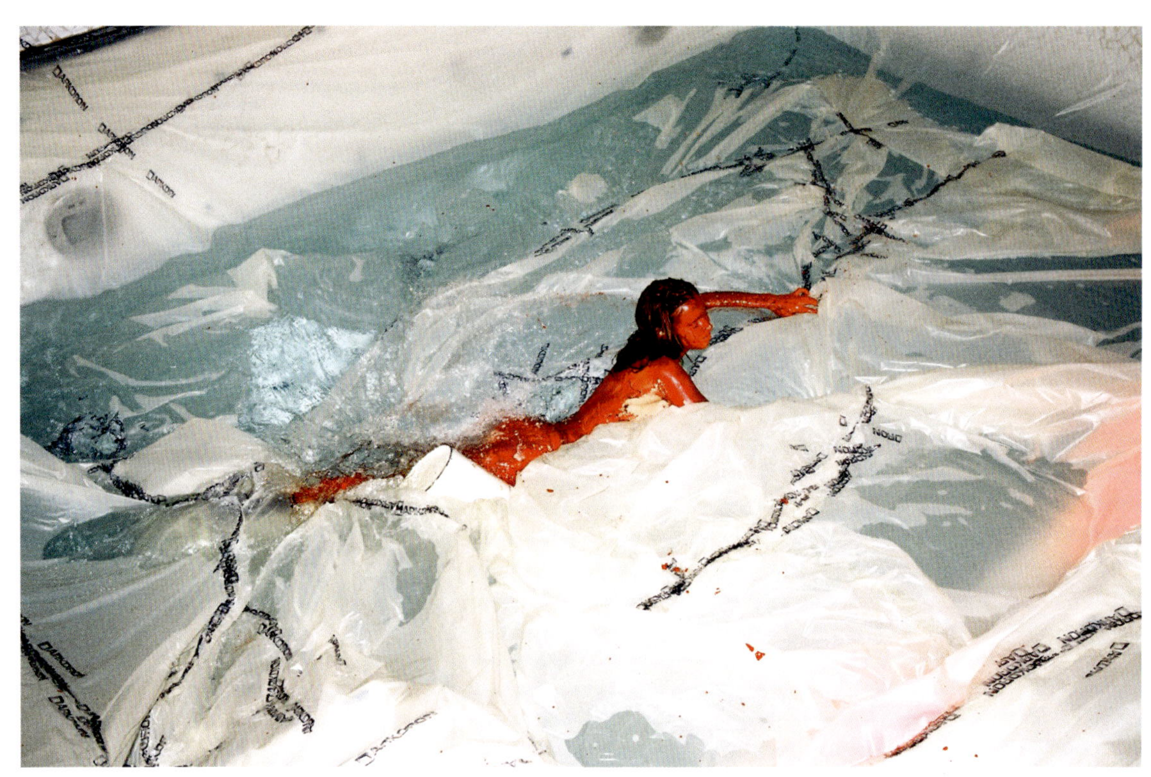

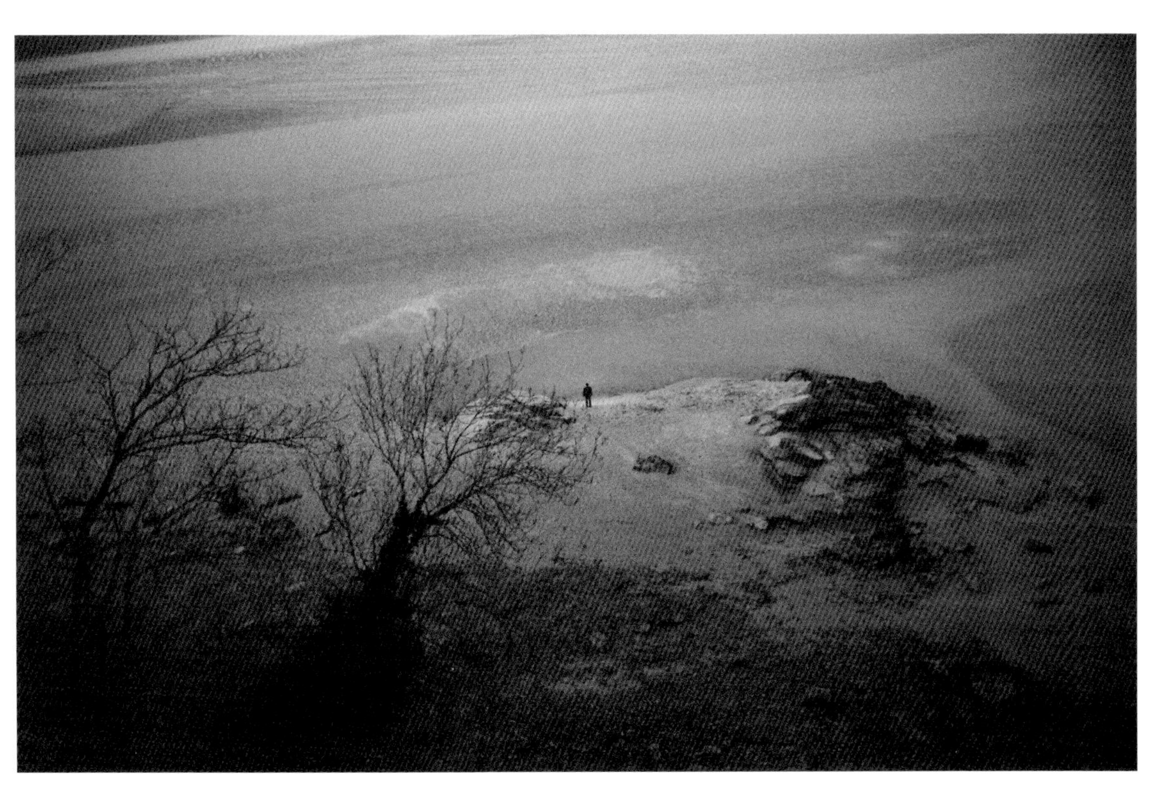

Charlie's mourning, Mont Saint-Michel, 2017

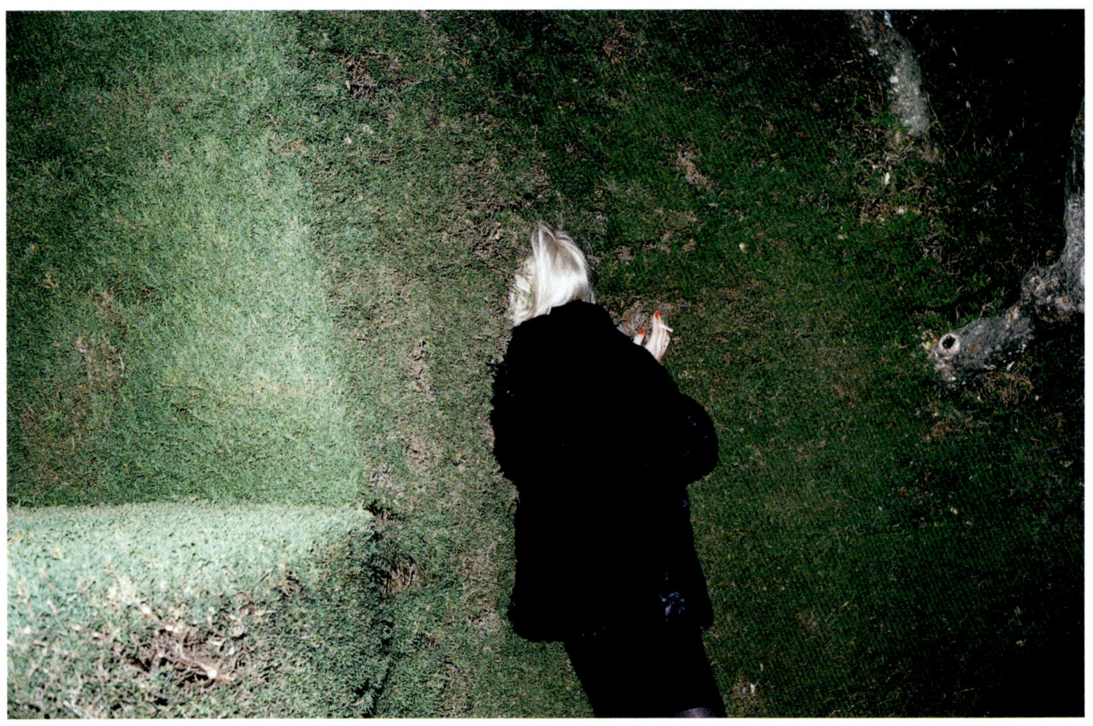

2017

Every night you wanna write to her.
You wanna hold her.
You go to bed alone and the sun is starting to shine on its own.
You close your door and stay in the dark.
You don't hear her comforting breath next to you under the blanket.
You hold your teddy bear really tight, sometimes you need two of them.
It's way too late to go to sleep.
You'll wake up terrified.
Feeling like you're walking on a tightrope.
You don't have too much vertigo and you enjoy the view from
there, but you're too clumsy to keep moving on that shit.
When you inhale it doesn't smell like her hair.
It smells more like you should wash your sheets.
And when you breathe out only smoke comes out of your mouth.
And it's cold beside you.
You use her pillow to feel something touching your skin.
You don't leave a note on the kitchen table to wish her a good day before going to sleep.
And when you finally wake up, you only have your mess to contemplate.
And you think about her, alone, in her own bed a few blocks away.
But you can't really. Your skin and your heart starts to remember her too vividly.
And your eyes get too wet and blurry to see what you're typing anyway.

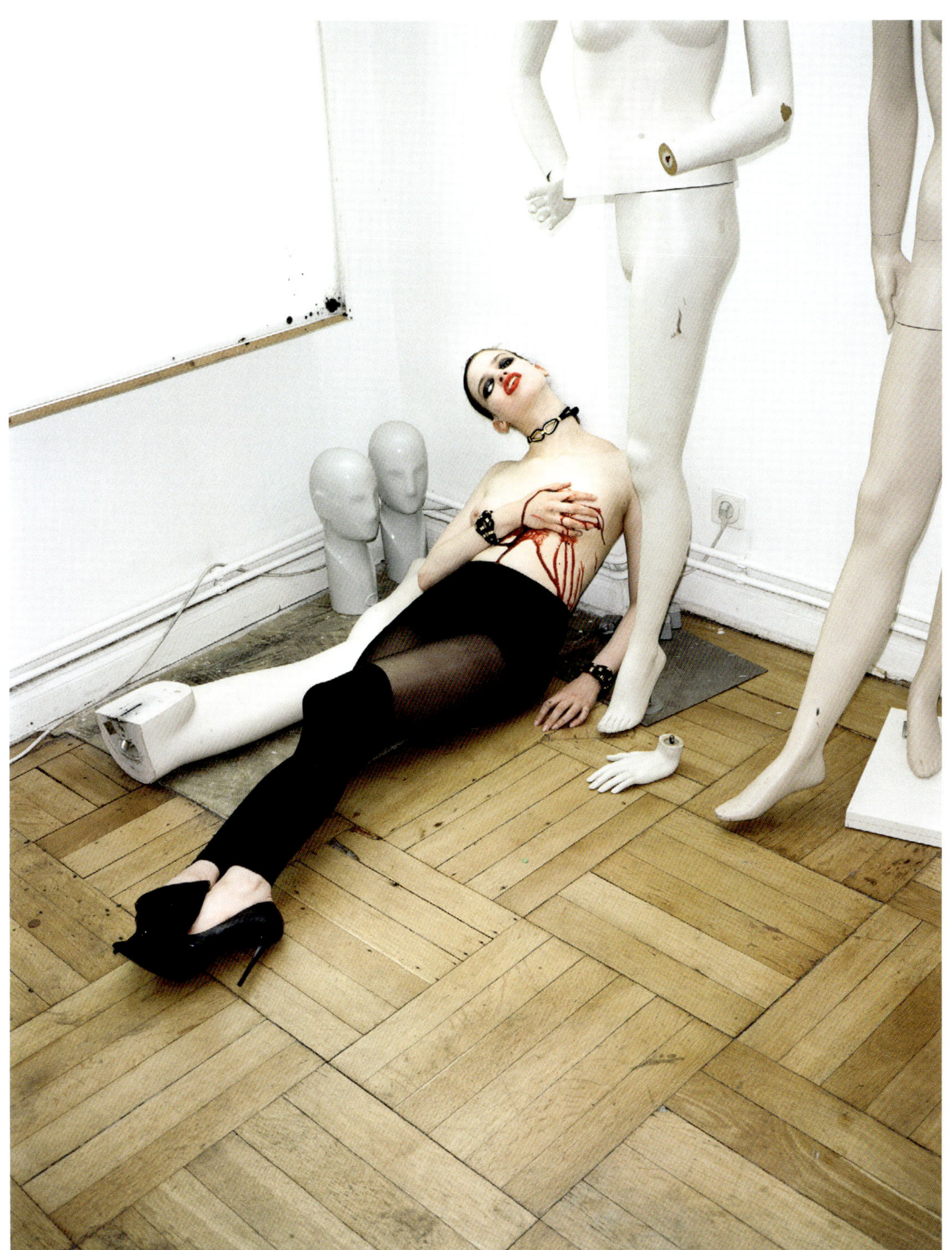

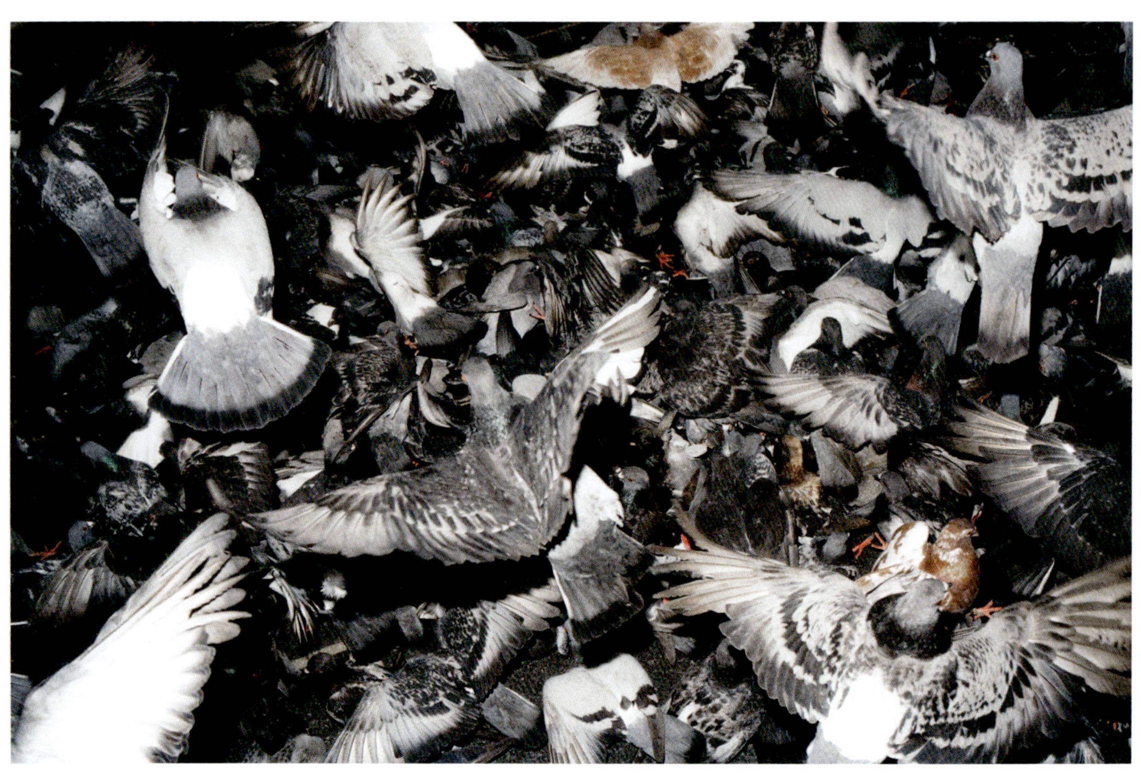

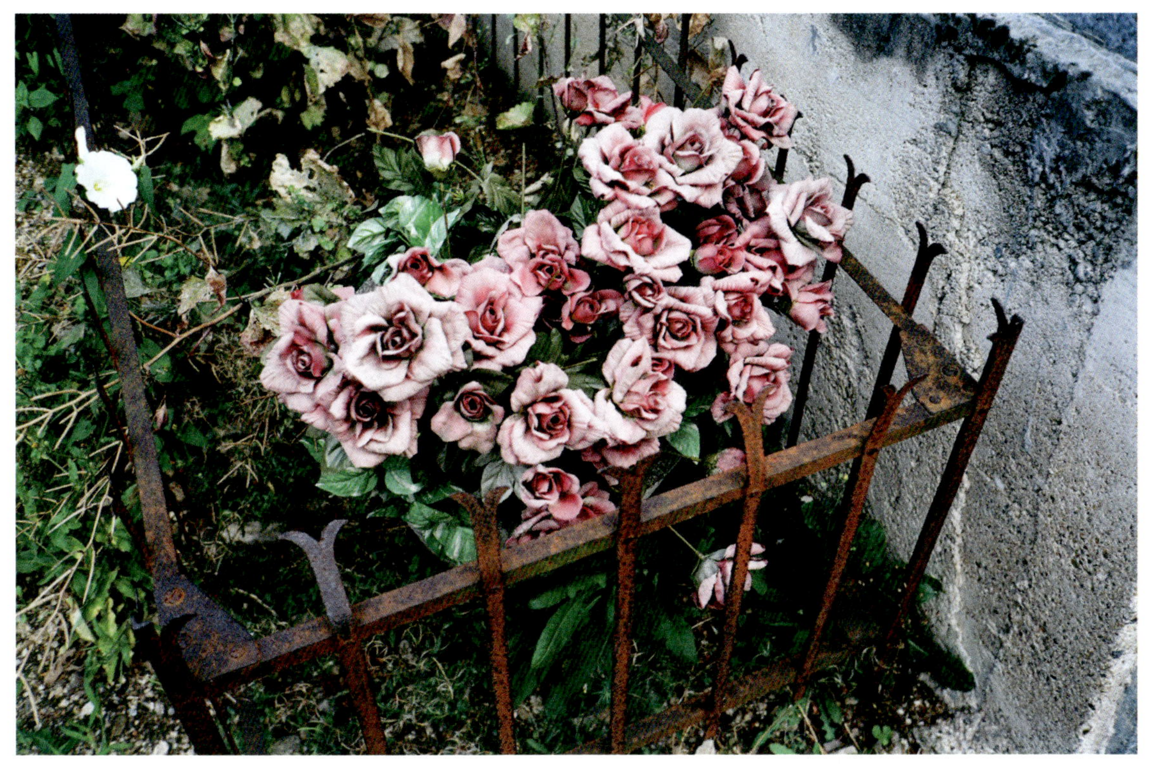

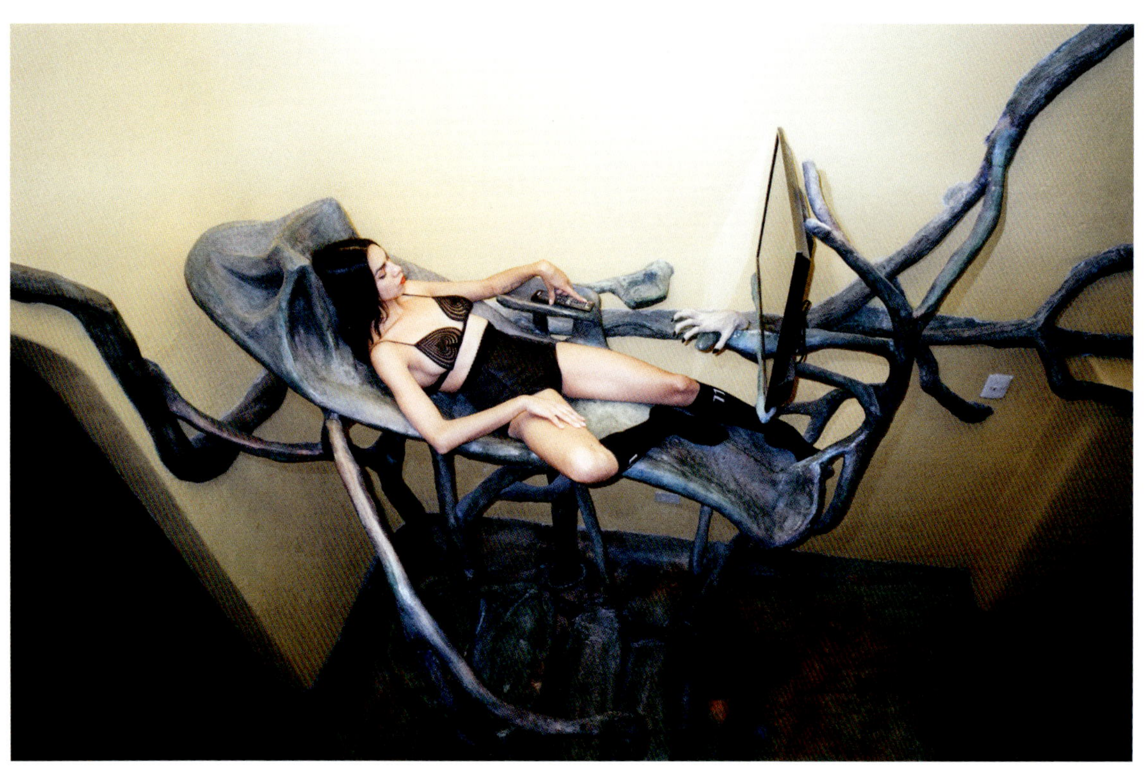

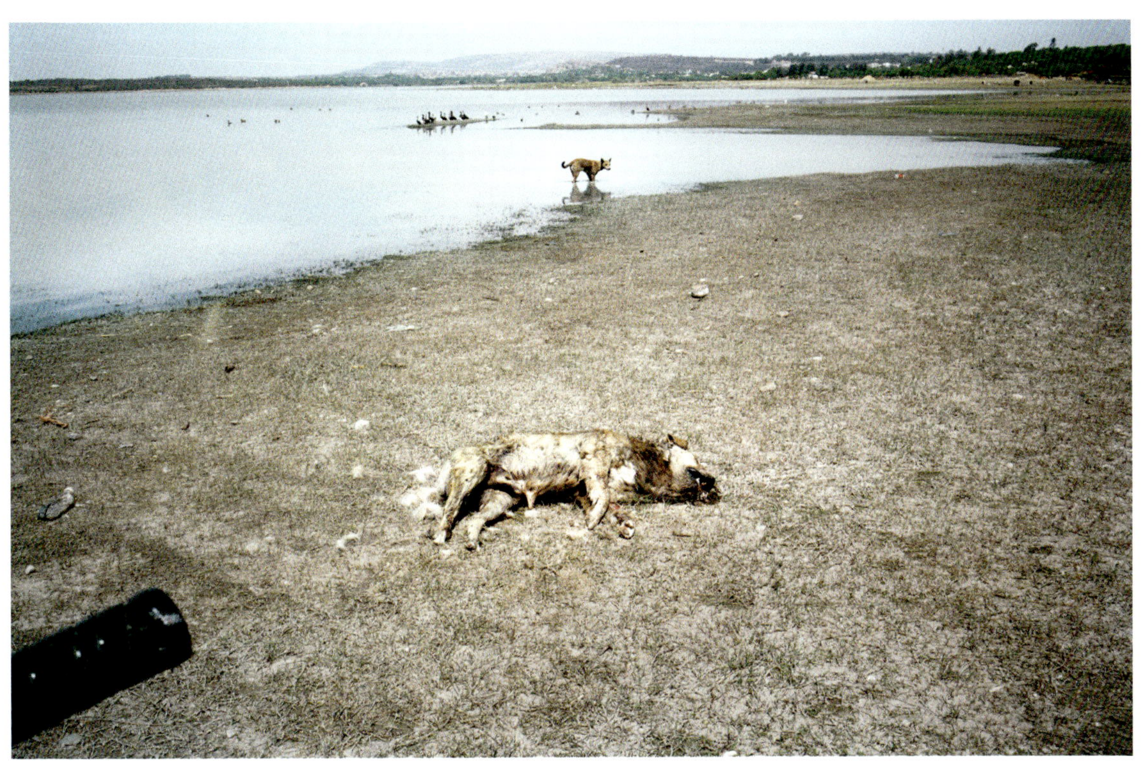

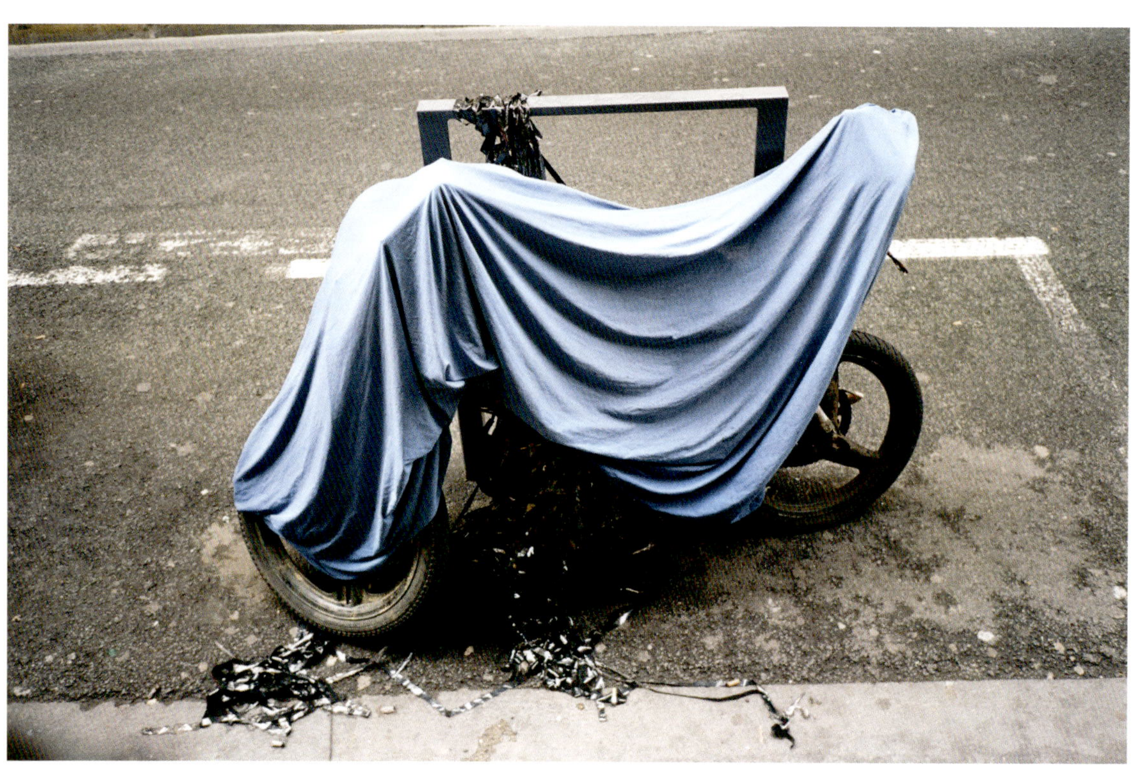

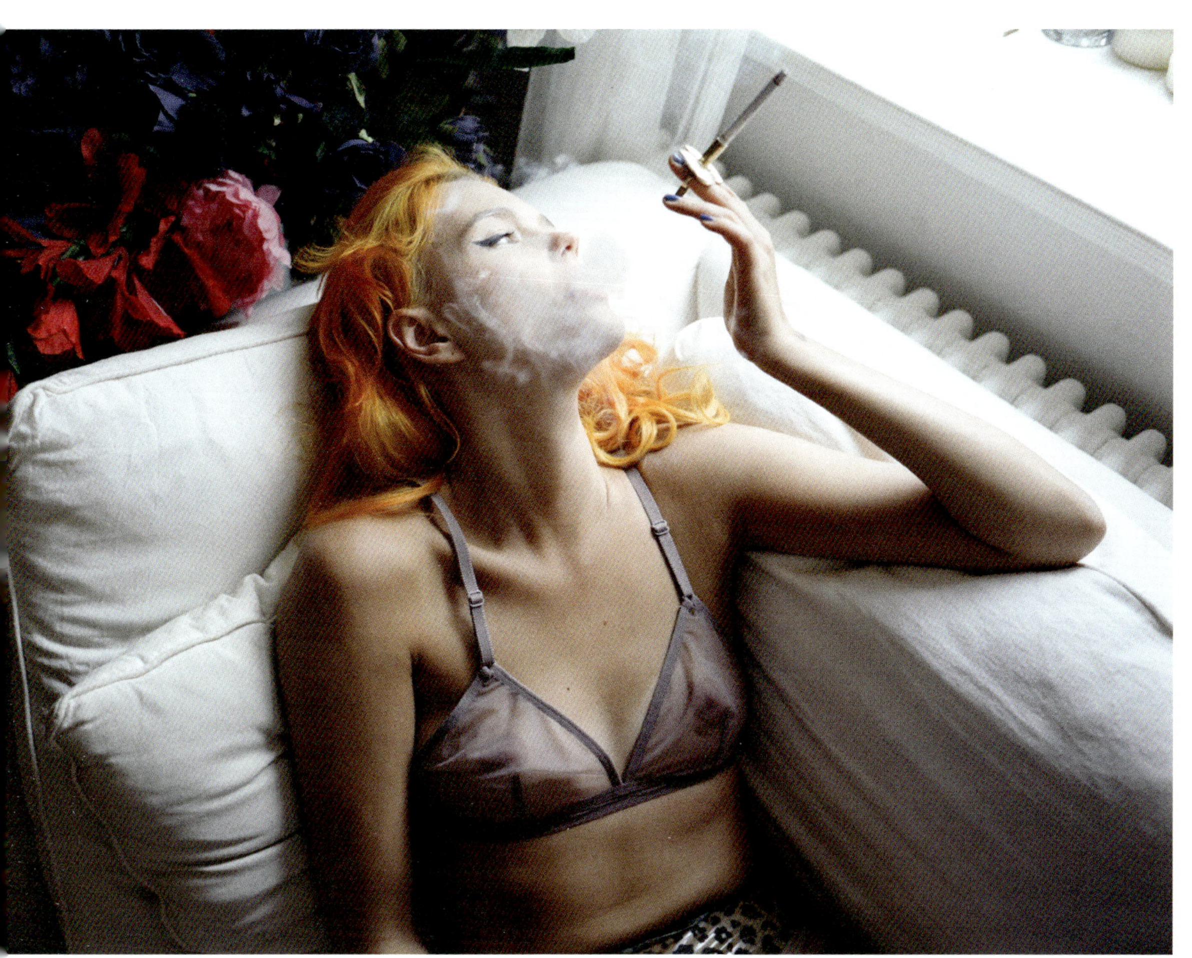

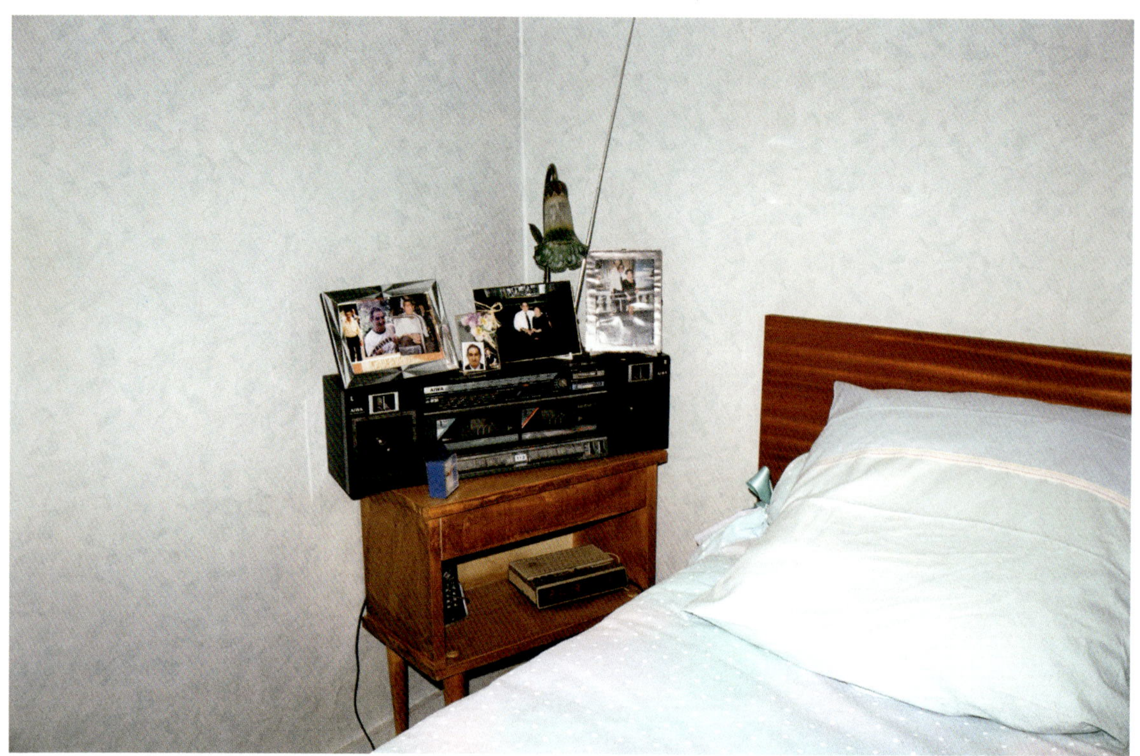

2006 Many things could have
turned his life upside-down
but he preferred to stay
locked in the bathroom.

2006 Beaucoup de choses auraient
pu bouleverser sa vie
mais il avait préféré rester
enfermé aux toilettes.

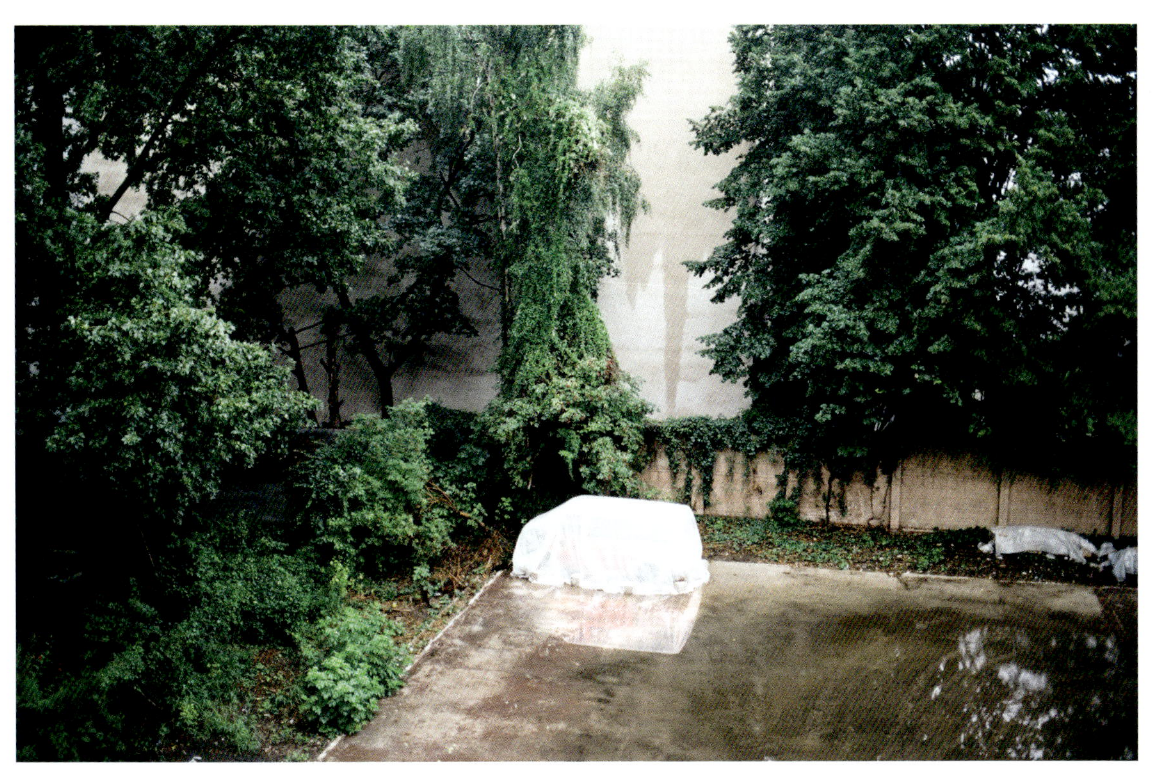

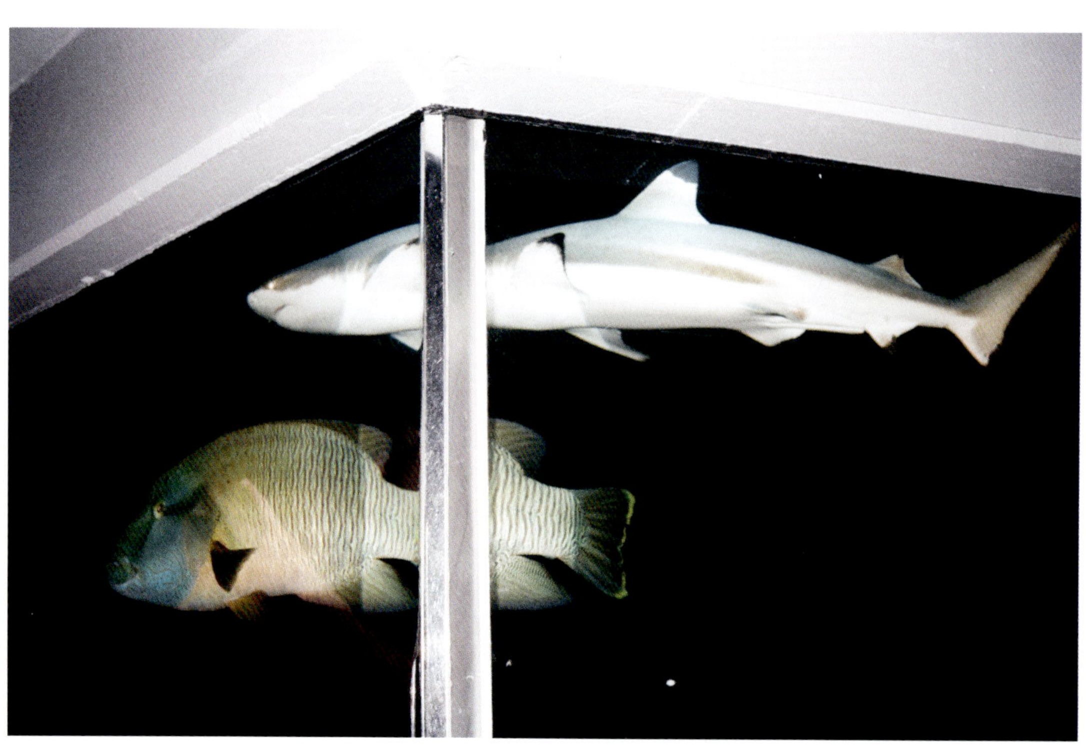

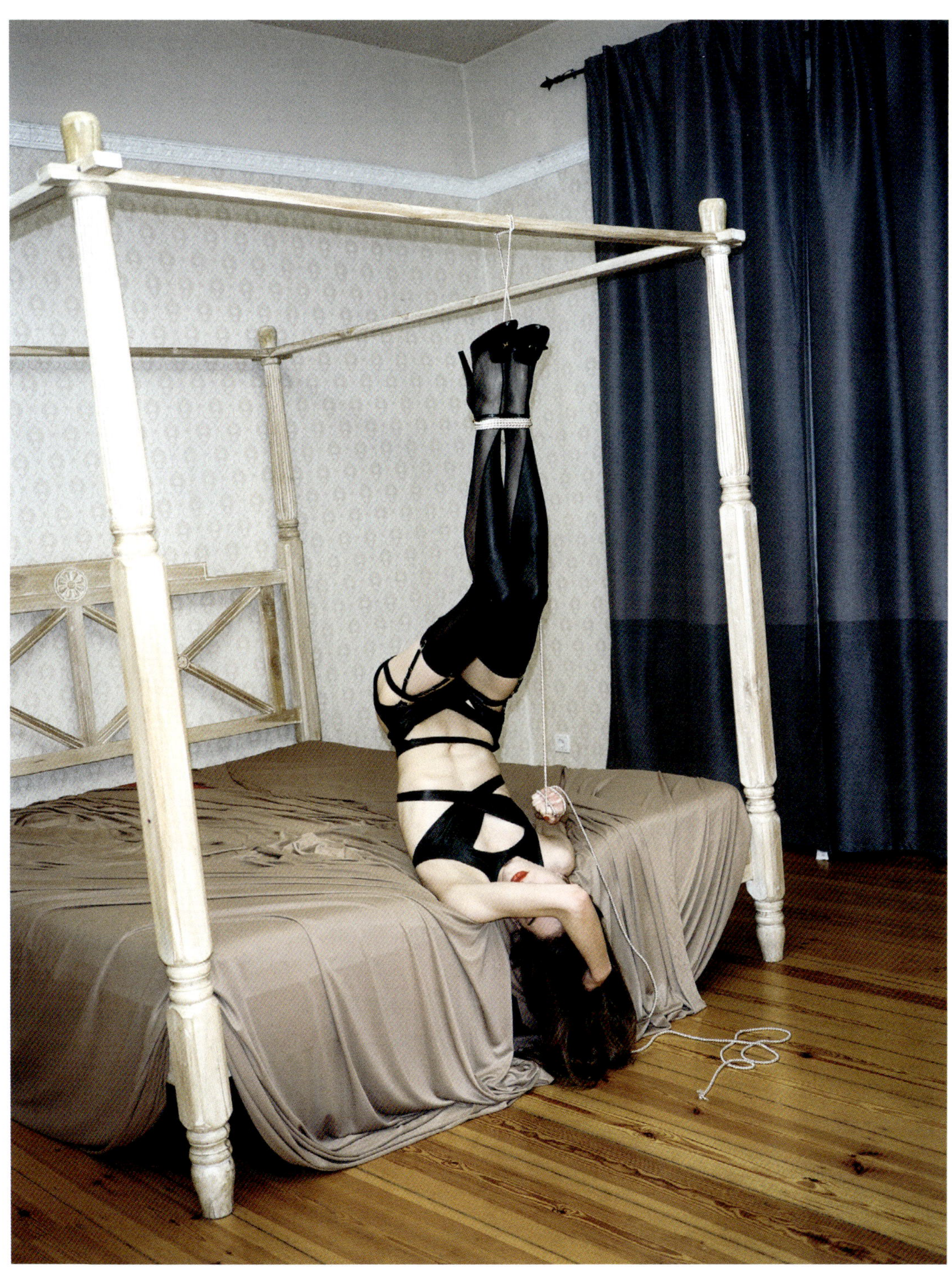

home alone, Berlin, 2016

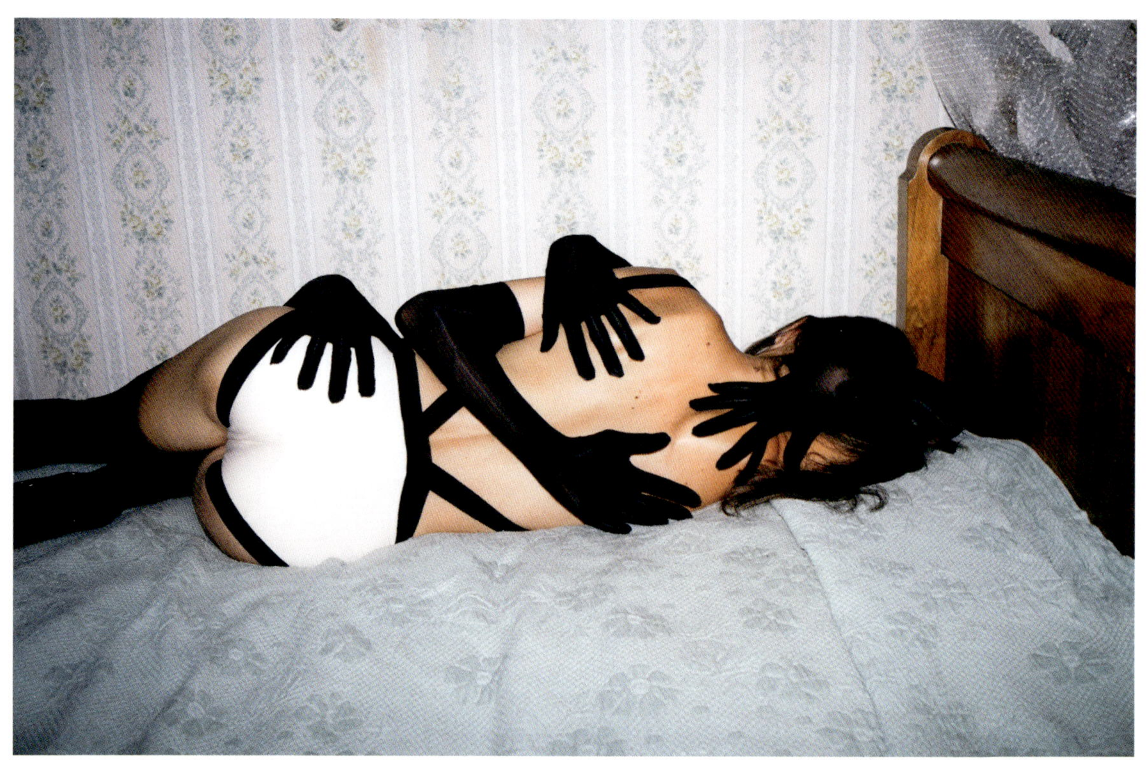

2007 What do you need?
You are not sad.
You just don't want to.
To have lunch, to stay here, to go home, to visit your mother, to go to a bar with no matter who.
To make love, to go outside.
To go back to France.
To work.
To listen to this fucking song.
To sleep again.
You can't find your smile anymore.
Your body repulses you.
Your head does not knock out your ass on the ground.
It does not jump up.
It shrinks slowly. Calmly.
Becoming dry it creaks like an awful parquet.
There is nothing left to please you.
What you usually cling to seems to be dark bullshit.
You go to prepare your breakfast.
You never eat savory in the morning but today you cook cabbage and sausages, with some eggs.
You listen to the steps on the stairs.
It is not her.
You want to puke your nerves and the sausages.
Things seem less and less interesting to you.
Even your emotions don't surprise you anymore.
You endure them quietly. You sit down and you roar. Like an old deer.
Vaulted and strained by these big heavy antlers.

2007 De quoi as-tu besoin?
Tu n'es pas triste.
Tu n'as juste pas envie.
De déjeuner, de rester ici, de retourner chez toi, de rendre visite à ta
mère, d'aller au bar avec untel. De faire l'amour, de sortir dans la rue.
De rentrer en France.
De travailler.
D'écouter cette putain de chanson.
De dormir encore.
Tu n'arrives pas à retrouver ton sourire.
Ton corps te repousse. Ta tête ne se cogne pas le cul par terre.
Elle ne rebondit pas. Elle se resserre doucement.
Calmement. Devient sèche et craque comme un affreux parquet.
Il ne reste plus rien pour te faire plaisir. Ce à quoi tu t'accroches
d'habitude te semble n'être que de sombres conneries.
Tu vas préparer ton petit déjeuner.
Tu ne manges jamais salé le matin mais aujourd'hui tu
fais du choux et des saucisses, avec des œufs.
Tu écoutes les pas dans l'escalier.
Ce n'est pas elle.
Tu as envie de gerber tes nerfs et les saucisses.
Les choses te semblent de moins en moins intéressantes.
Tu n'es même plus étonné par tes réactions.
Tu les subis sagement. Tu t'assois quelque part et tu râles.
Comme un vieux cerf. Vouté et encombré par de ces gros bois lourds.

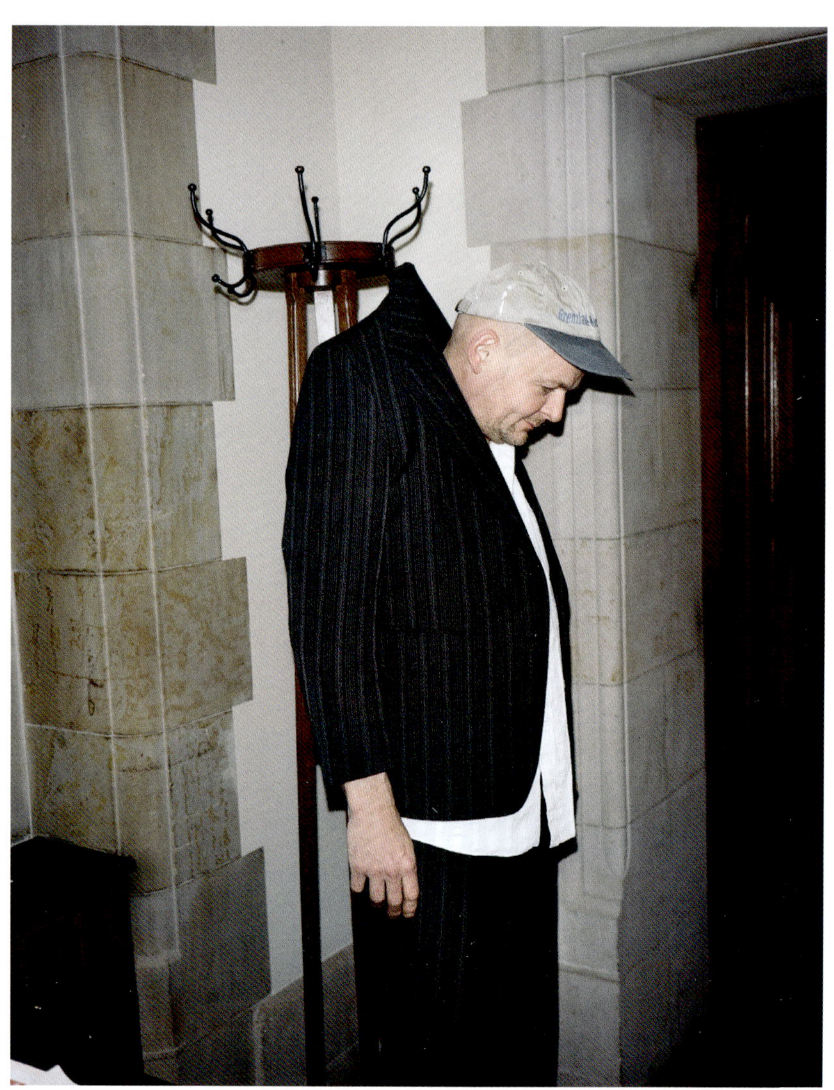

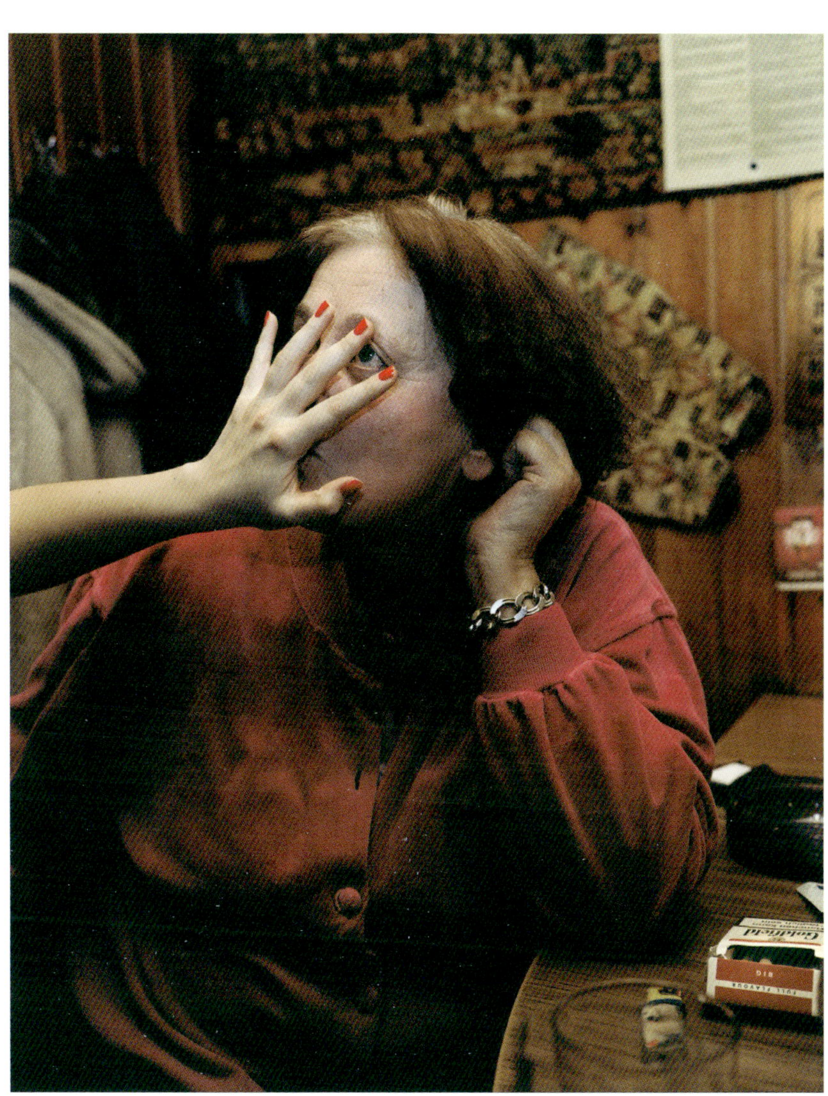

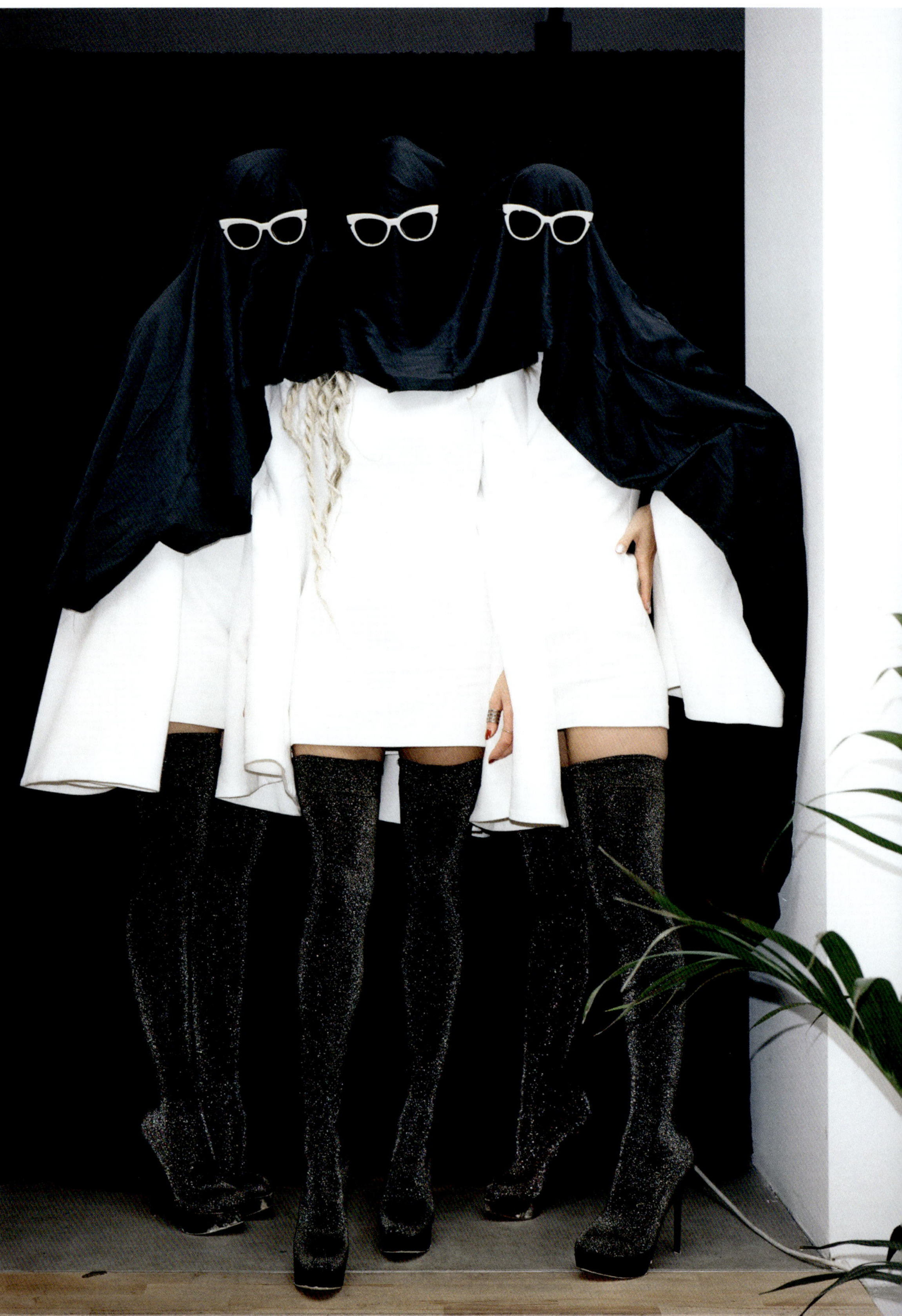

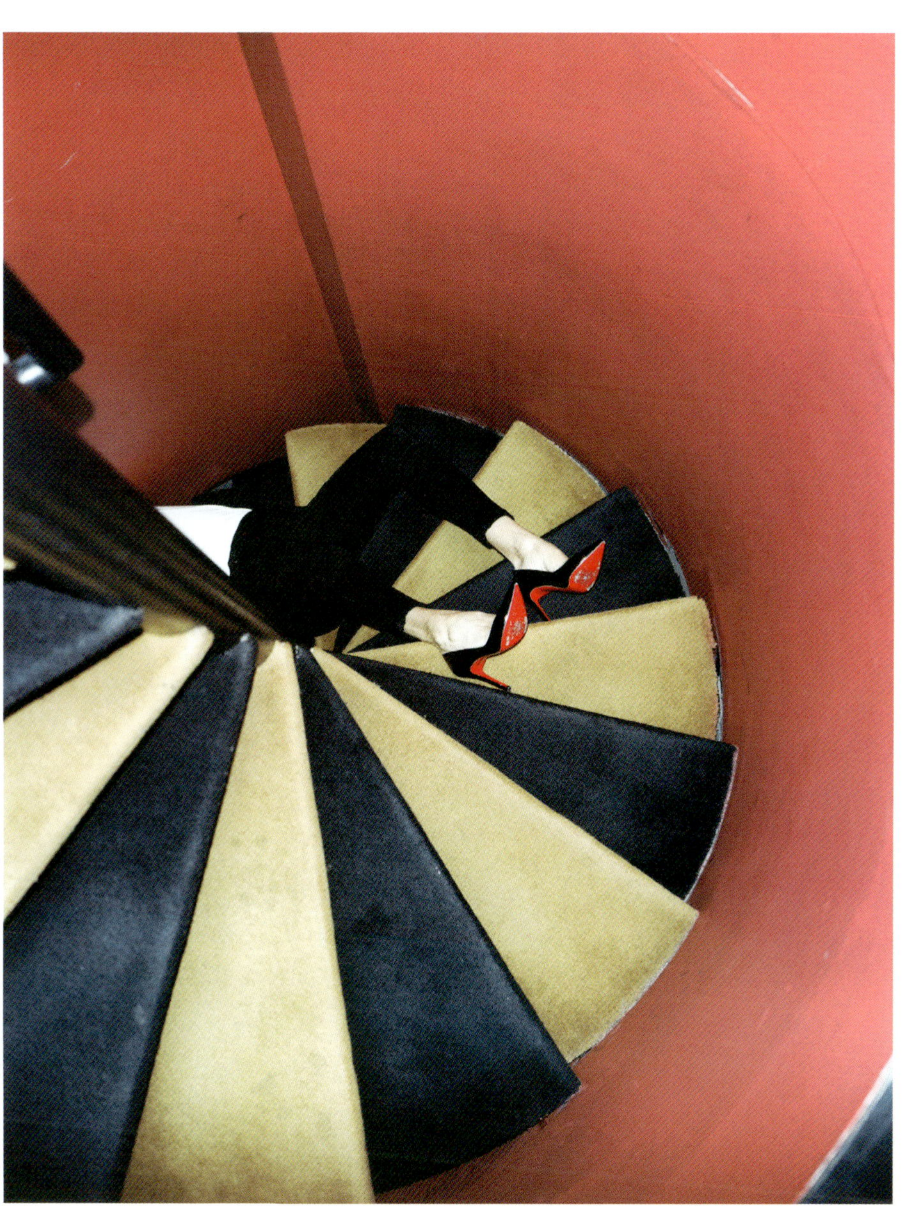

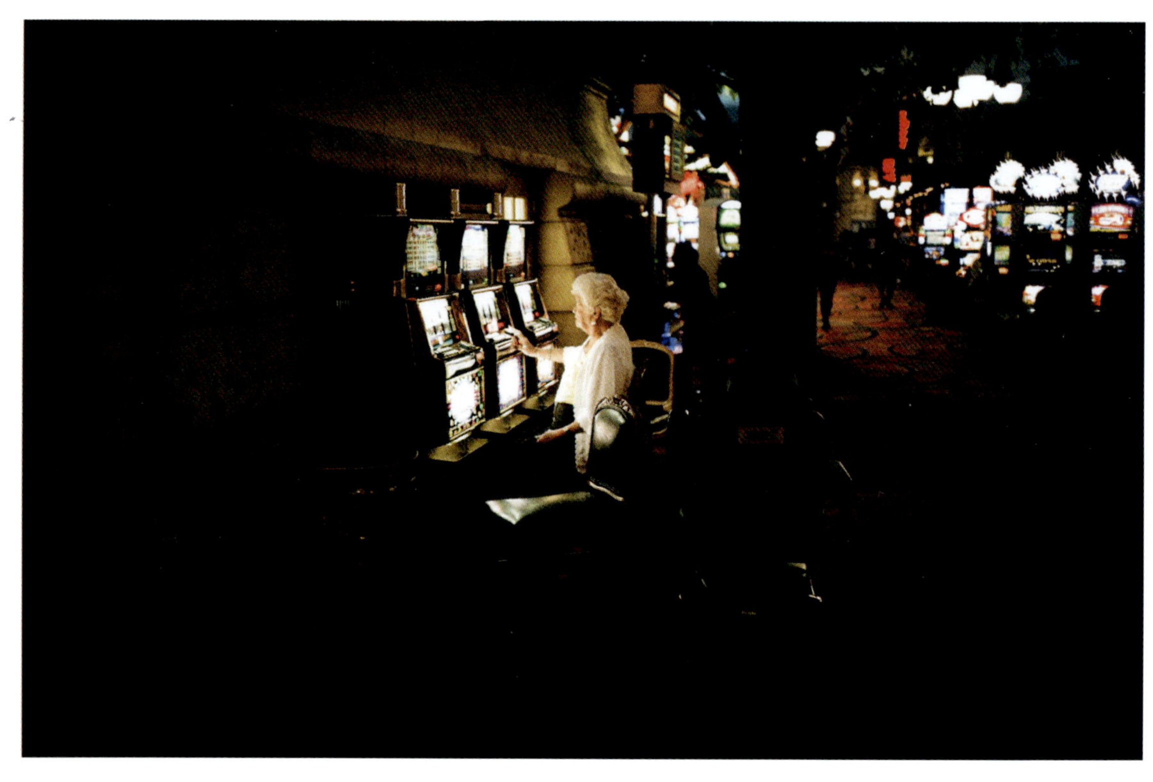

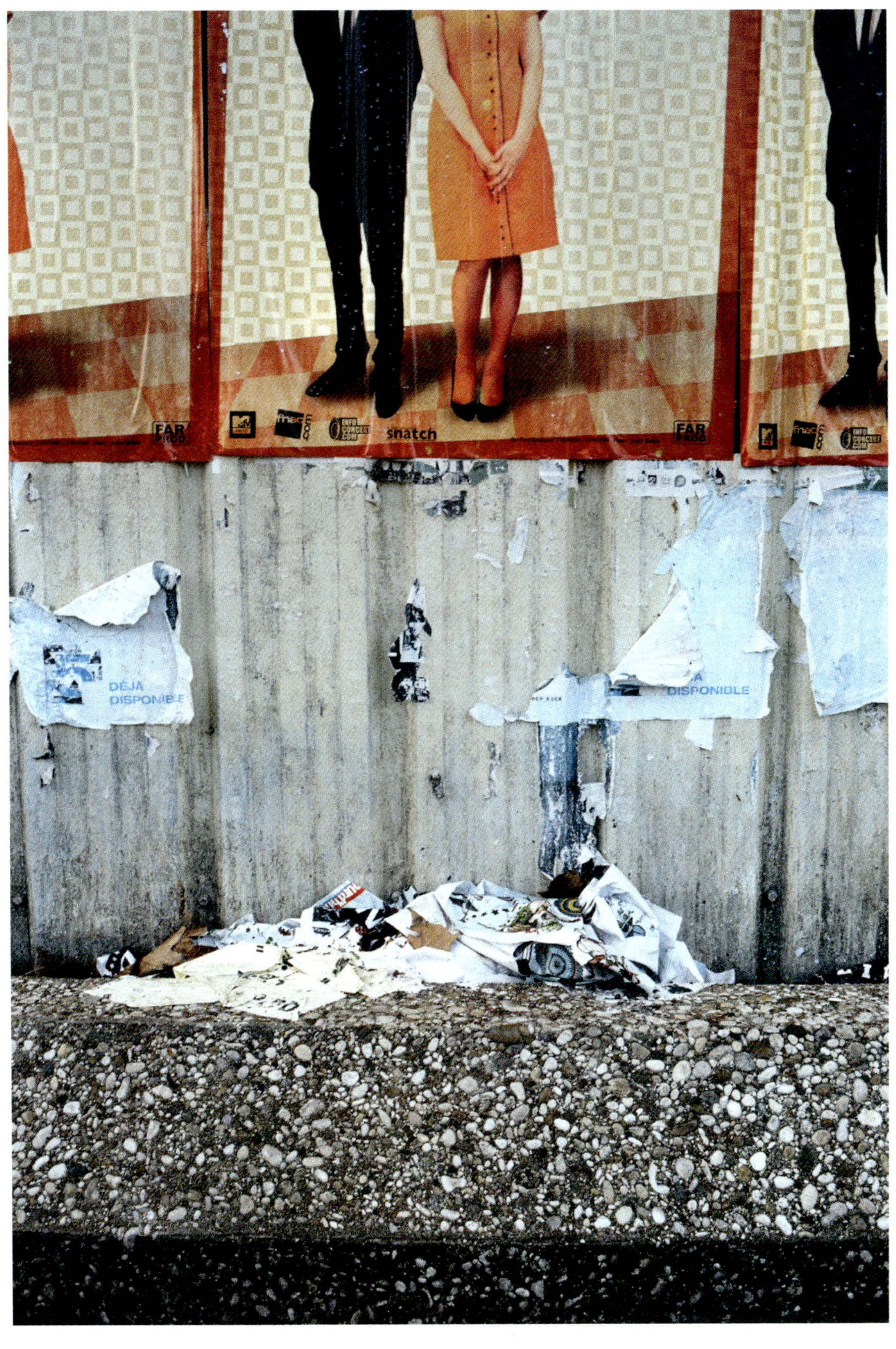
snatch
DÉJA
DISPONIBLE

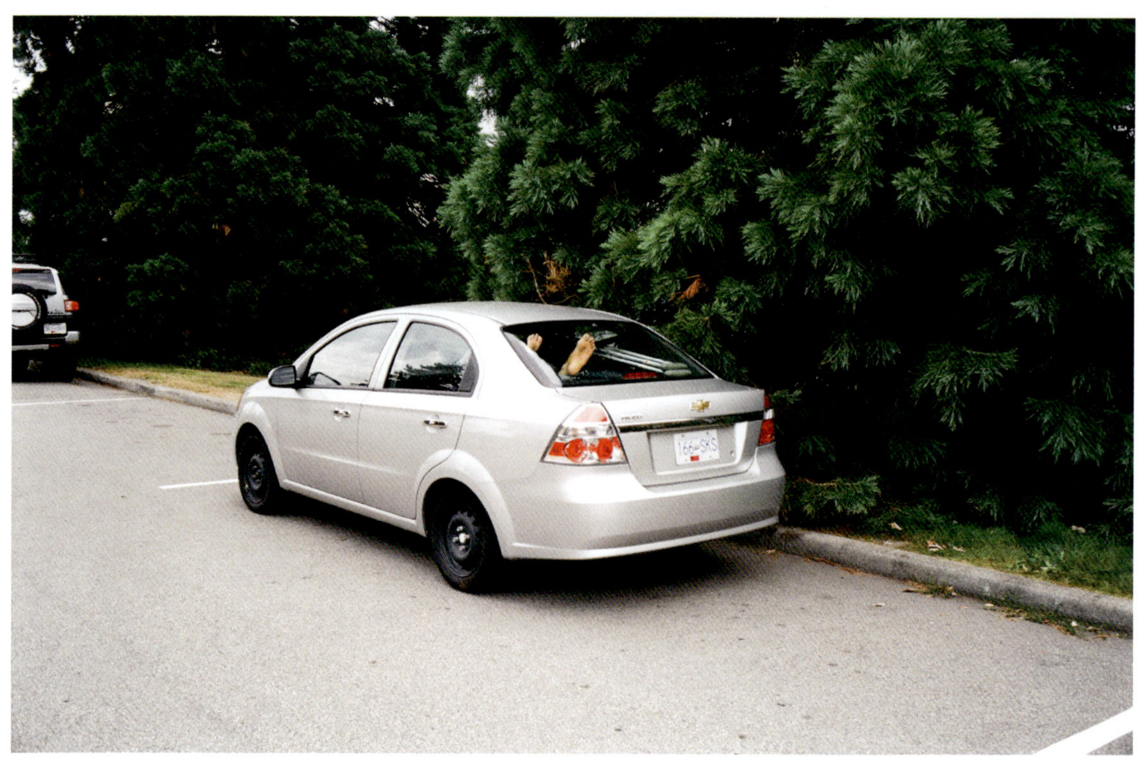

2006 Giving a name to his genitals
might seem ridiculous,
but for Pierre,
it was the start of a new life as a couple.

2006 Donner un nom à son sexe
pourrait paraître être une chose ridicule,
mais pour Pierre,
c'était le début d'une nouvelle vie à deux.

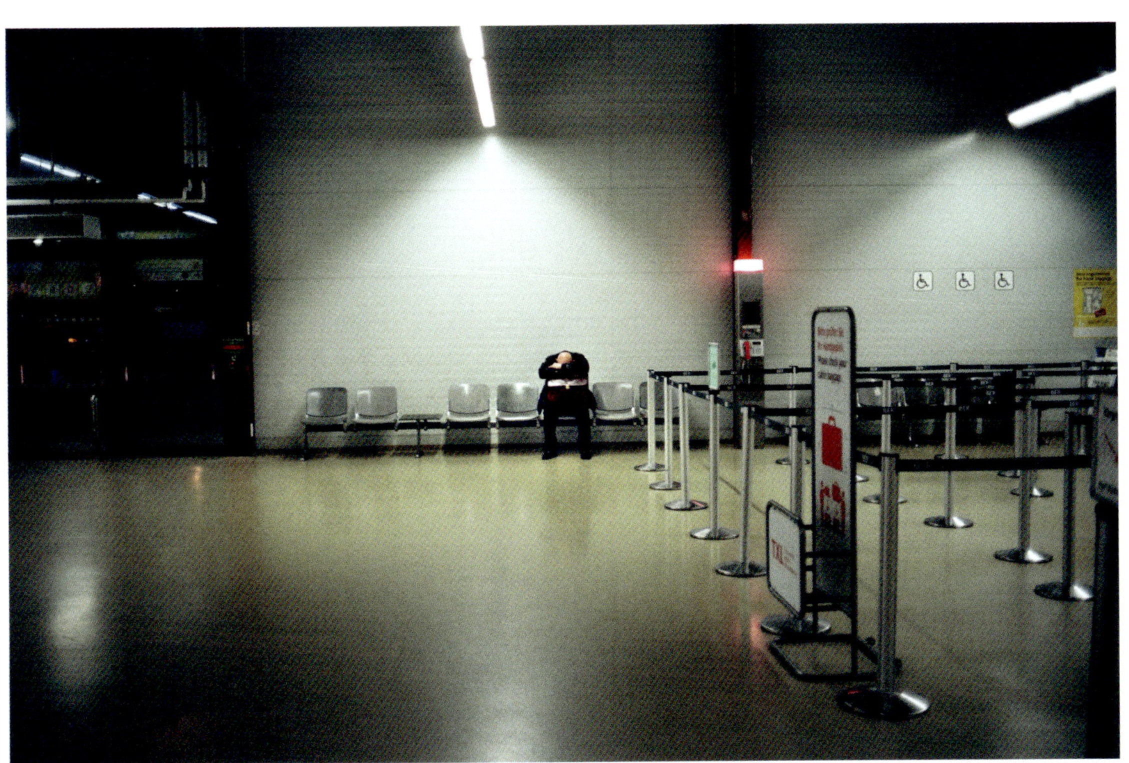

Reveries

2004

There is nothing more to say. All that is left to do is imagine. Imagine that you are alive. Imagine that you are the absolute. If you know what the absolute is. Imagine a young woman sitting. A young woman sitting and doing nothing. She does not even realize that she is sitting. And that you are imagining her. Then you can, for example, light a cigarette and stay like this. You will not even smoke. Then the young woman will be standing and she can walk. She would be beautiful. It would seem natural that she's beautiful. But you are intrigued. You are intrigued because you are a pike. A slimy pike. Slimy and flabby. You are incredibly ugly. But despite your incredible ugliness you like to look at her. You like to imagine that you are looking at her. But you are so flabby that it is very difficult for you to keep your eyelids open. And it is so hard to breathe out of the water, that each inhalation is a bitter torture that you like to inflict upon yourself. The asphyxia is slow. The asphyxia makes you uglier. You are swelling. You are swelling sitting on the only chair in your clammy apartment. Your smell is bothering the young woman. Because you stink. You are swelling and stinking so badly. And from your obese eye you observe her delicate step. You observe her pulling her very thin heels out of your so flabby pike body. You have no more air but you're still swelling. Your arms are coming off your body. You are upset, you surely will not be able to knot your tie as well as you used to. You are a pike and you are incredibly ugly and you stink. You are slimy and flabby. You don't have arms anymore, you are swelling, inflating and stinking even more. You are sitting on the only chair in your clammy and greenish apartment. And you yearn.

2004

Il n'y a rien à dire de plus. Il ne reste plus qu'à imaginer maintenant. Imaginer que tu es vivant. Imaginer que tu es l'absolu. Si tu sais ce qu'est l'absolu. Imaginer une jeune femme assise. Une jeune femme assise qui ne fait rien. Qui ne pense même pas qu'elle est assise. Et que tu l'imagines ainsi. Ensuite tu peux t'allumer une cigarette par exemple et rester comme ça. Tu ne fumeras même pas. Alors la jeune femme serait debout et elle pourrait marcher. Elle serait belle. Il te semblerait naturel qu'elle soit belle. Mais tu es intrigué. Tu es intrigué car tu es un brochet. Un brochet visqueux. Visqueux et flasque. Tu es incroyablement laid. Mais malgré ton incroyable laideur tu aimes la regarder. Tu aimes imaginer que tu la regardes. Mais tu es si flasque qu'il t'est très difficile de rester les paupières ouvertes. Et tu respires si difficilement hors de l'eau, que chaque inspiration est une torture amère que tu aimes pourtant t'infliger. L'asphyxie est lente. L'asphyxie te rend encore plus laid. Tu gonfles. Tu gonfles sur la seule chaise de ton appartement moite. La jeune femme est dérangée par ton odeur. Car tu pues. Tu enfles et tu pues terriblement. Et de ton œil obèse tu observes son pas délicat. Tu l'observes dégager ses talons si fins de ton corps de brochet si flasque. Tu n'as plus d'air mais tu gonfles encore. Tes bras se détachent de ton corps. Tu es déçu car tu ne réussiras sûrement plus aussi bien tes nœuds de cravate. Tu es un brochet et tu es incroyablement laid et tu pues. Tu es visqueux et flasque. Tu n'as plus de bras et tu gonfles, tu enfles et tu pues encore plus. Tu es assis sur la seule chaise de ton appartement moite et verdâtre. Et tu bailles.

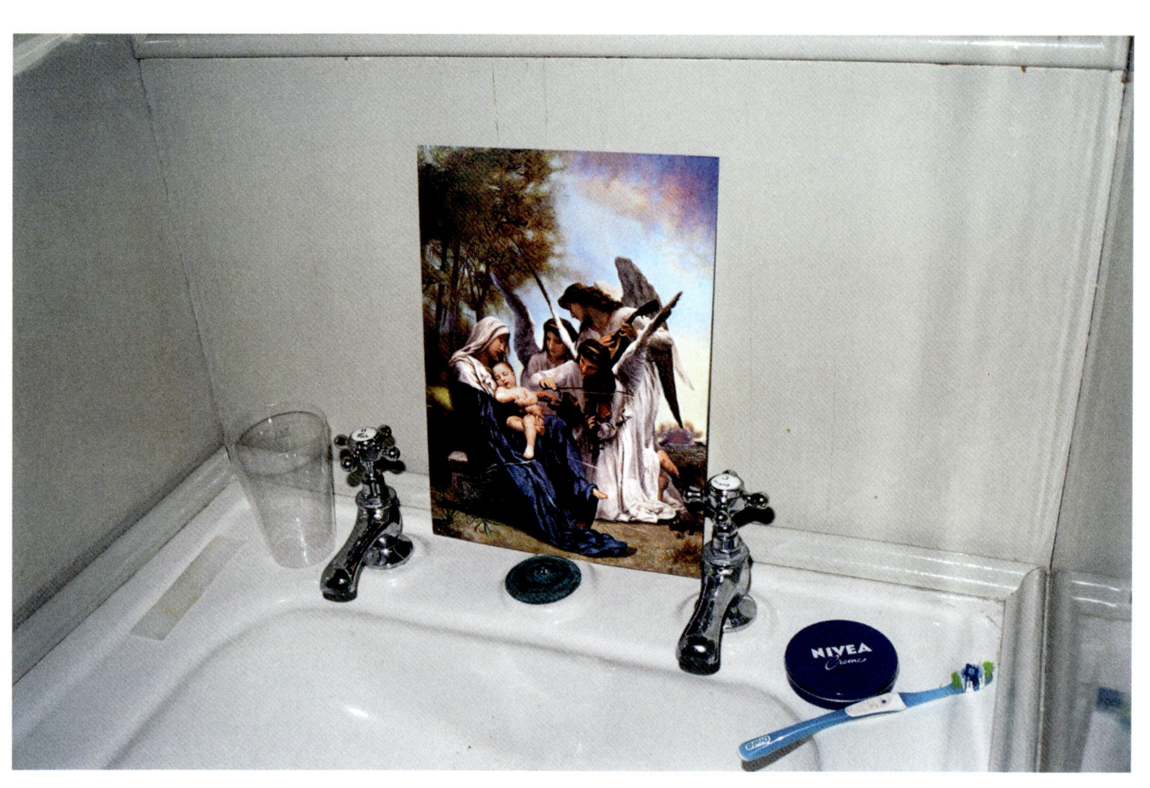

morning sonata, Berlin, 2014

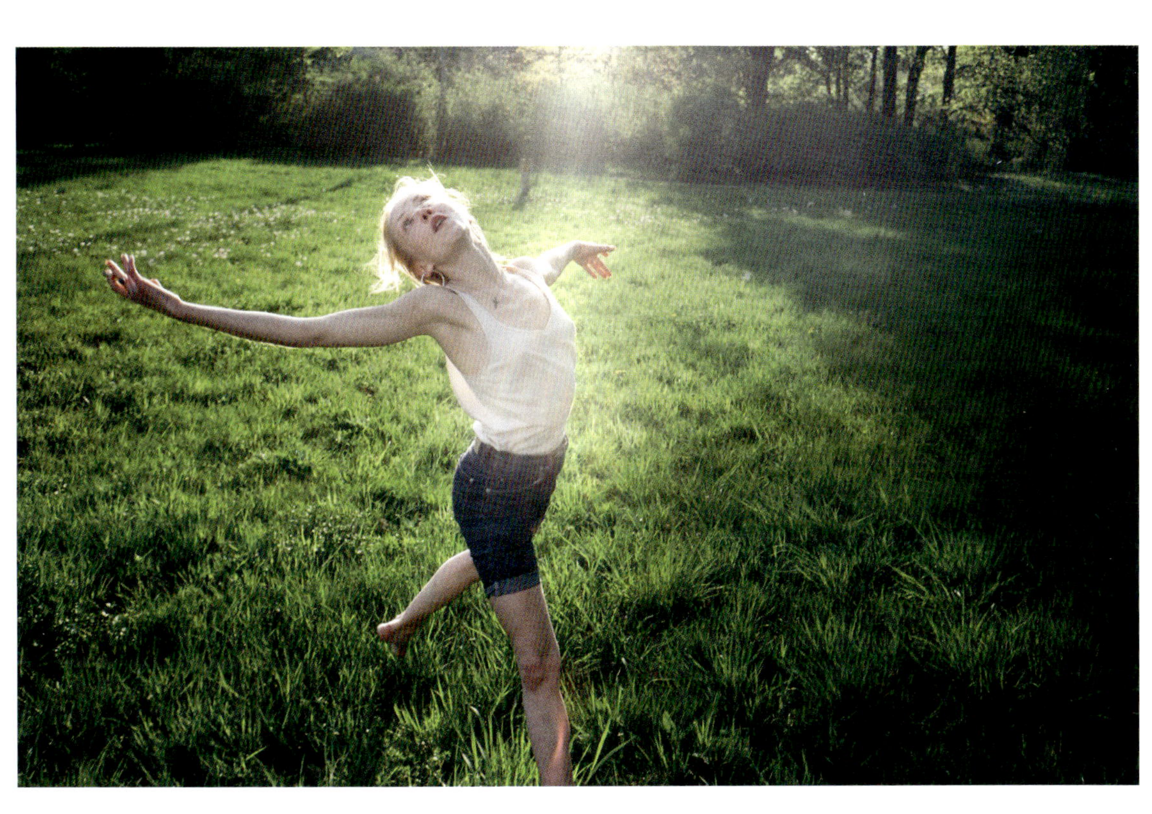

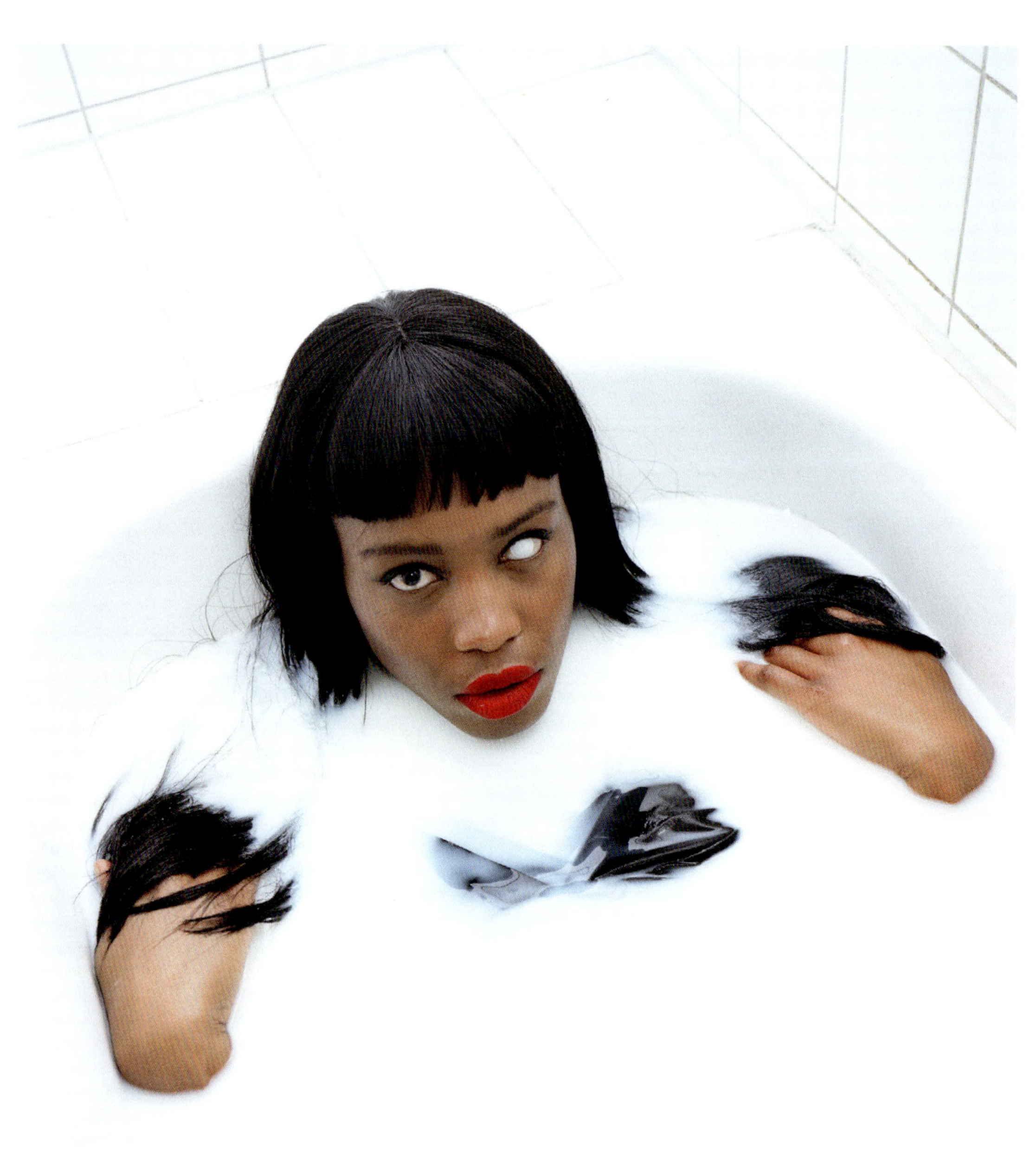

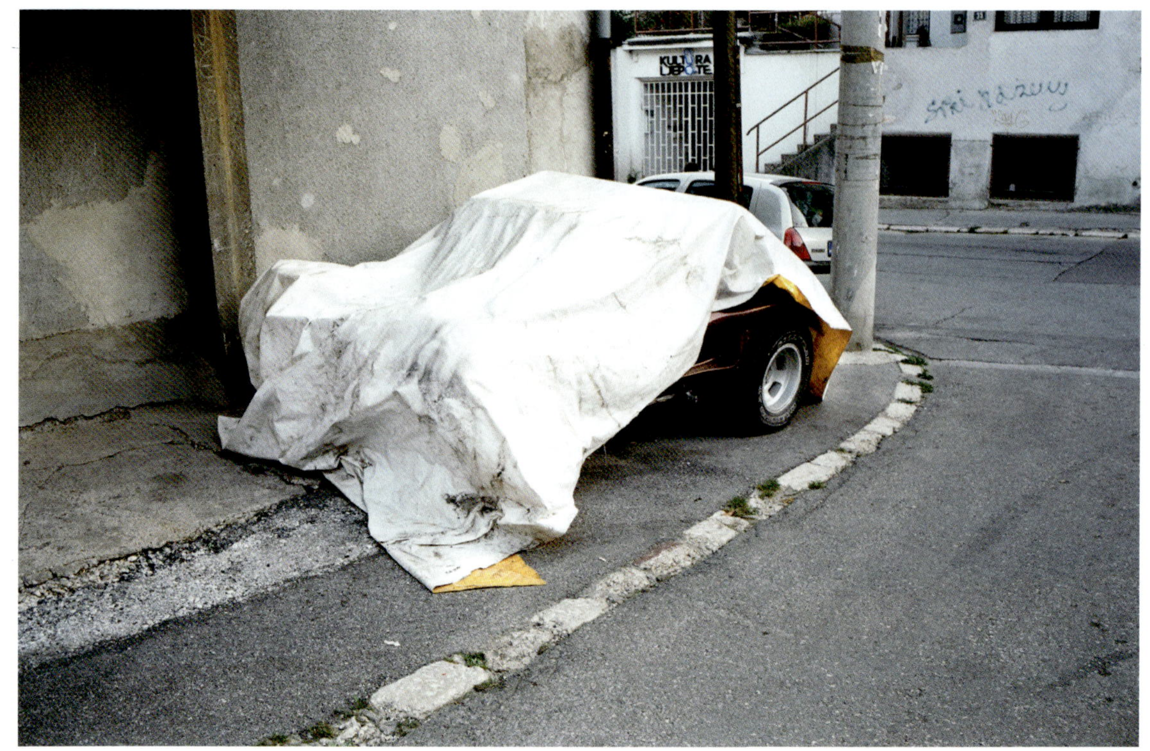

2006 It may be a year since there's been a pin missing from the poster above your bed.
Only today you notice that the upper right corner falls and covers a quarter of the picture.
You can be sure, though, that it
has been like that for a long time,
a year maybe.

2006 Voilà peut être un an qu'une punaise manque à l'affiche en face de ton lit.
Tu ne remarques qu'aujourd'hui que le coin supérieur
droit tombe et recouvre un quart du poster.
Tu peux malgré tout affirmer que c'est comme ça depuis longtemps,
peut être un an.

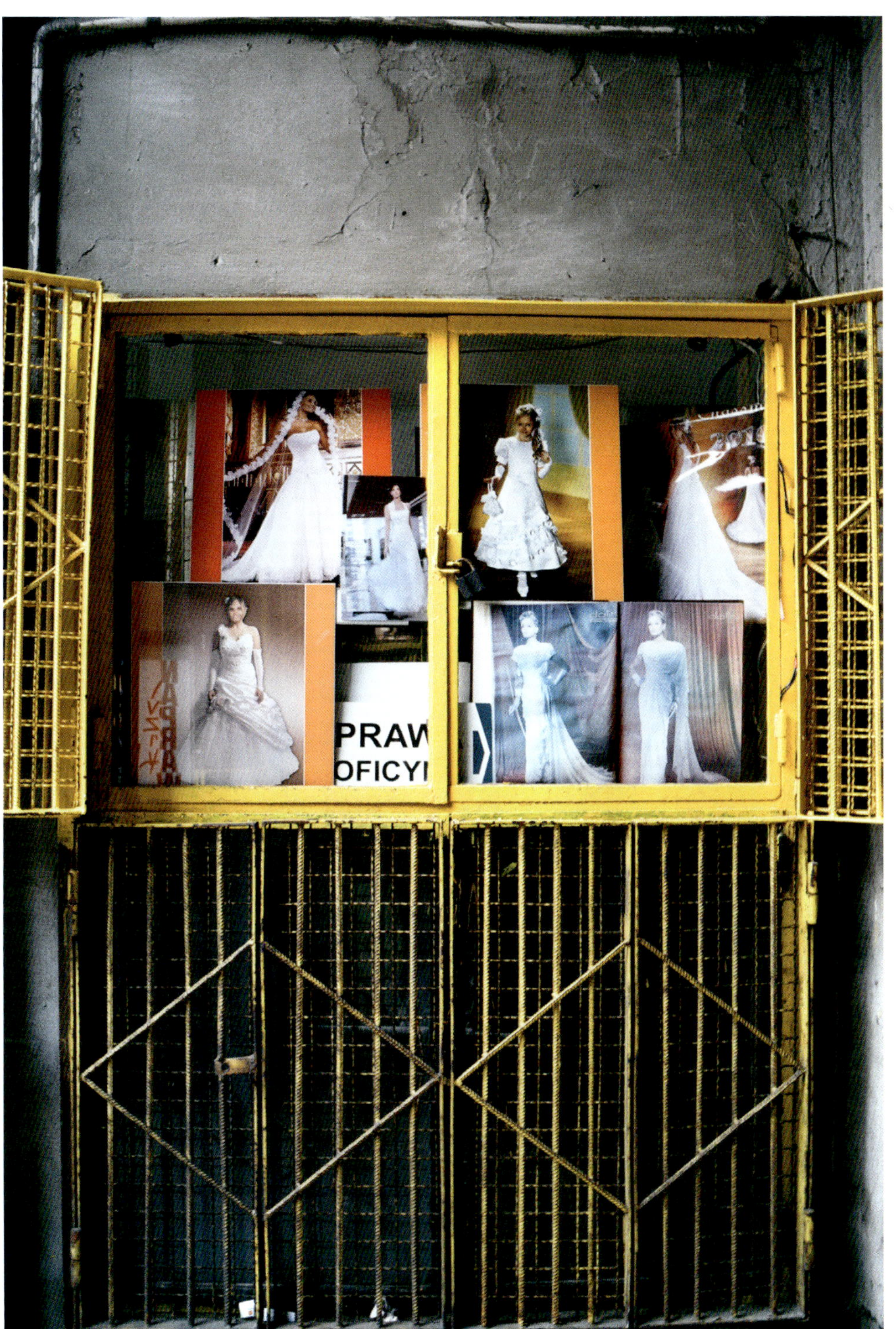
PRAW
OFICY

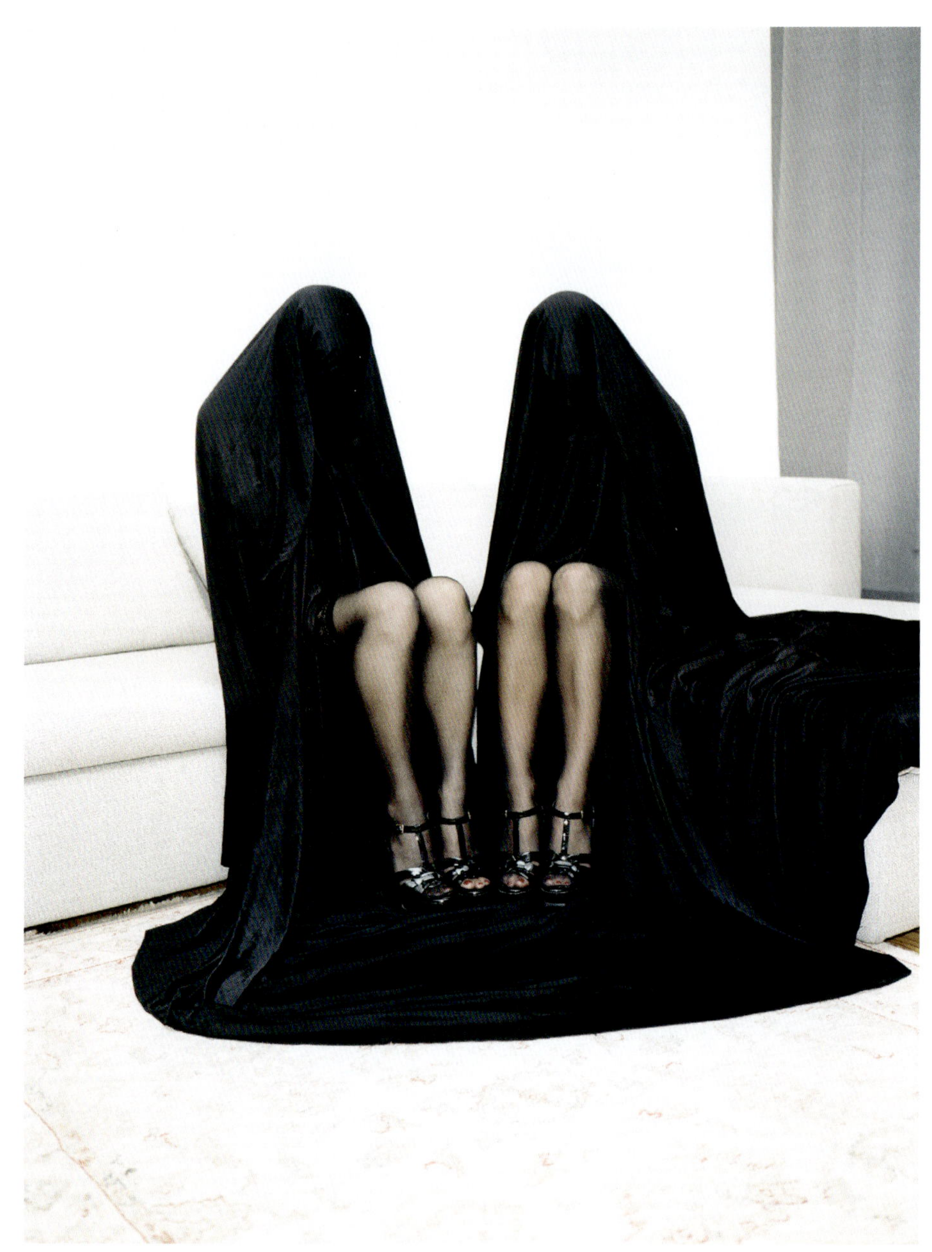

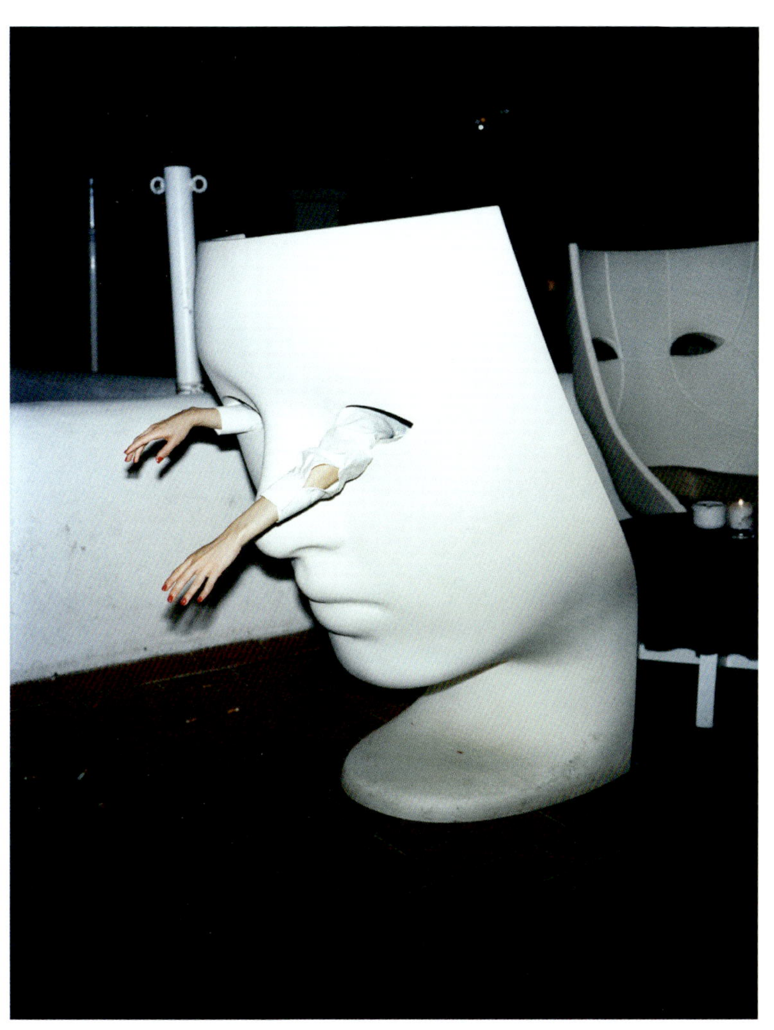

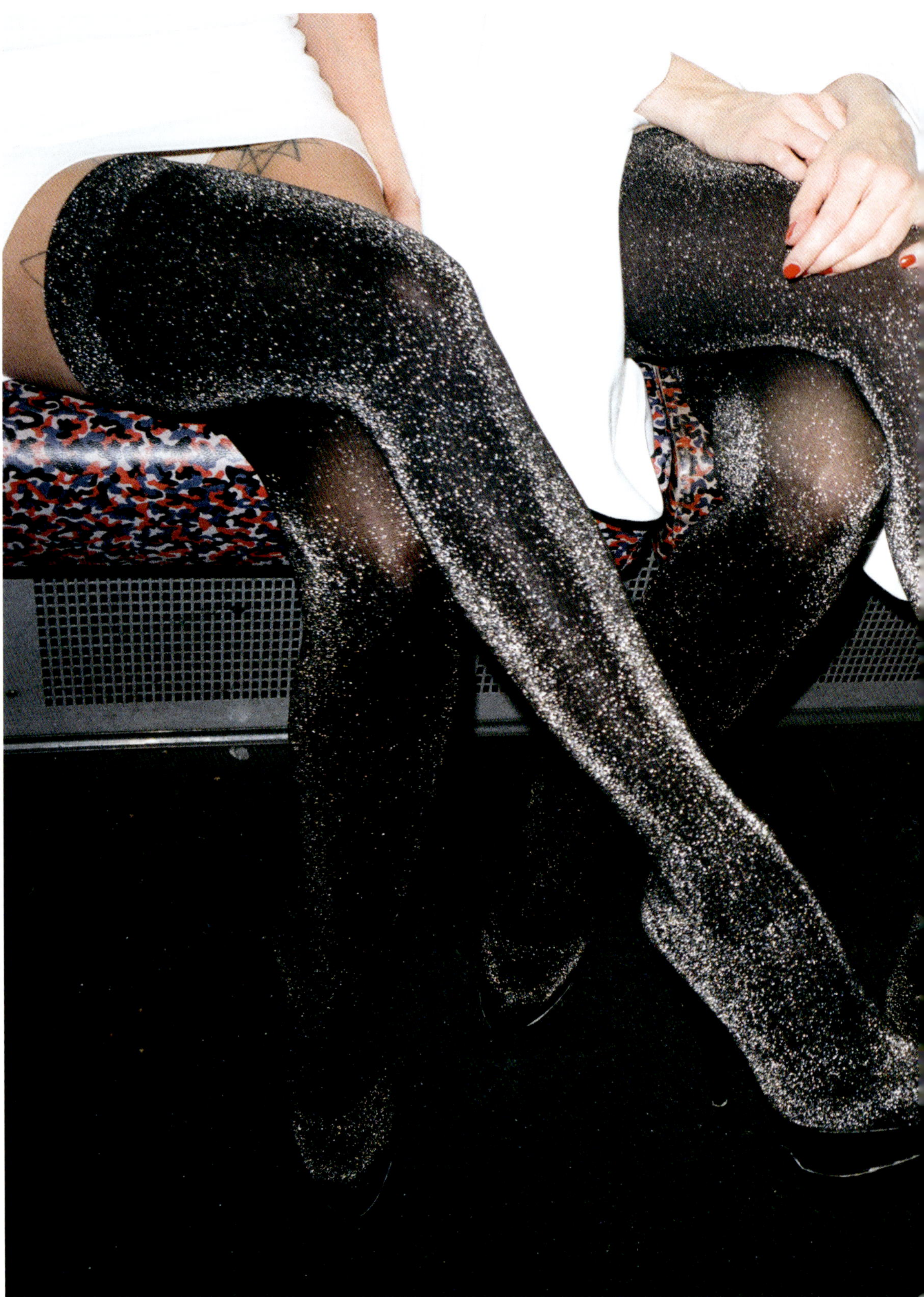

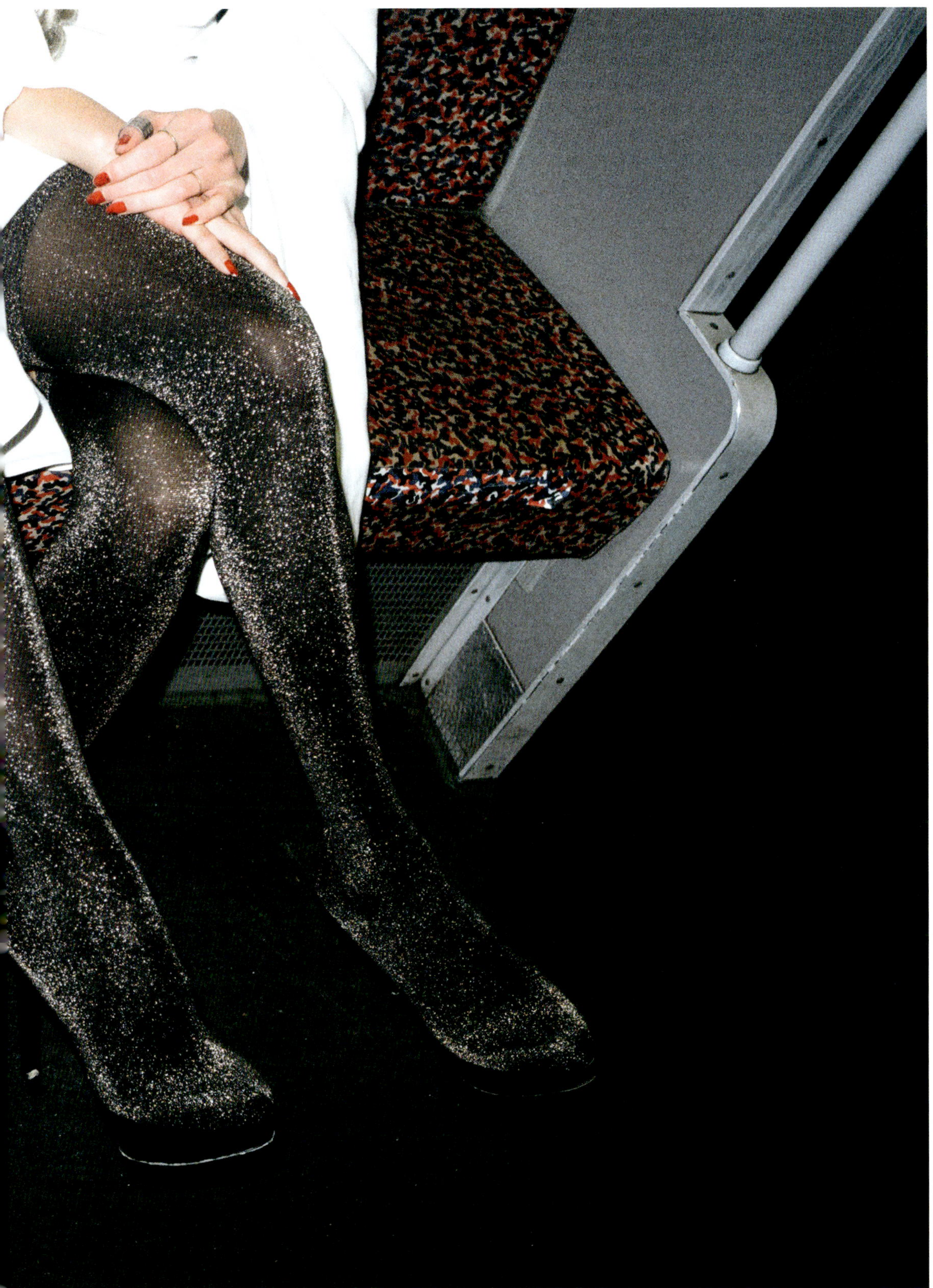

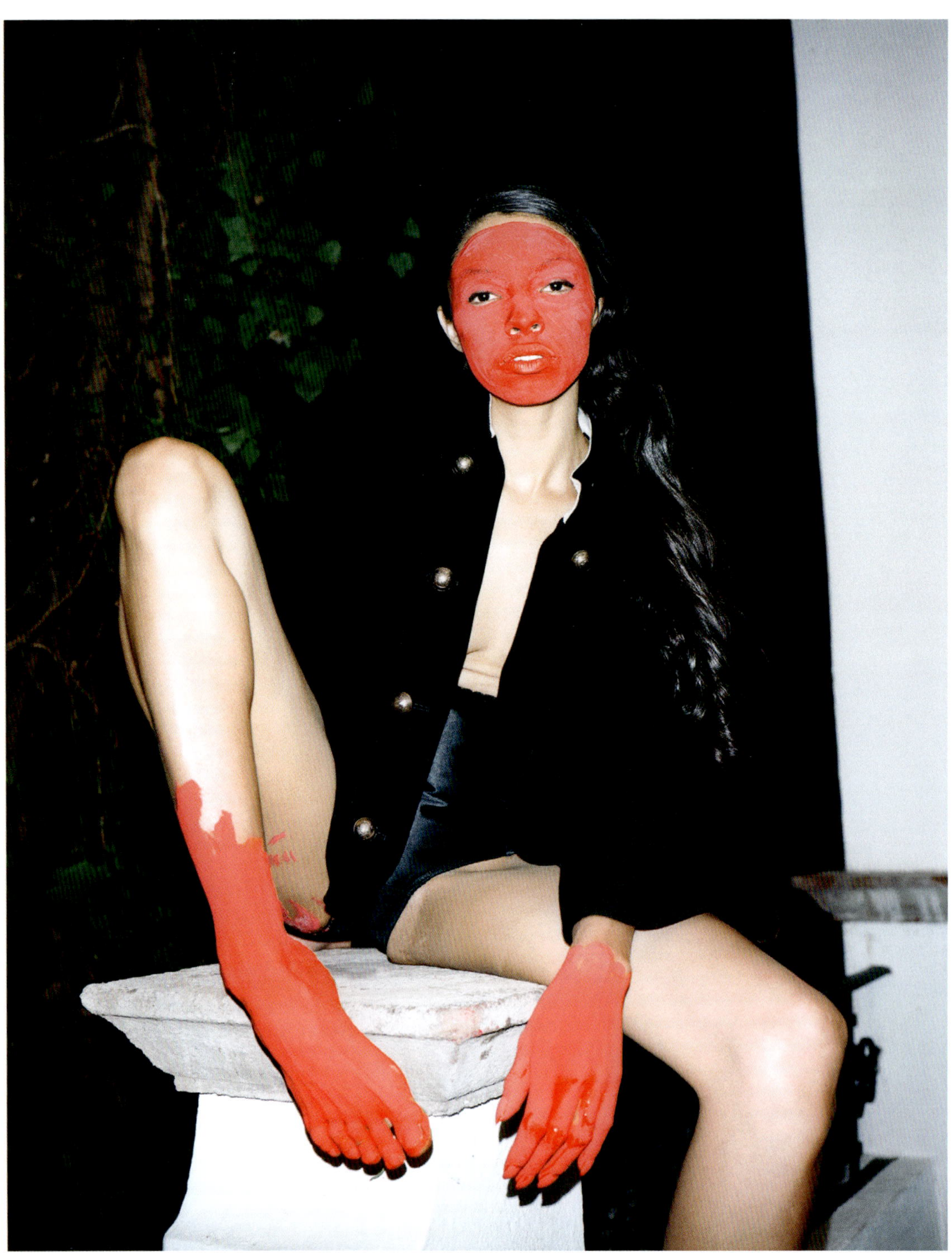

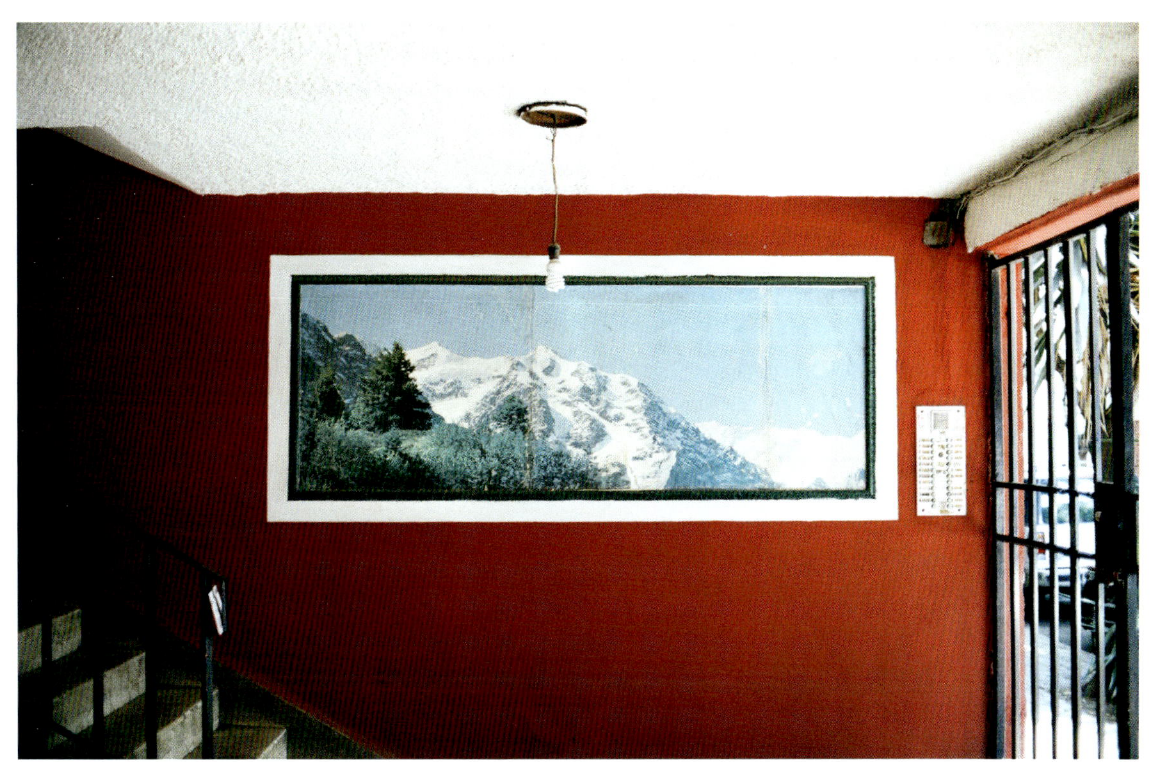

2014 Pierre would have gone to the seaside this summer, but he was
afraid he'd get his cellphone wet.
It's decided, he will stay home,
and count his pimples.

2014 Pierre serait bien parti à la mer cet été, mais il avait
peur de mouiller son portable.
C'est décidé, il restera à la maison,
et comptera ses boutons.

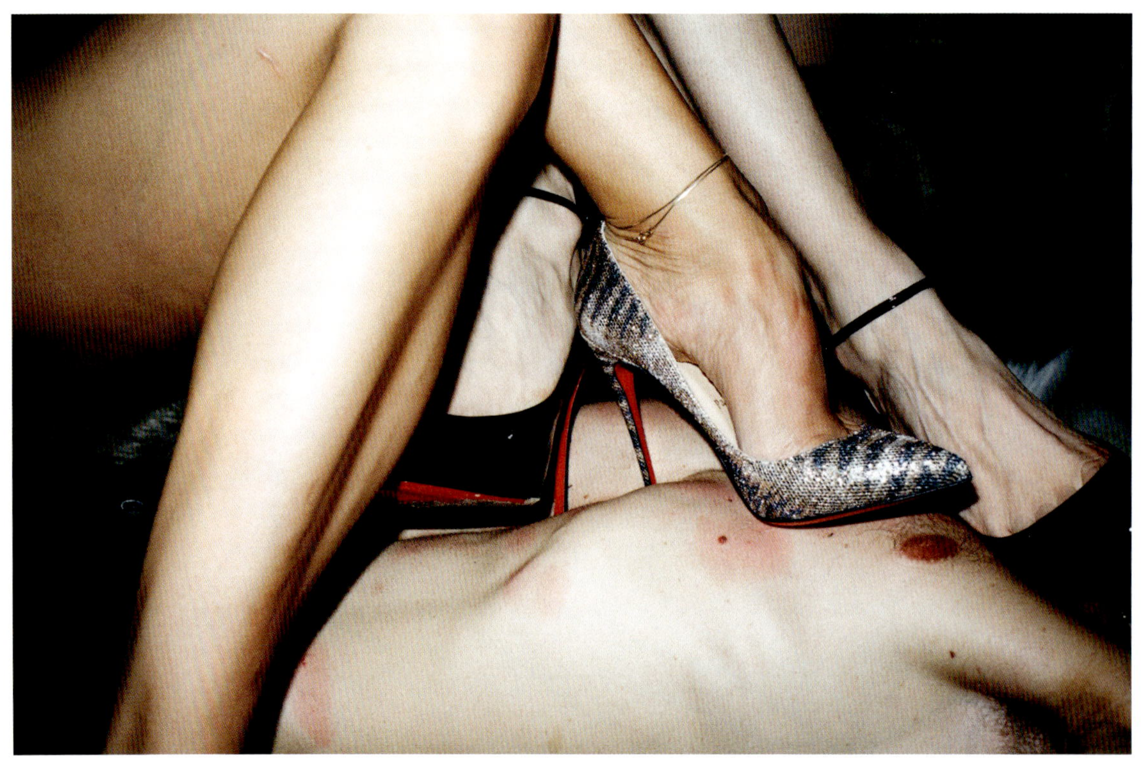

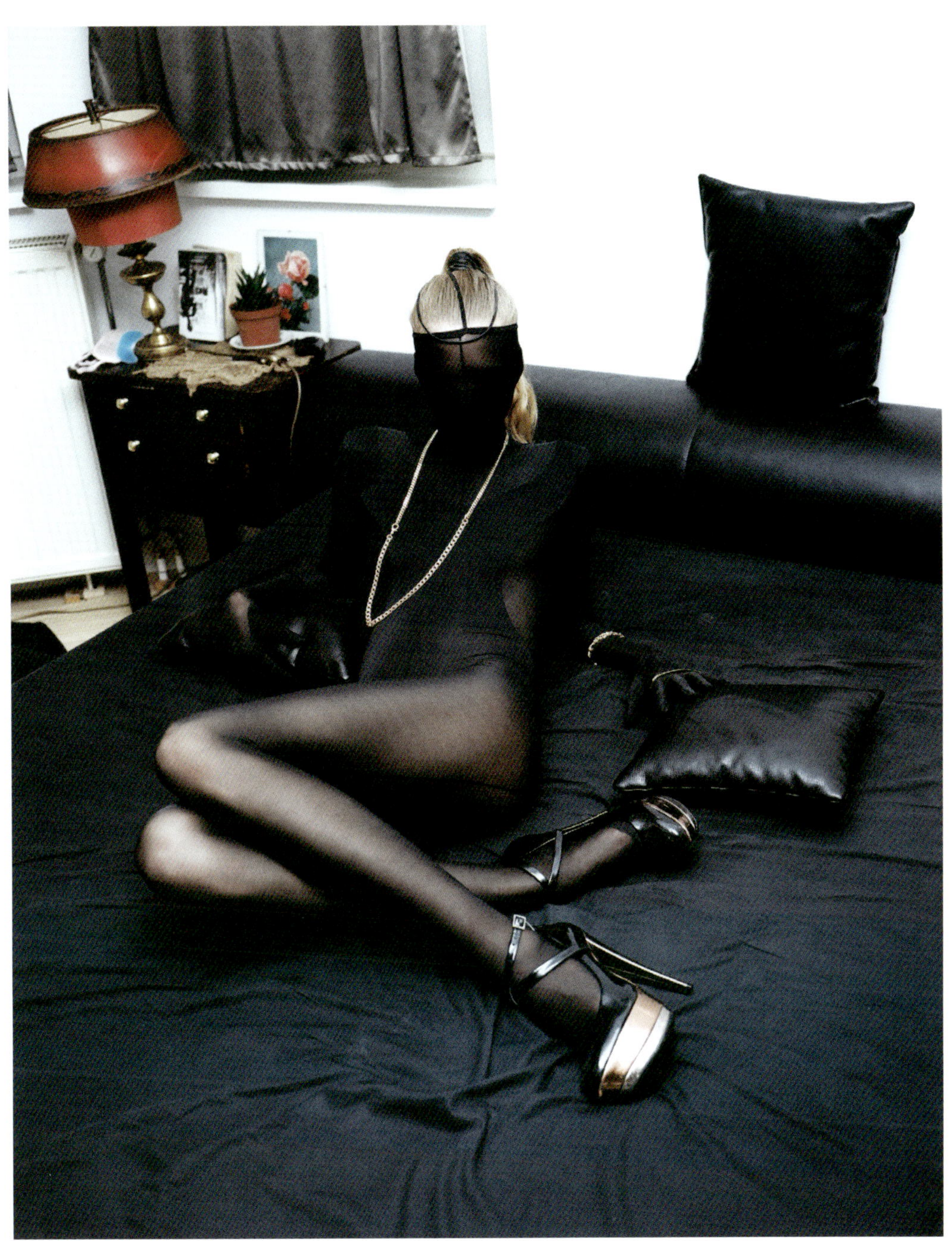

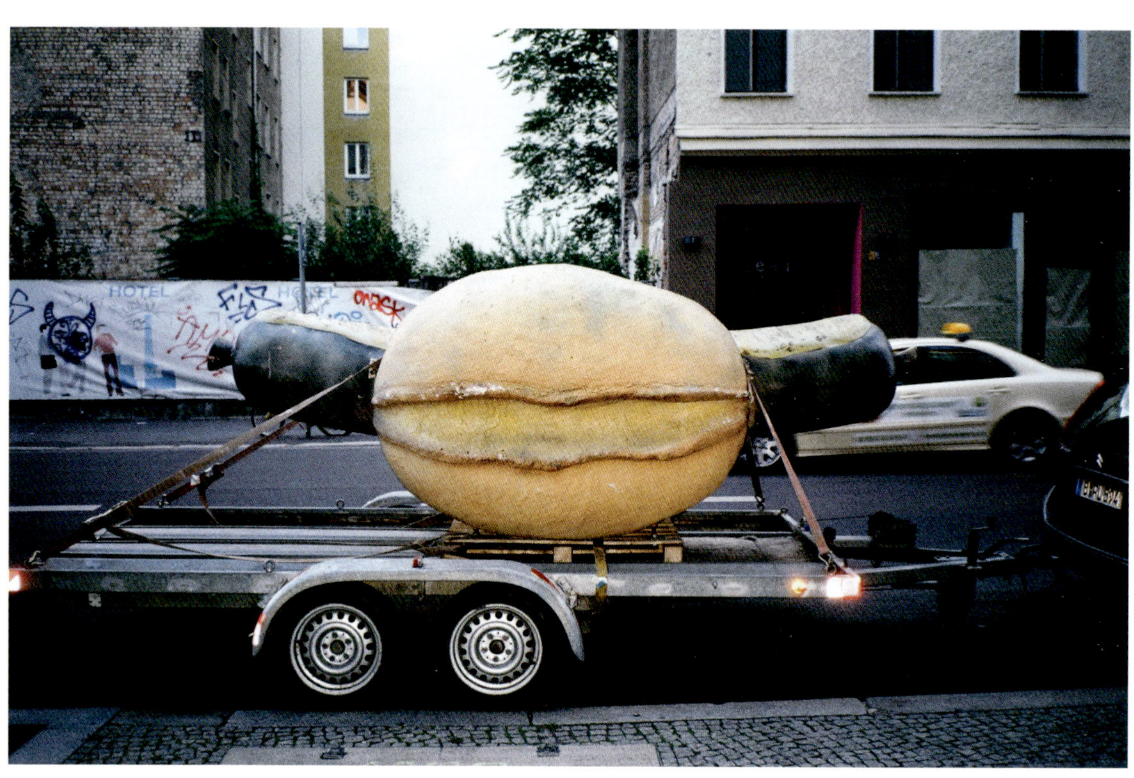
HOTEL

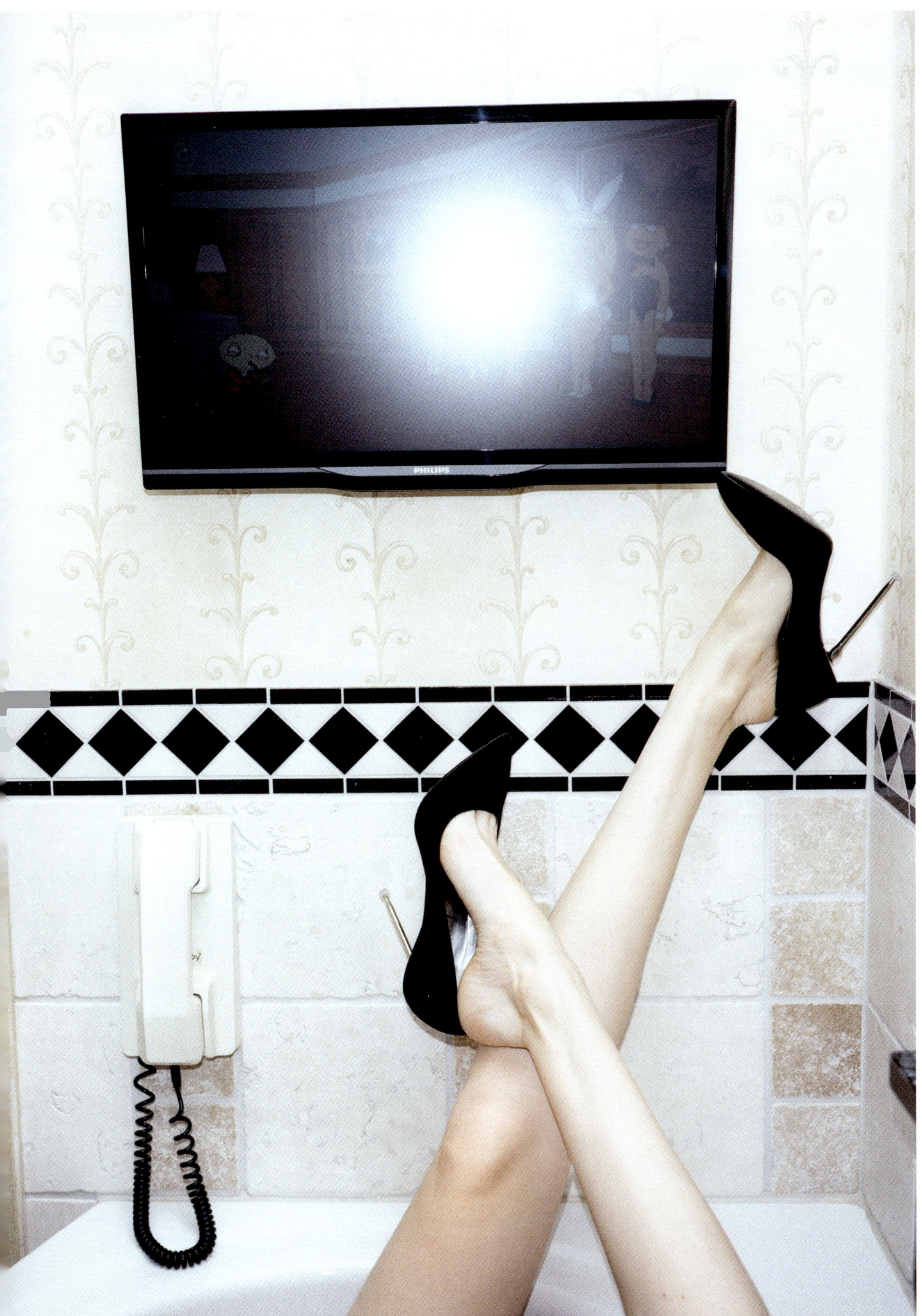
PHILIPS

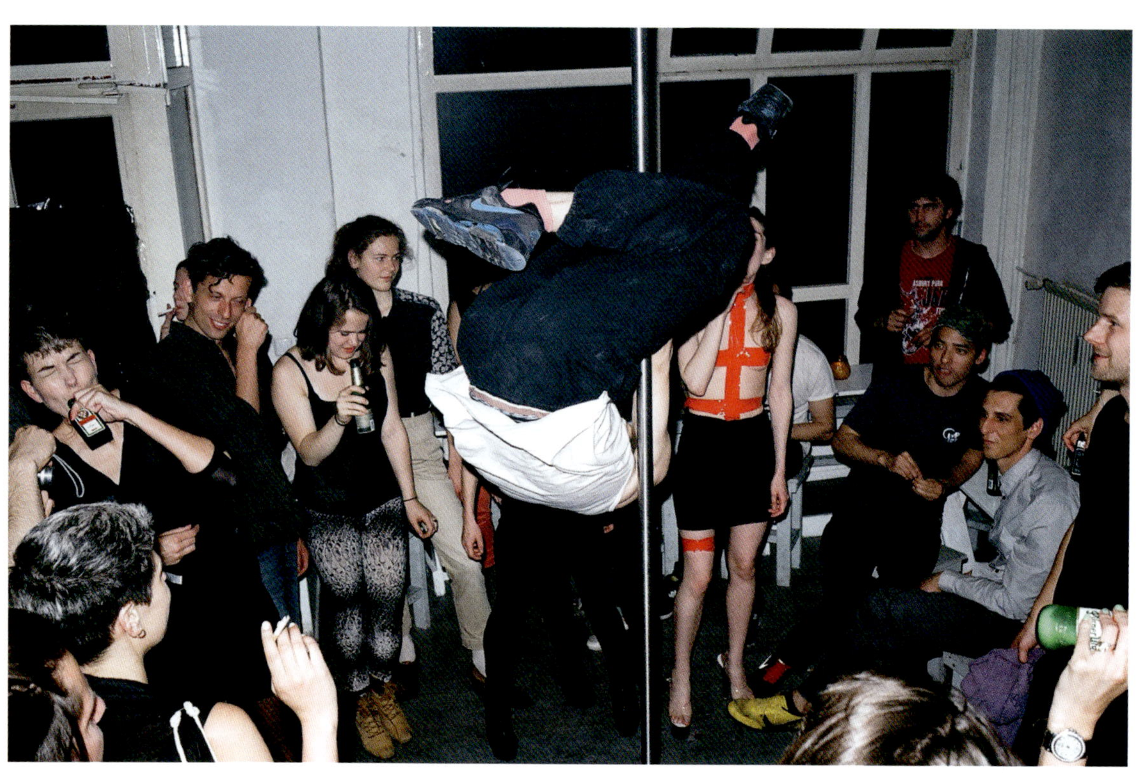

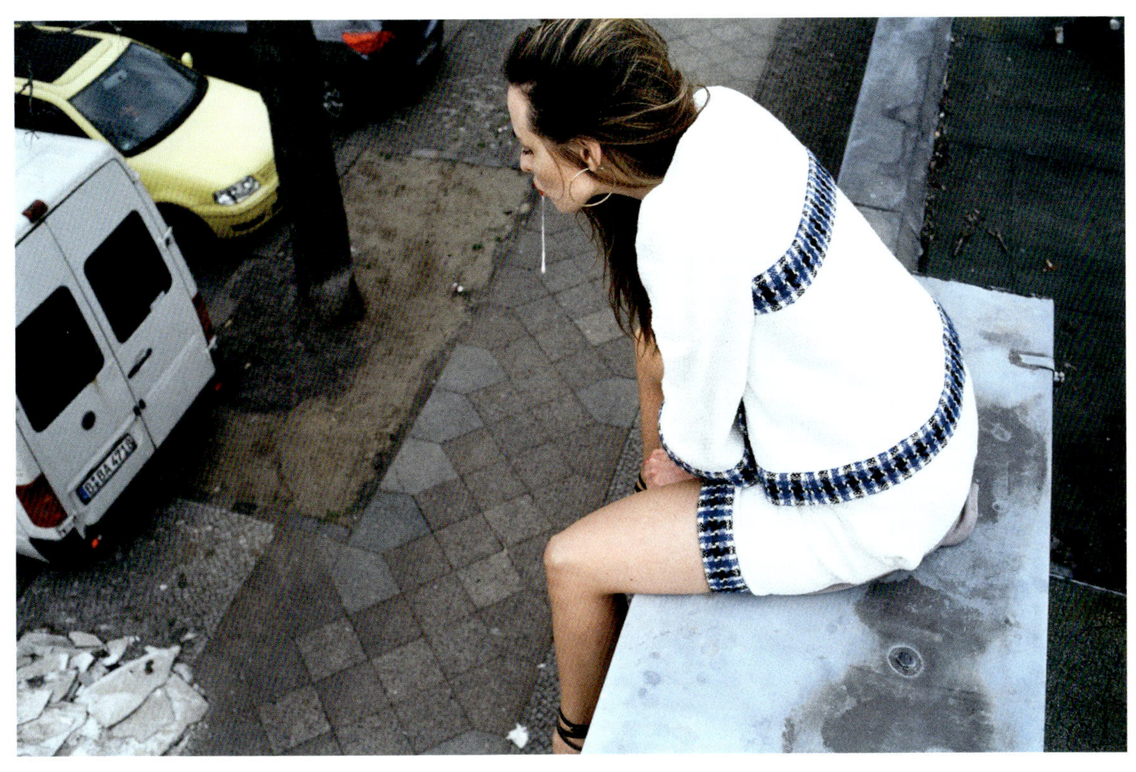

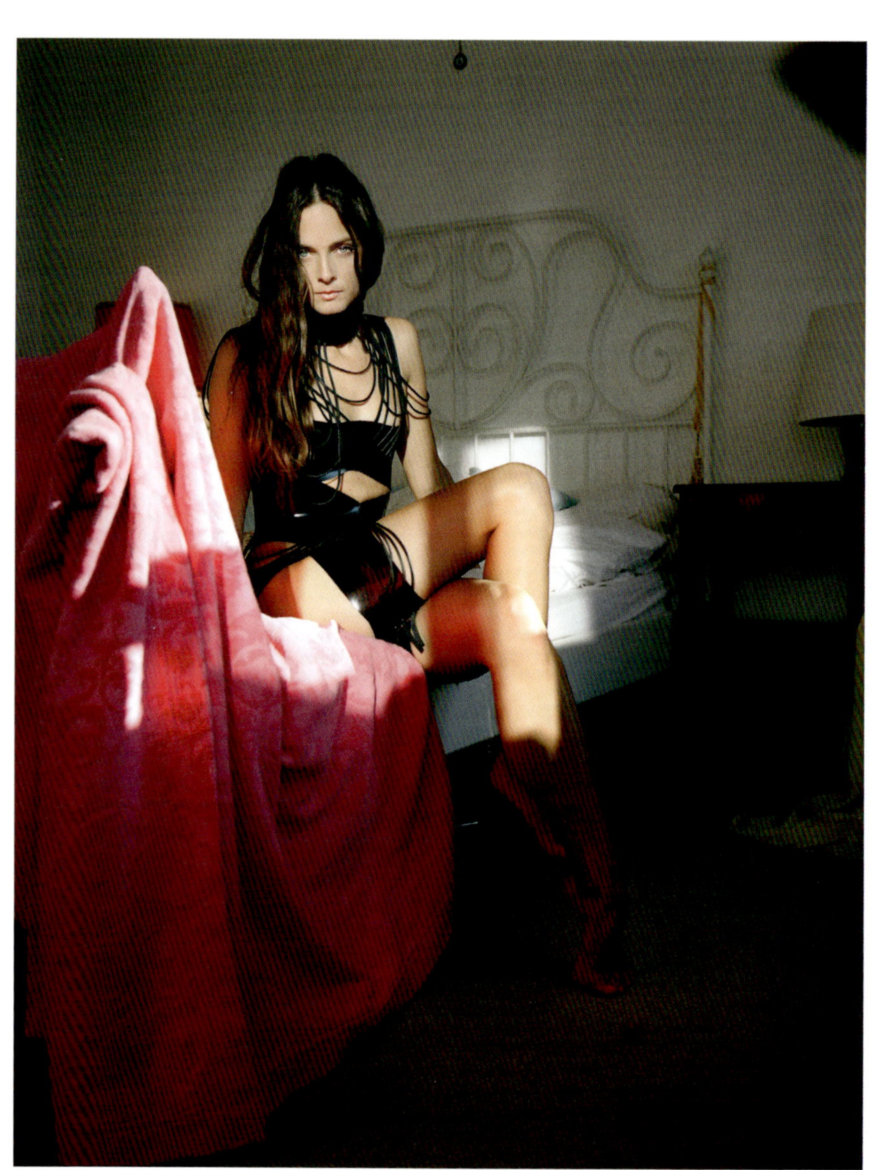

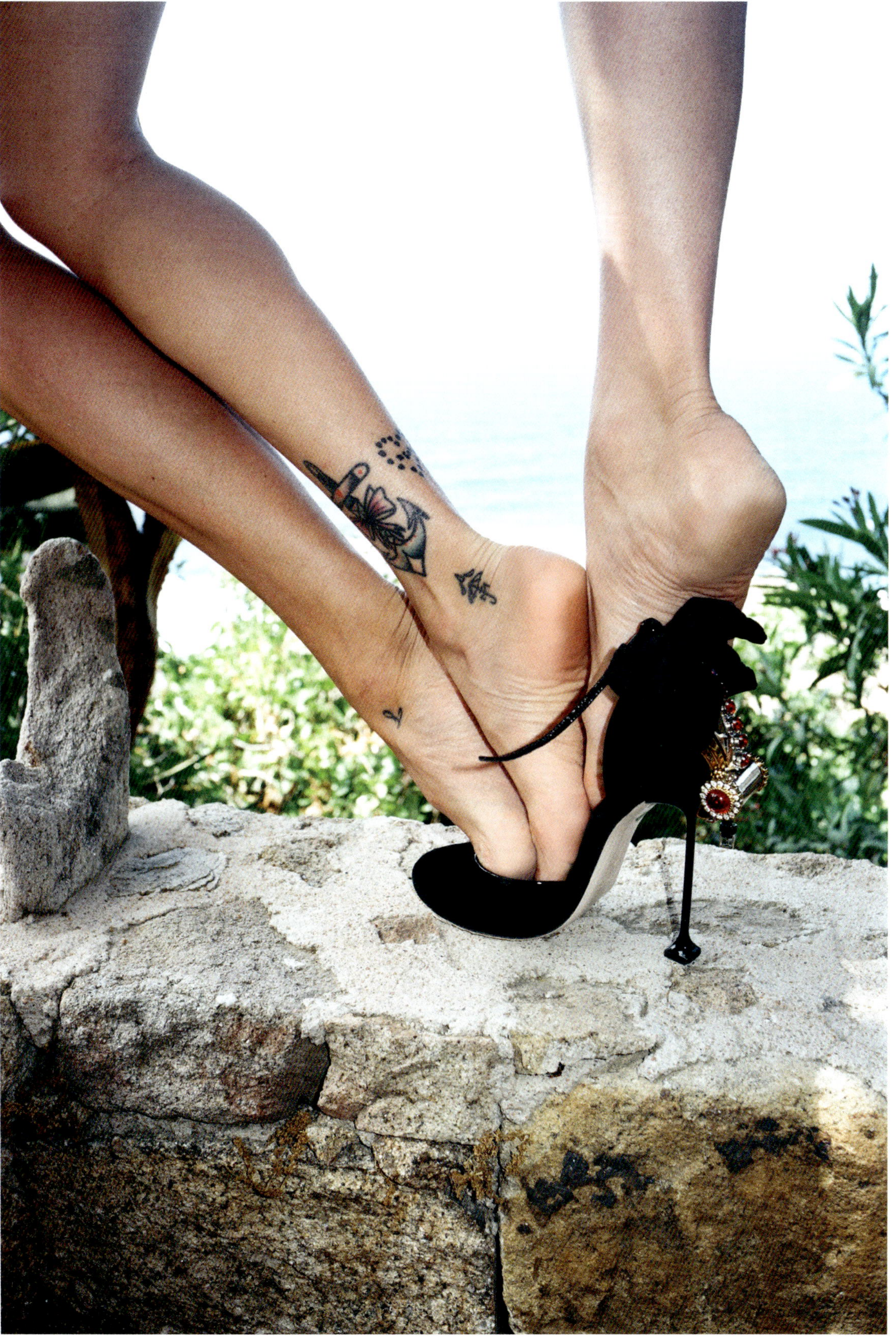

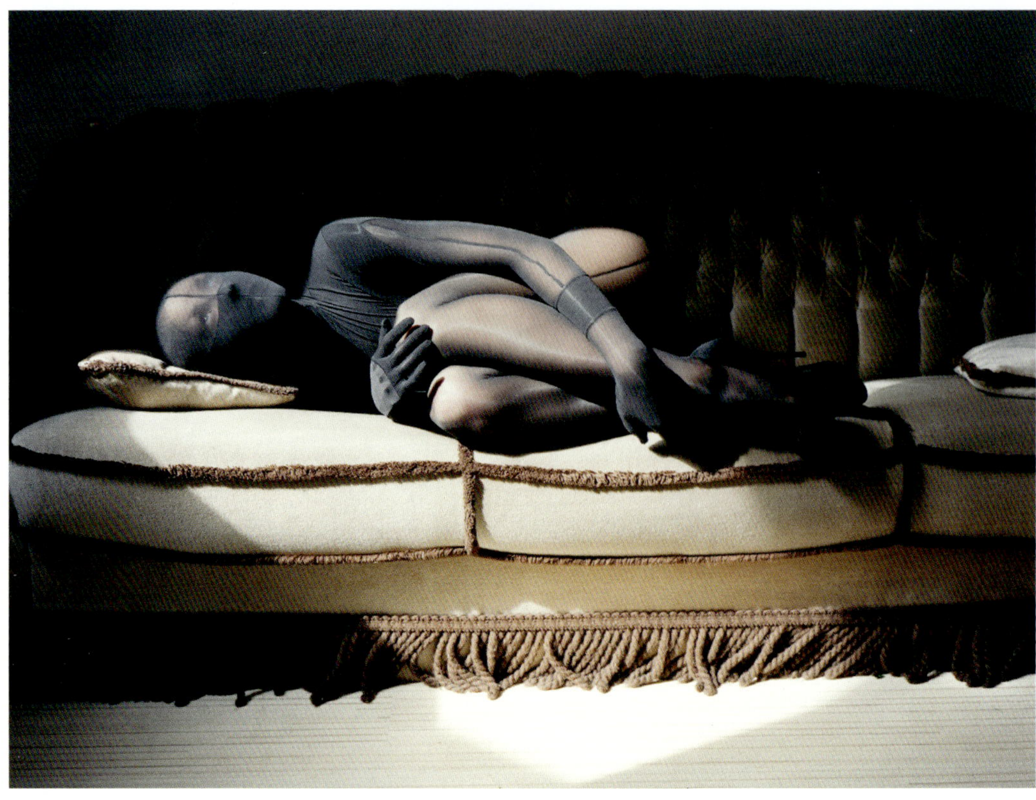

2008

You are fearful.
You are afraid to lift your head a little.
You are afraid to make love to this girl.
And a bit less with this one. You are afraid to speak foreign languages. You are afraid of the park. You are afraid that a snout will grow between your lips. You crawl slowly on all fours. No one can understand what you are trying to say anymore. They pet you but you bellow so loud that people go to wash their hands. Muddy on your bed you try in vain to pull your blanket up. It slips on your still too smooth hooves. Tomorrow you will go to pick up straw. You don't have any teeth anymore and you comb your hair. Maybe you put a cap on to look normal. You can still count to fifteen and recognize your name when someone calls you.

2008

Tu es peureux.
Tu as peur de lever un peu la tête.
Tu as peur de faire l'amour à cette fille.
Et un peu moins avec celle-là. Tu as peur de parler d'autres langues. Tu as peur du parc. Tu as peur qu'un groin te pousse entre les lèvres. Tu marches lentement sur tes quatre pattes. Plus personne ne peut comprendre ce que tu essaies de dire. On te caresse mais tu beugles si fort de bonheur que les gens partent se laver les mains. Boueux sur ton lit tu essaies en vain de remonter ta couette. Elle glisse sur tes sabots encore trop lisse. Demain tu iras cueillir de la paille. Tu n'as plus de dents et tu te recoiffes. Tu mets peut être une casquette pour avoir l'air naturel. Tu peux encore compter jusqu'à quinze et reconnaitre ton prénom lorsqu'on t'appelle.

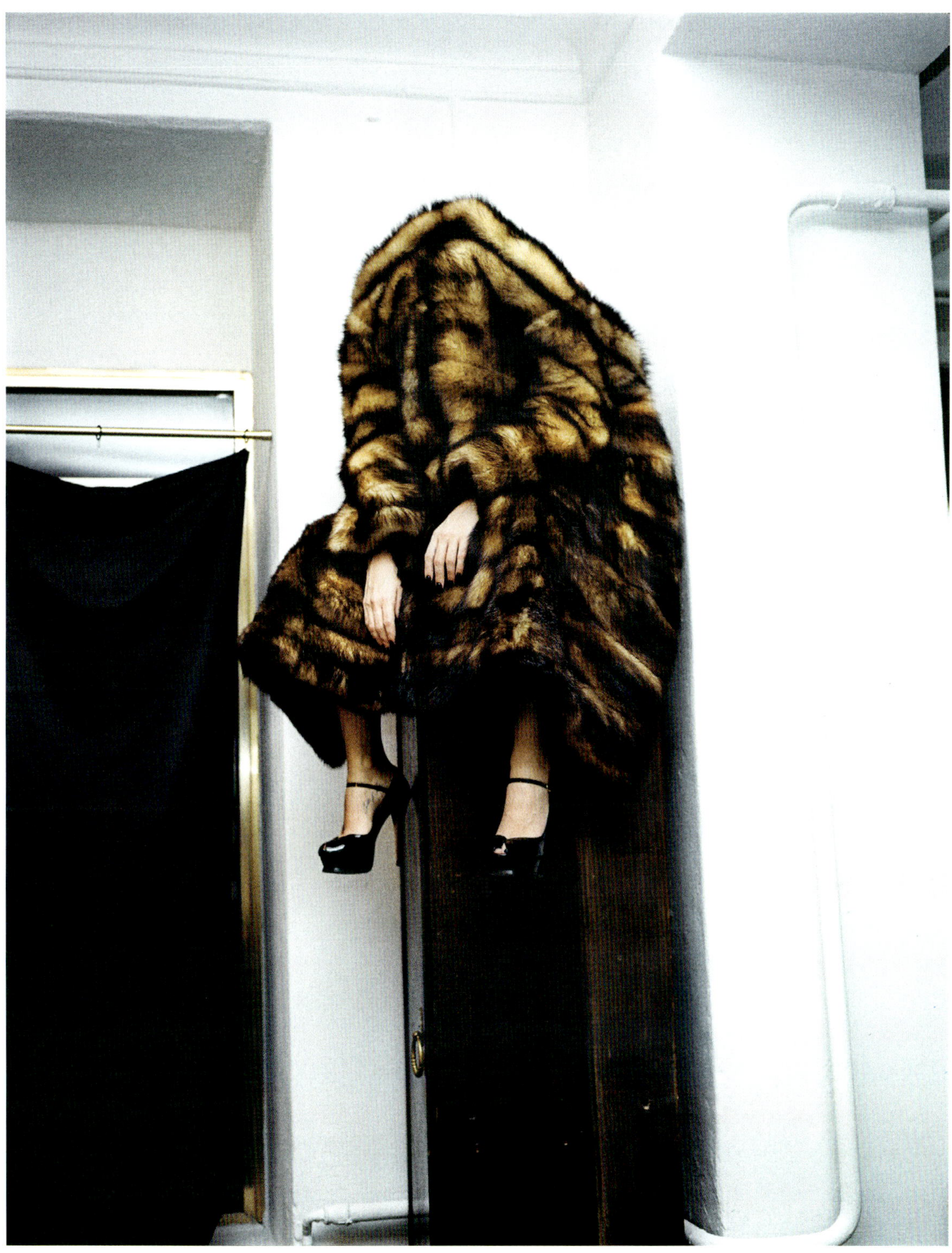

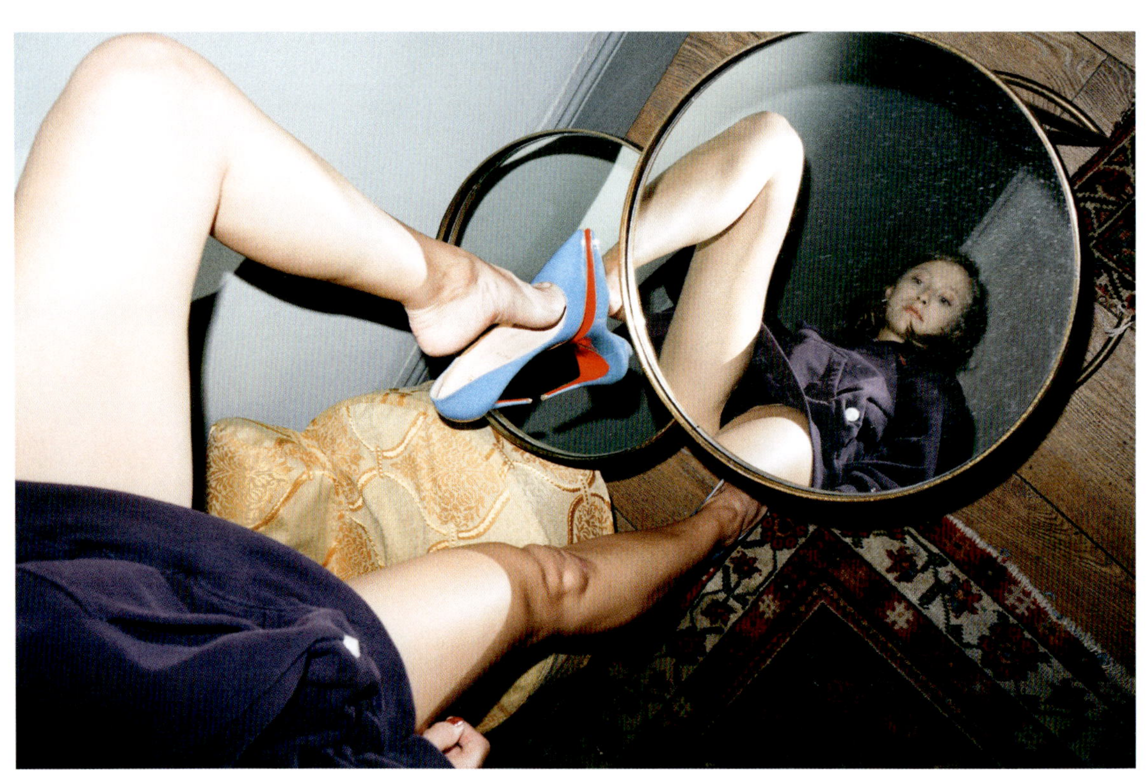

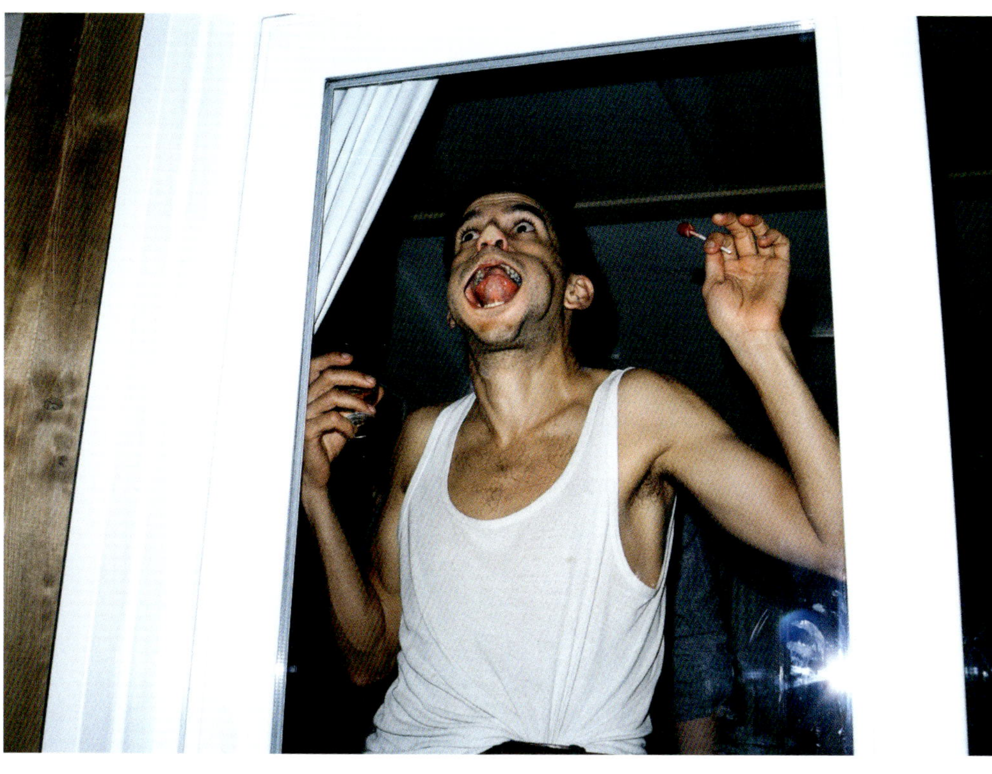

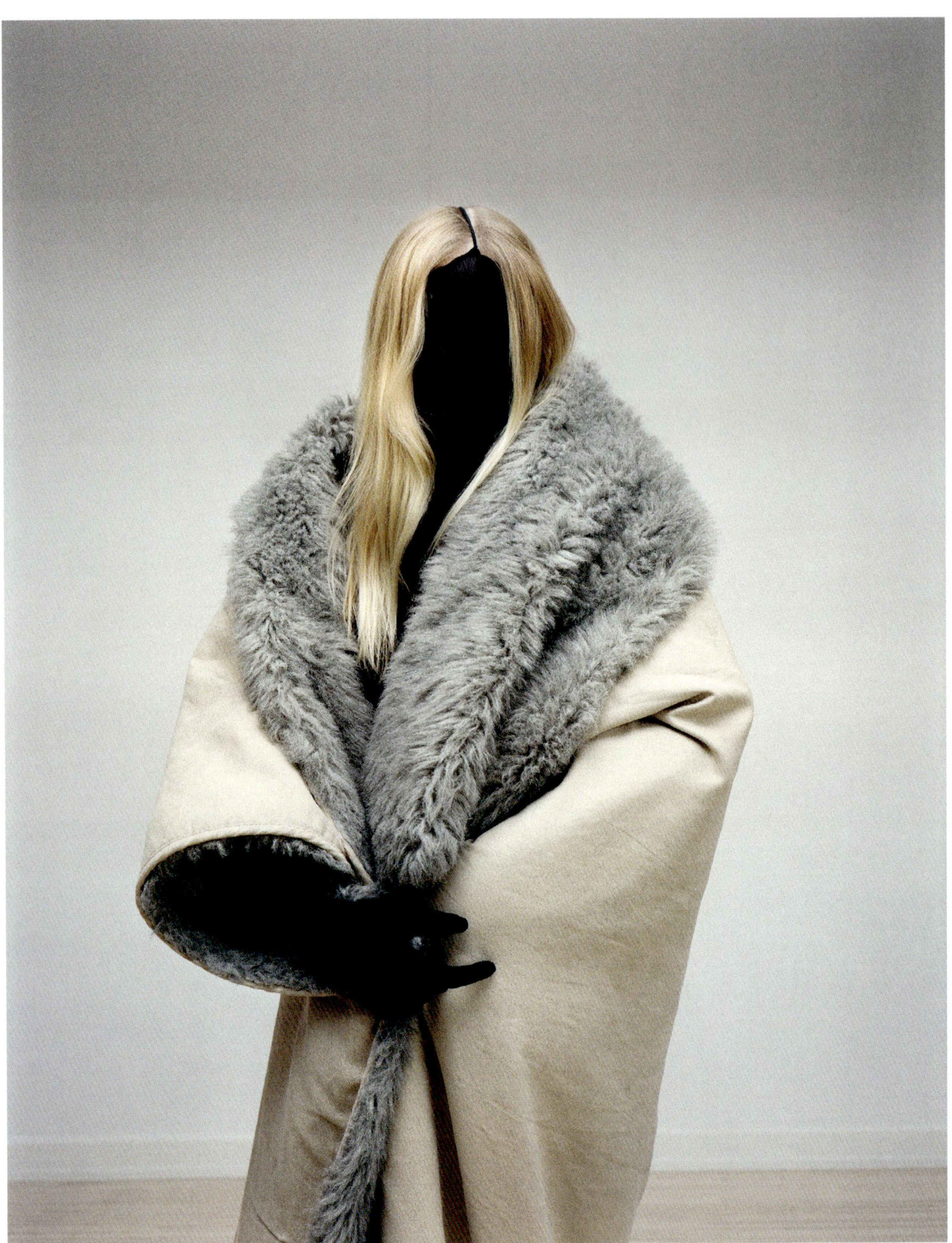

the broken muse, 2012

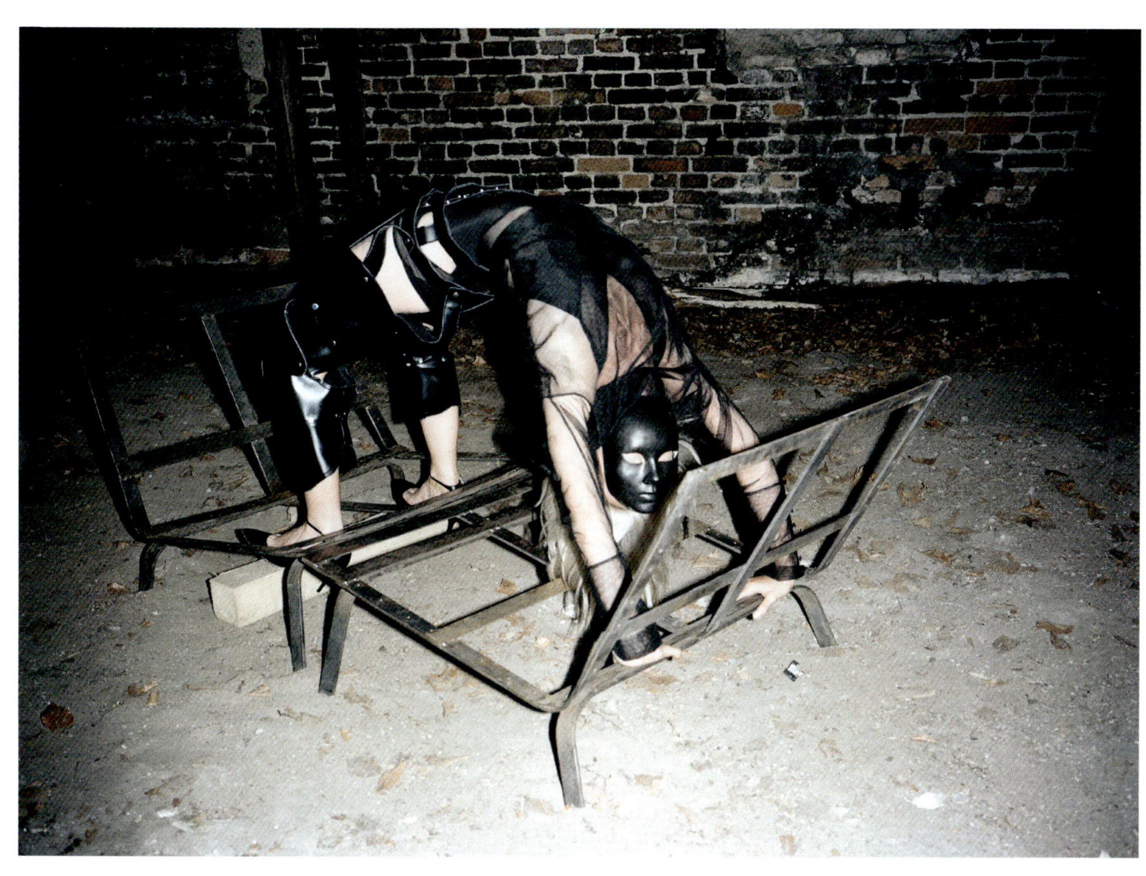

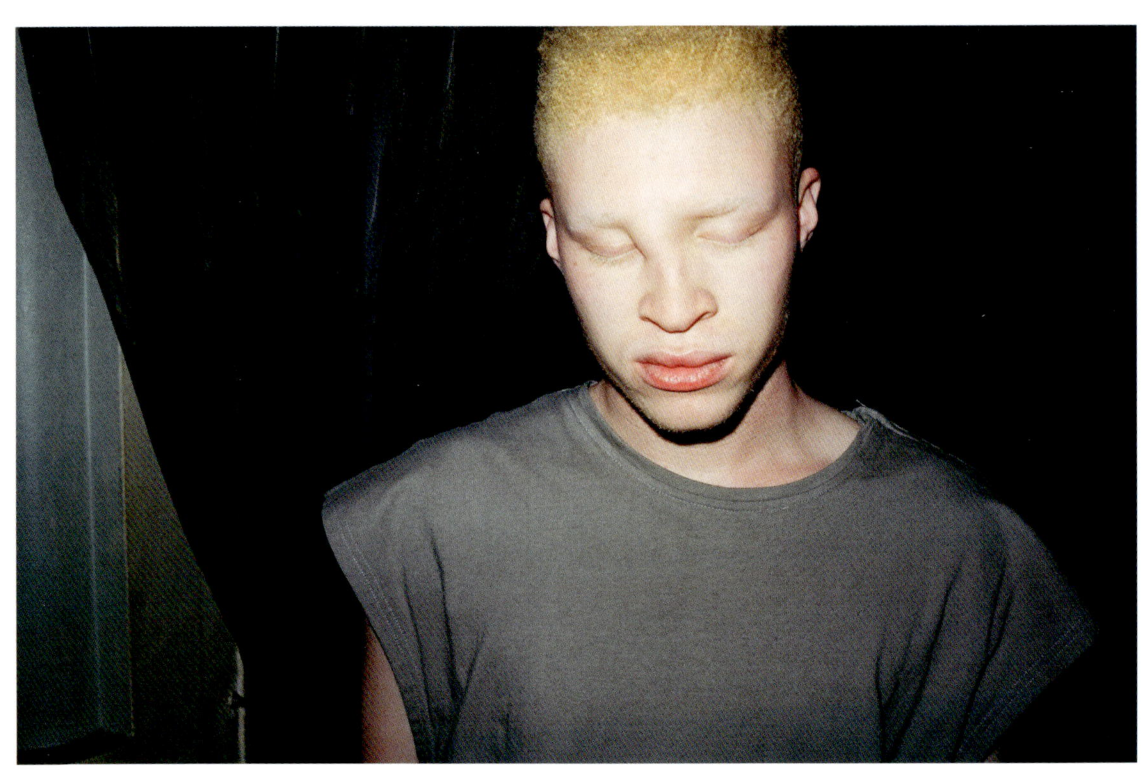

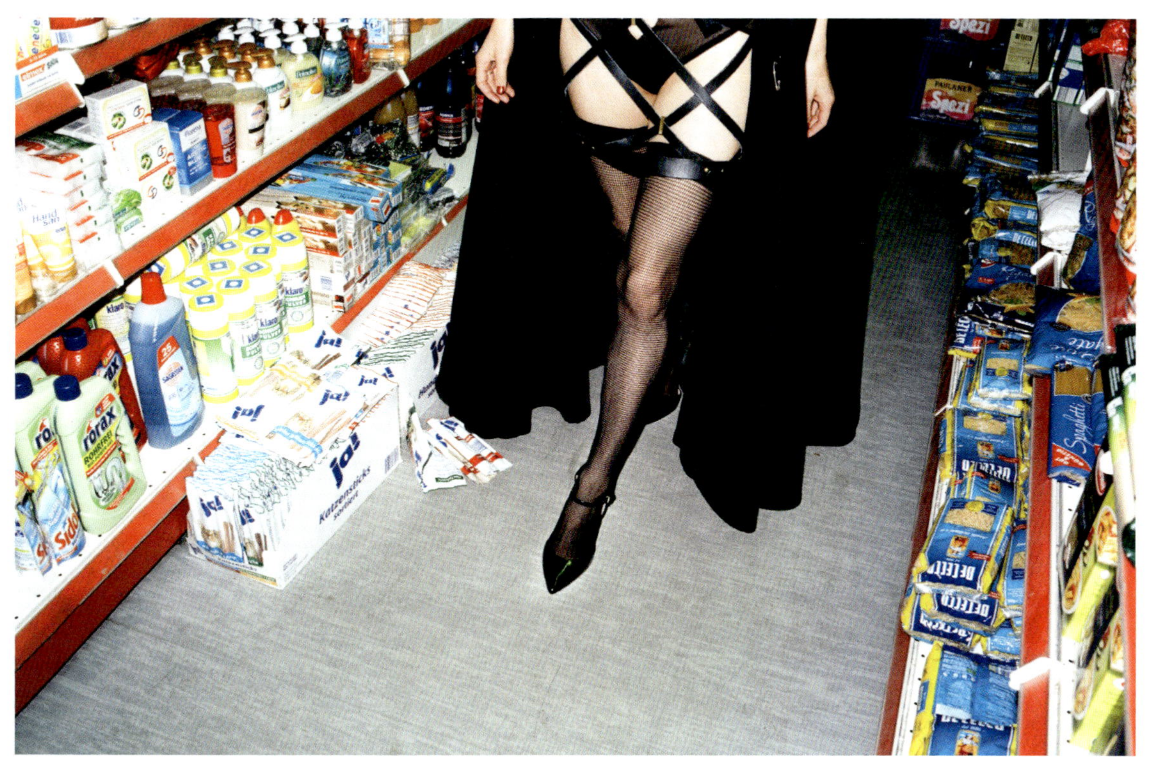

Spezi
rorax
ja!
Katzensticks
Spaghetti

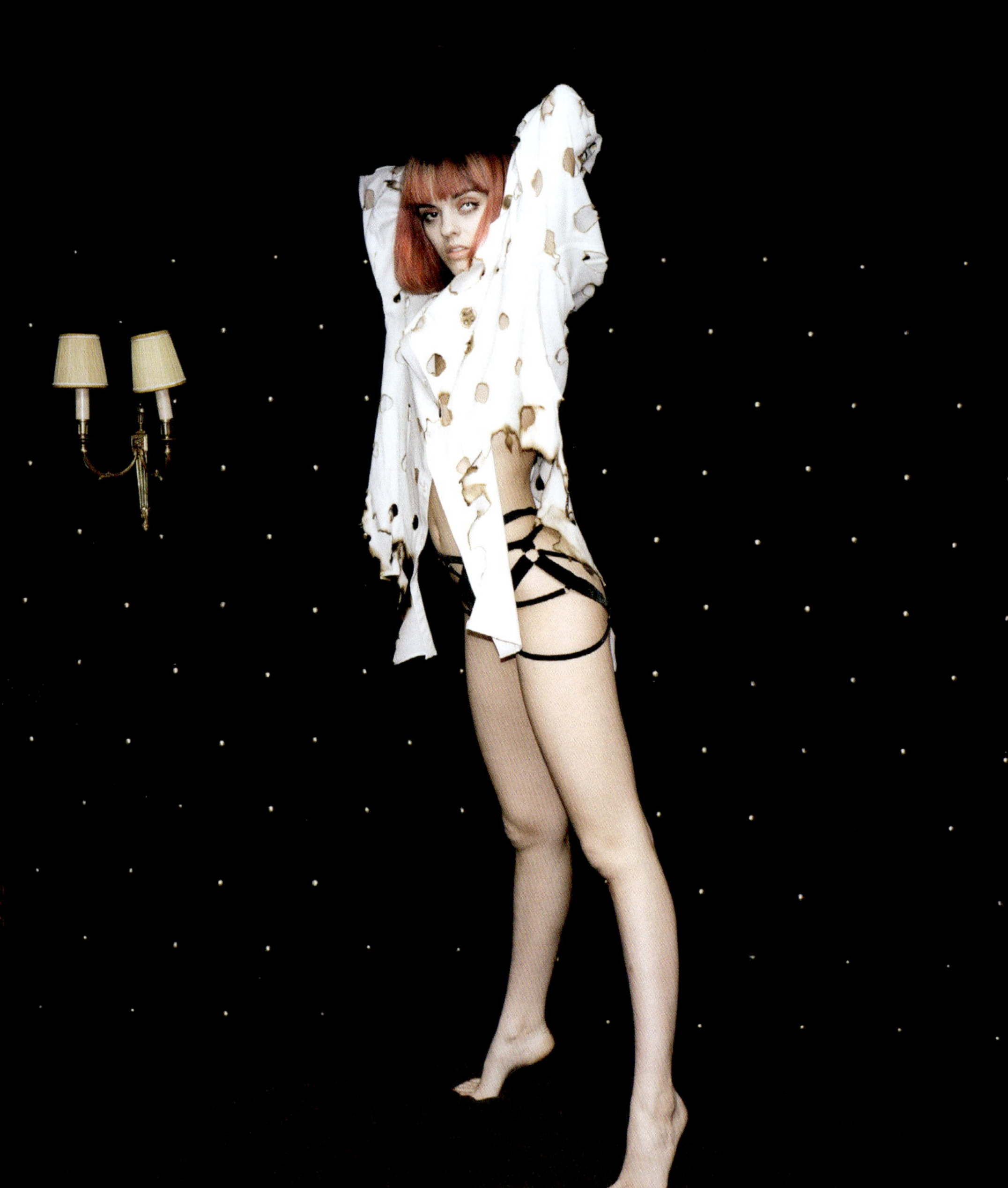

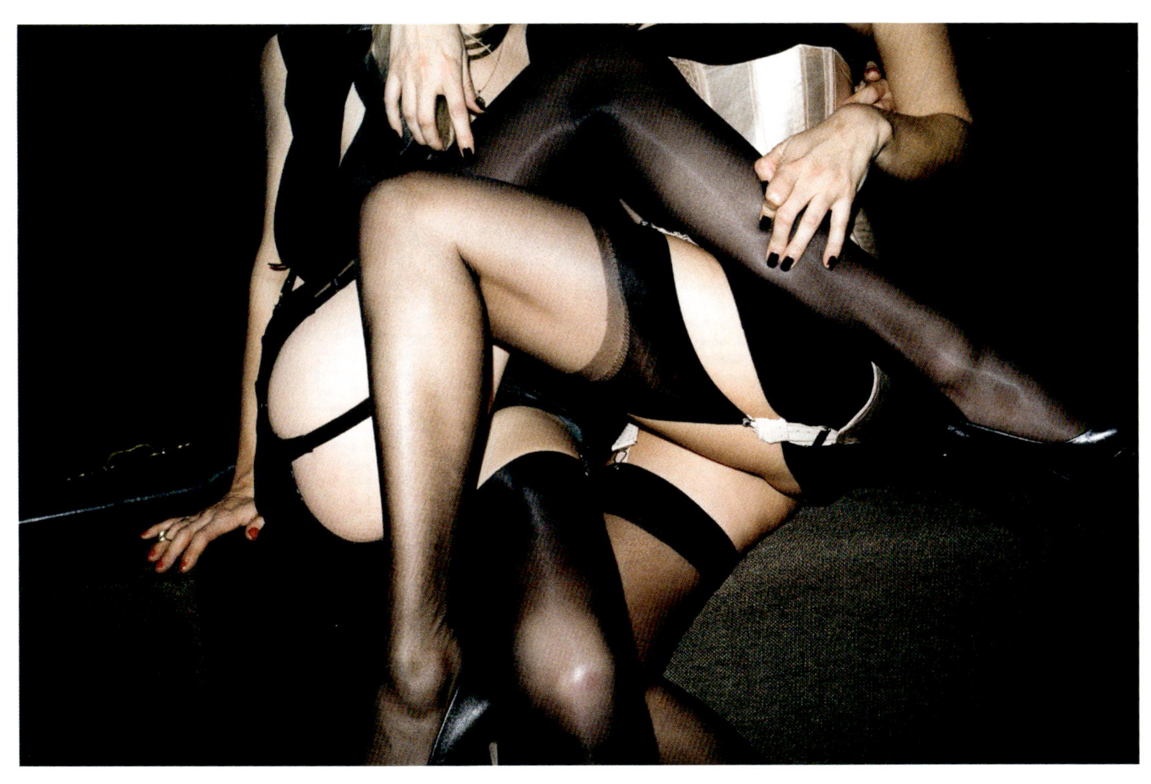

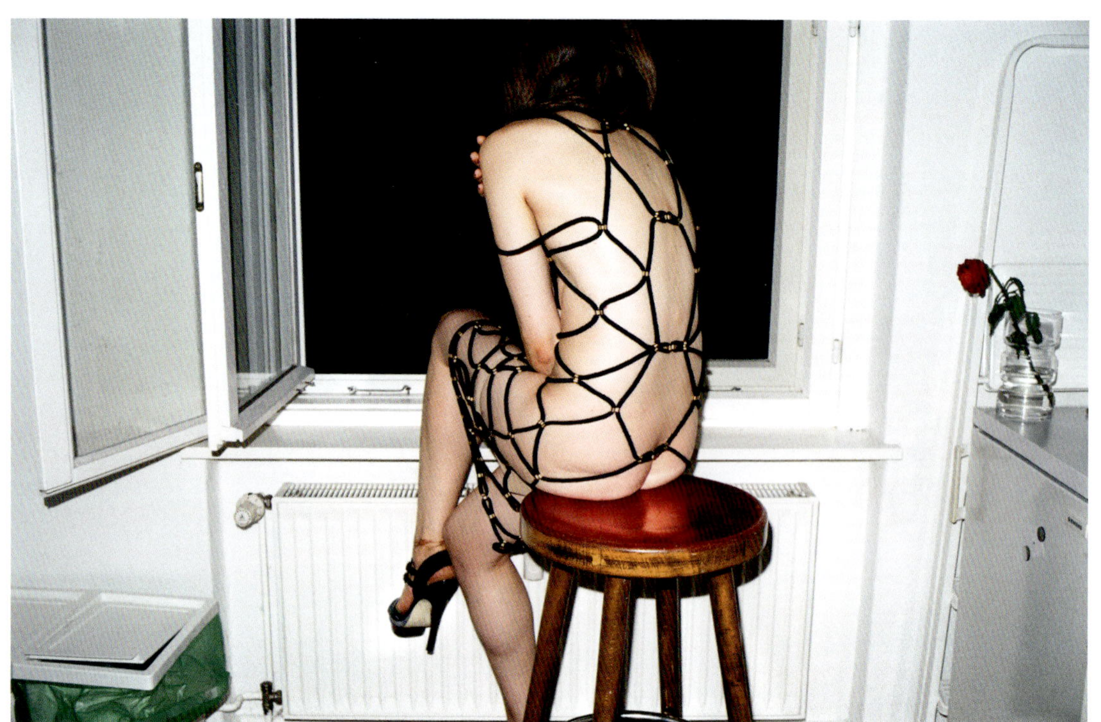

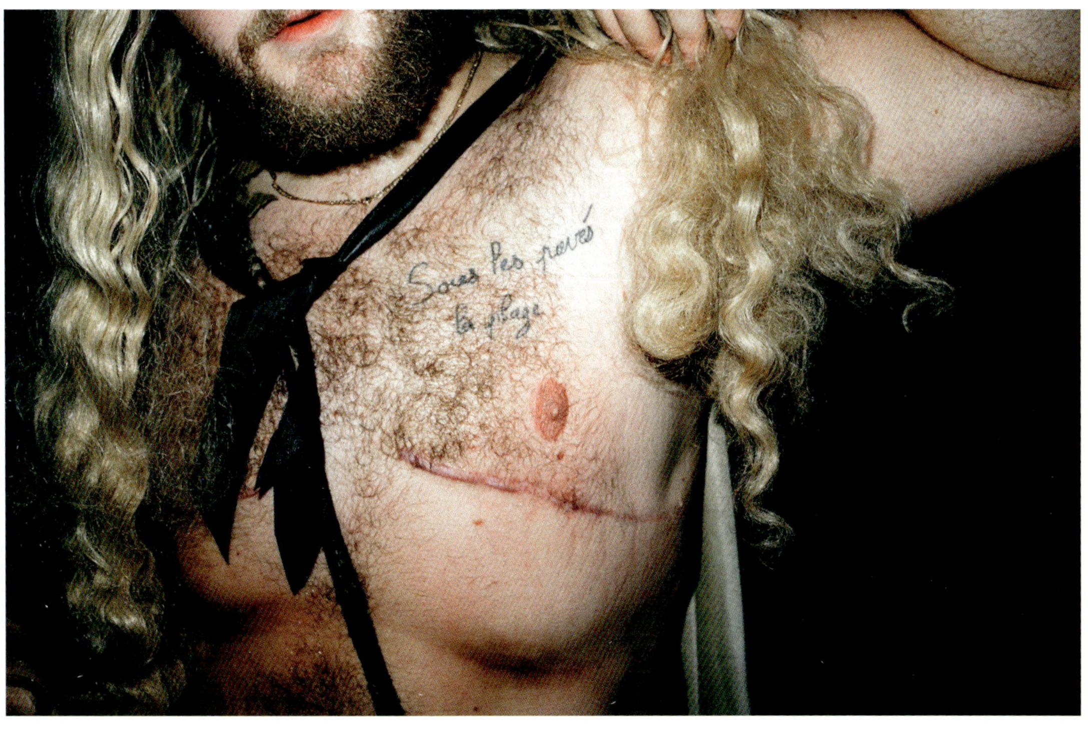

2011 J. sleeps restlessly on the bed, dressed and wearing heels over the covers.
It is winter but strangely it's not very cold.
Not even very grey. Days pass and you are more and more broke,
you find less and less solutions. Actually, you don't really try.
You hope. You wait quietly.
(...)
Somebody knocks. You don't know who it is. You open the
switchblade that you keep nailed to the door. It's the downstairs
neighbor, his flat is flooded. He came to check how it was at yours.
You hide the knife and put it discreetly back in its place.
J. does not wake up. She has slipped under the duvet. It is 5 o'clock in the morning.

2011 J. dors d'un sommeil agité dans le lit, tout habillée en talons sur les couettes.
C'est l'hiver et bizarrement il ne fait pas très froid.
Il ne fait meme pas très gris. Les jours filent et tu es de plus
en plus fauché, tu trouves de moins en moins de solutions.
Tu n'en cherches pas énormément non plus.
Tu espères. Tu attends gentiment.
(...)
Quelqu'un sonne. Tu ne sais pas qui c'est. Tu ouvres le cran d'arrêt
que tu gardes cloué à la porte. C'est le voisin du dessous, il y a une
inondation chez lui. Il vient voir ce qu'il en est chez toi. Tu caches le
couteau et le remet discrètement à sa place.
J. ne se réveille pas. Elle s'est glissée sous les couettes. Il est cinq heures du matin.

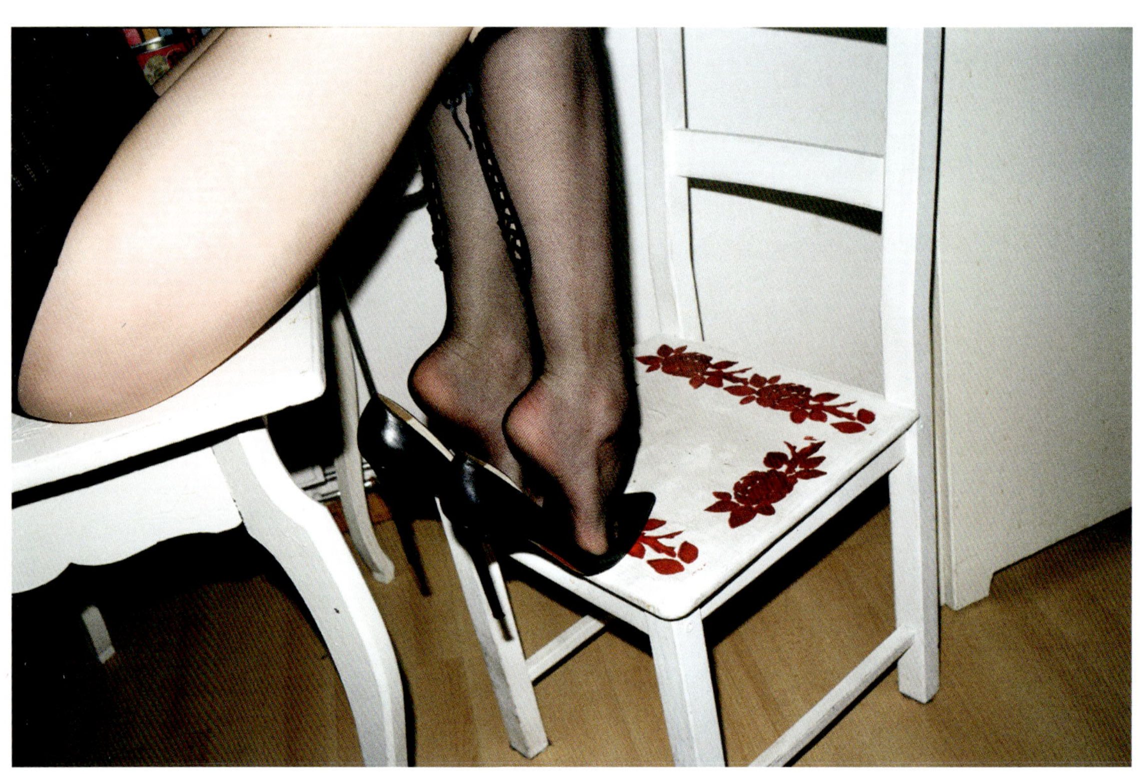

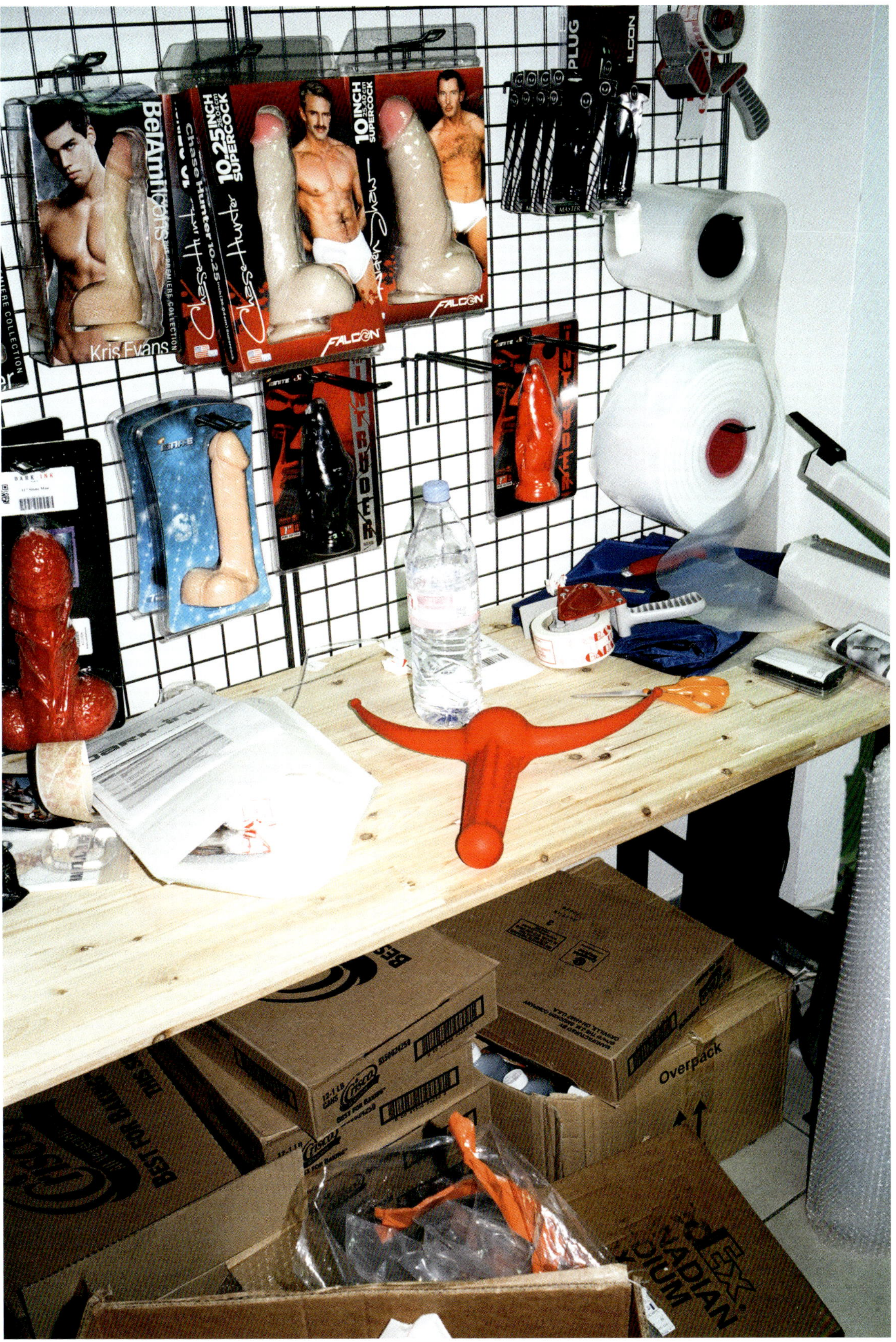

BelAmi Icons
Kris Evans
Chase Hunter
10.25 INCH
SUPERCOCK
FALCON
10 INCH
SUPERCOCK
FALCON
PLUG
Overpack

Le sordide et le sublime

Cracks

2007 He is sweating from all his pores. He must have been a handsome man
before. Before slacking off and reading *Le Point* stuck in a seat getting
smaller and smaller. Now he is dragging his huge suitcases
behind his huge butt.
He stayed joyful. And crammed into his massive shirt
he stayed beautiful.

2007 Il sue de tous ses pores. Il a dû être bel homme
avant. Avant de se laisser aller à lire *Le Point* coincé dans un siège de plus en plus étroit.
Maintenant il traine ses valises énormes
derrière son cul énorme.
Il est resté joyeux. Et engoncé dans sa chemise immense
il est resté beau.

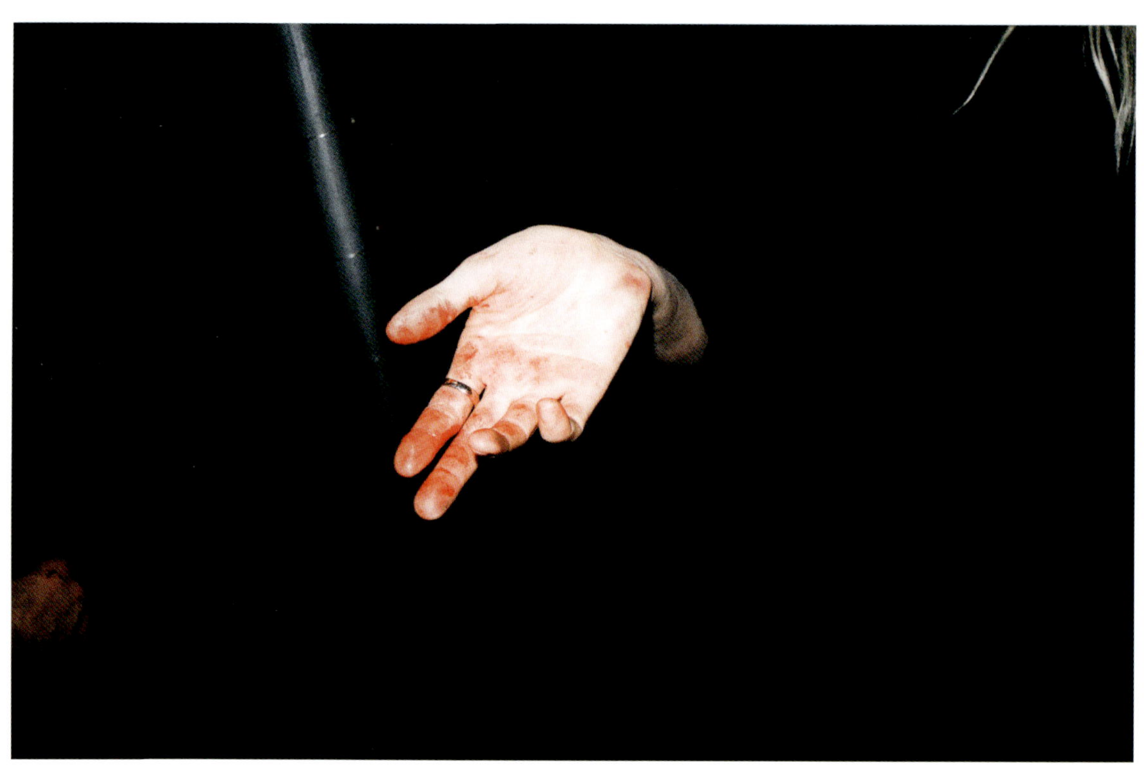

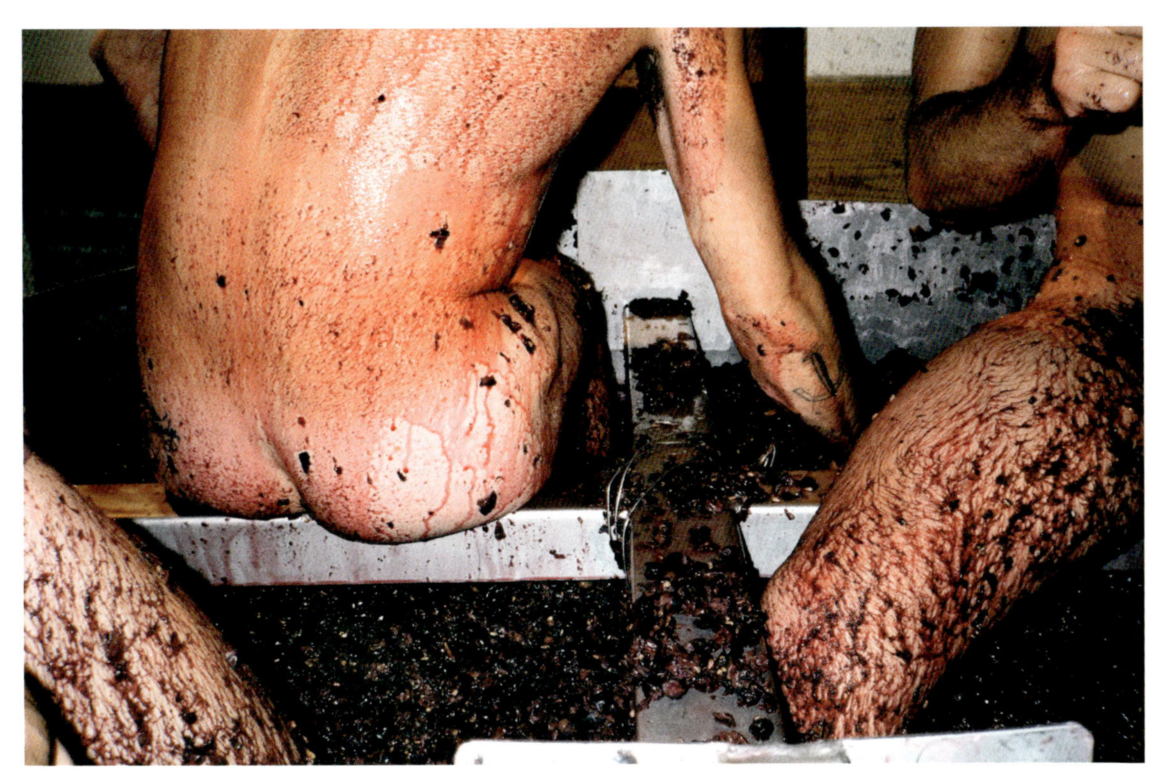

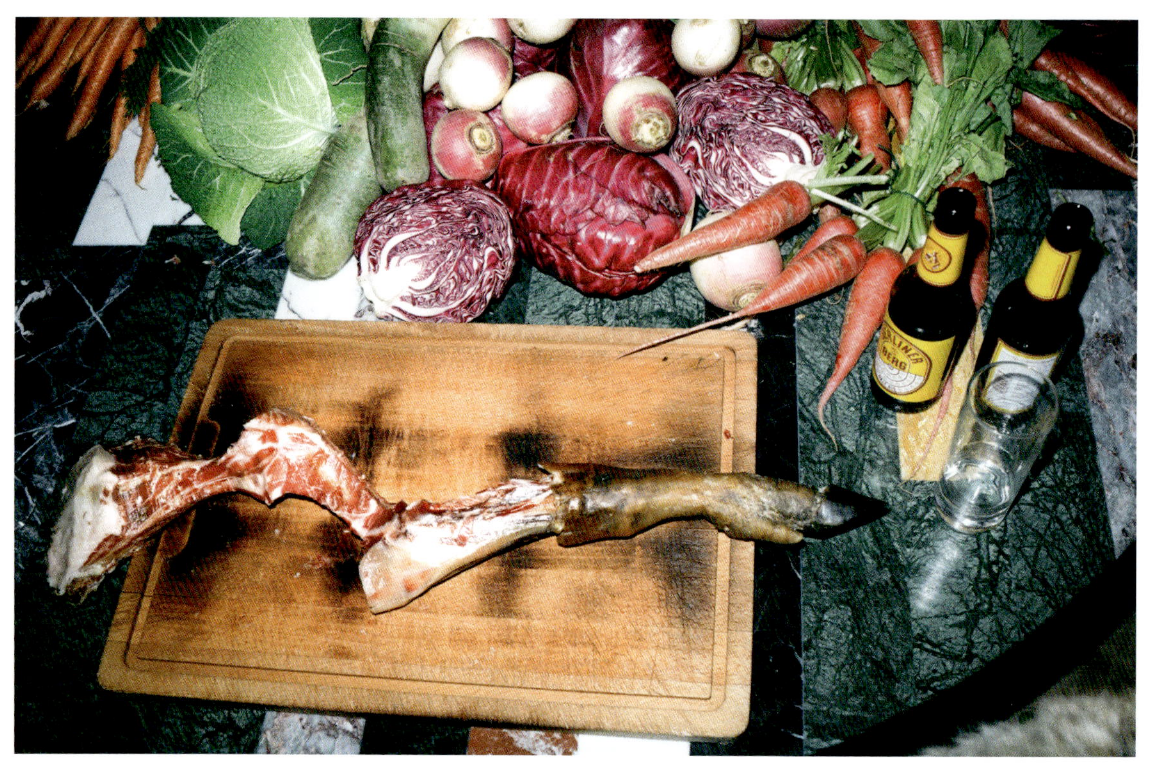

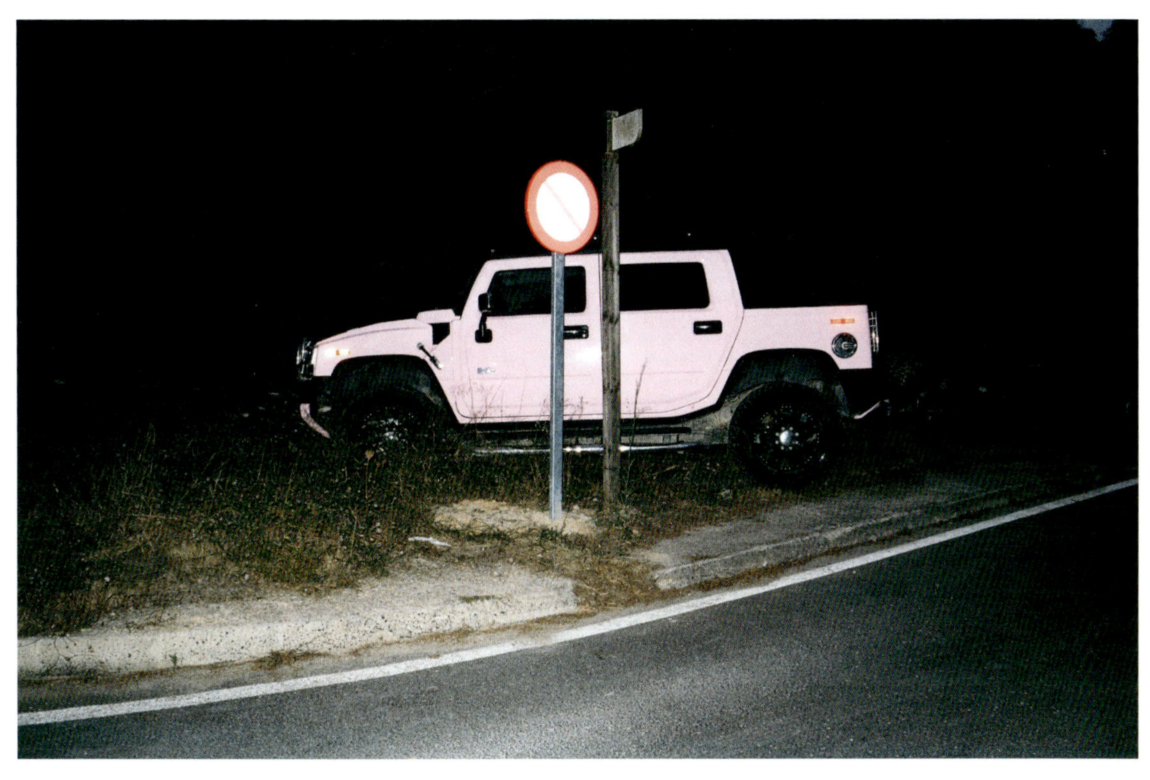

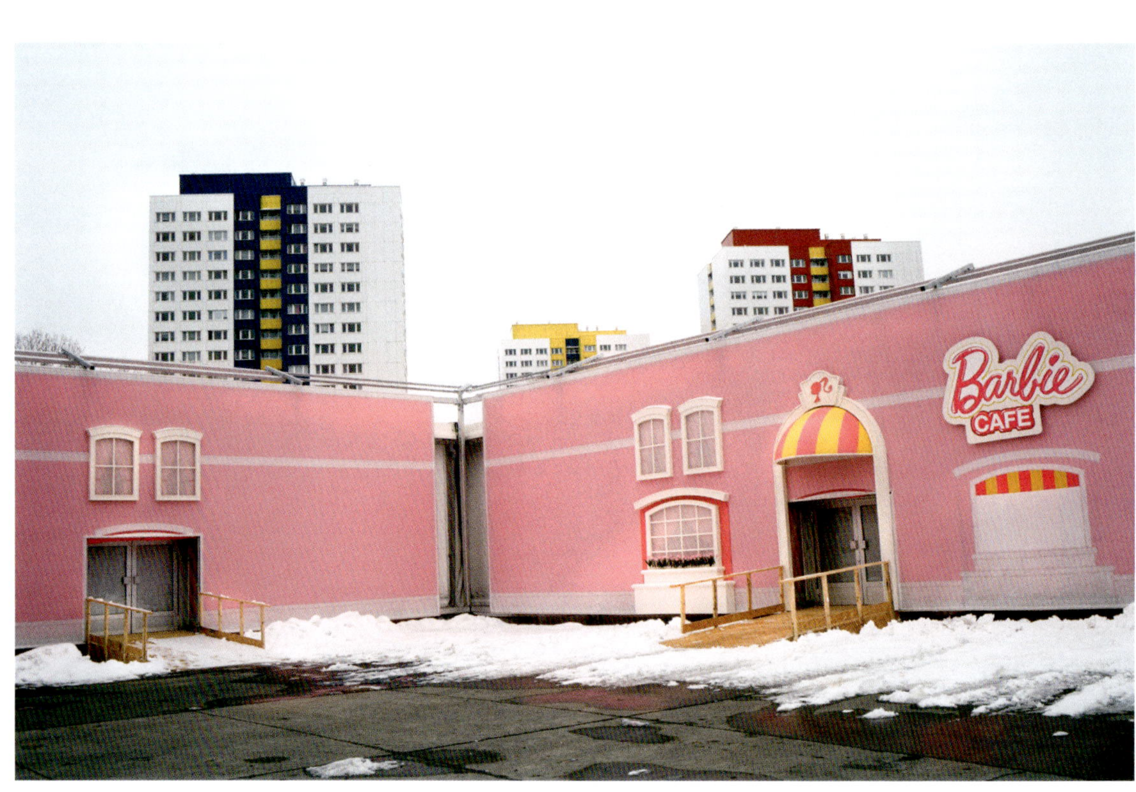
Barbie
CAFE

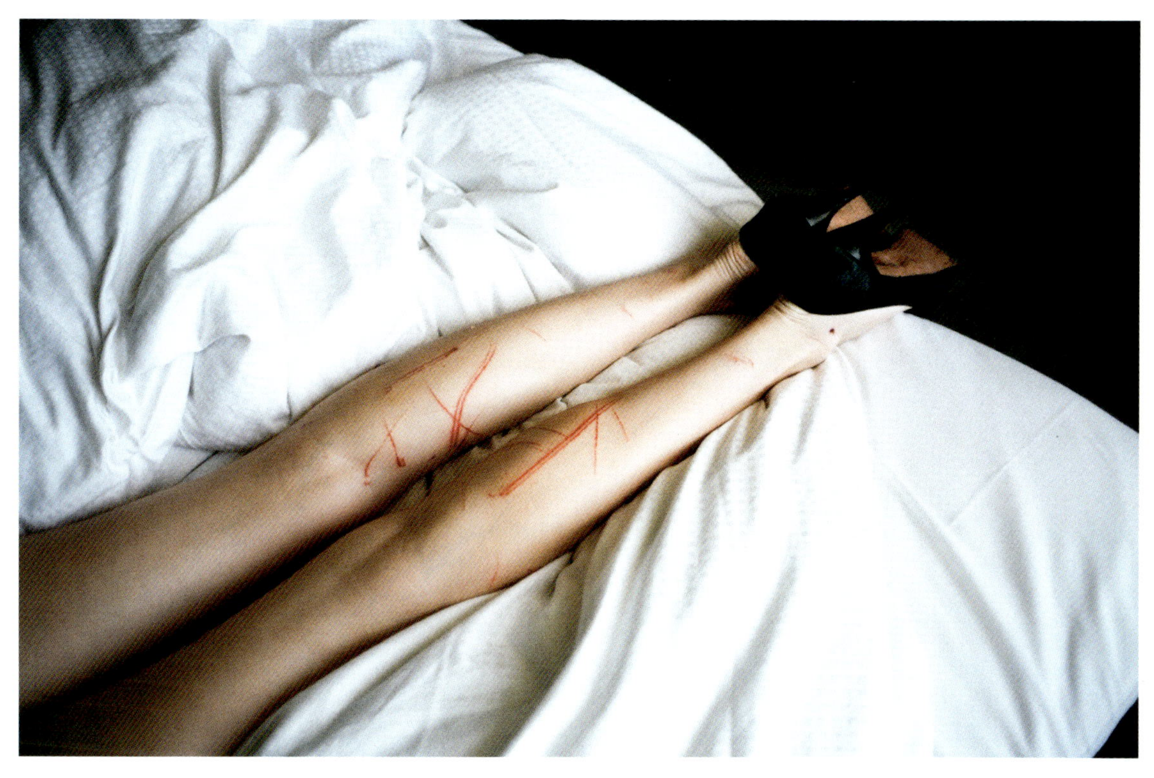

nuit blanche, Stockholm, 2015

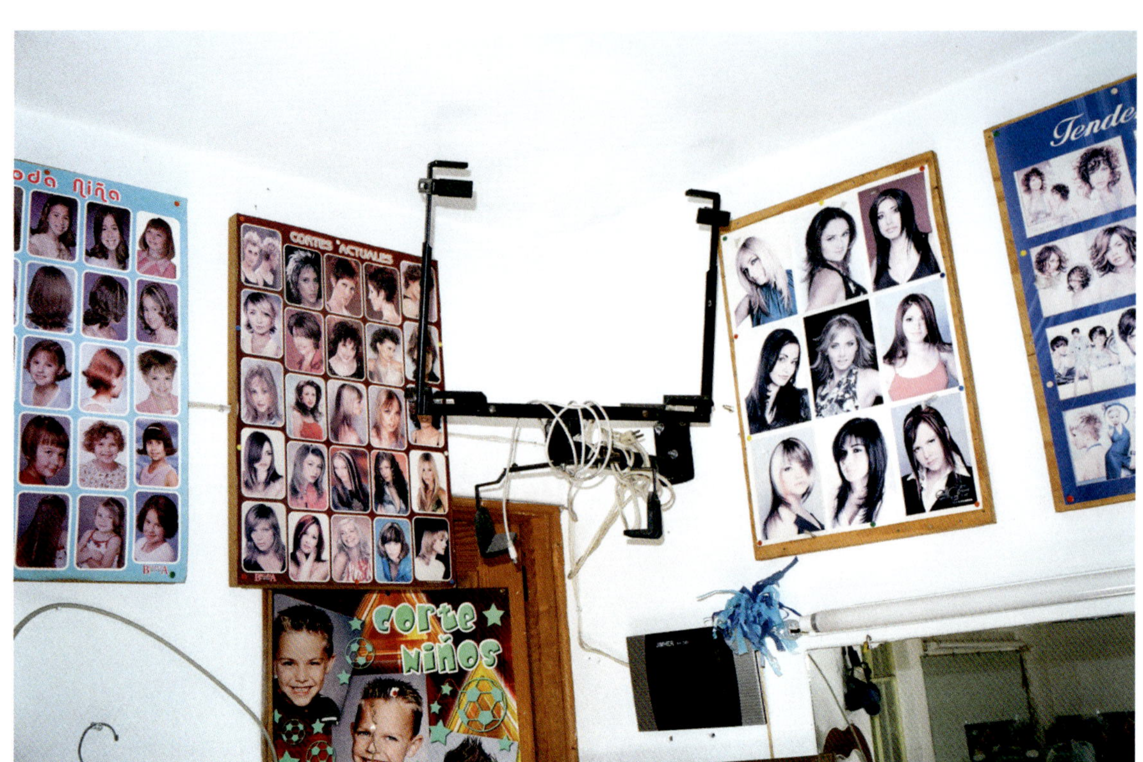
Niña
CORTES ACTUALES
corte niños

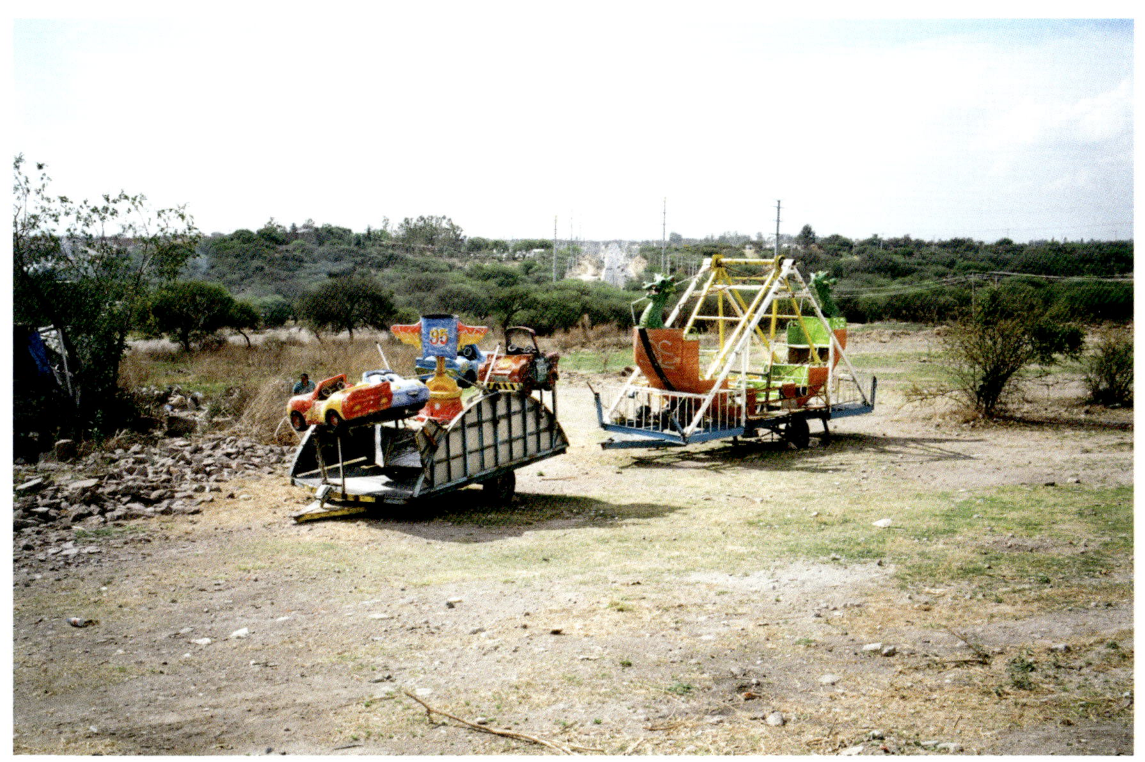

2007

You are not at home here anymore. In this city you managed to tame. You can hardly clear your path forward. People scare you. You lower your head. You do not know where you are going anymore. You don't have any more coffee. You can't stop walking. You can't sit down. Is your asshole in its place, at least? Every street corner awakens a memory. Sweet ones. The roofs of Saint-Jean you climbed on to make love and dream. The small squares where you were doing circus acts with F. for some coins. The never-closing bakery. And Fourvière. And all the hidden corners that once belonged to you. Your bench. Your seat in the funicular. The stairs. The bars at Place Sathonay. The dusty book and record shops. The streets you wandered down till morning. The 10-francs-cookie from the bakery at the corner. The first metro train. And all the rest. A kind of inane romanticism that you were carrying around the city. You have lost all that. You've been gone for too long. You came back too late. You like to get lost in places you don't know;

but not here.

2007

Tu n'es plus chez toi ici. Dans cette ville que tu avais réussi à apprivoiser. Tu te frayes difficilement un chemin. Les gens t'effraient. Tu baisses la tête. Tu ne sais plus où tu vas. Tu n'as plus de café. Tu ne peux plus t'arrêter de marcher. Plus t'assoir. Ton trou du cul est il seulement à sa place? Chaque coin de rue réveille un souvenir. Doux. Les toits de Saint-Jean où tu grimpais pour faire l'amour et rêver. Les petites places où tu faisais du cirque avec F. contre quelques pièces. La boulangerie qui ne ferme jamais. Et Fourvière. Et les coins cachés qui t'appartenaient. Ton banc. Ta place dans le funiculaire. L'escalier. Les bars place Sathonay. Les librairies et les disquaires poussiéreux. Les rue où tu errais jusqu'au matin. Le biscuit à dix francs de la boulangerie au coin. Le premier métro. Et le reste. Un genre de romantisme niais que tu trimballais partout dans cette ville. Tu as perdu tout ça. Tu es partis trop longtemps. Tu es revenu trop tard. Tu aimes te perdre dans les lieux que tu ne connais pas.

Mais pas ici.

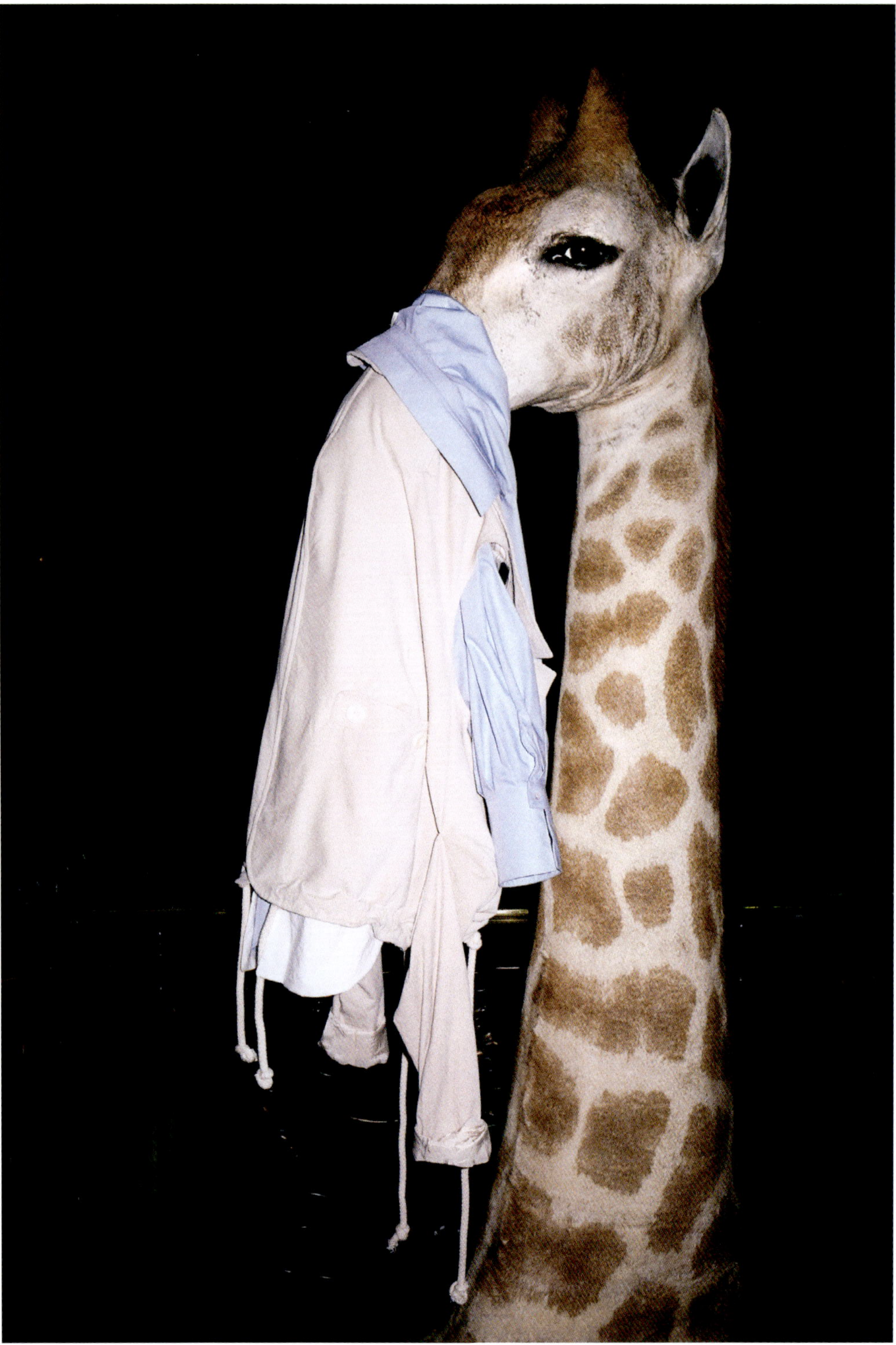

sniffles, Paris, 2015

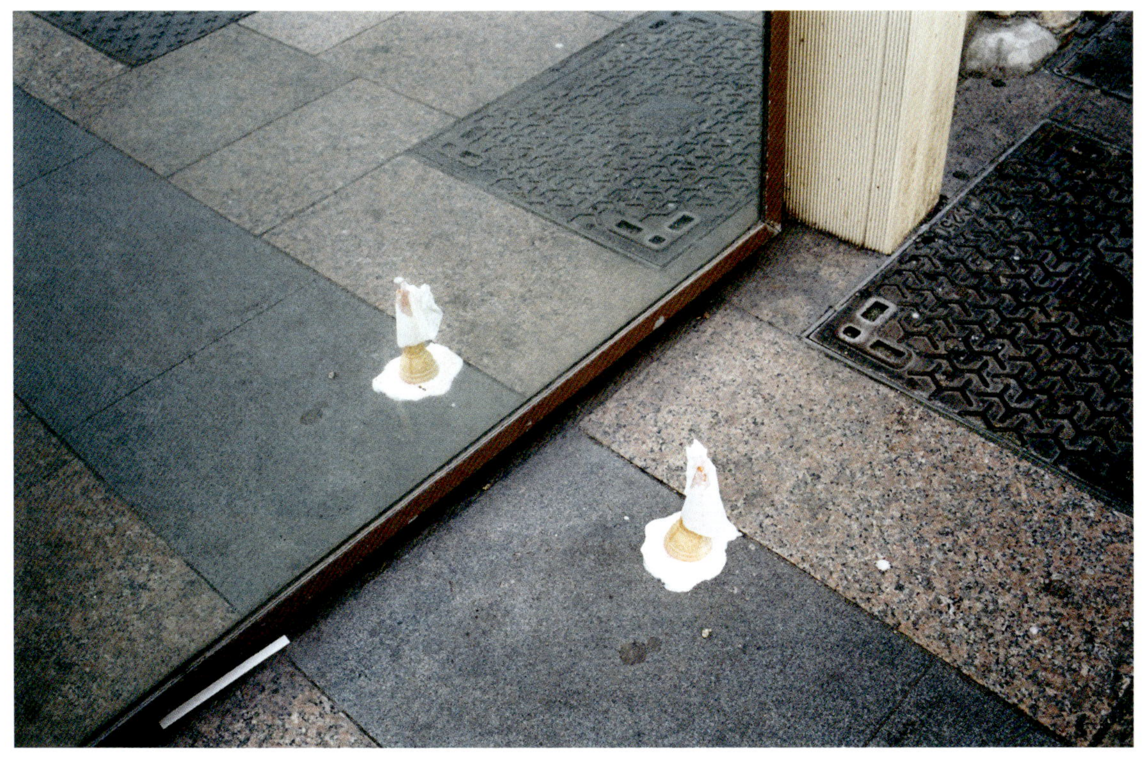

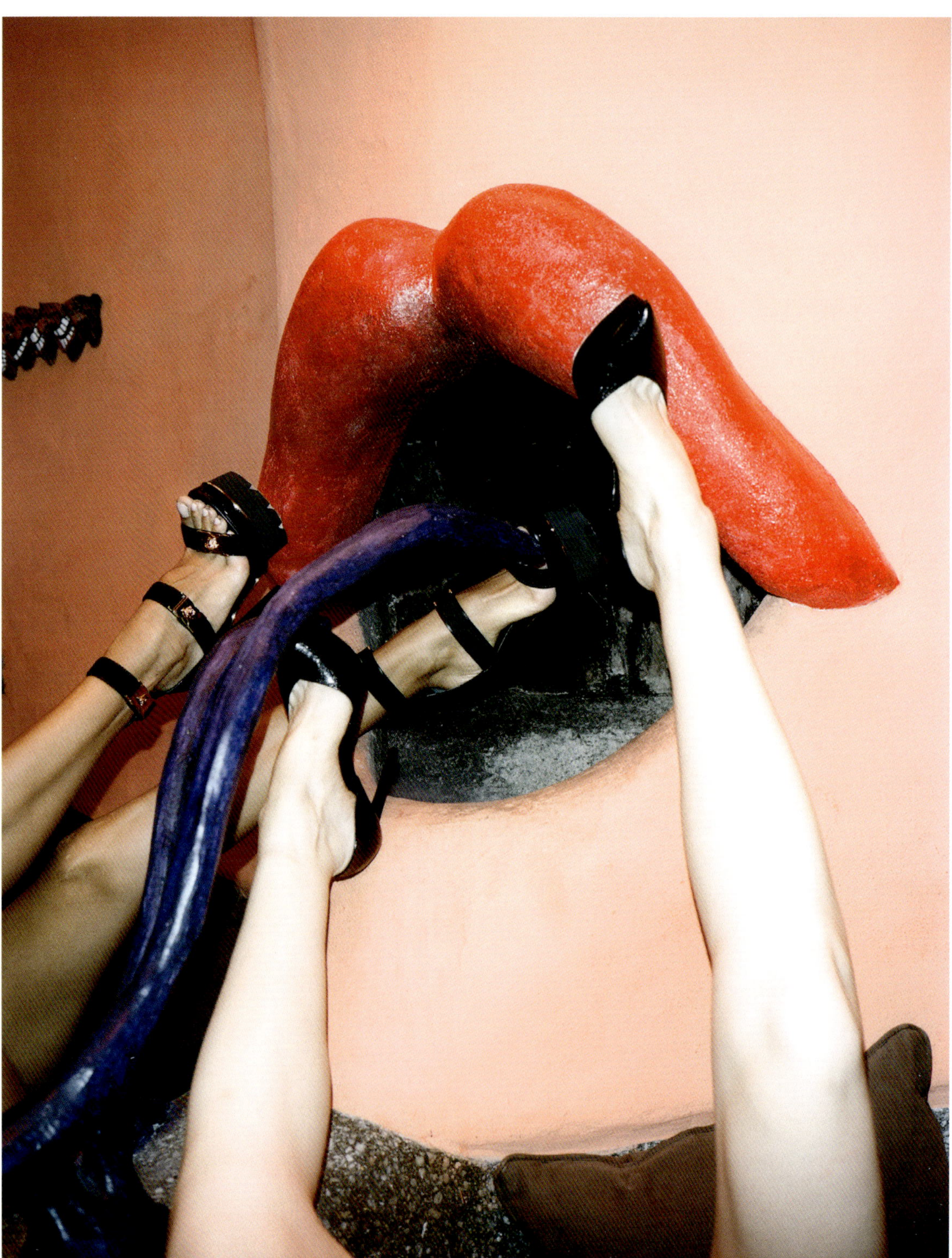

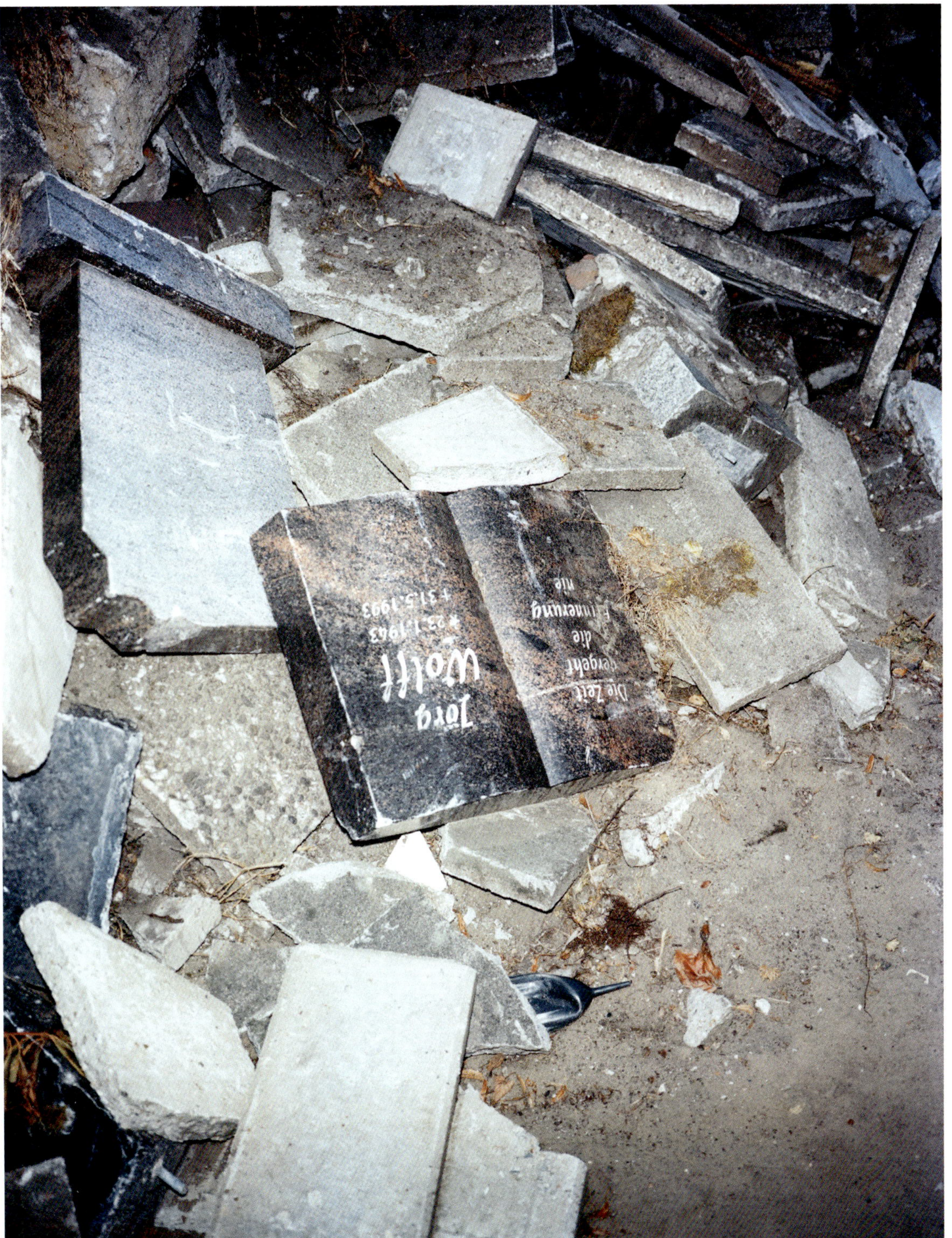
Jorg
Wolff
* 23.1.1943
+ 31.5.1993
Die Zeit
vergeht
die
Erinnerung
nie

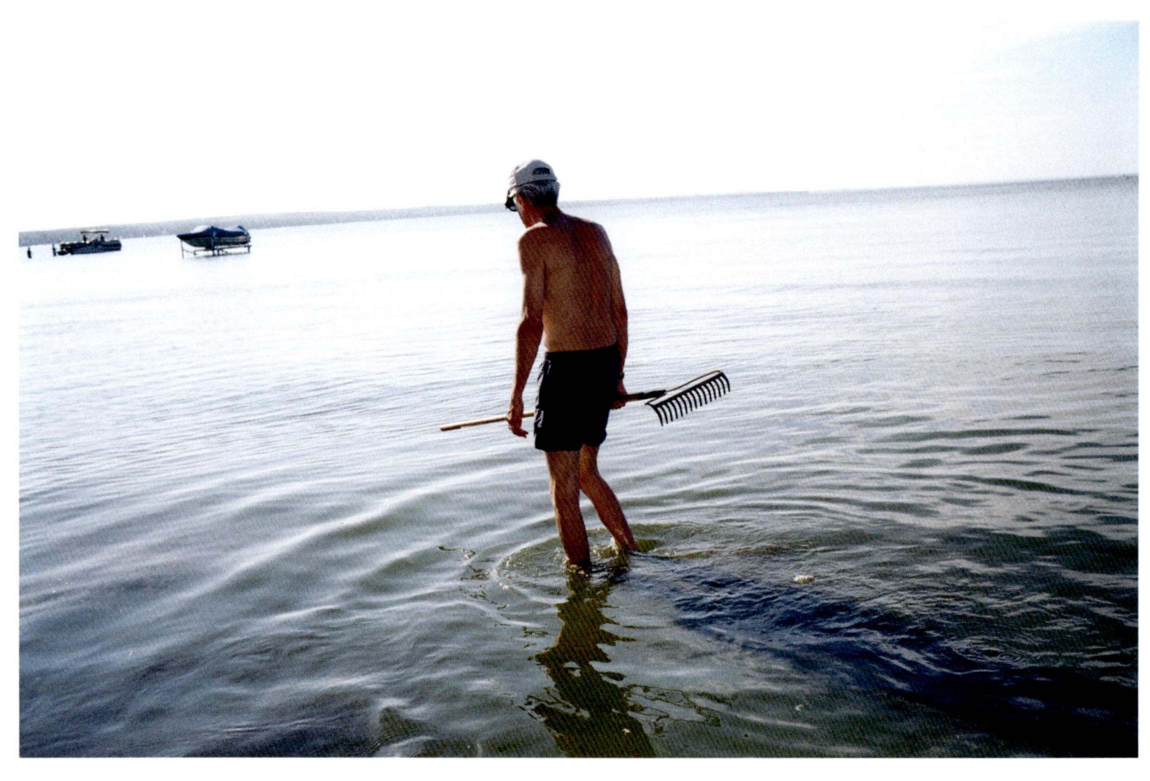

infinite garden, Ma-me-mo Beach, AB, 2012

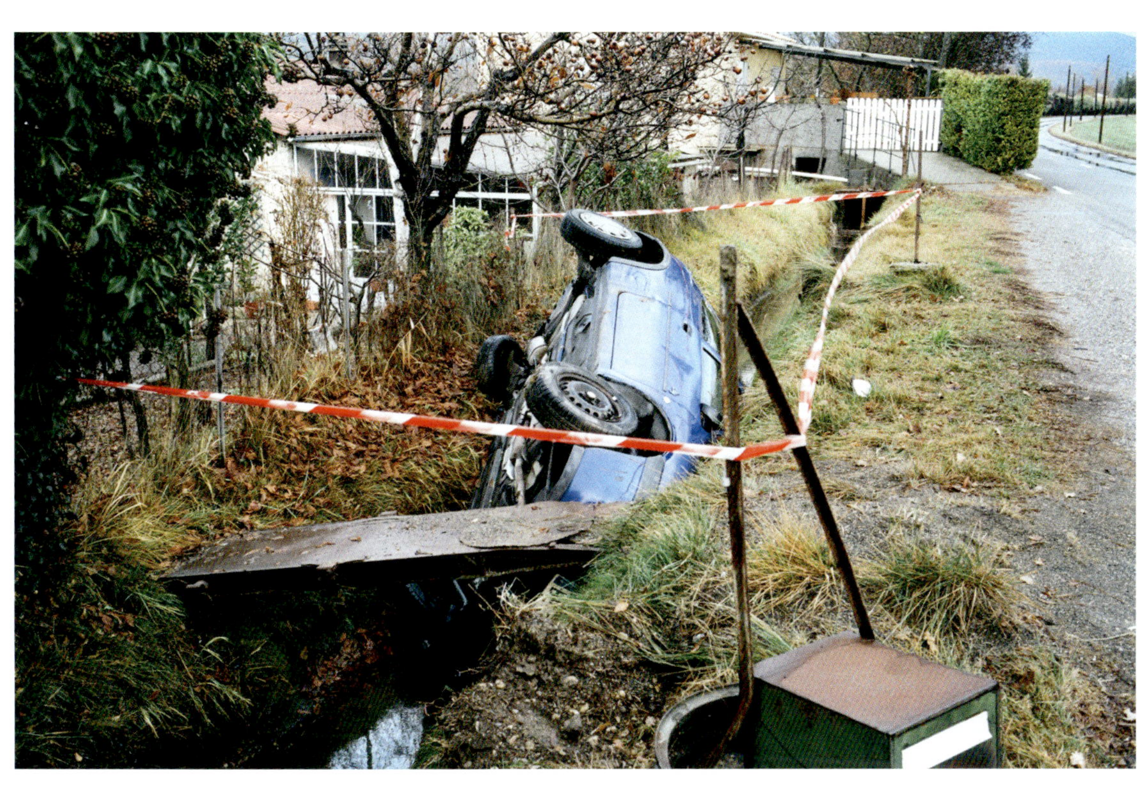

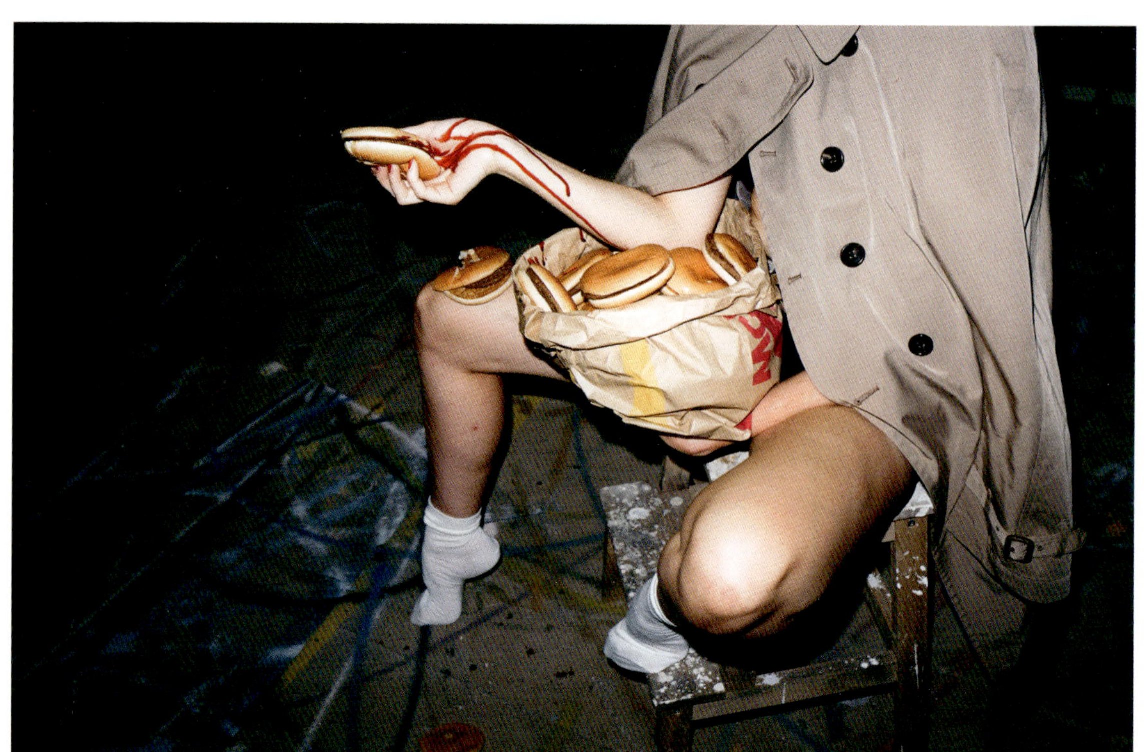

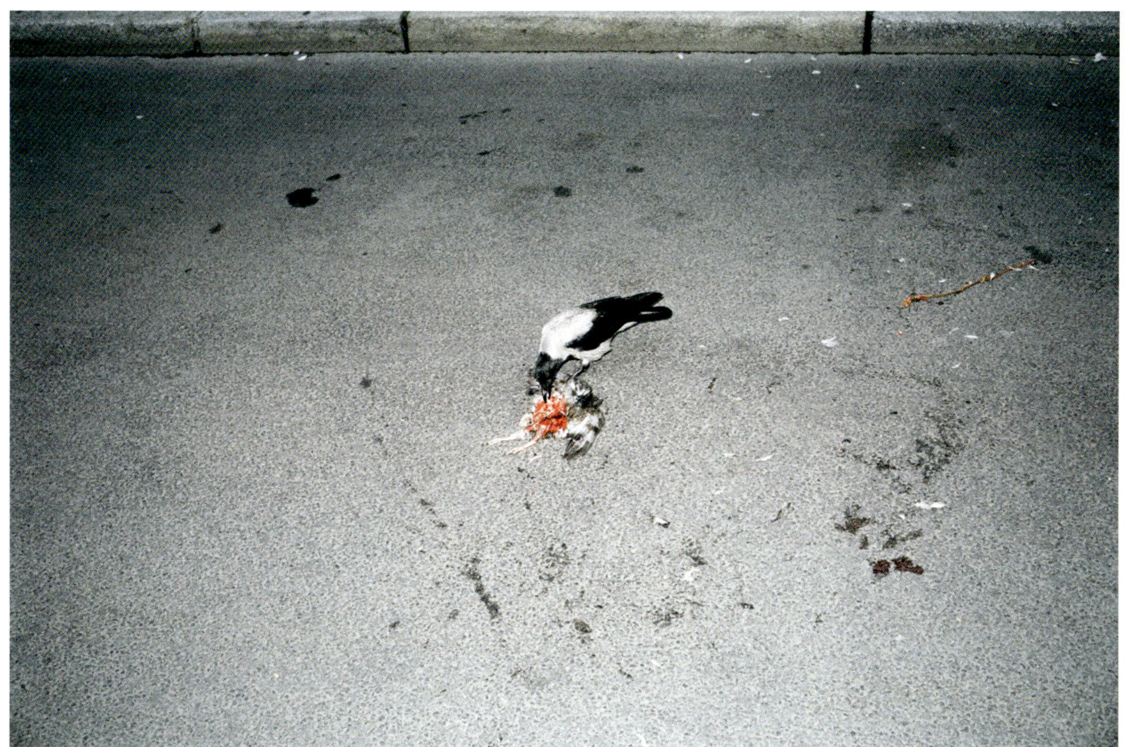

2017 You think of death, of your death, lightly. Almost affectionately, almost out of habit.
This idea calms you, as it always has. At least as far as your head,
your half-empty memory, can recall. A boy of 7 or 8 years, with an
uncharged rifle in the mouth. Before you grew up and slowly tamed this
idea. Making it a friend of yours, your protégée. Lift its dark, disgusting
and blinding cape to discover only your own reflection, barely fogged.
Your only freedom, so precious.
To each his faith.
The birds start singing outside, the sky always black and grey, turning to blue.
So you see, a new day begins.

2017 Tu penses à la mort, à ta mort, de manière légère.
Presque affectueusement, presque par habitude.
Cette idée t'apaise, elle l'a toujours fait. Au moins aussi loin que ta tête à
moitié vide de souvenirs peut remonter. Un gamin de sept ou huit ans, une
carabine sans plombs dans la bouche. Avant que tu ne grandisses et
n'apprivoises tout doucement cette idée. En fasse ton amie, ta protégée.
Soulève sa cape noire, déguelasse et aveuglante pour n'y découvrir que
ton reflet, à peine embué.
Ta seule liberté, si précieuse.
A chacun sa foi.
Les oiseaux commencent à chanter dehors, le ciel toujours noir et gris, tournant au bleu.
Alors tu vois, une nouvelle journée commence.

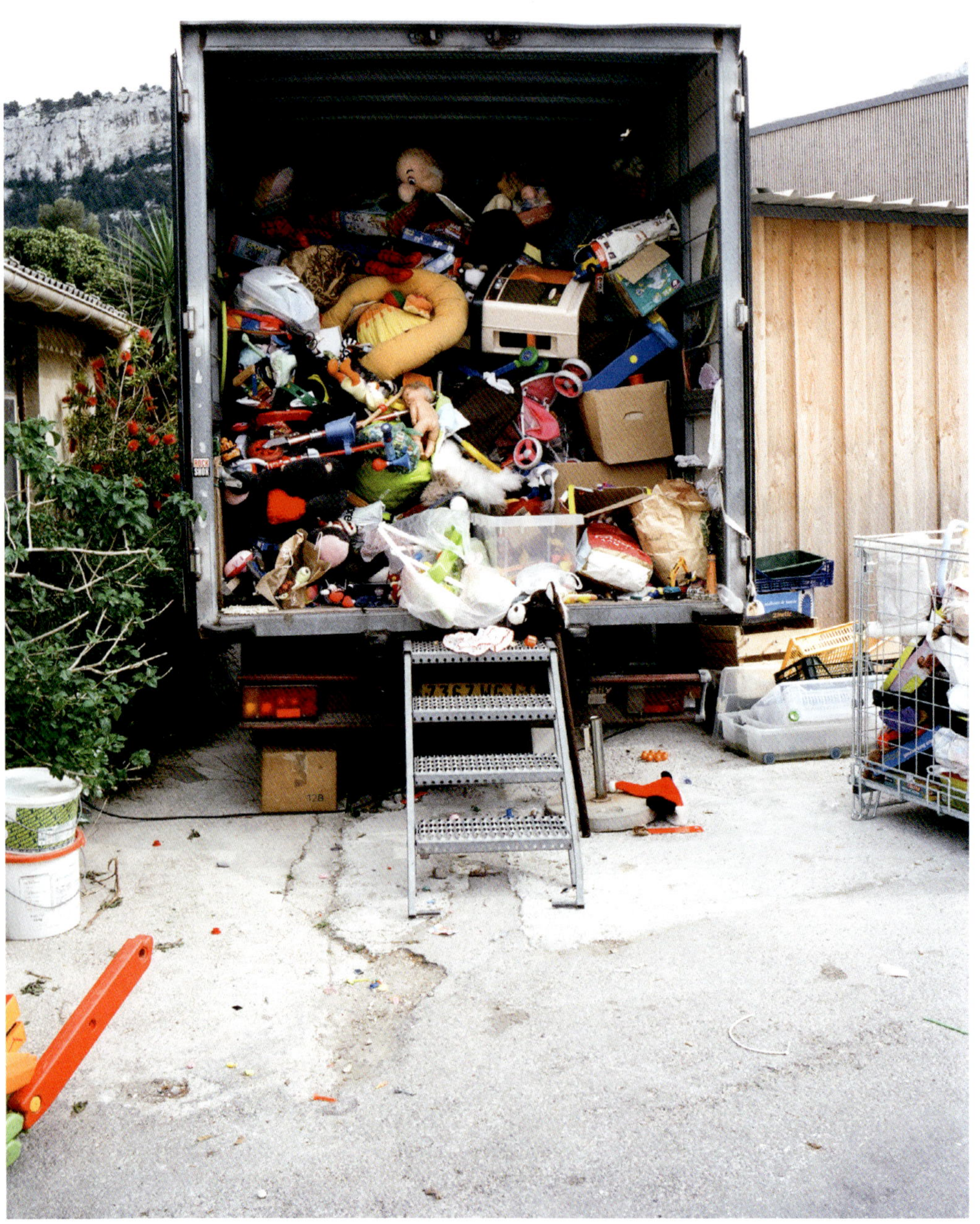

broken dreams, Marseille, 2015

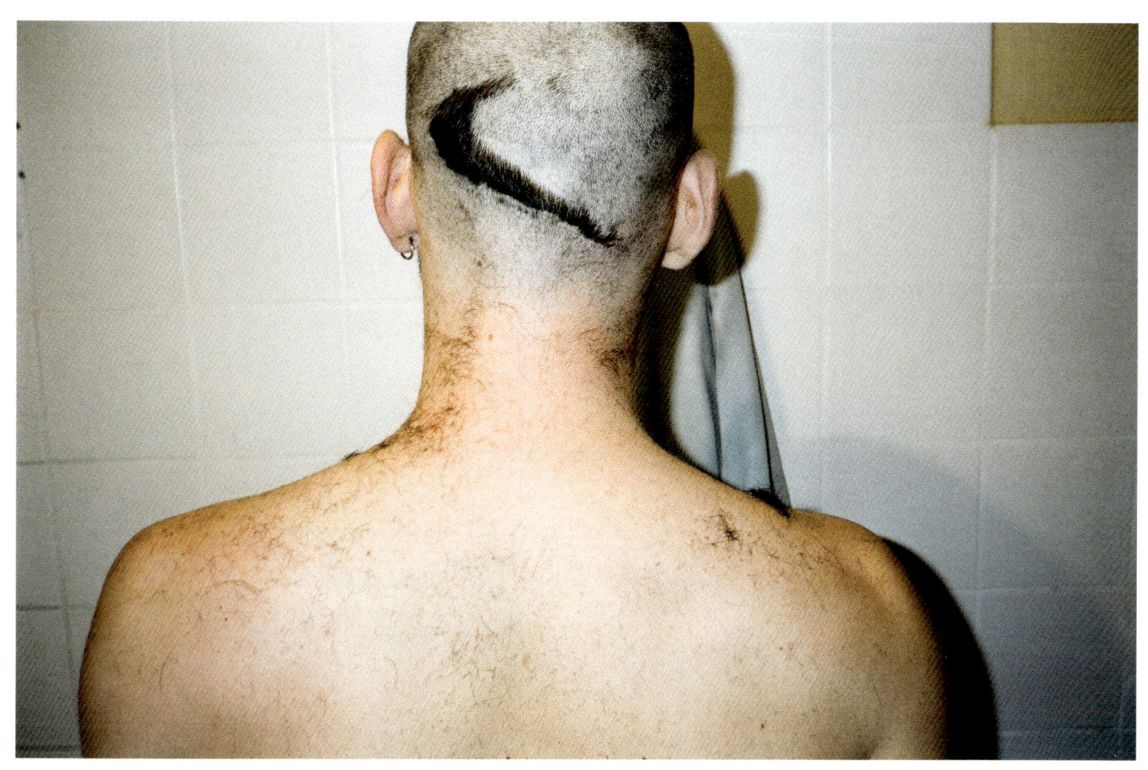

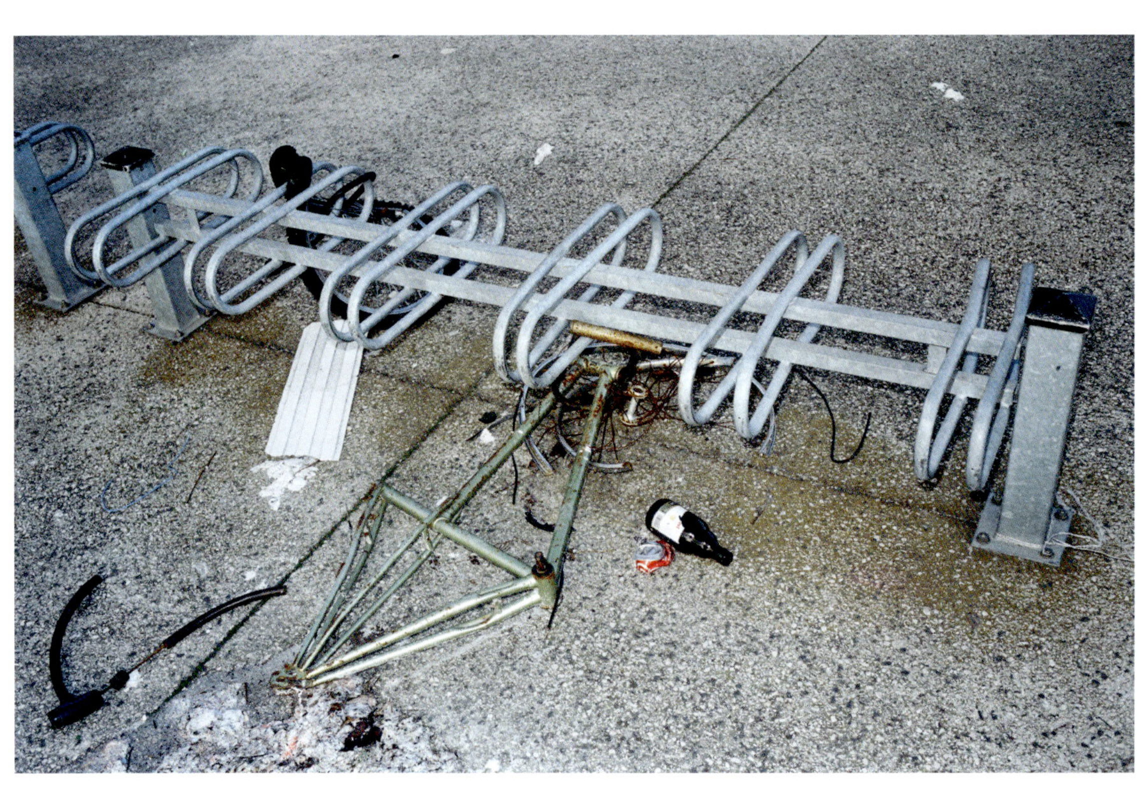

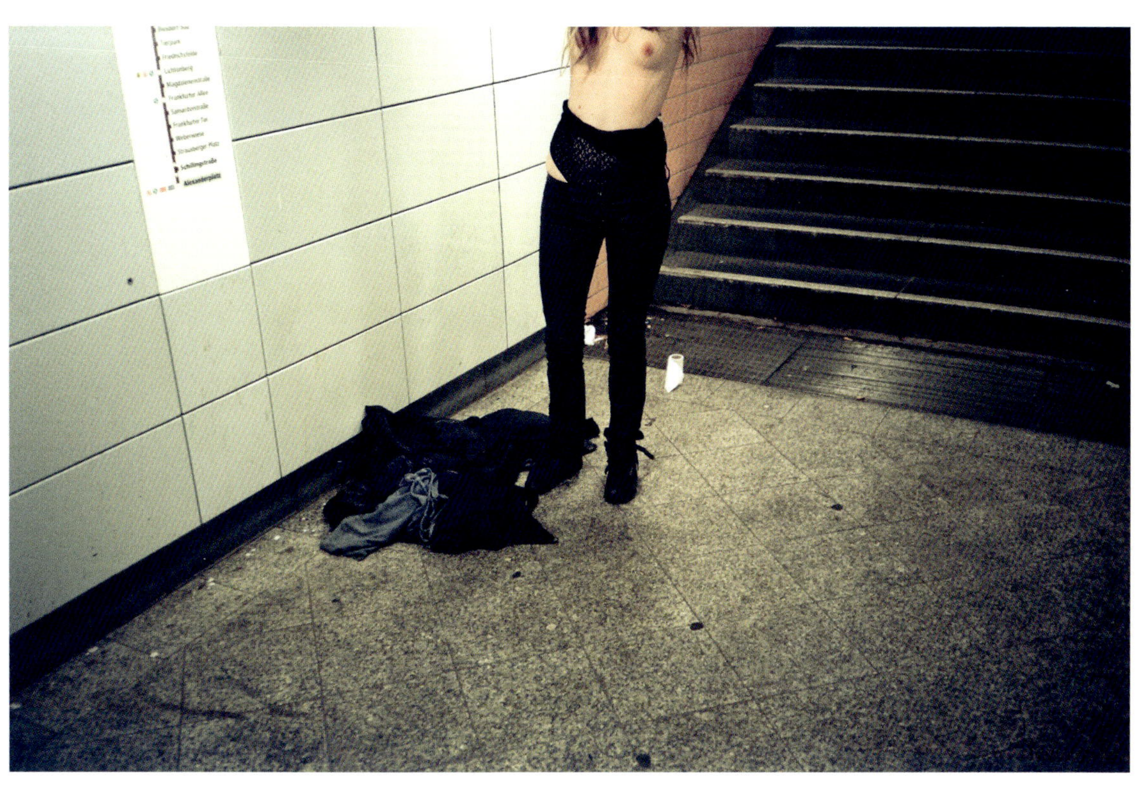
Frankfurter Tor
Schillingstraße
Alexanderplatz

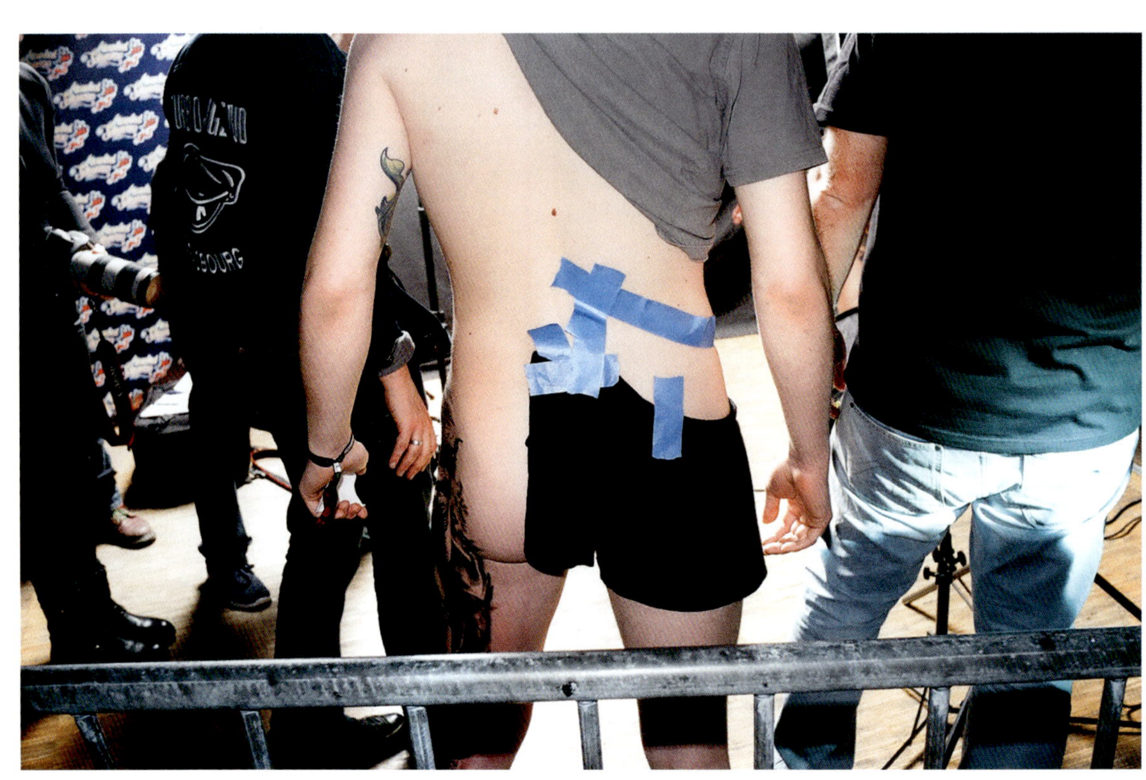

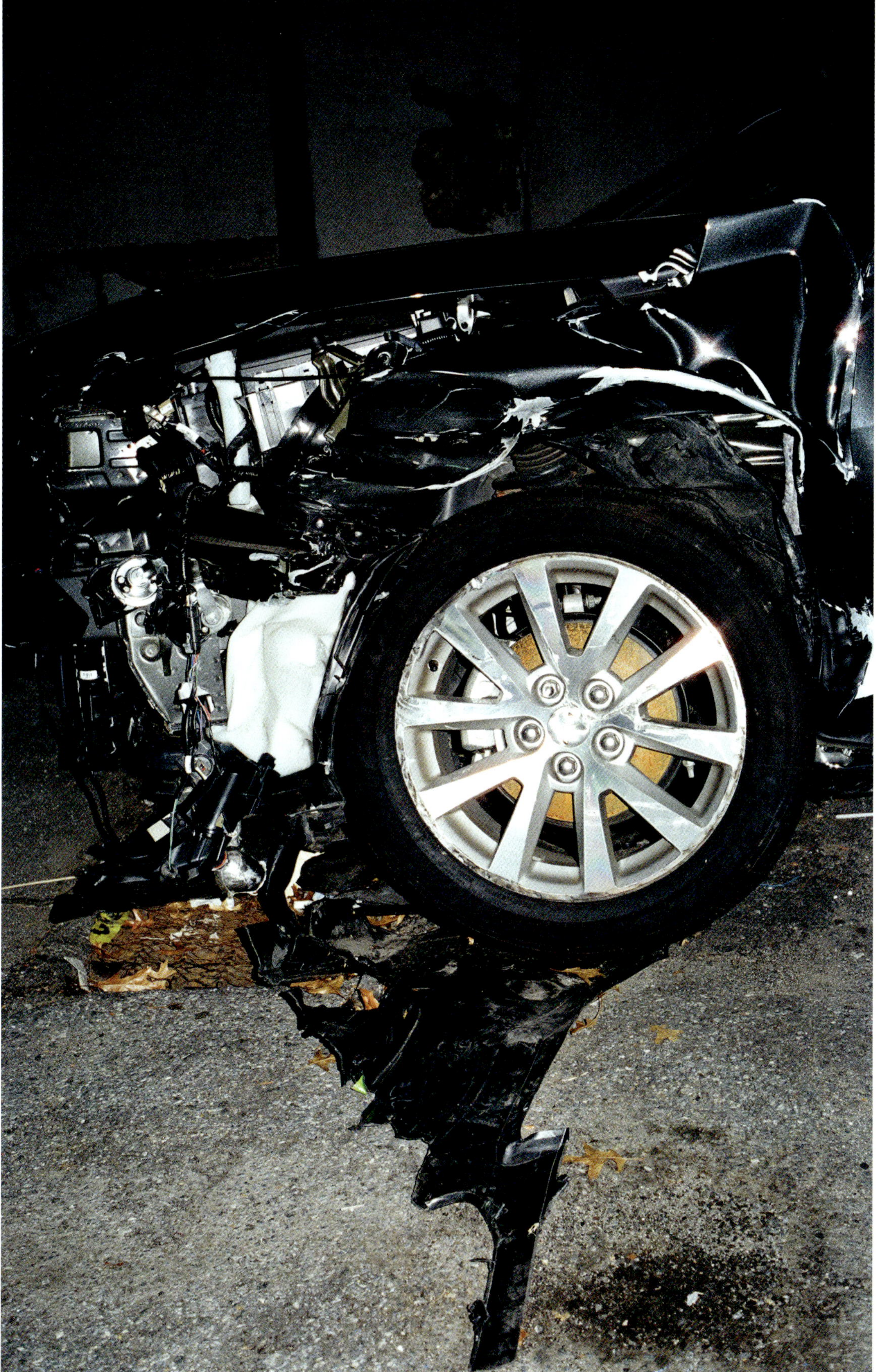

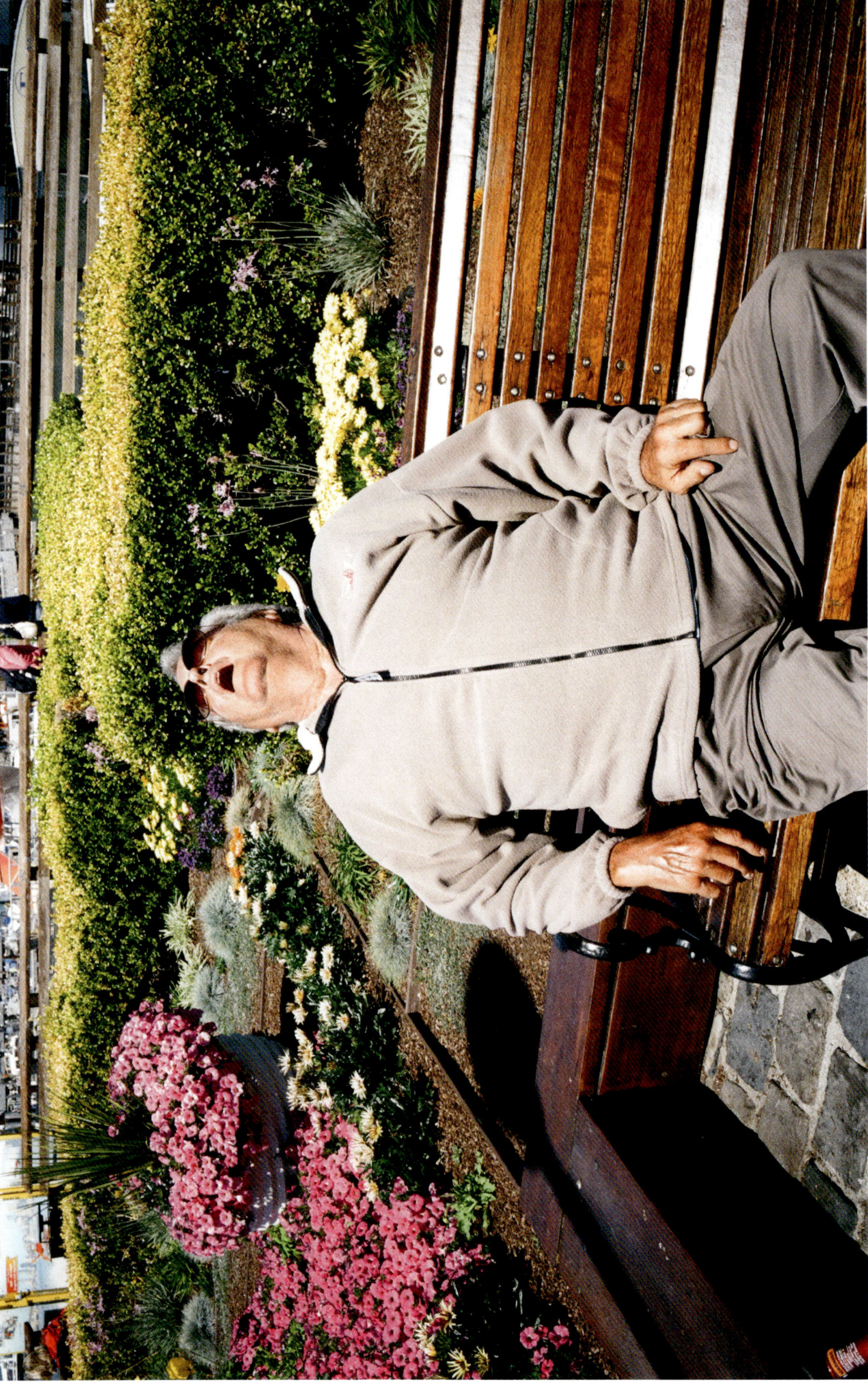

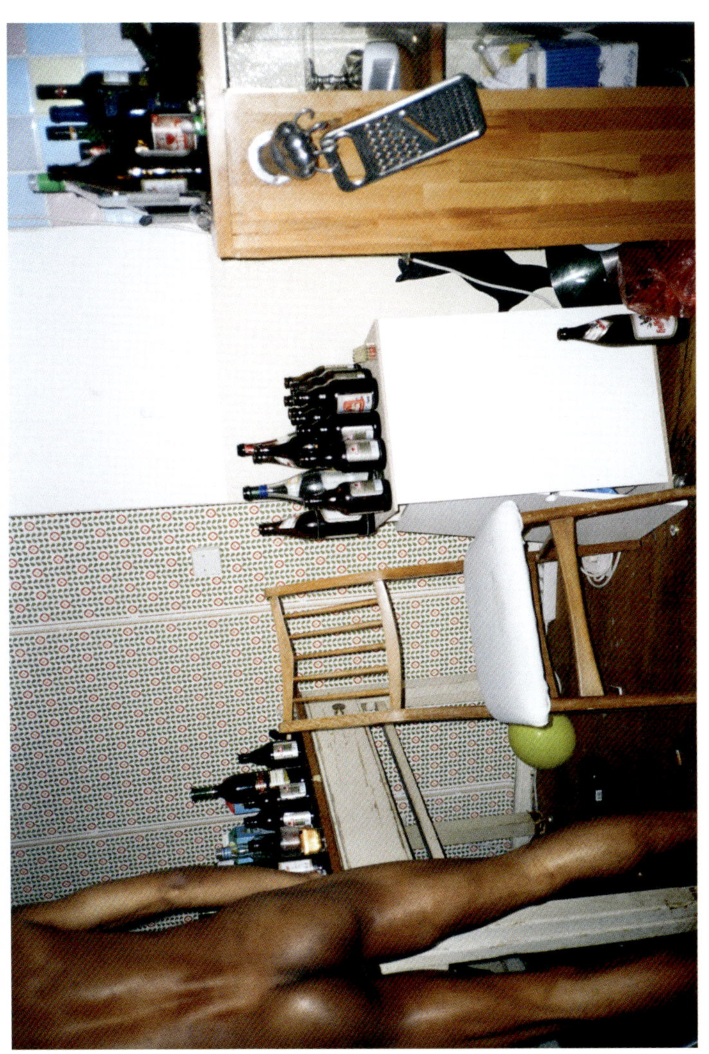

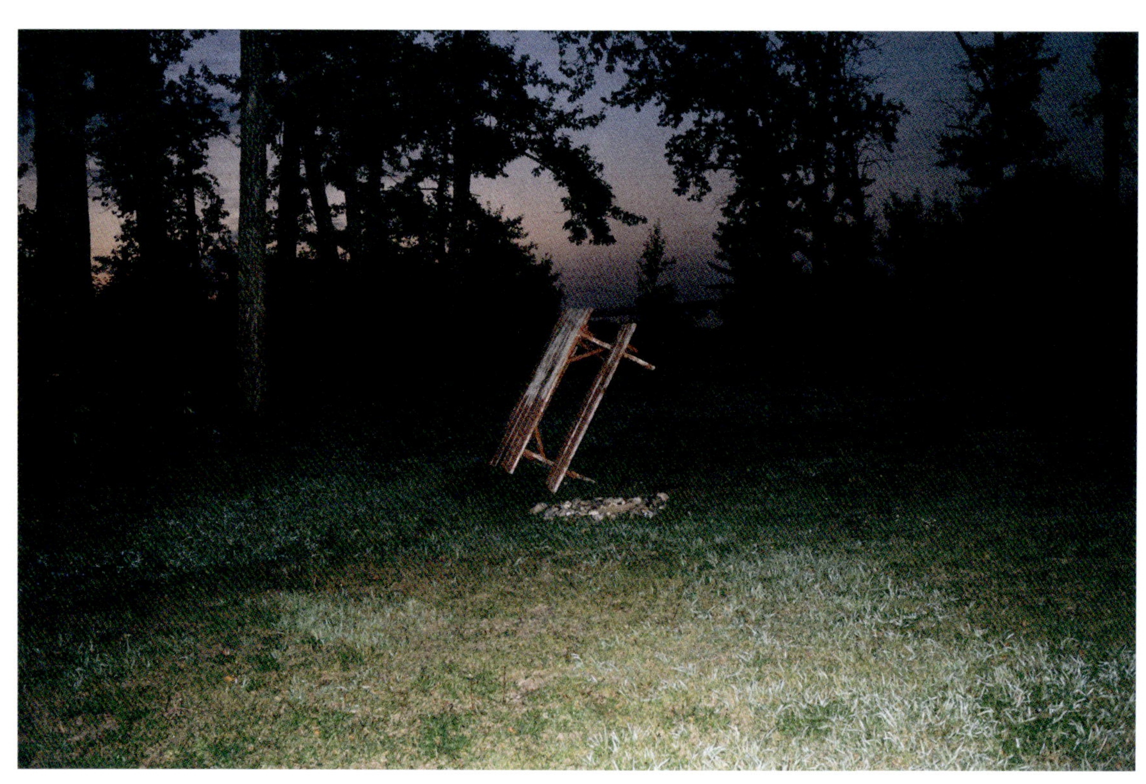

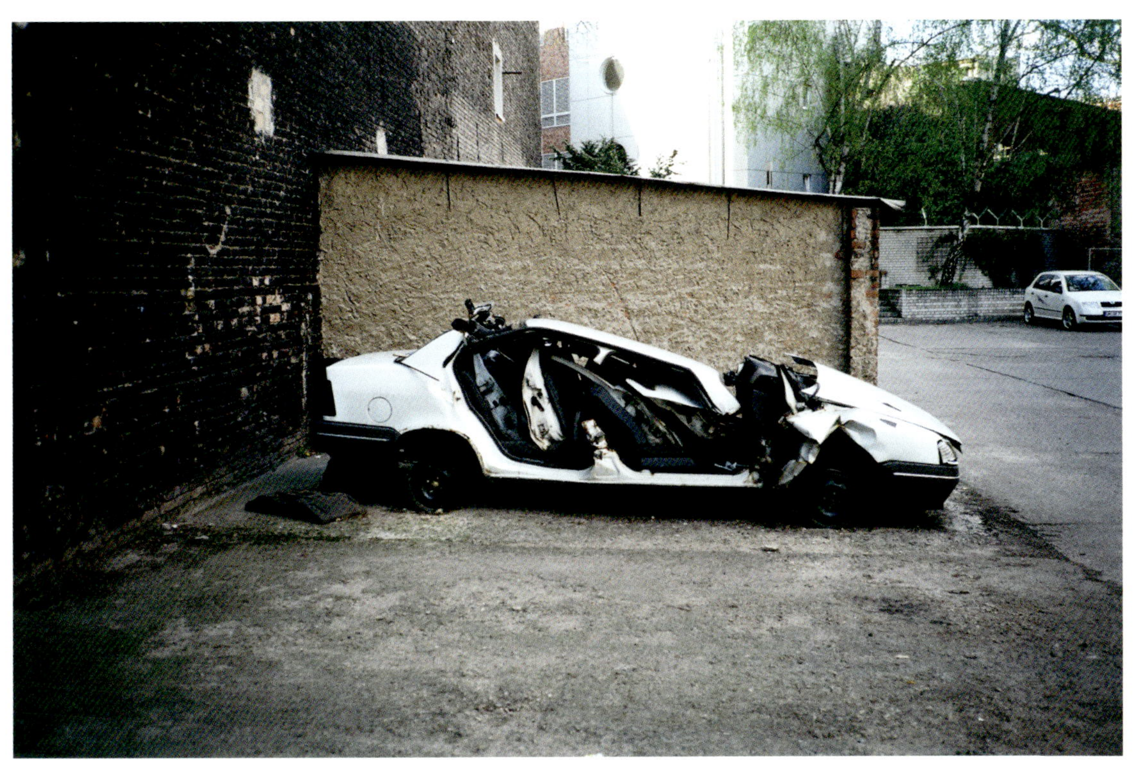

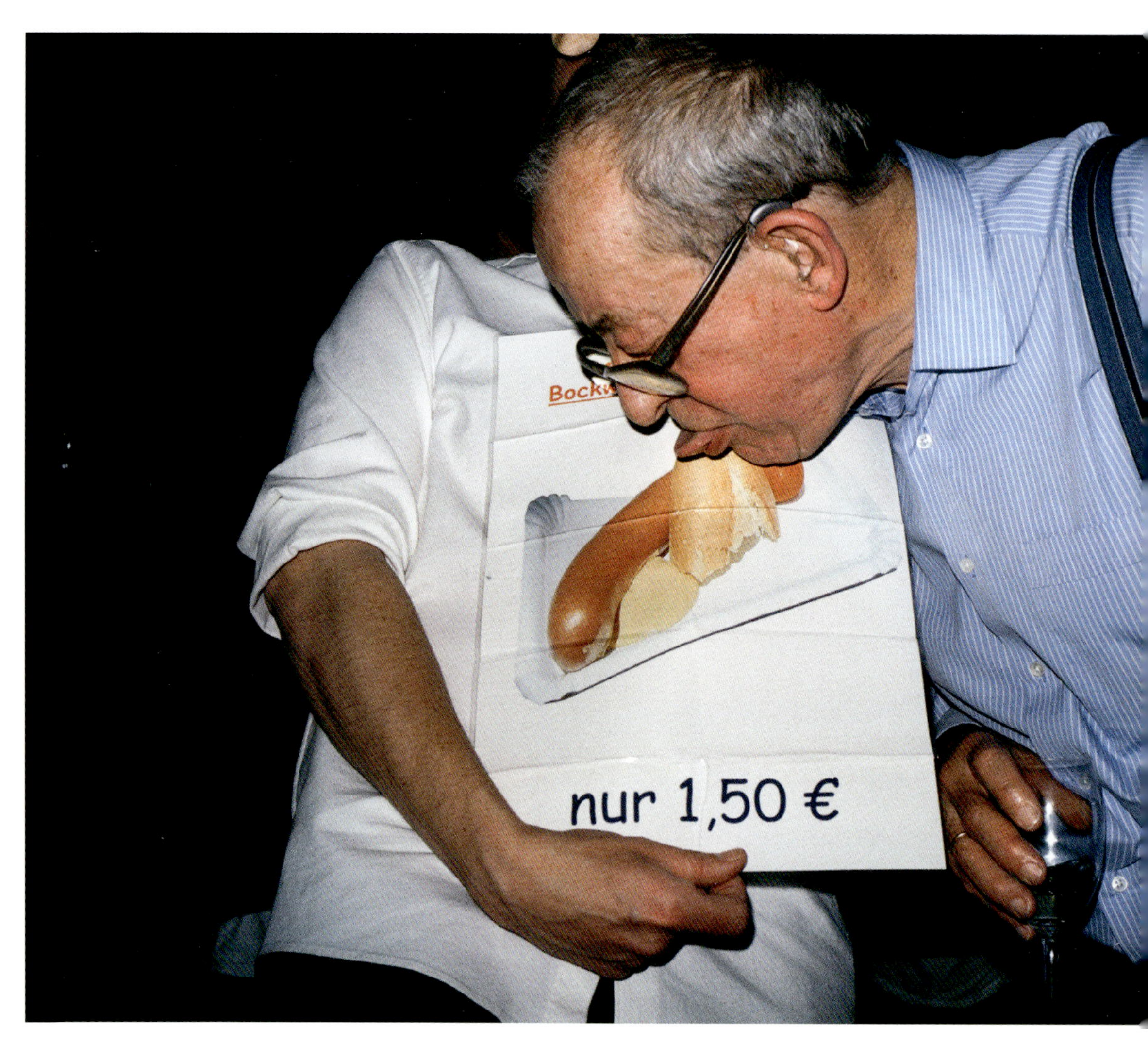
nur 1,50 €

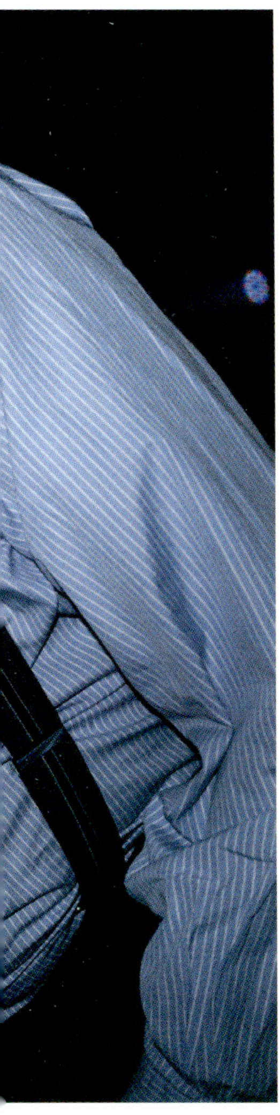

2007 You're driving very fast, for a very long time. Actually, for two days.
You don't sleep well.
Drunk, you collapse by the side of the road and cannot stand up.
You stay drunk for a long time.
You make a fire with F.
You talk and dream.
About the East.
About the North.
About the cold and the night.
You meet S., here, two years later. Her voice has changed. Her face has hardened.
Tonight you take M-J to the train station.
You move your bed a bit to the left.
And the pollution produces something white and heavy. It's never really night.
You are not cold.
You have a mini rosebush and a music box. C. gave it to you long ago.
You keep it open next to your bed and you look at it a lot.
Your two suitcases are open at the other end of
the room and your clothes on the floor. Dry paint
has fallen off the ceiling.
And
You look through the window at the night that never comes.
You're maybe waiting to cut your hair to start this life.

2007 Tu conduis très vite, très longtemps. En fait pendant deux jours.
Tu dors mal.
Tu t'effondres par terre, ivre sur le bord de la route sans pouvoir te relever.
Tu reste saoul longtemps.
Tu fais du feu avec F.
Tu parles et tu rêves.
De l'Est.
Du Nord.
Du froid et de la nuit.
Tu revois S., ici, après deux ans. Sa voix a changé. Son visage s'est durci.
Ce soir tu raccompagnes M-J à la gare.
Tu décales un peu ton lit vers la gauche.
Et la pollution produit quelque chose de blanc et lourd. Et il ne
fait jamais vraiment nuit.
Tu n'as pas froid.
Tu as un mini rosier et une boite à musique. Celle que C. t'a
donné il y a longtemps. Elle est ouverte près de ton lit et tu la
regardes beaucoup.
Tes deux valises sont ouvertes à l'autre bout de la pièces et tes
vêtements par terre. De la peinture sèche est tombée du plafond.
Et
Tu regardes par la fenêtre la nuit
qui n'arrive jamais.
Tu attends peut être de te couper les cheveux pour commencer cette vie.

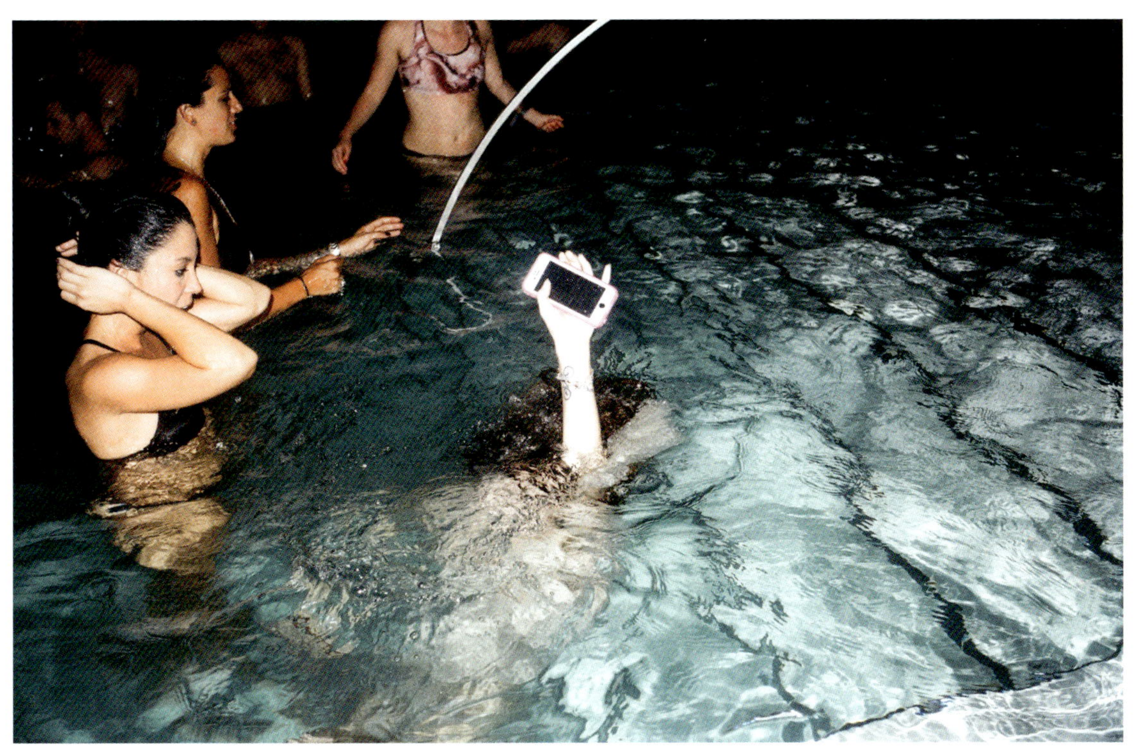

221 — 256

Blue tears

Falsehoods

2005 He was proud and
serene like an old goat,
disemboweled.

2005 Il était fier et
paisible comme un vieux bouc
éventré.

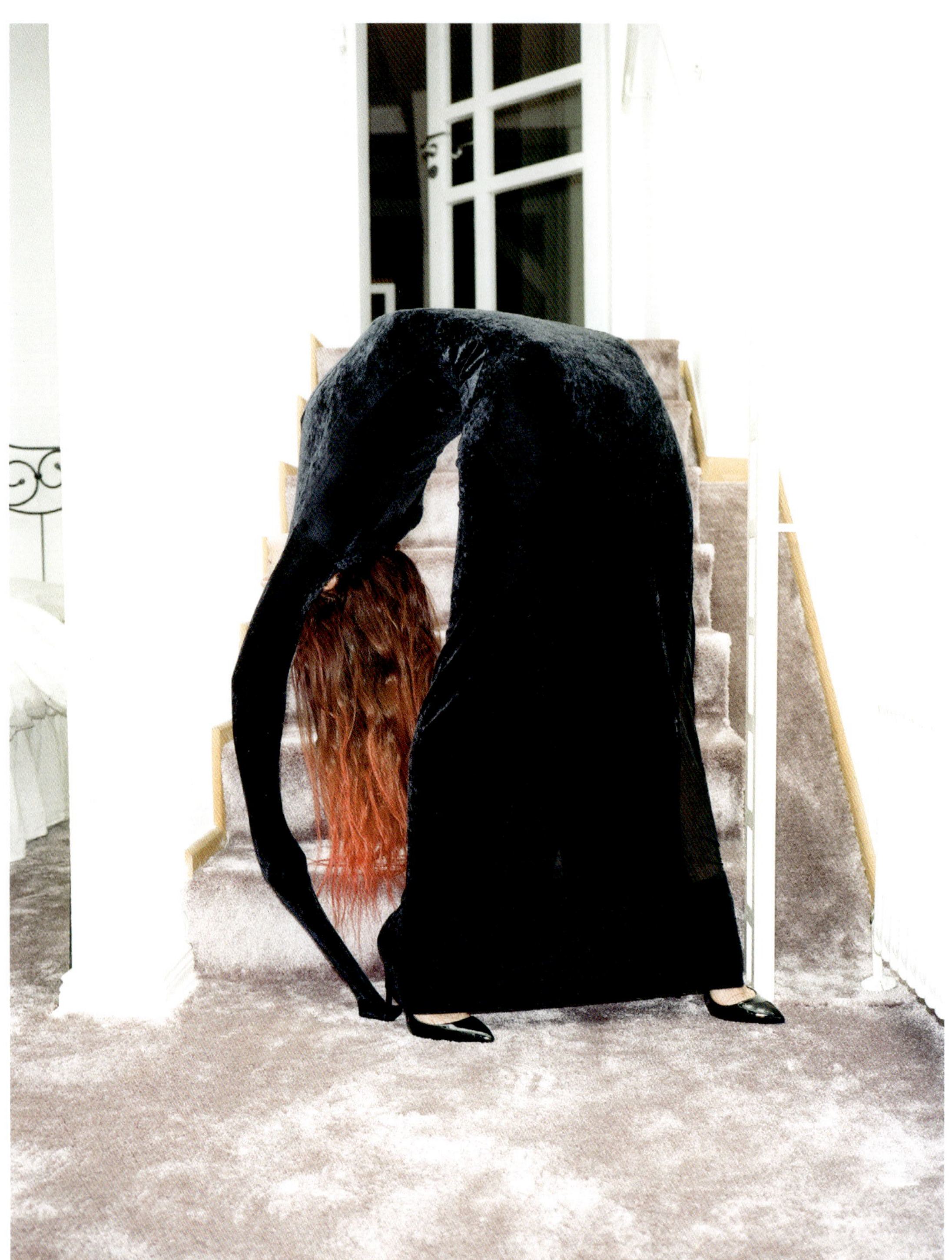

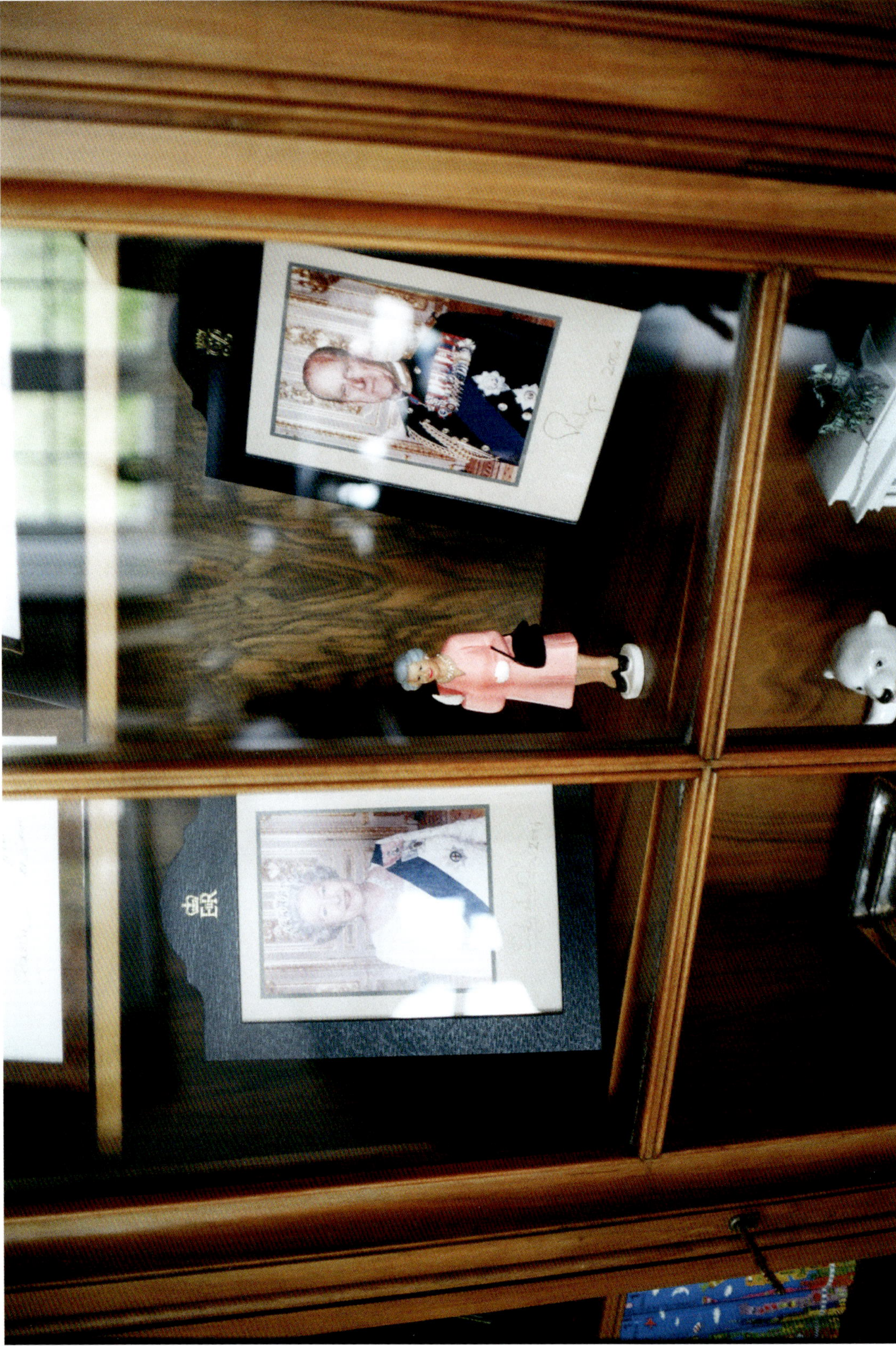

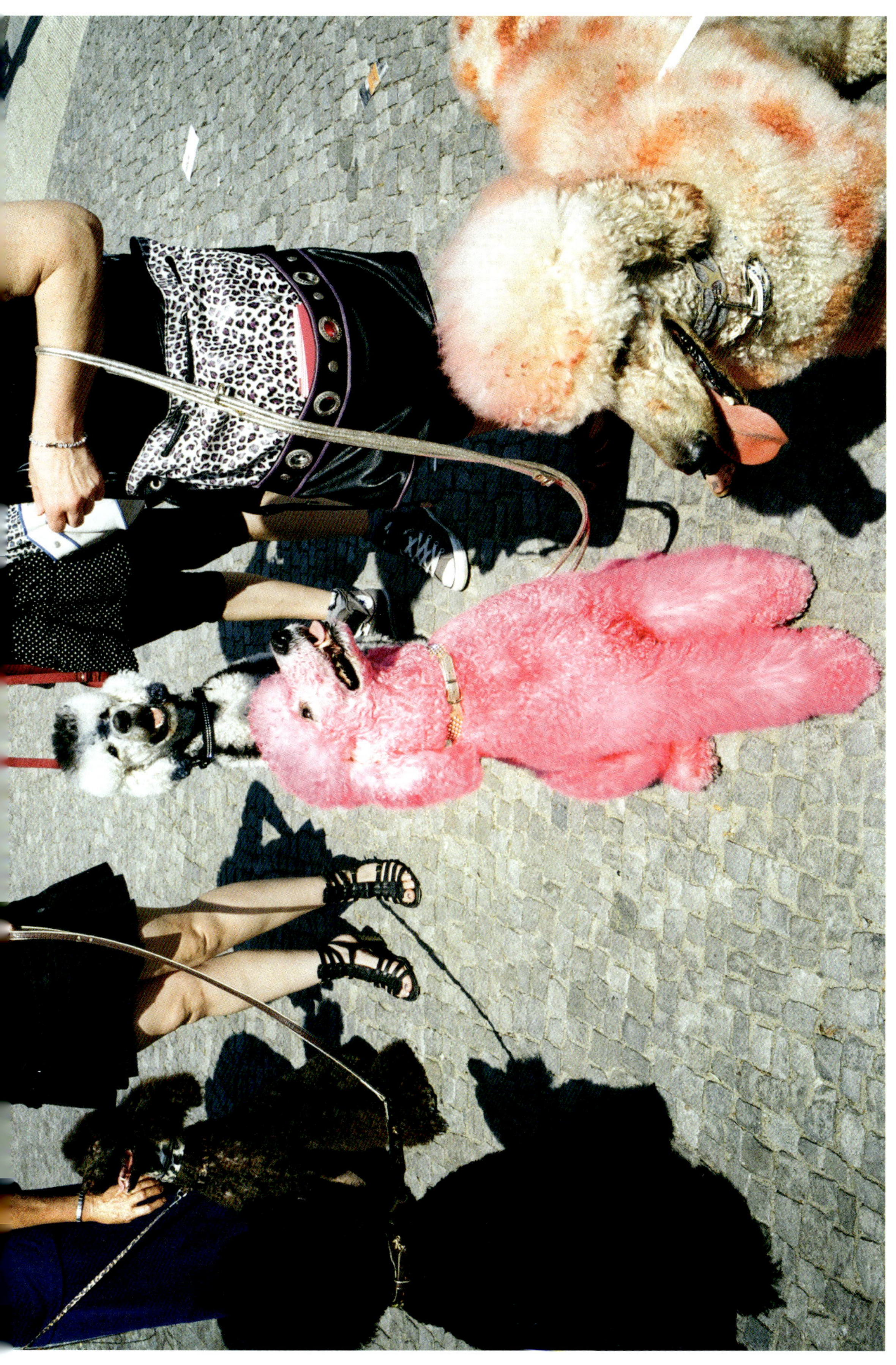

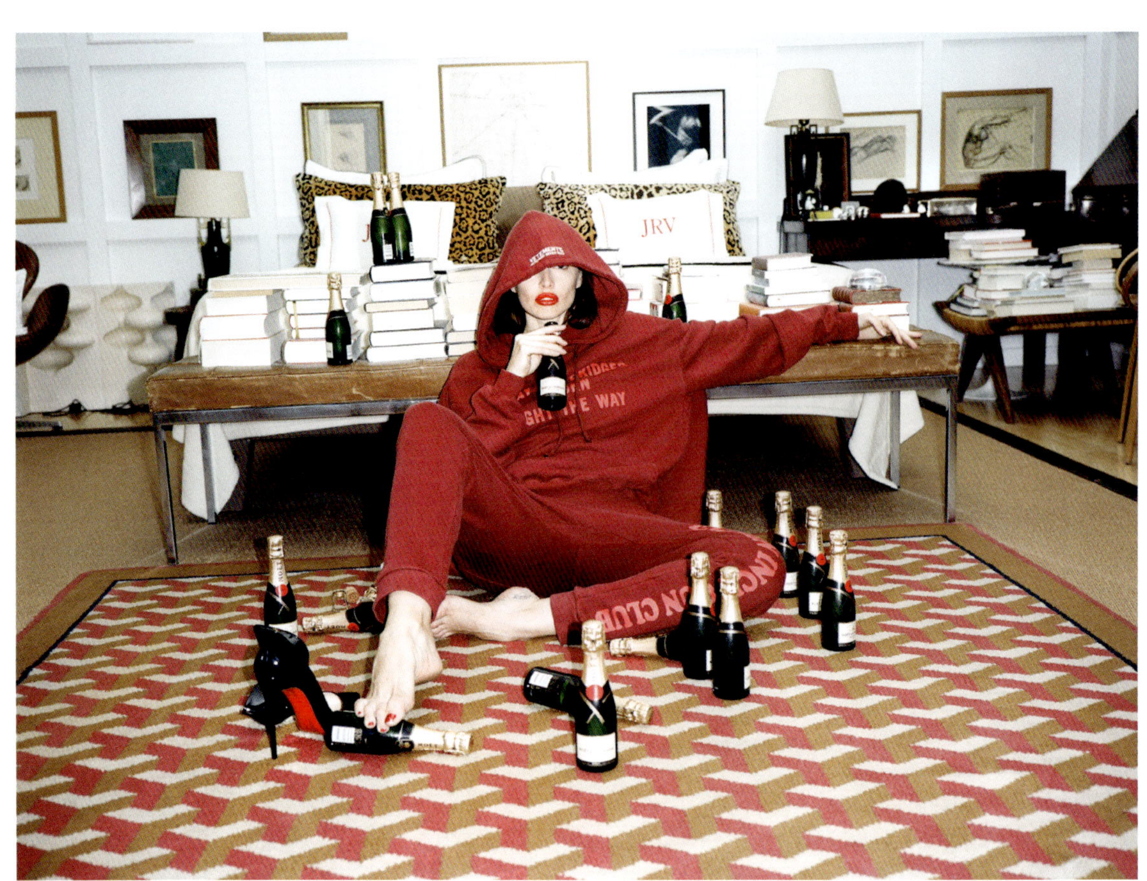
JRV

2006 Sitting at a table, you ask yourself:
would we be less stupid if there was less bullshit on TV and in magazines, or would there be less bullshit on TV and in magazines if we were less stupid?

2006 À table tu te demandes:
est-ce que nous serions moins cons s'il y avait moins de conneries à la télé et dans les magazines, ou, est-ce qu'il y aurait moins de conneries à la télé et dans les magazines si nous étions moins cons?

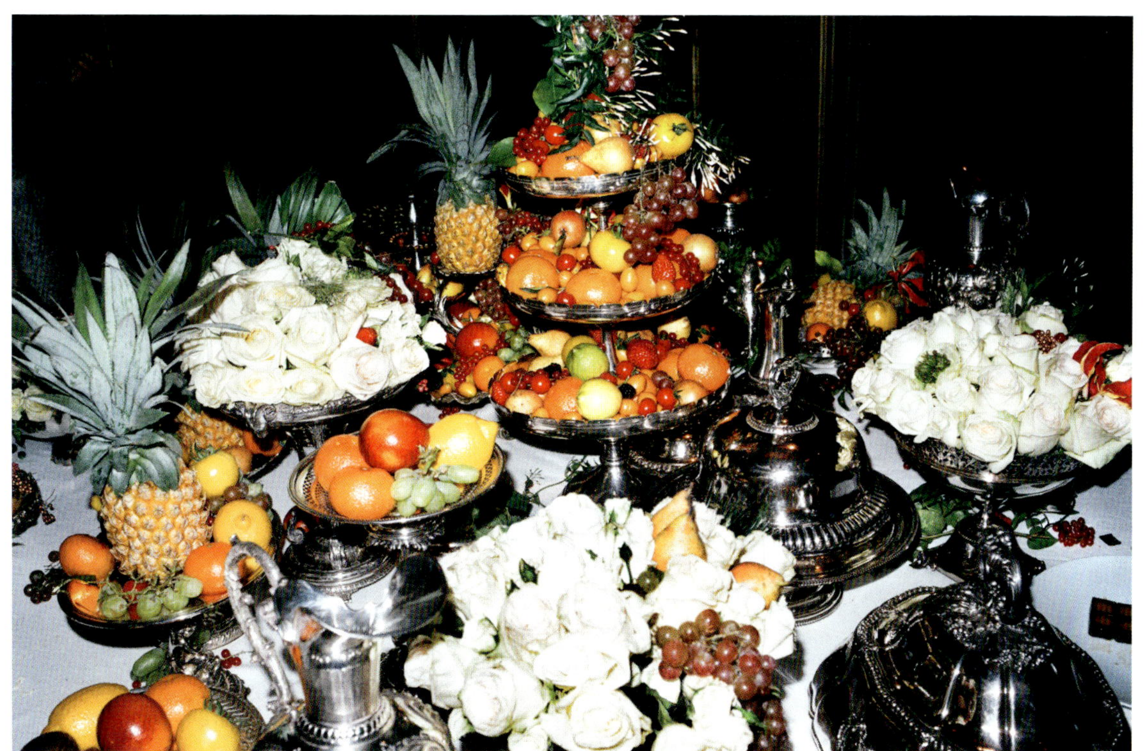

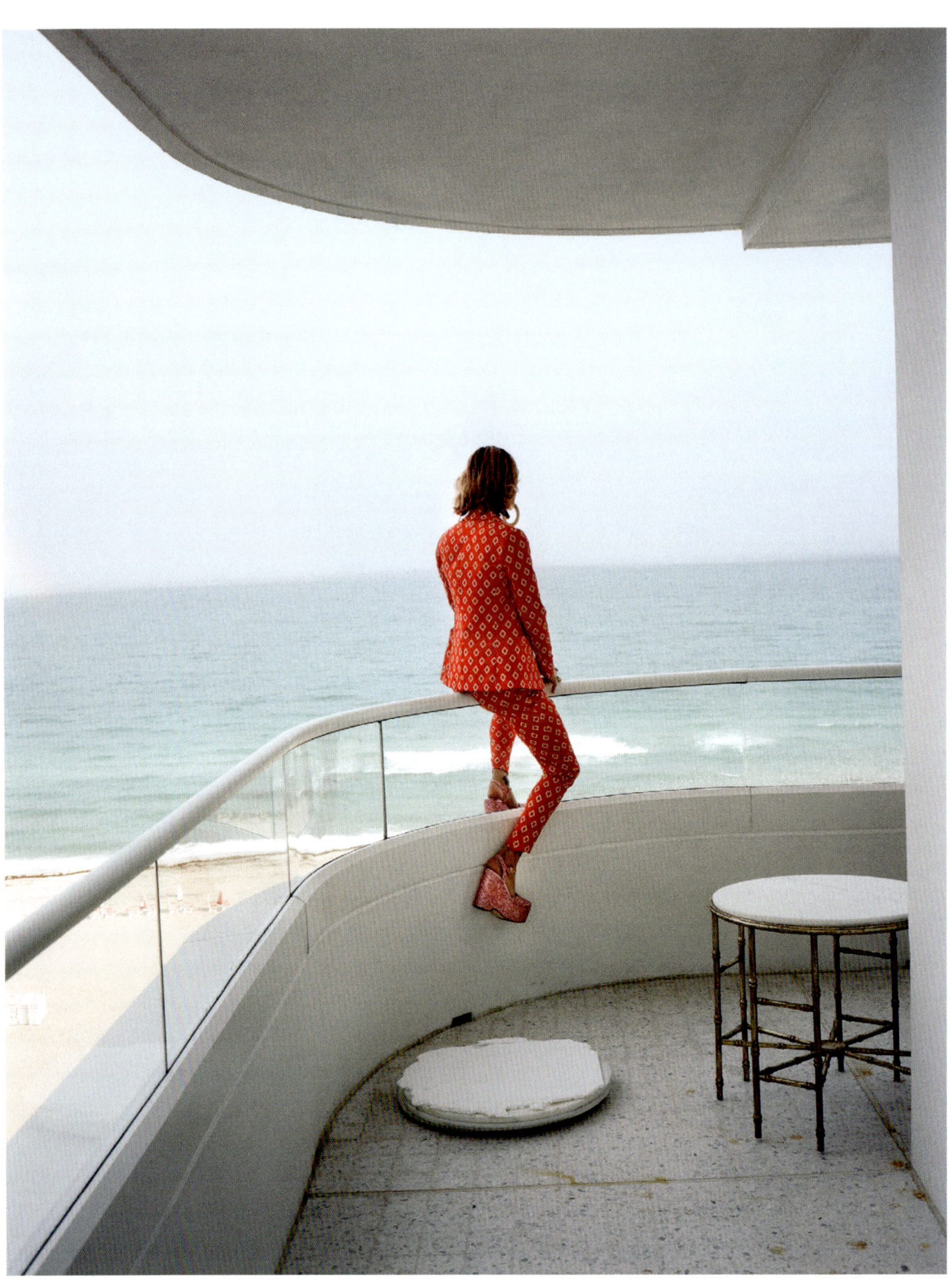

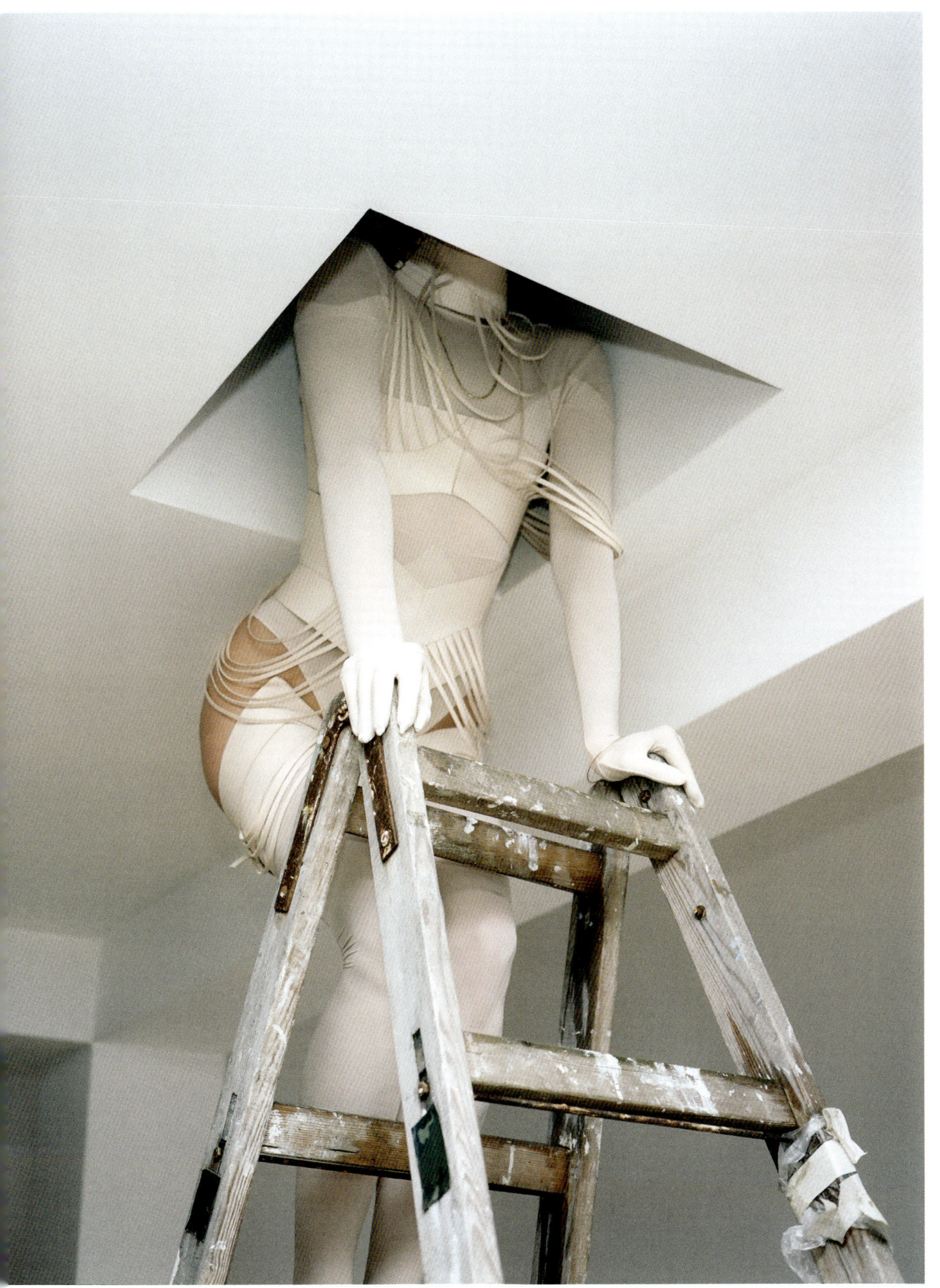

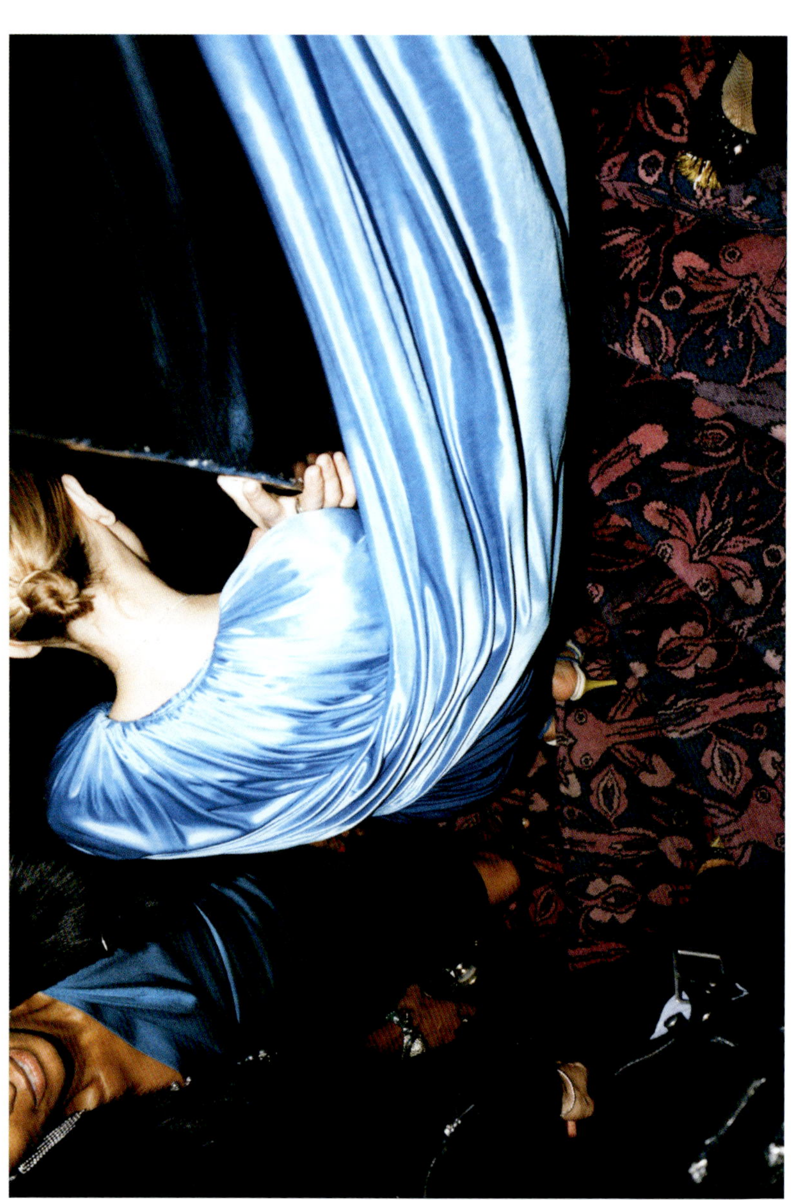

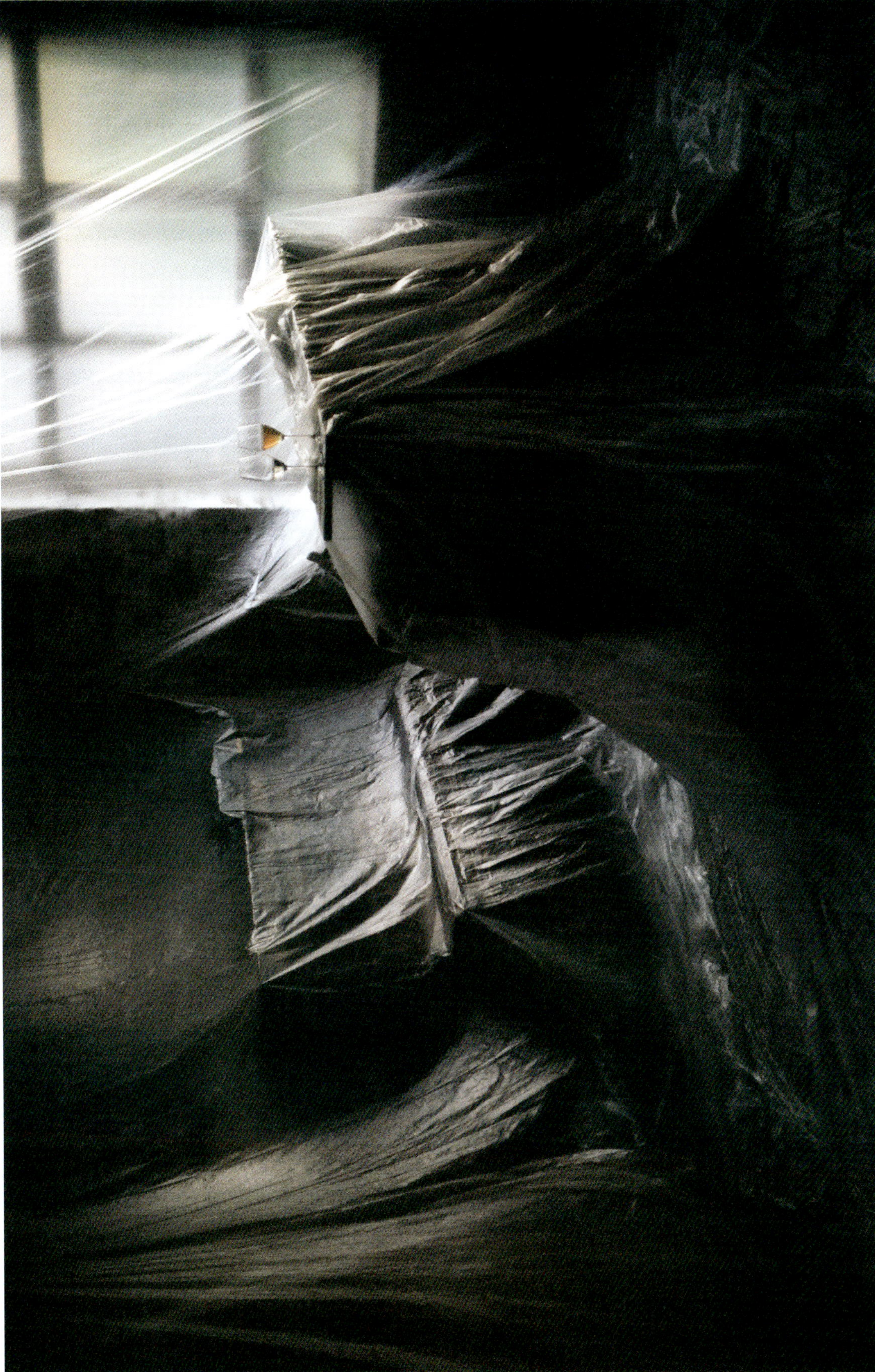

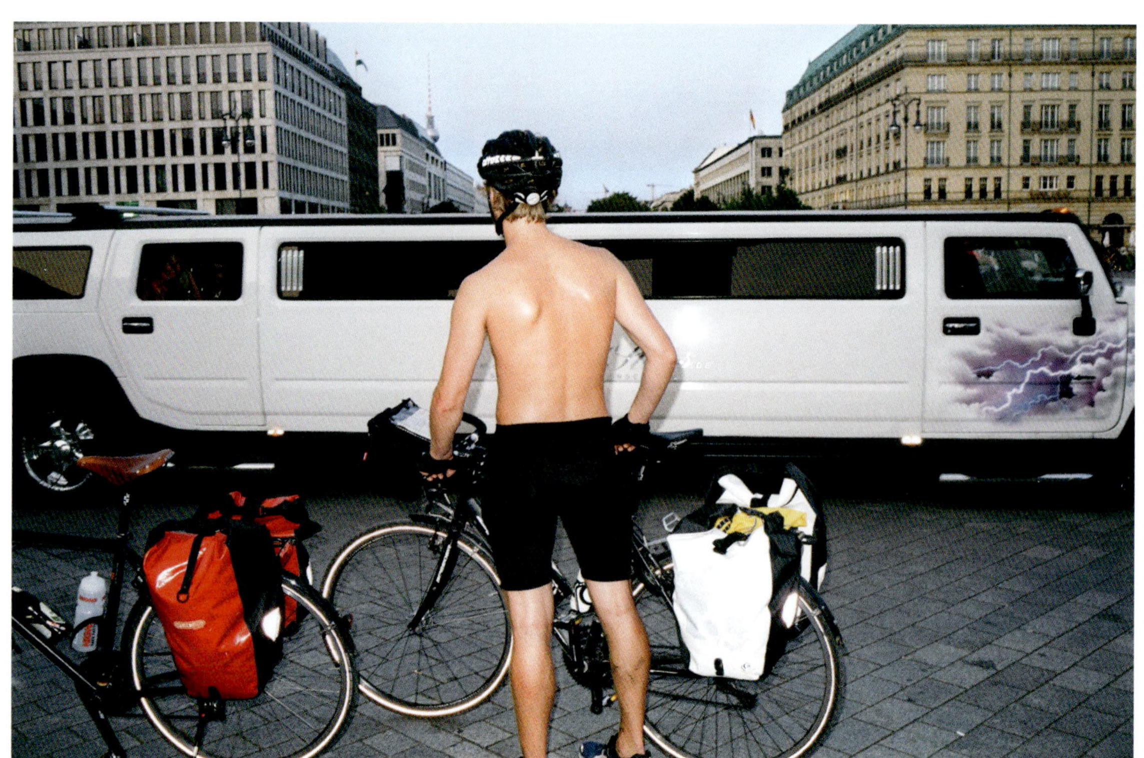

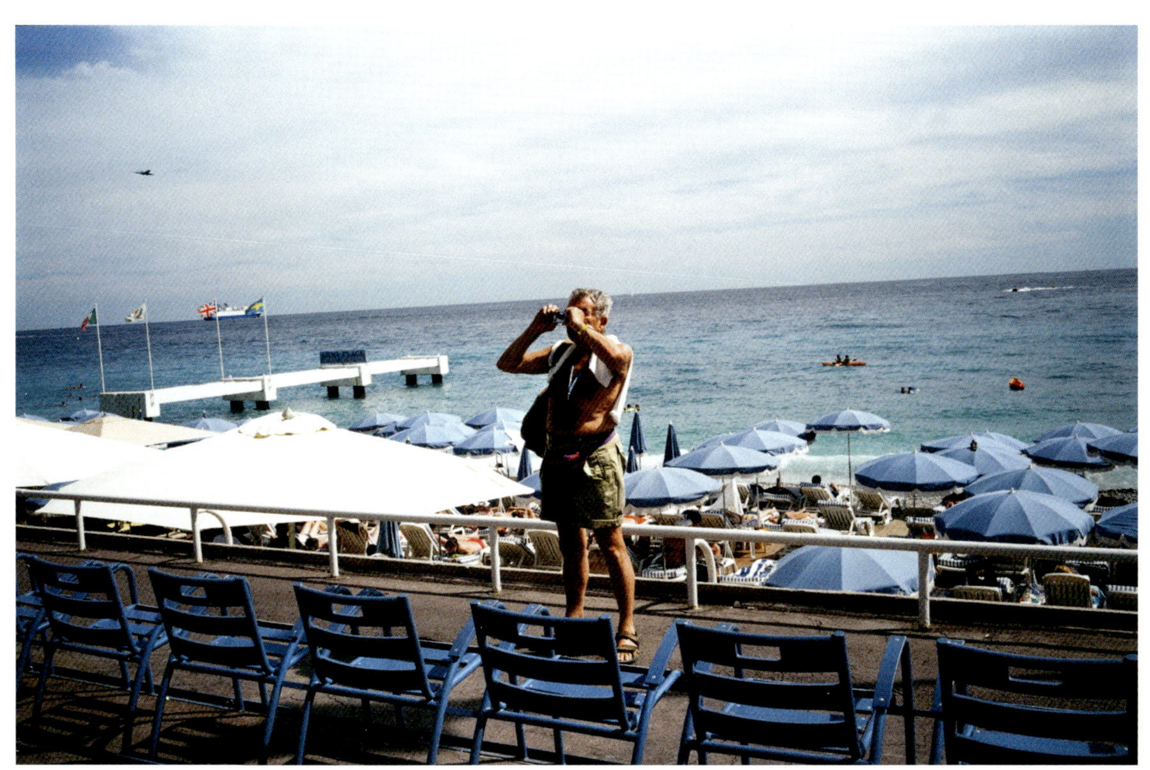

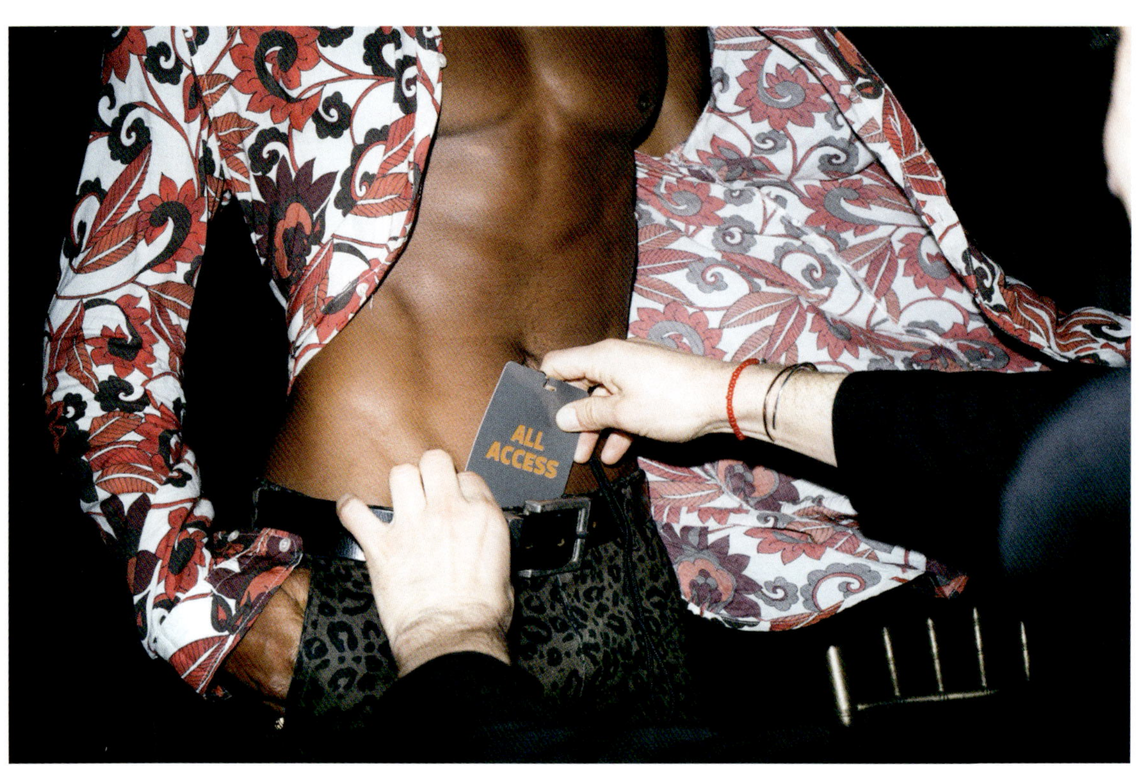
ALL
ACCESS

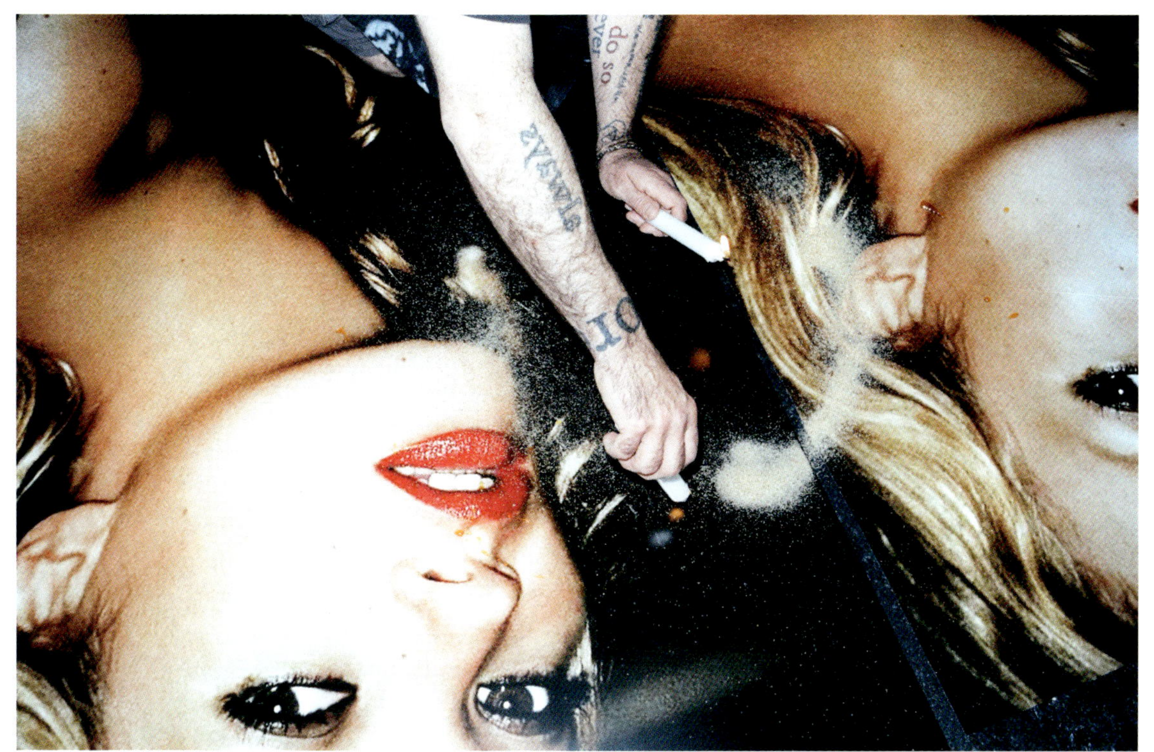

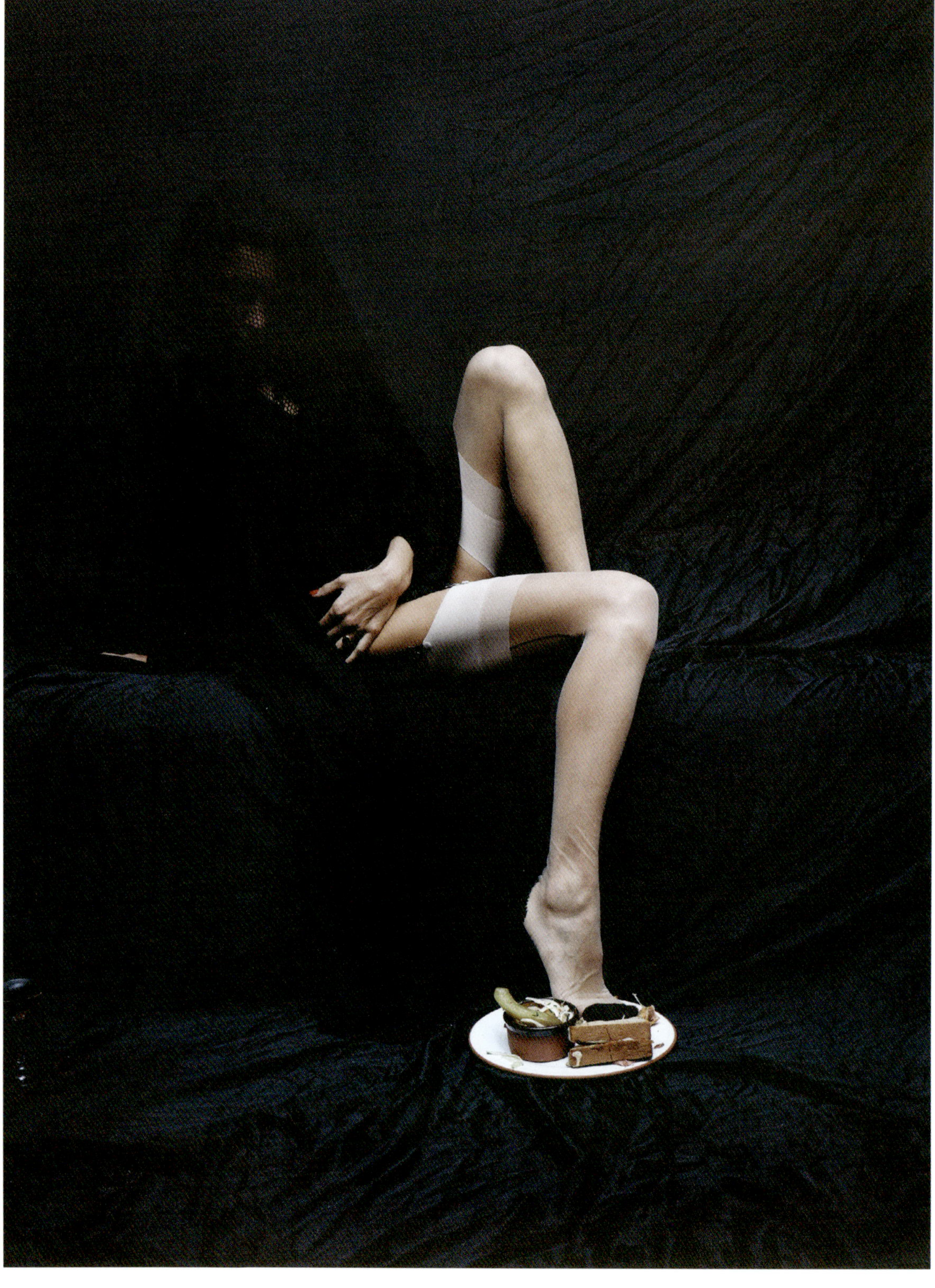

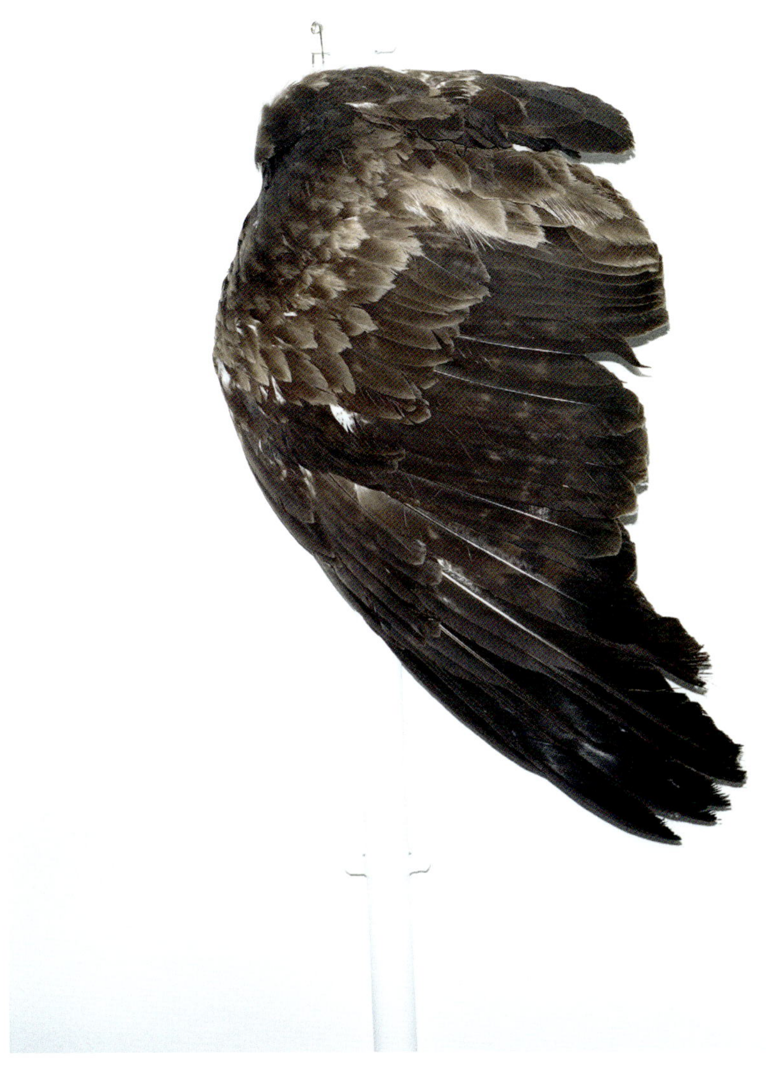

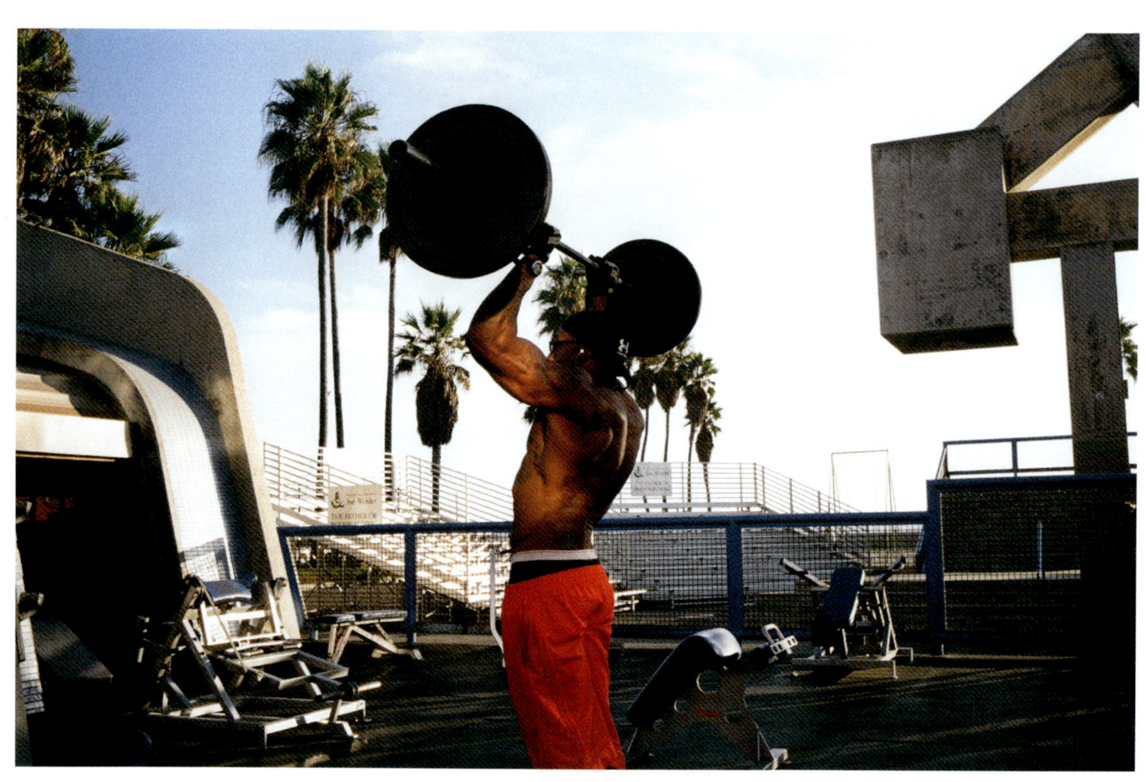

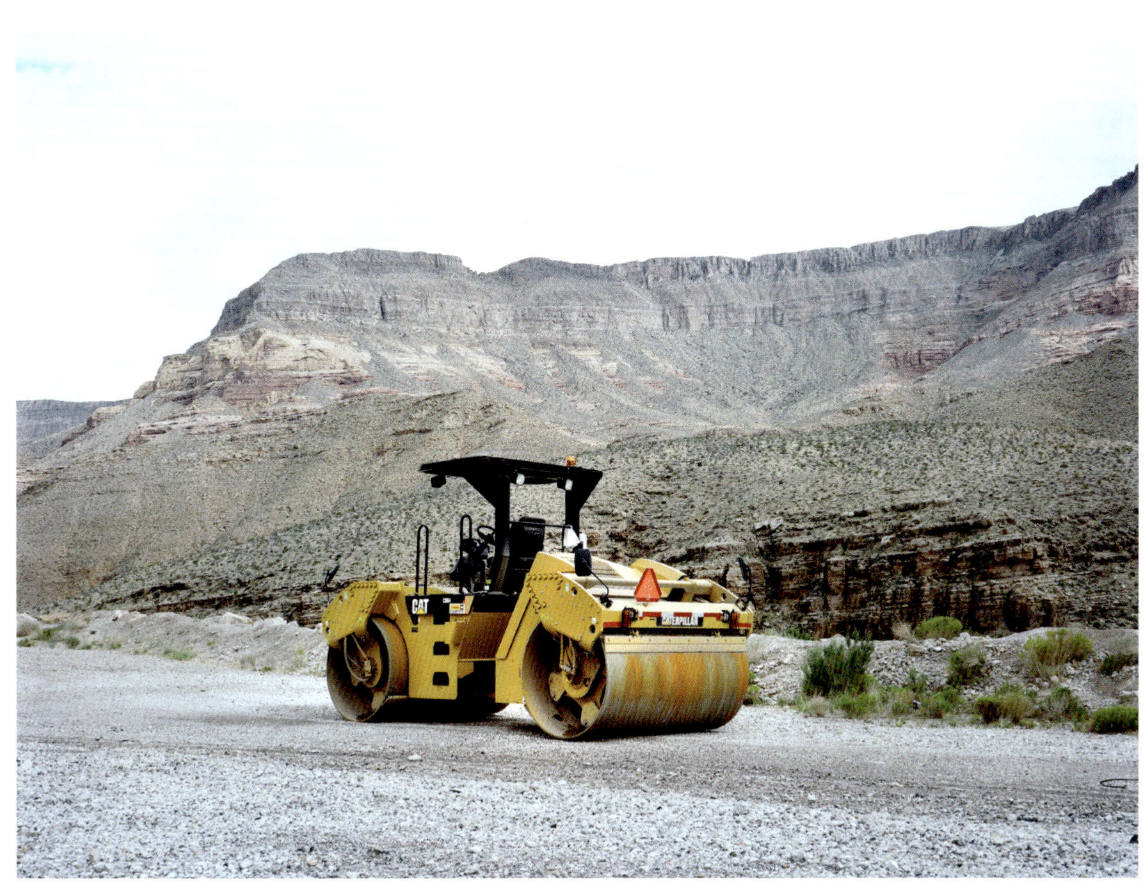
CAT
CATERPILLAR

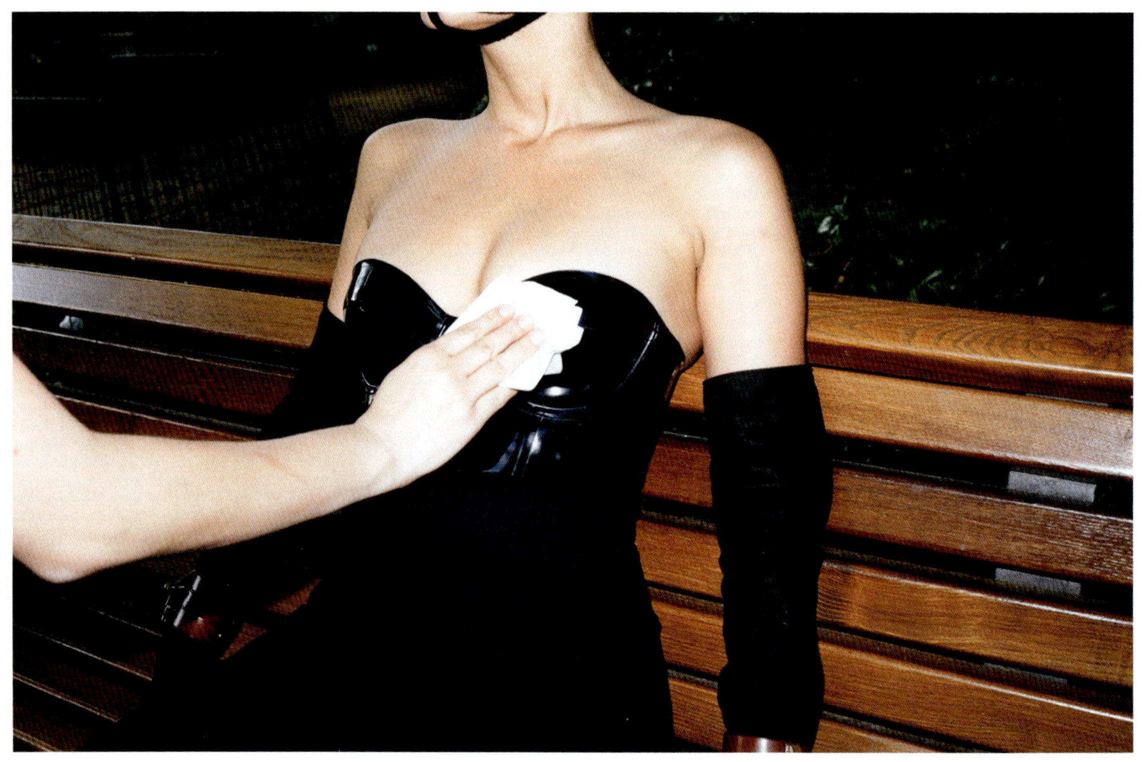

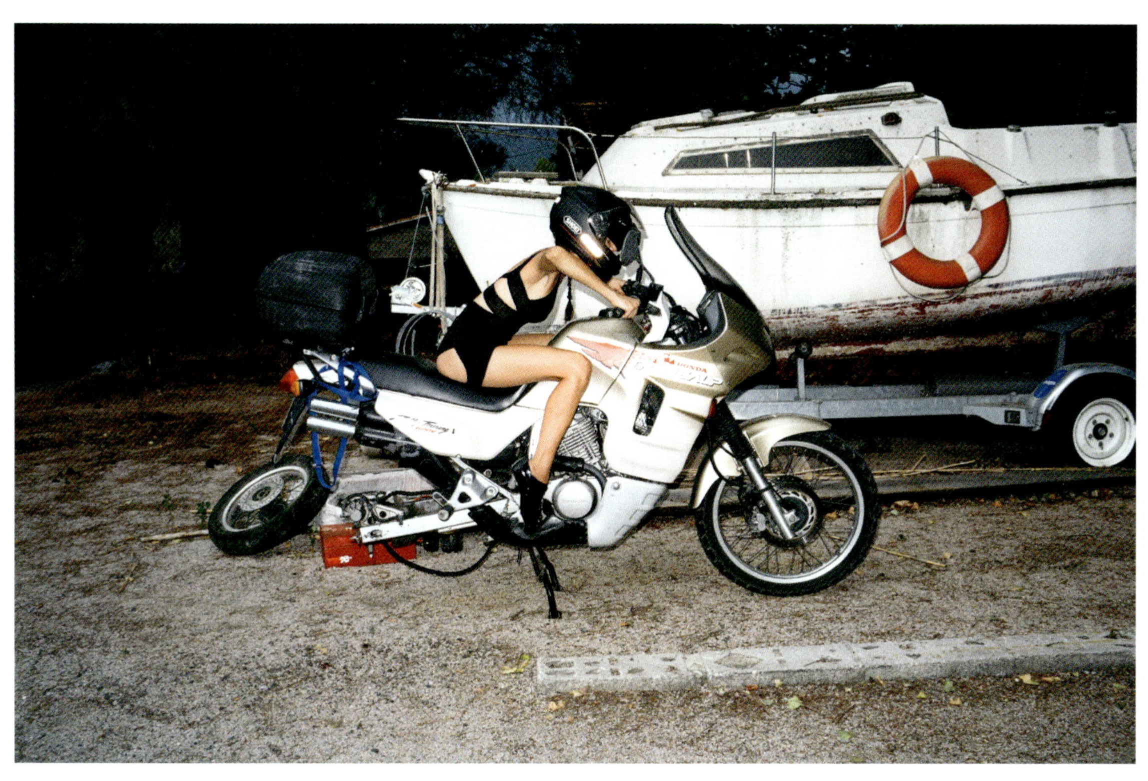

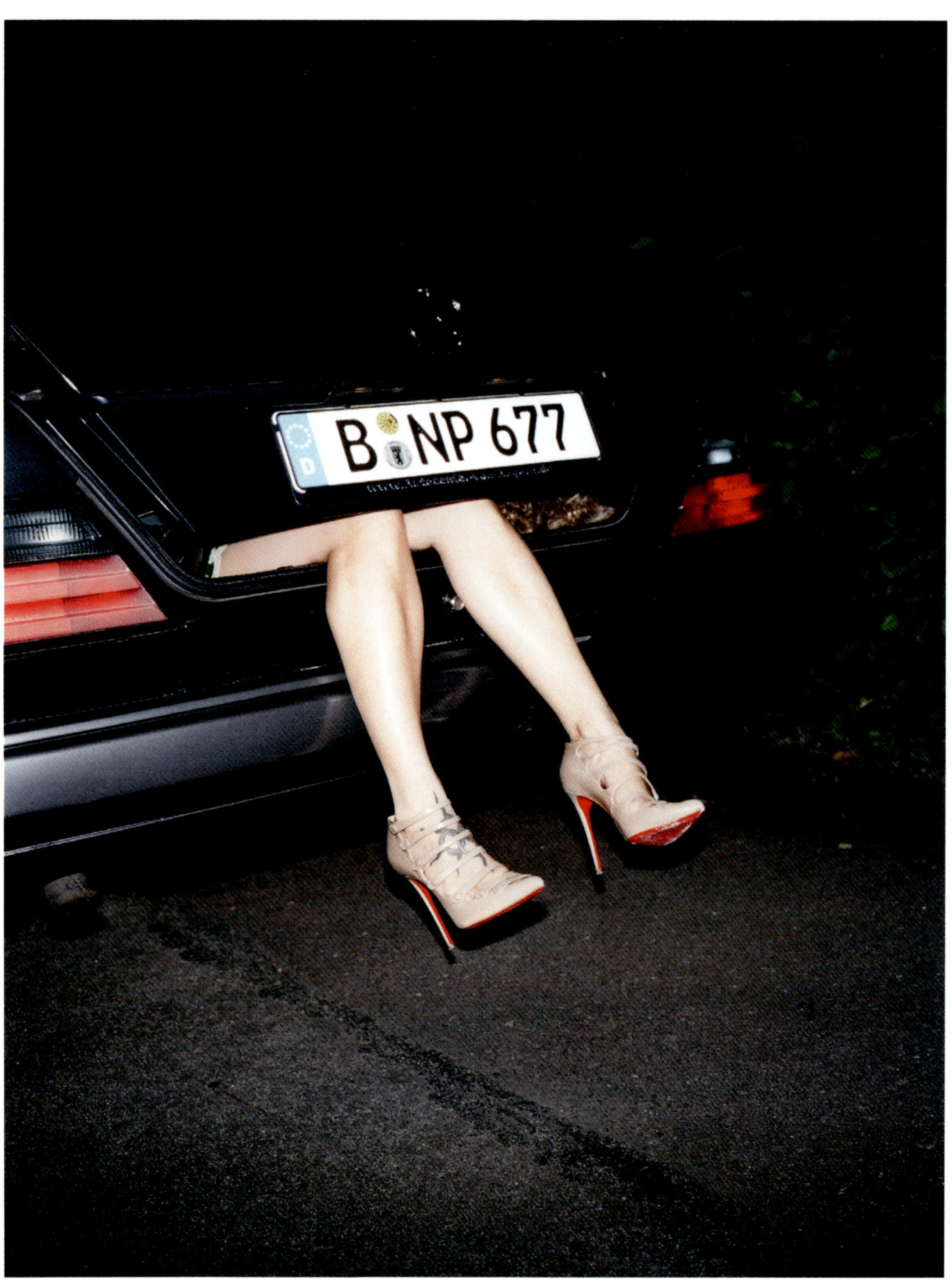
D
B NP 677

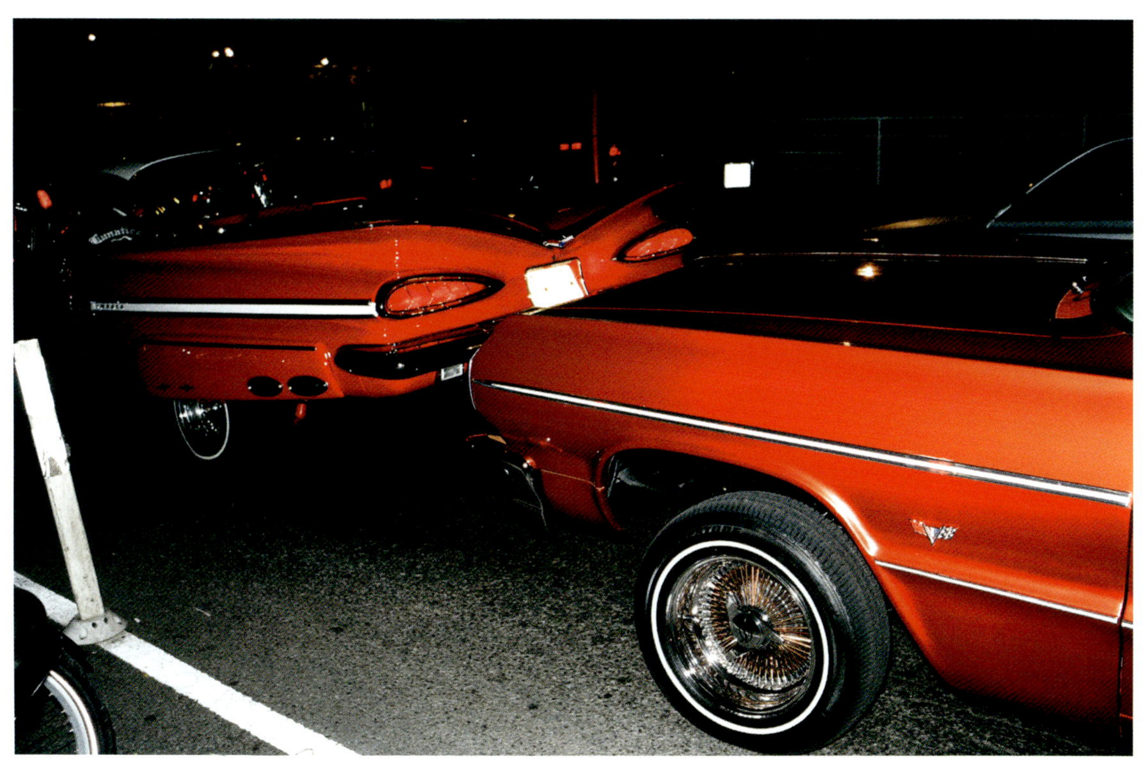

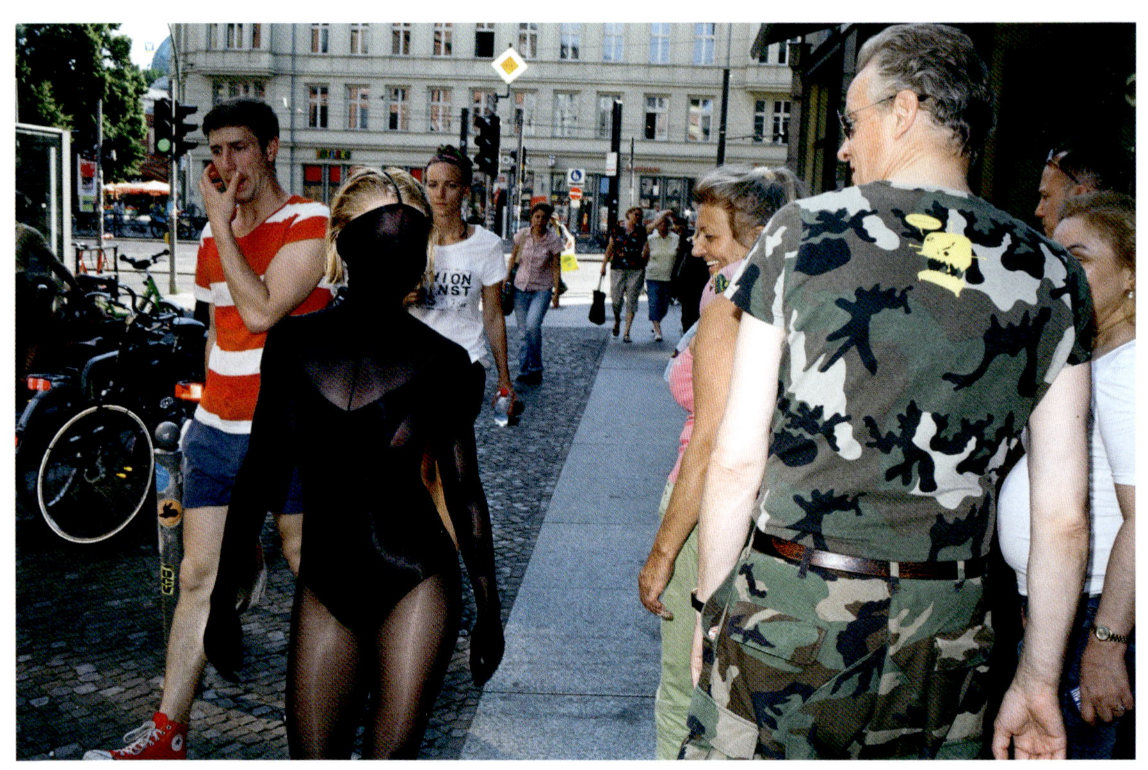

2006 It seems that you have become a well-oiled machine.

You don't even consider the fact that you might as well not exist at all. You choose your clothing carefully. You feel unique. You are sure that you are choosing. This morning you put on a white top under your fine-striped shirt. You tucked it half into your new jeans. Then you slipped on thin socks and patent leather shoes that you didn't lace.

You put on your net cap and a more or less matching jacket. Now you really feel like you exist. Especially since you have fresh breath. It will be a good day because yesterday you saw a gorgeous girl in a fashion magazine casually wearing the same cap you have now on your head, and you don't doubt your taste anymore.

You flaunt. Your movements are fluid.

You are walking with elegance. You are contented. Your anus is dilating loudly. You are the spokesperson of your ass. Through funnels you pour your droppings on the little heap of flesh that you usually call your head.

Your face sinks slowly under the atrocious weight of your shit and you seriously start to look like a magpie. Even though you are wearing patent leather shoes.

2006 Il semble que tu sois déjà un mécanisme bien huilé.

Tu ne te poses même plus de questions sur le fait que tu pourrais aussi bien ne pas exister. Tu choisis avec soins toutes tes tenus. Tu te sens unique. Tu es persuadé de choisir. Ce matin tu as mis un débardeur blanc sous ta chemise à rayures fines. Tu l'as rentré à moitié dans ton nouveau jean. Ensuite tu as enfilé des chaussettes fines et des chaussures vernies que tu n'as pas lacées. Tu as mis une casquette à filet et une veste plus ou moins assortie. Maintenant tu as vraiment l'impression d'exister.

D'autant que tu as bonne haleine. La journée sera bonne car la veille tu as vu dans un magazine à la mode une fille ravissante porter avec nonchalance la casquette que tu as en ce moment même sur la tête, et depuis tu ne doutes plus de ton goût.

Tu t'étales. Tes gestes sont fluides.

Tu marches avec allure. Tu es comblé. Ton anus se dilate bruyamment. Tu es le porte-parole de ton cul. À l'aide d'entonnoirs tu additionnes ta fiente au petit monticule de chair que tu appelles habituellement ta tête.

Ton visage s'affaisse doucement sous le poids atroce de ta merde et tu commences sérieusement à ressembler à une pie. Bien que tu portes des chaussures vernies.

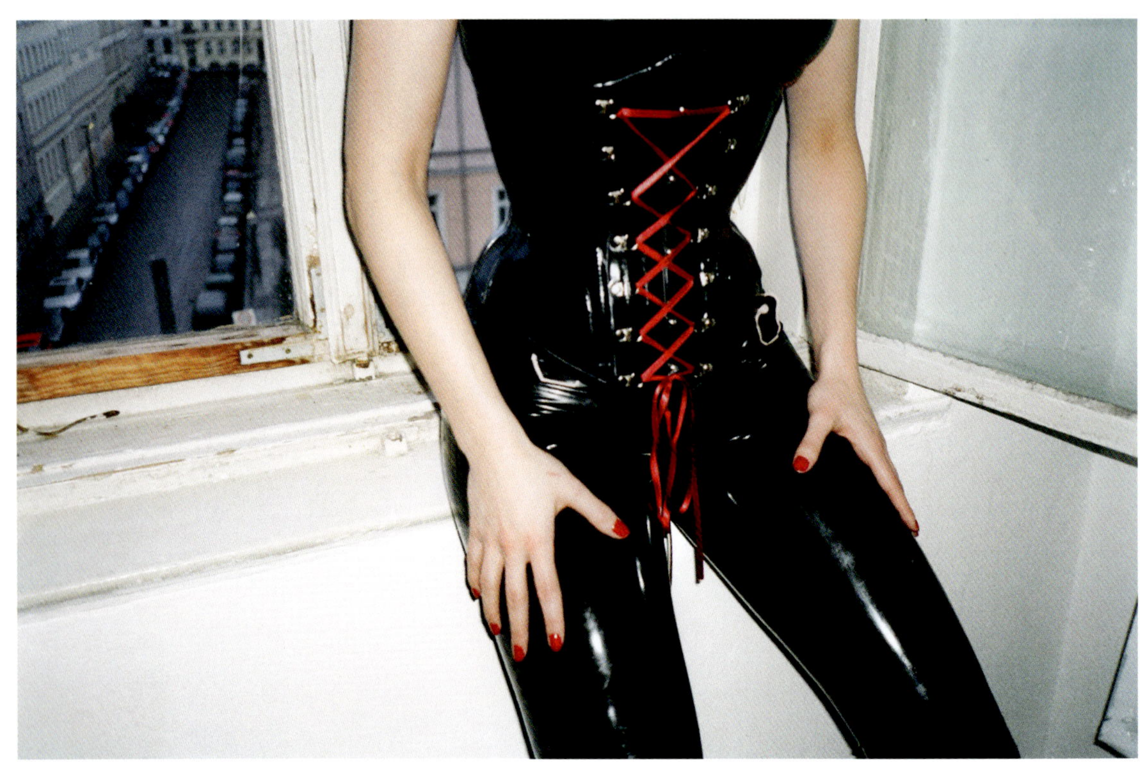

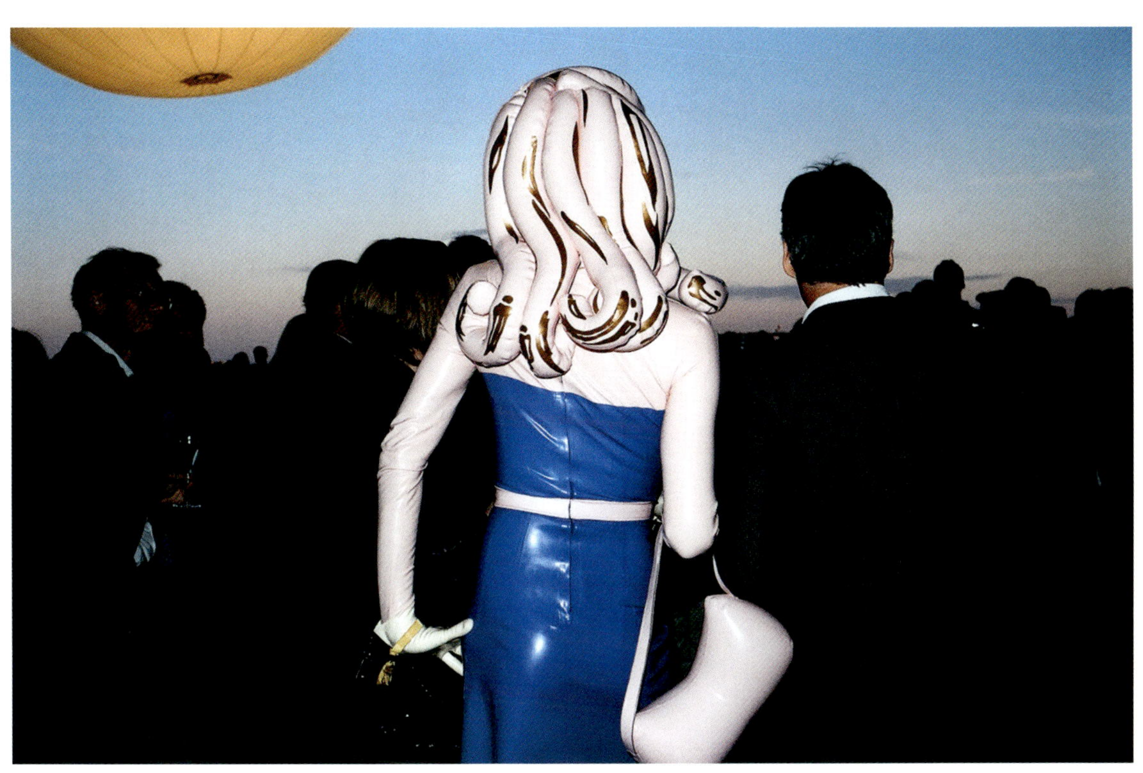

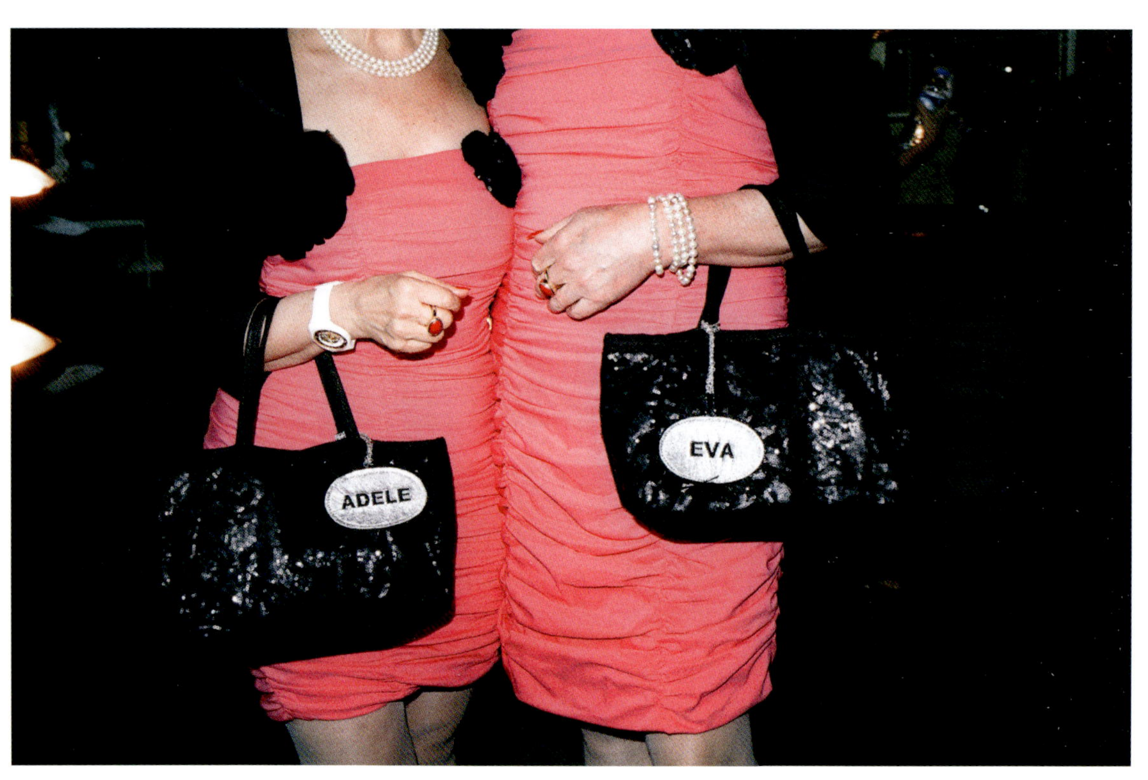
ADELE
EVA

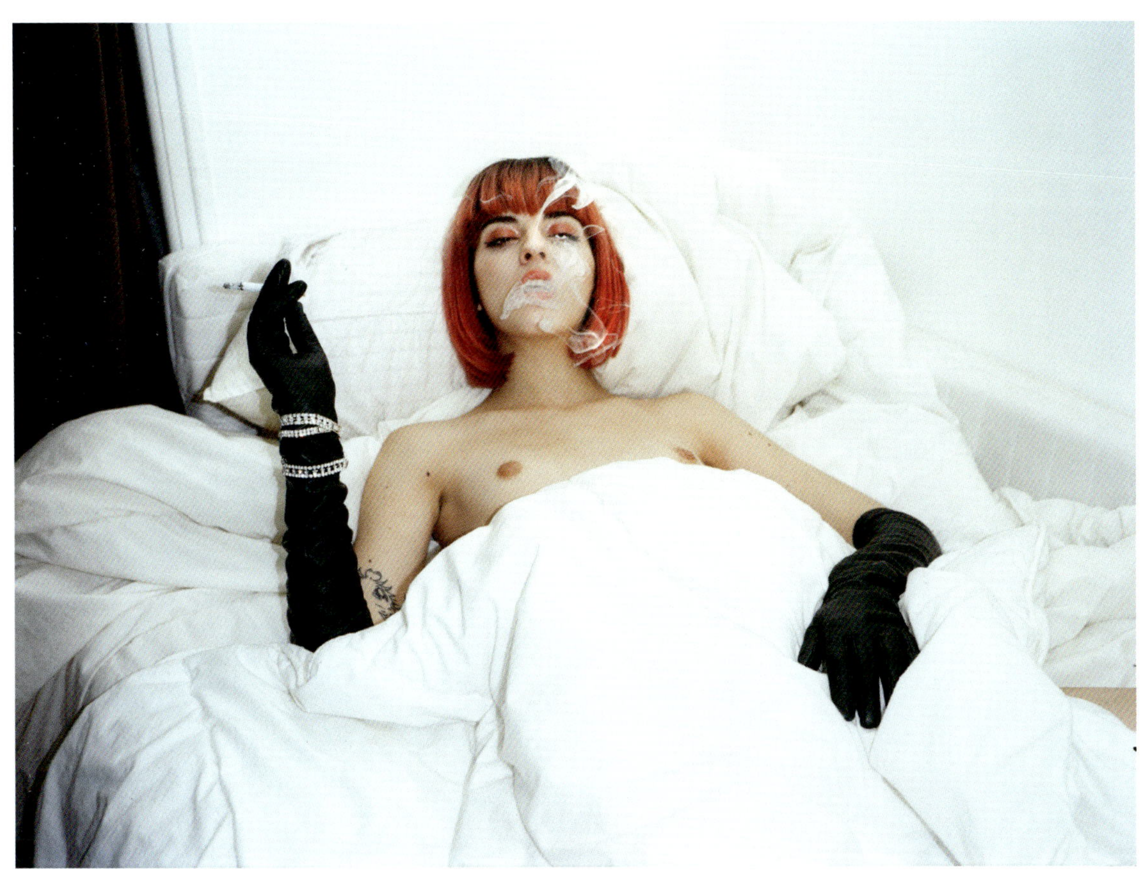

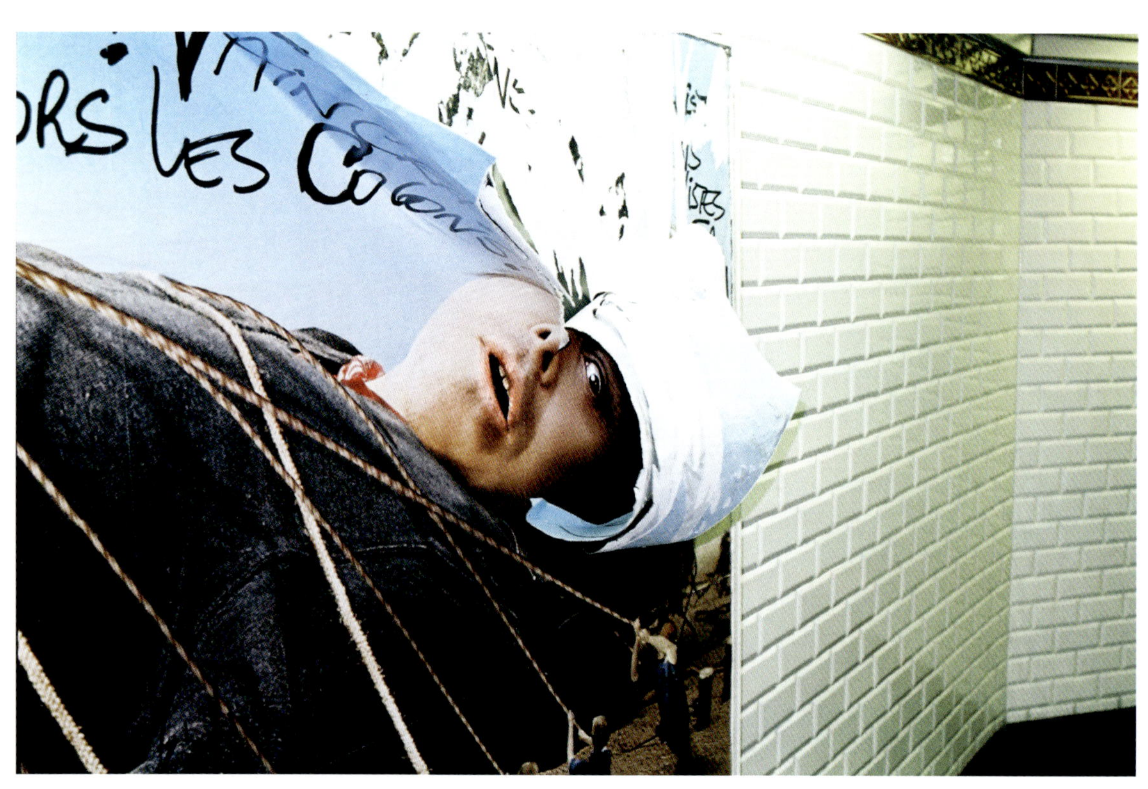

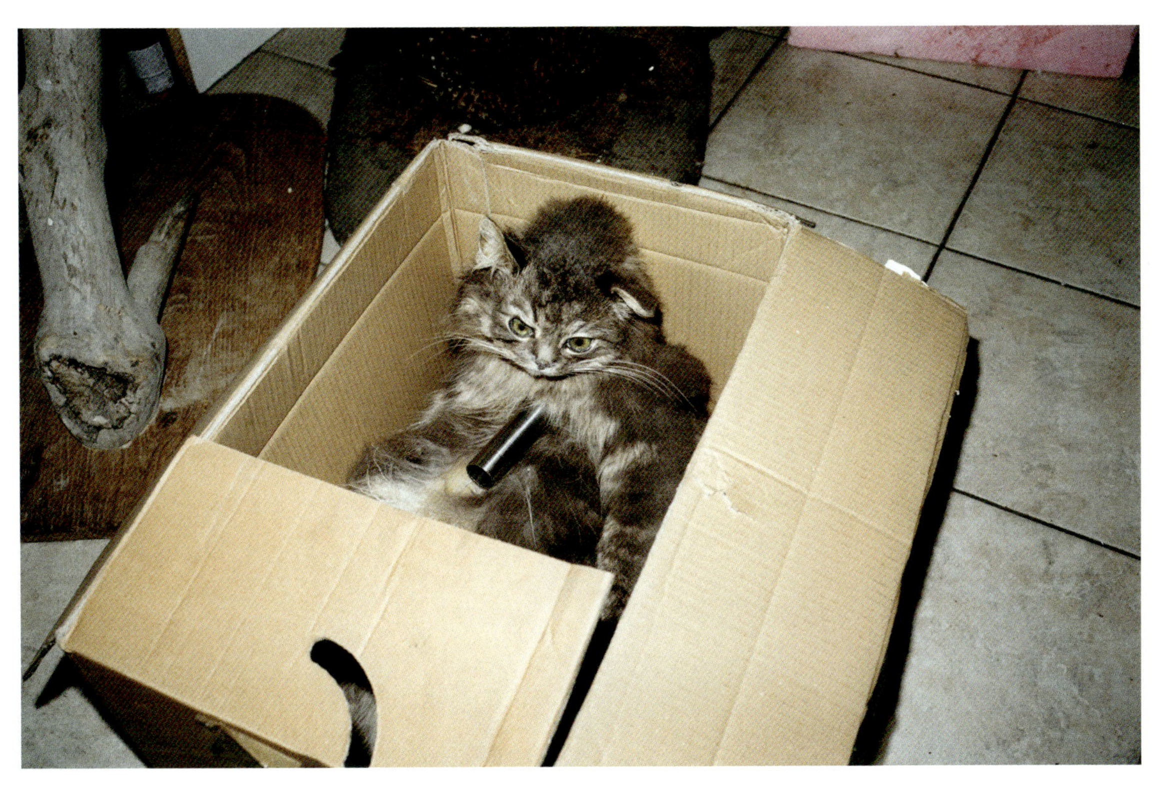

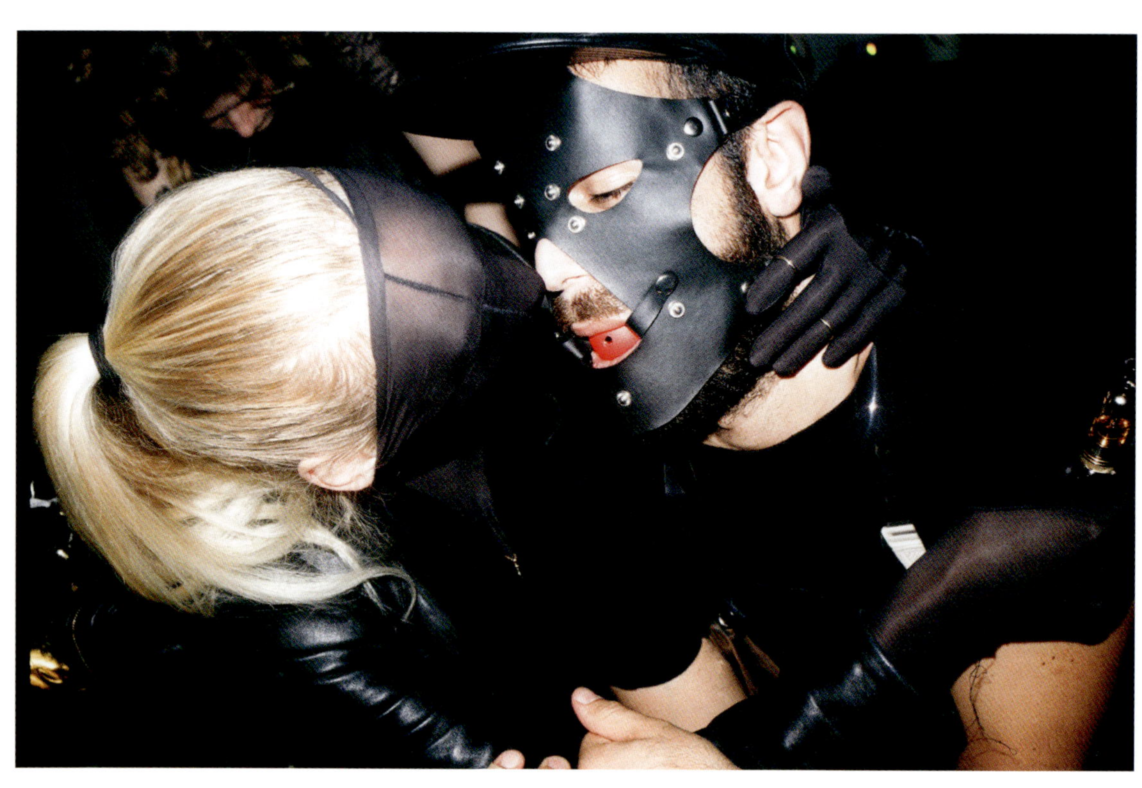

silent romance, Berlin, 2014

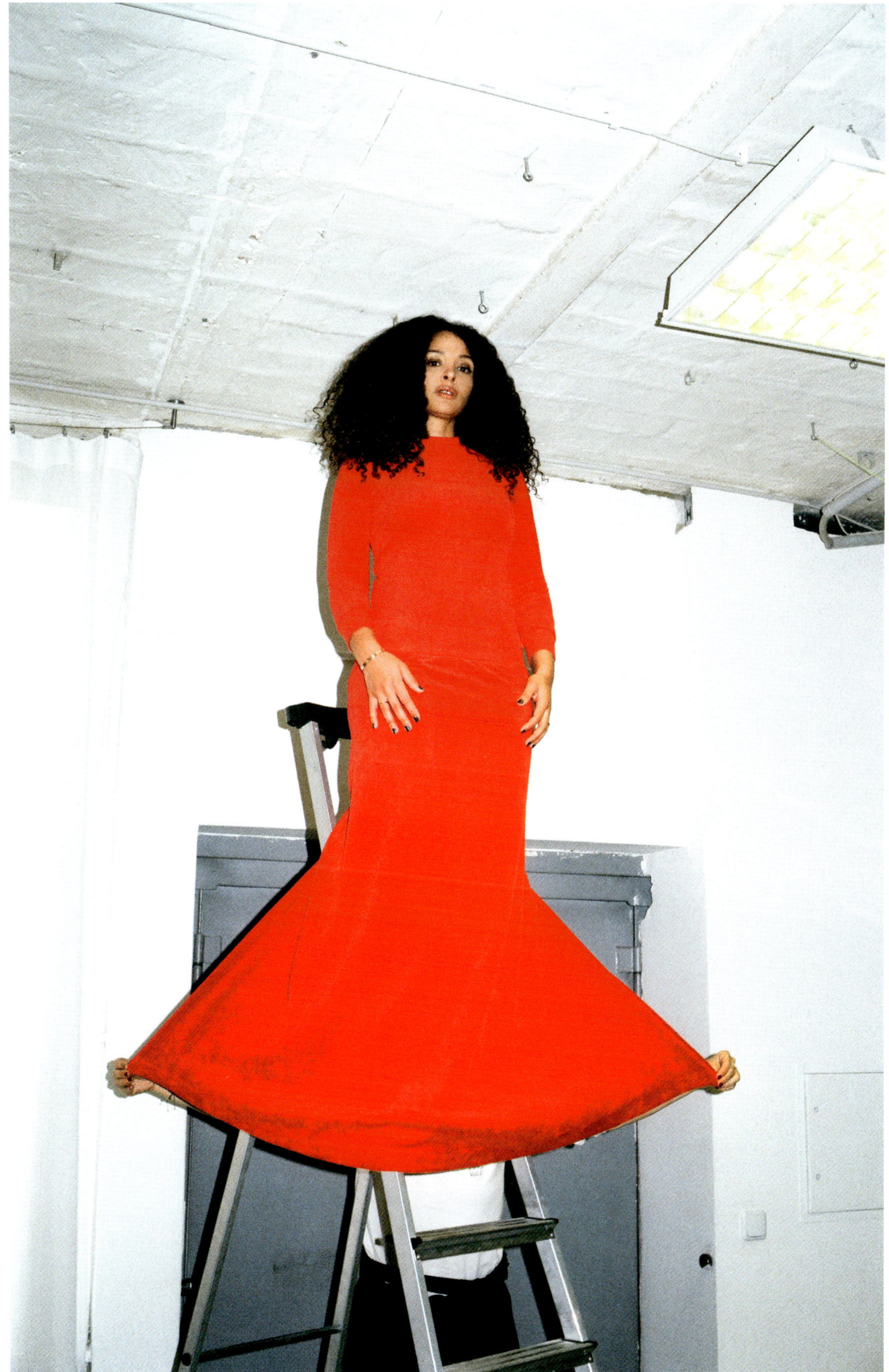

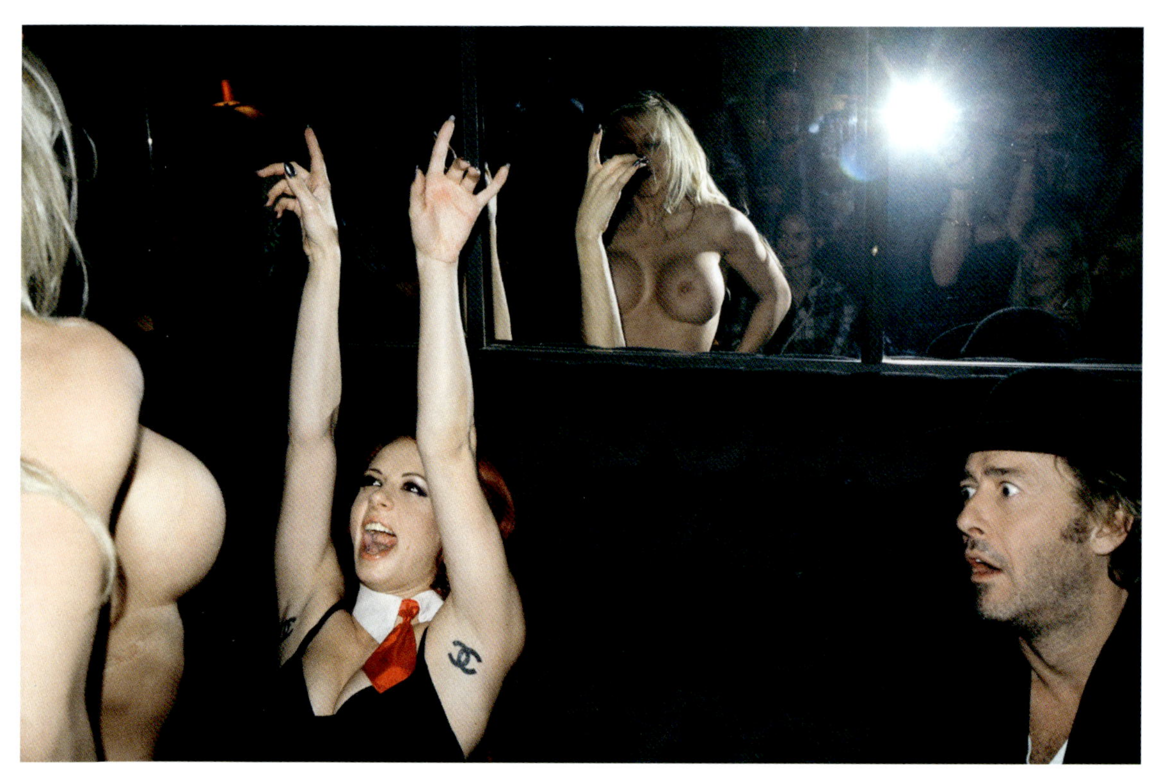

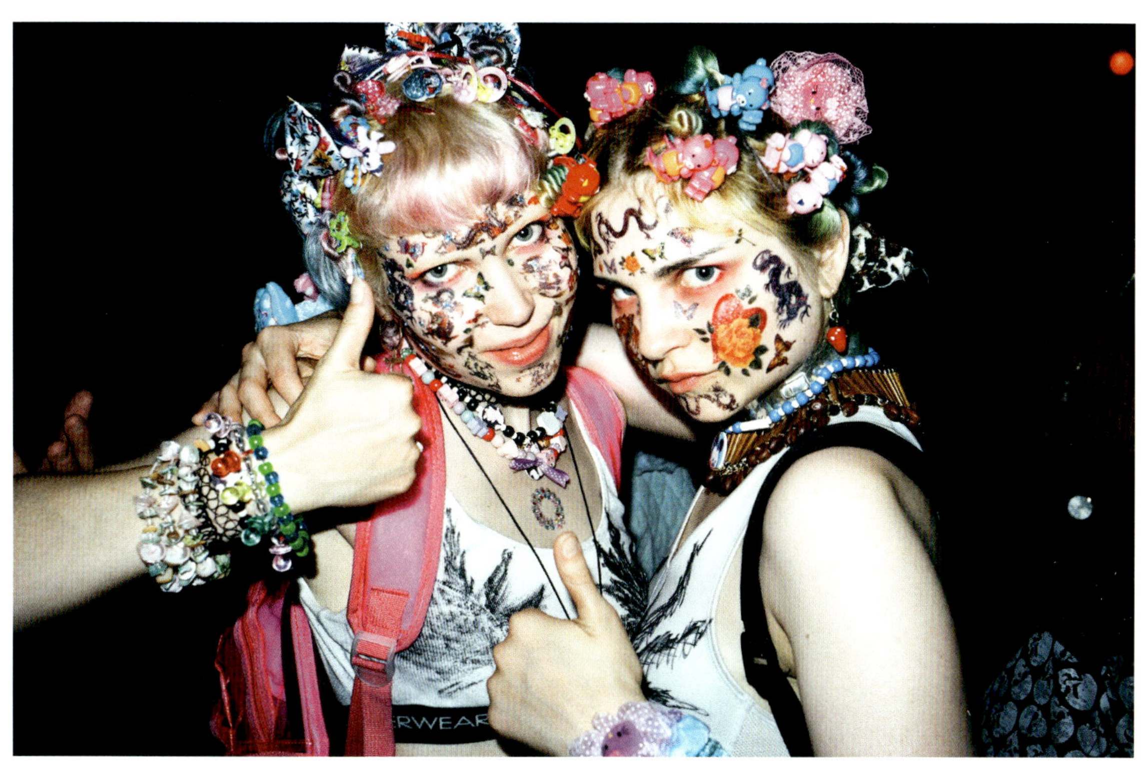

Index

009 — 046

Battles

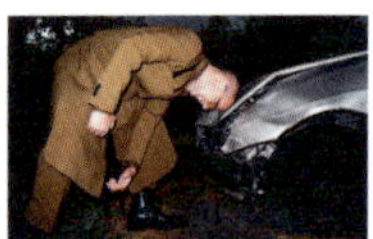

010. *Marc*
Berlin, 2017

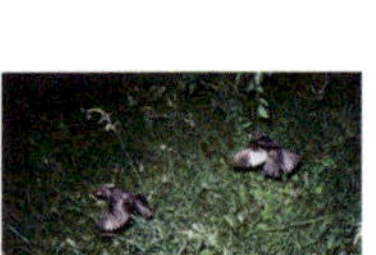

011. *birds fighting*
Berlin-Dahlem, 2014

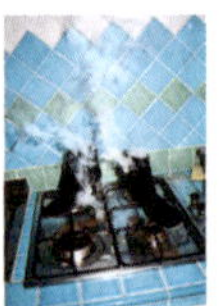

012. *warm afternoon*
Costa Paradiso, 2016

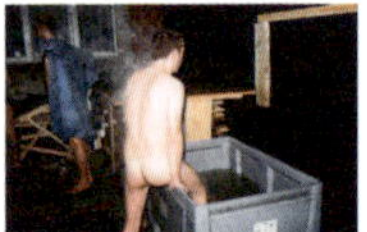

013. *winter ghosts*
Berlin-Weissensee, 2017

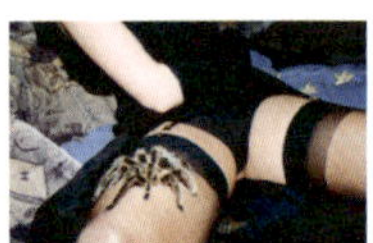

014. *first date*
Berlin-West, 2013

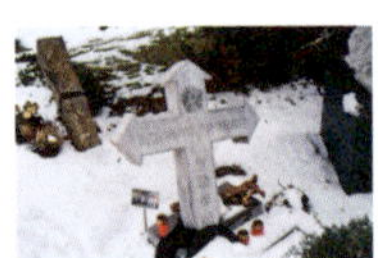

015. *it's time to fight*
Berlin, 2013

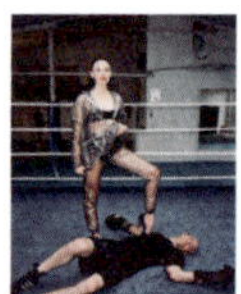

017. *love at first sight*
Berlin, 2016

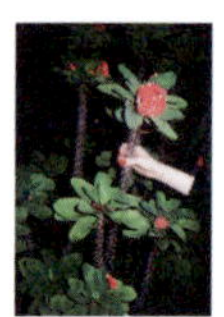

018. *dialogue de sourds*
Miami, 2015

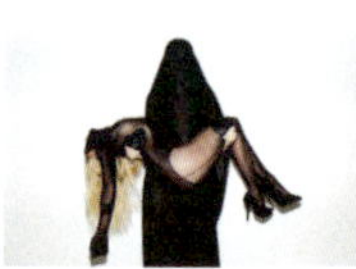

020. *la chute*
Berlin, 2012

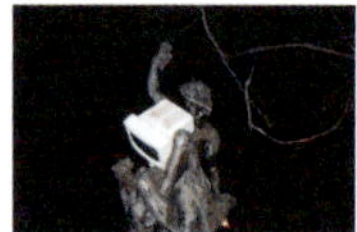

021. *battle*
Saint Etienne, 2013

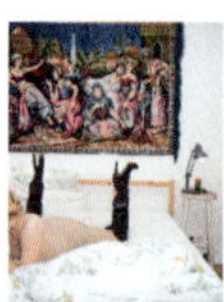

022. *tea time*
Berlin-Wedding, 2017

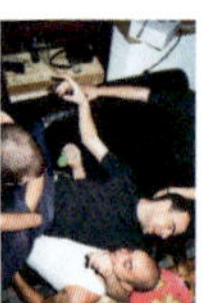

023. *golden ratio*
Marseille, 2015

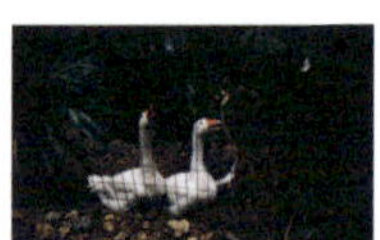

024. *opera*
Haute Provence, 2016

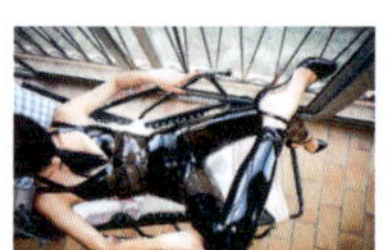

025. *sunbath*
Prades, 2016

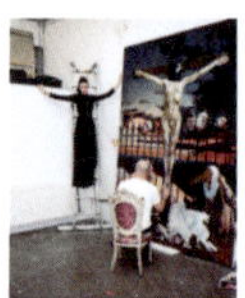

027. *crepuscule*
Berlin, 2016

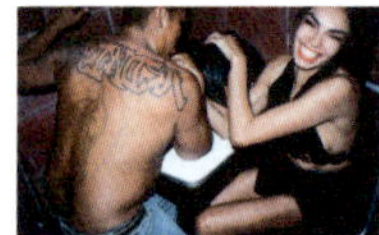

028. *heat wave*
Mexico, 2016

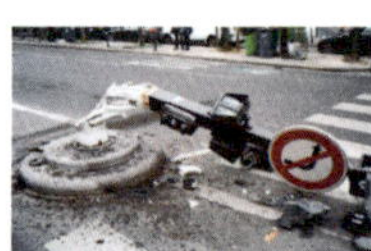

029. *wrong turn*
Paris, 2015

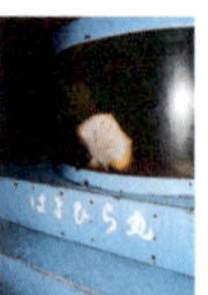

030. *take away*
Itō, 2014

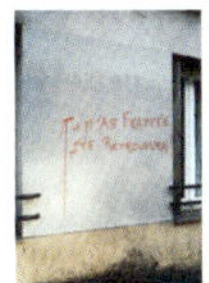
031. *promise*
Paris, 2015

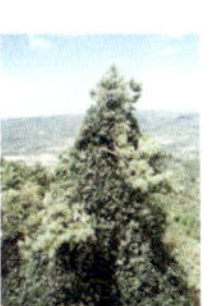
032. *l'arbre-montagne*
Provence, 2011

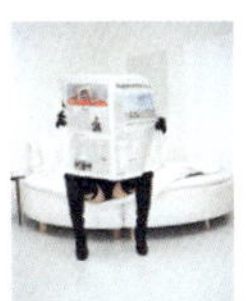
033. *zeitgeist*
Berlin, 2015

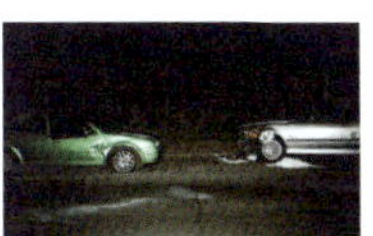
034. *dégradé de vert jusqu'à gris, métalisé*
Berlin, 2010

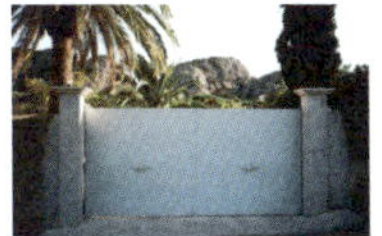
035. *paysage du sud*
Marseille, 2011

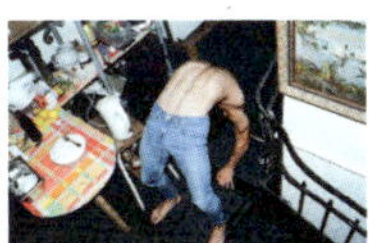
036. *swans in the staircase*
Berlin, 2014

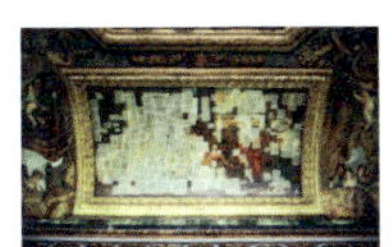
037. *pixelation*
Versaille, 2015

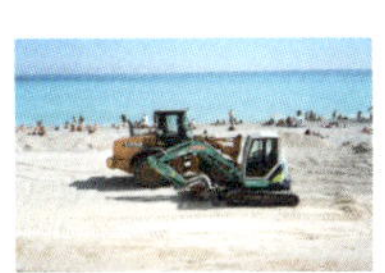
038. *beach*
Nice, 2010

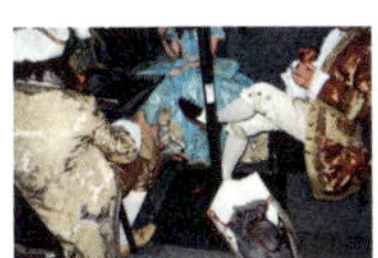
039. *lunch break*
Venice, 2015

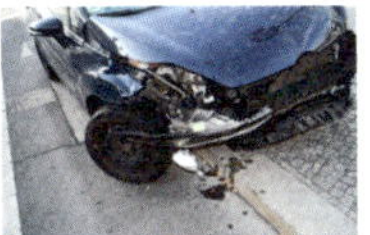
040. *disformed clouds*
Berlin, 2013

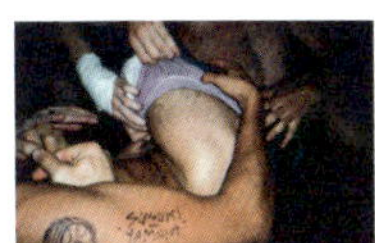
041. *ritual*
Condrieux, 2009

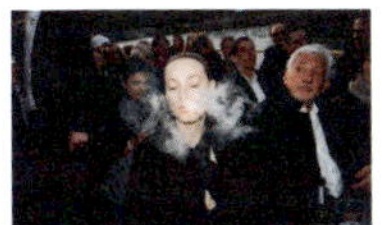
042. *Jen dans les nuages*
Berlin, 2016

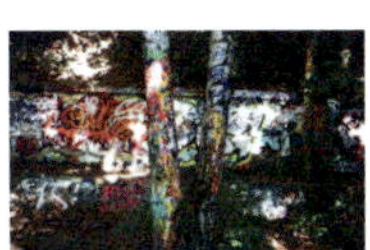
043. *graphittis*
Berlin-Schöneberg, 2013

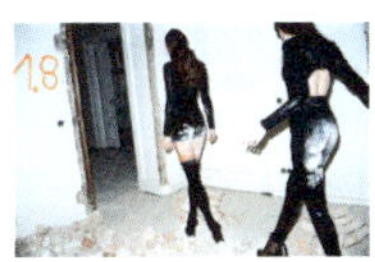

044. *dusty bench*
Berlin, 2014

047 — 082

The 3000 days before

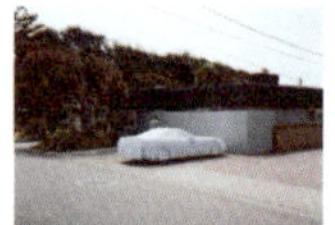
048. *the house of fun*
Morro Bay, 2012

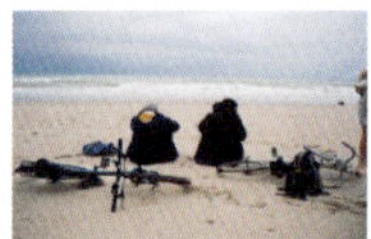
050. *en attendant la marée*
Varengeville-sur-Mer, 2012

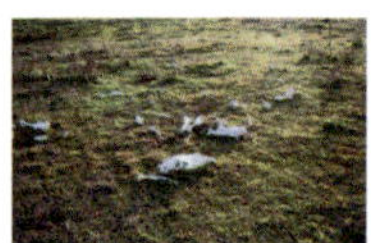
051. *wild horses in the sky*
Andalusia, 2017

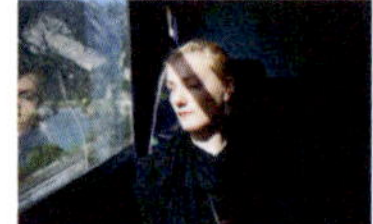
052. *Jen as her own sundial, stopping time in the train*
Provence, 2010

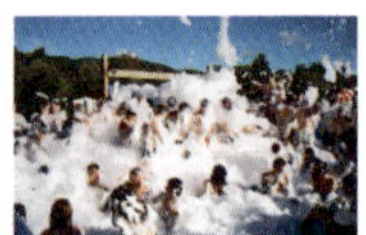
053. *cloudy afternoon*
Volonne, 2016

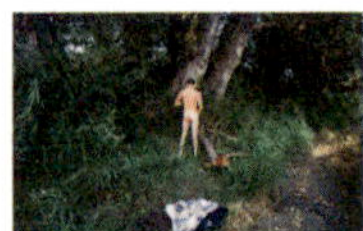
054. *Fred à poil au bord du Rhône,* 2009

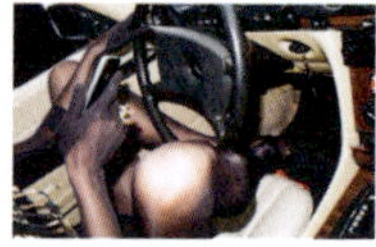
055. *soft ride*
Brandenburg, 2013

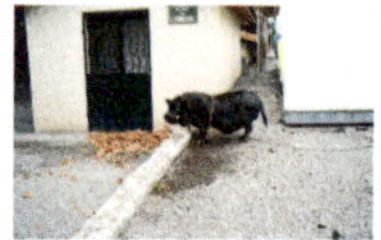
056. *mirror*
Haute-Provence, 2014

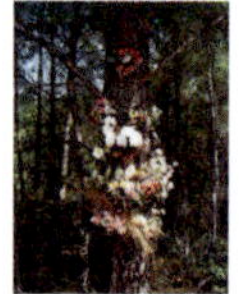
057. *birth of a tree*
2011

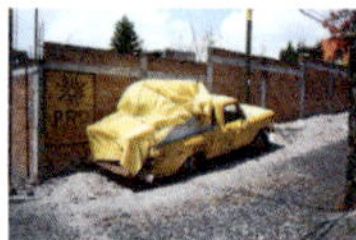
058. *nap*
Mexico, 2016

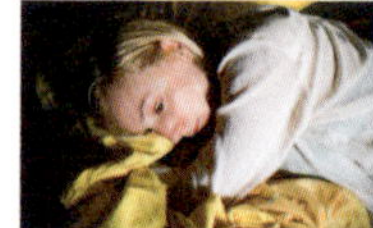
059. *Jen froissée dans les draps jaune*
San Miguel, 2011

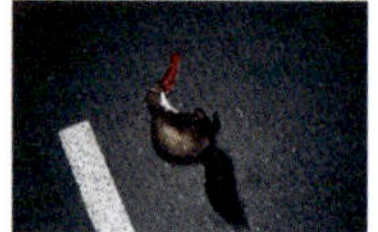
060. *insomnia*
Malijai, 2010

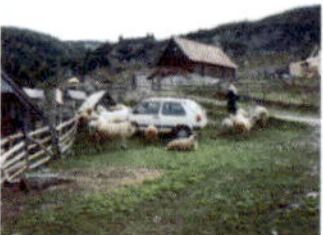
061. *drive-in*
Prokoško, 2015

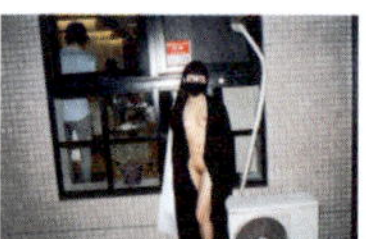
062. *armor*
Tokyo, 2014

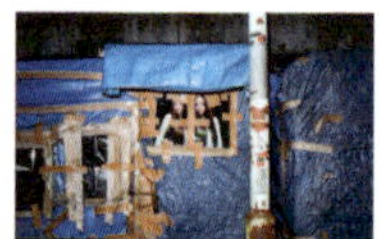
063. *twins under the bridge*
Tokyo, 2014

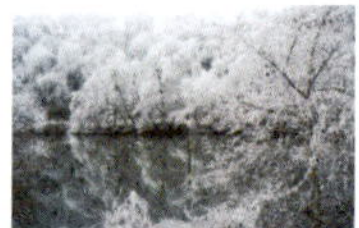
064. *crystals*
Andouillé, 2017

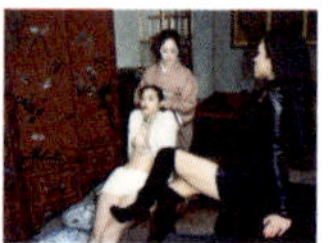
065. *family affairs*
Tokyo, 2014

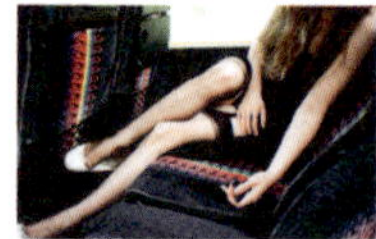
066. *soft journey,*
Provence, 2009

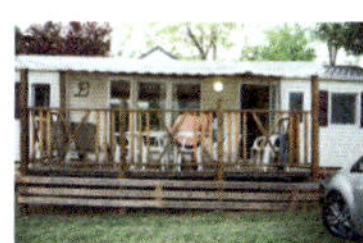
067. *pleine lune*
Volonne, 2012

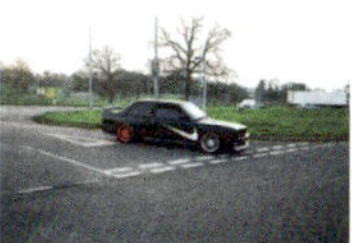
068. *road to Manchester*
2015

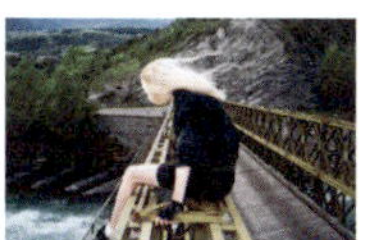
069. *Jen on a bridge*
Embrun, 2013

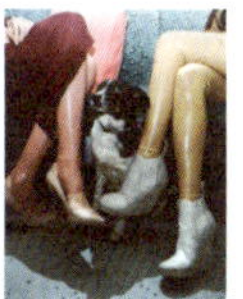
070. *dog with pearl eyes*
Berlin, 2012

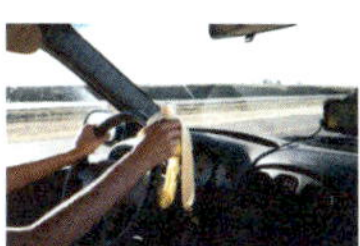
071. *slow highway*
Sunburst, MT, 2012

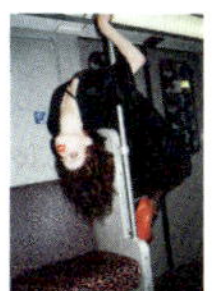
072. *Lily in the U-Bahn*
Berlin, 2015

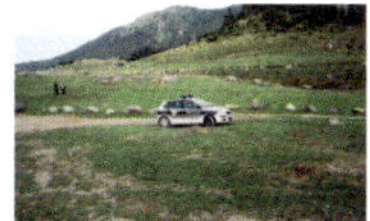
073. *mystery lake*
Bosnia and
Herzegovina, 2015

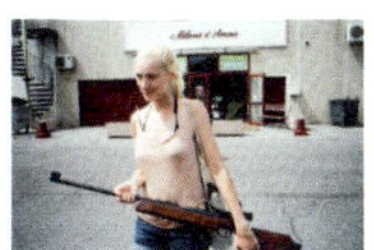
074. *Jen killing time*
Digne, 2011

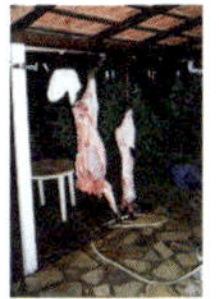
075. *clothesline at the neighbors*
Volonne, 2013

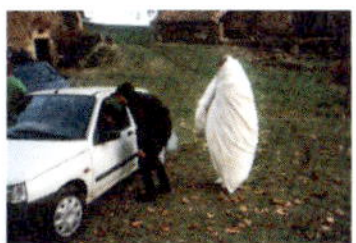
076. *apparition*
Ardèche, 2009

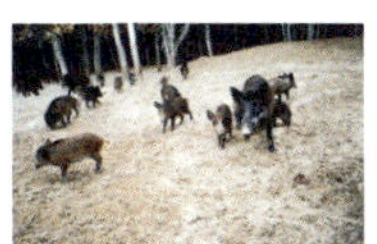
078. *summer camp*
Haute-Provence, 2016

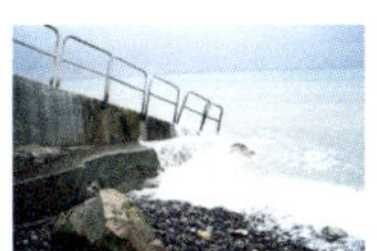
079. *hug*
Normandy, 2012

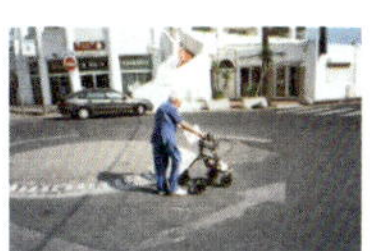
080. *shortcuts*
Poussan, 2016

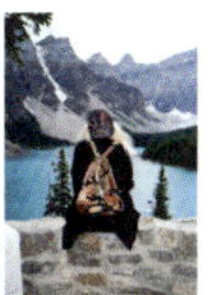
081. *flat lake*
Banff, 2012

083 — 122

Des après-midi à la fenêtre

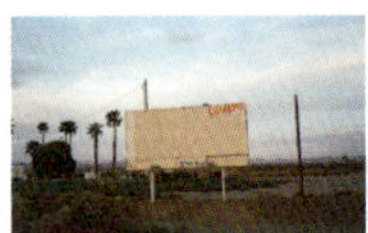
084. *self-titled*
CA, 2012

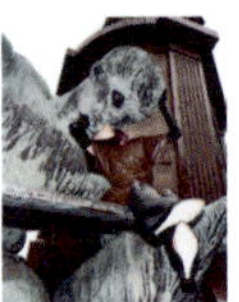
085. *bronze's tenderness*
Berlin, 2012

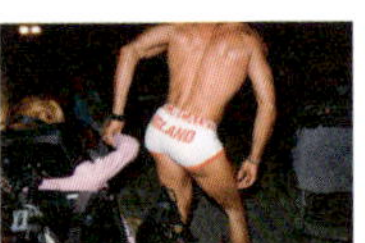
086. *party time*
Peipin, 2013

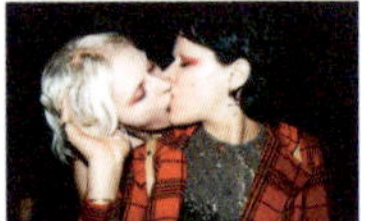
087. *red shadows*
Ibiza, 2015

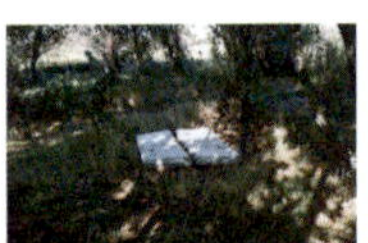
088. *king size*
Montpellier, 2010

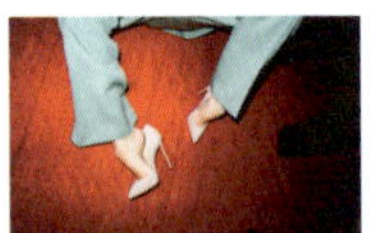
089. *burning bridges*
Berlin, 2016

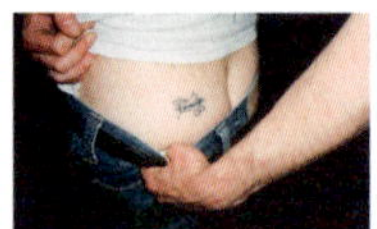
090. *Benjo et regrets*
Saint Etienne, 2009

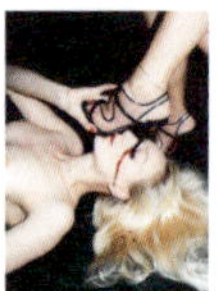
092. *first love*
Berlin, 2014

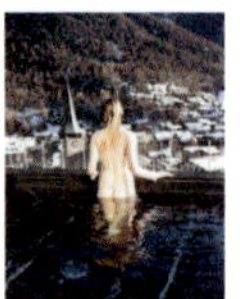
093. *winter siren*
Zermatt, 2016

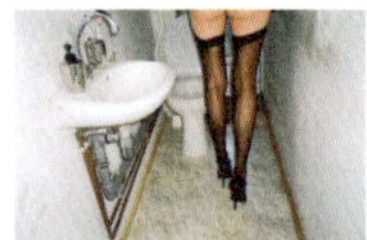
094. *parallelism*
2009

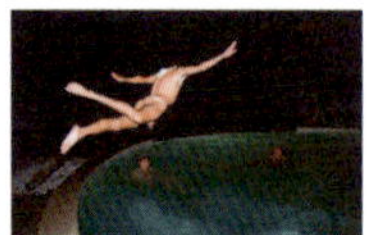
095. *infinity jump*
Haute Provence, 2013

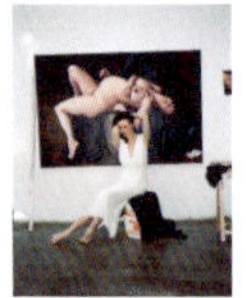
096. *Celyn*
Berlin-Weissensee, 2014

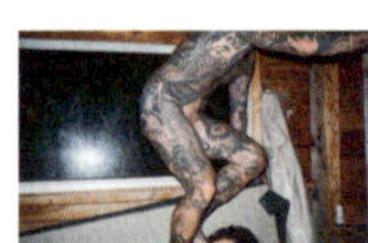
097. *twerk*
Haute-Provence, 2013

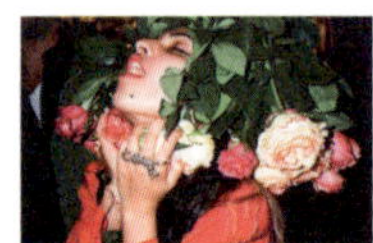
098. *Ameena and flowers*
Berlin, 2011

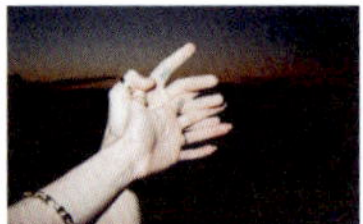
099. *wishes*
Volonne, 2016

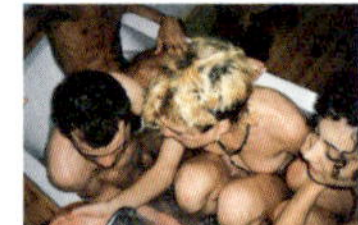
100. *baptizing*
Berlin, 2009

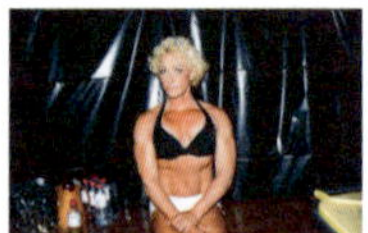
101. *Beate*
Berlin, 2013

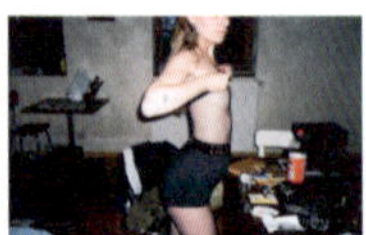
102. *VV*
Saint Etienne, 2009

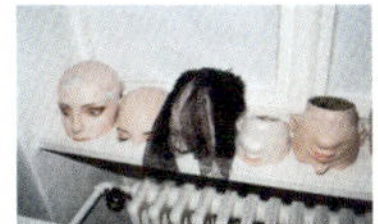

103. *half-bride*
Berlin, 2013

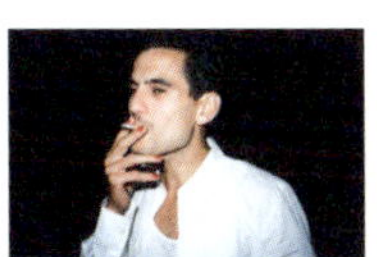

104. *Jon*
Haute-Provence, 2013

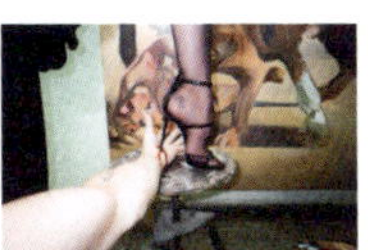

105. *love letter*
Berlin, 2016

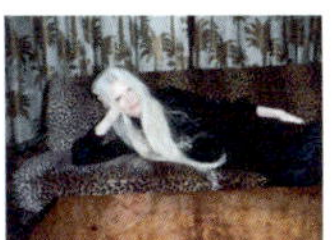

106. *Kristen*
Miami, 2016

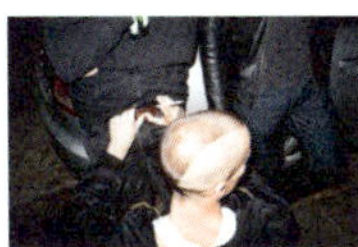

107. *initiatives*
Paris, 2016

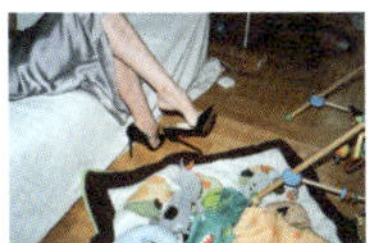

108. *rattles*
Berlin, 2013

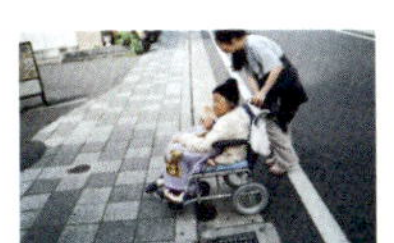

109. *glances lengths*
Kyoto, 2014

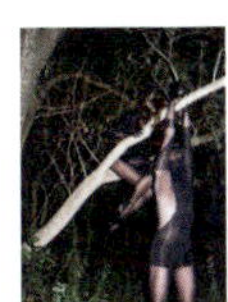

110. *treehouse*
Los Masos, 2016

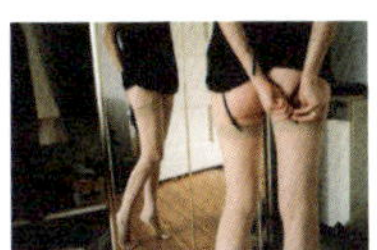

111. *mornings with Jen*
Berlin, 2011

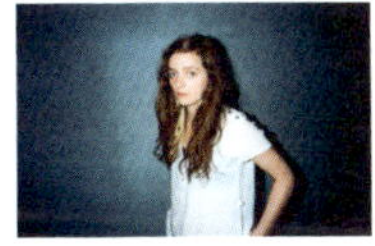

112. *Camille sur fond bleu*
Berlin, 2008

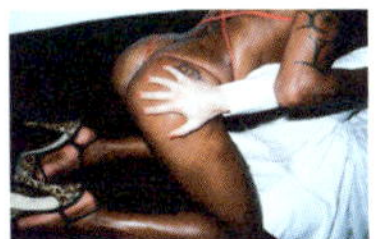

113. *apéritif*
Ibiza, 2014

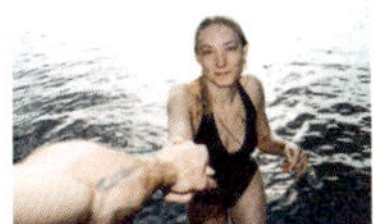

114. *Jen, starting to get cold*
Berlin-Tegel, 2014

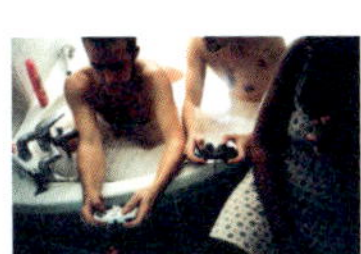

116. *mornings*
St Etienne, 2008

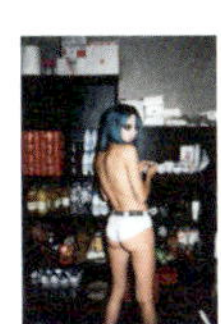

117. *Sita*
Paris, 2015

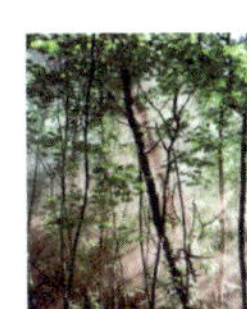

118. *fog*
Berlin, 2016

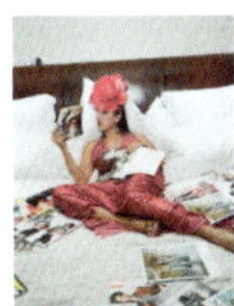

119. *Rossy*
Berlin, 2012

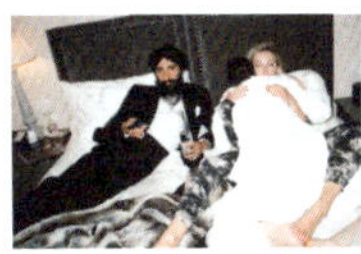

120. *bedtime stories*
Gstaad, 2015

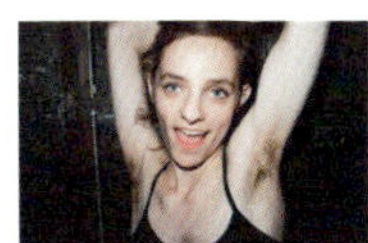

121. *Camille 4 ans après, au local*, Lyon, 2013

Marble bench

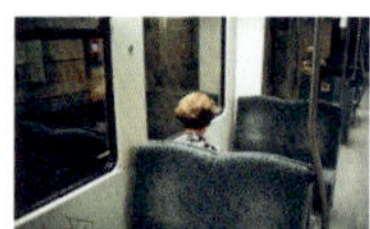
124. *les absents*
Berlin, 2014

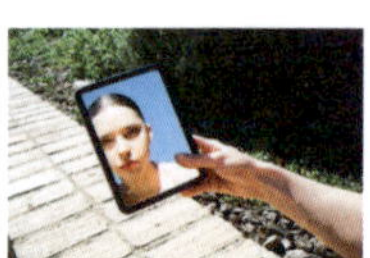
125. *Venus*
Andalusia, 2017

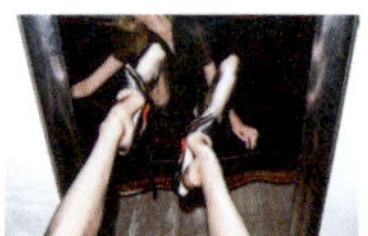
126. *nylon trap*
Berlin, 2017

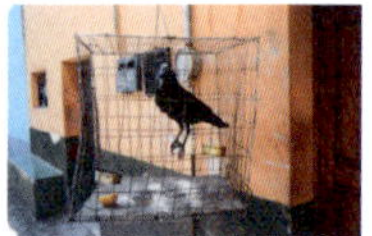
127. *the triumph of vanity*
Mexico, 2016

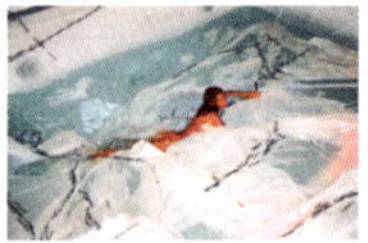
128. *Maya*
Paris, 2016

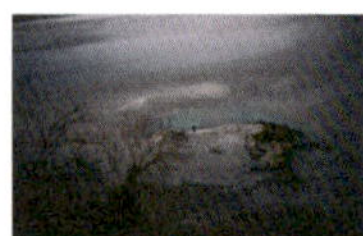
129. *Charlie's mourning*
Mont Saint-Michel, 2017

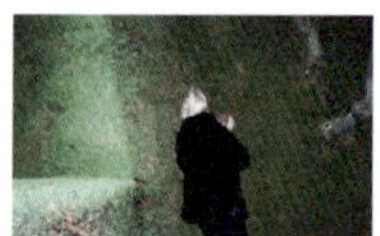
130. *free fall*
Roquebrune, 2013

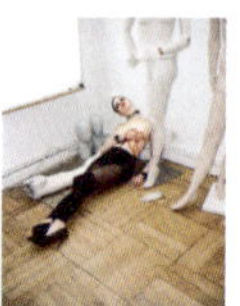
131. *peine de coeur*
Berlin, 2015

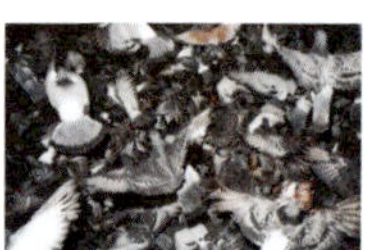
132. *distorting mirror*
Paris, 2015

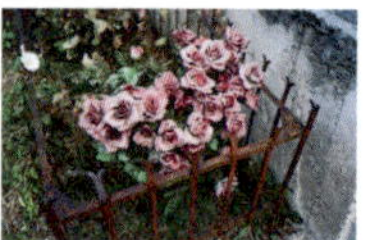
133. *roses, impression céramique*
2009

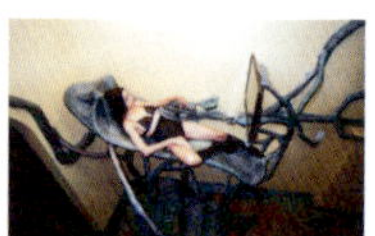
134. *tenacious claws*
Mexico, 2016

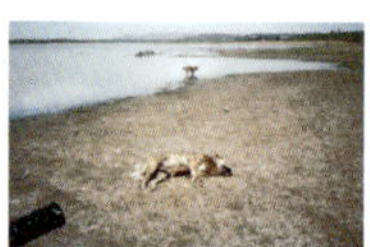
135. *dead and living dogs*
San Miguel, 2012

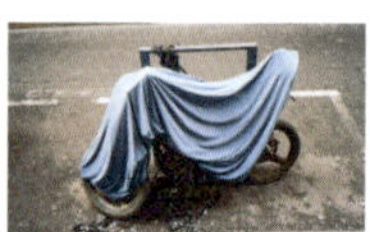
136. *mob*
Saint Etienne, 2009

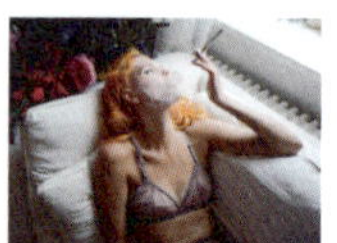
137. *Bonnie, ailleurs*
Berlin, 2012

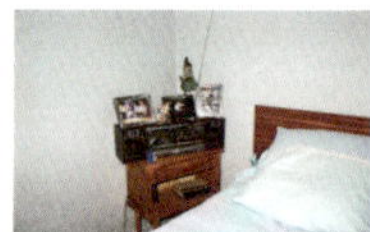
138. *9pm at grandma's, before they demolished the house*
Venissieux, 2012

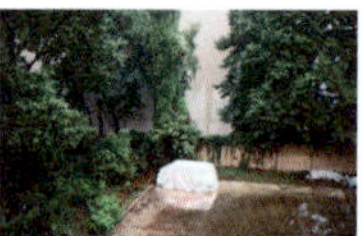
139. *camion et son spectre sous la pluie*
Berlin, 2011

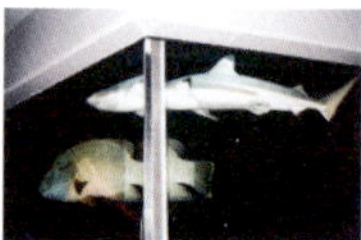
140. *cleavages*
Berlin, 2015

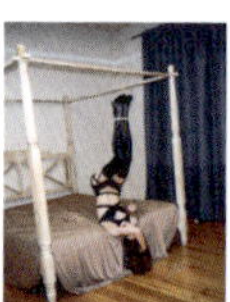
141. *home alone*
Berlin, 2016

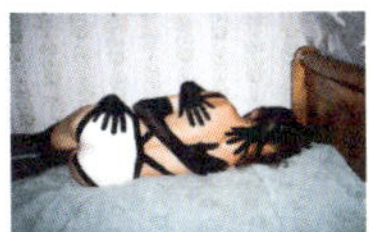

142. *lonely nights*
Prades, 2016

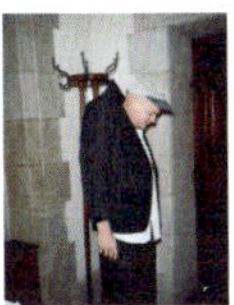

144. *break*
Kronberg, 2015

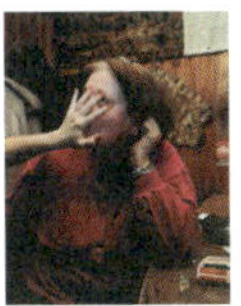

145. *stare*
Berlin-West, 2013

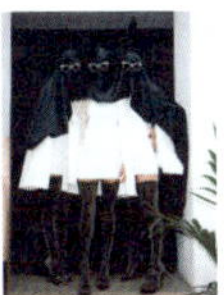

146. *singular plural*
Berlin, 2016

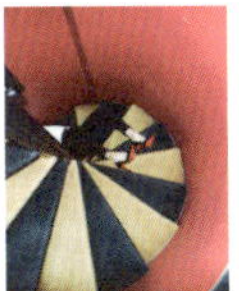

147. *chess*
Paris, 2015

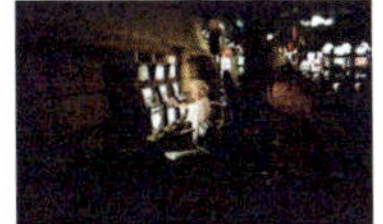

148. *the bright light*
Vegas, 2012

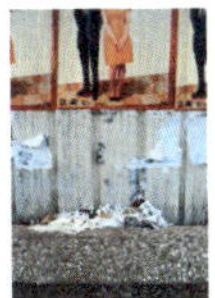

149. *couple*
Villeurbanne, 2013

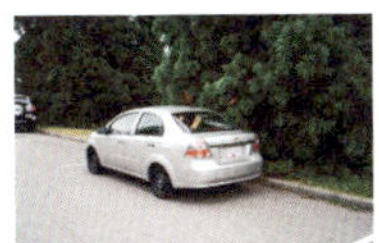

150. *parking*
Vancouver, 2012

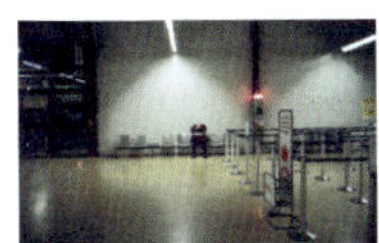

151. *last call*
Berlin, 2015

153 — 188

Reveries

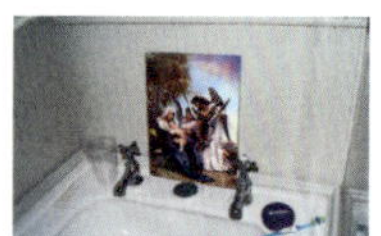

154. *morning sonata*
Berlin, 2014

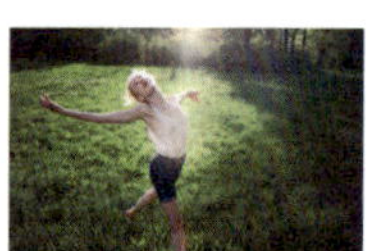

155. *Helga dancing*
Potsdam, 2009

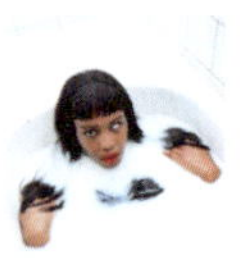

156. *Valerie*
Berlin, 2015

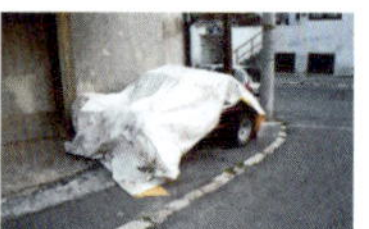

158. *silent horses*
Sarajevo, 2015

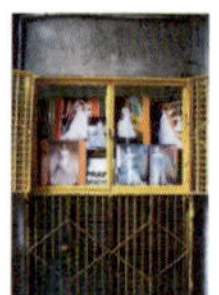

159. *fantasies*
Łódź, 2013

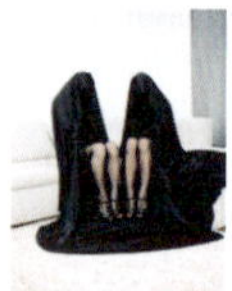

160. *trou noir*
Berlin, 2014

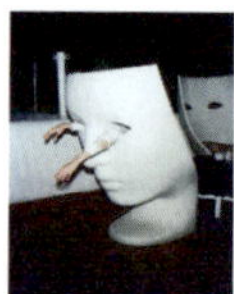

161. *deep glance*
Ibiza, 2013

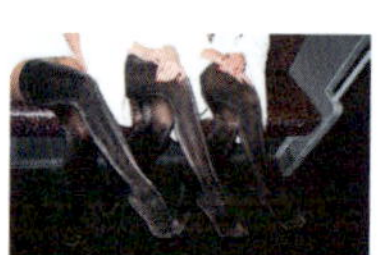

162. *milky way*
Berlin, 2016

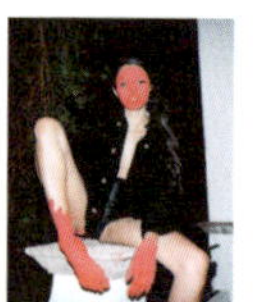

164. *full moon*
Mexico, 2016

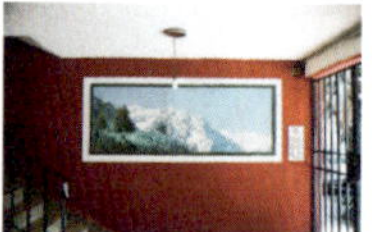

165. *glacier*
Mexico City, 2016

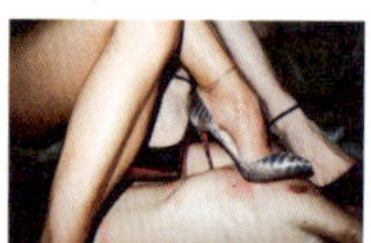

166. *acupuncture*
Berlin, 2014

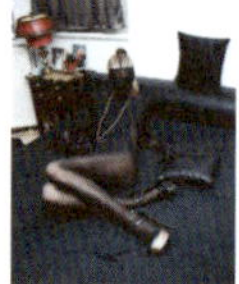

167. *Merle*
Berlin, 2012

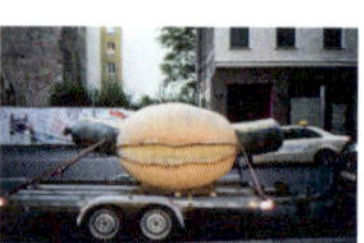

168. *food delivery*
Berlin, 2011

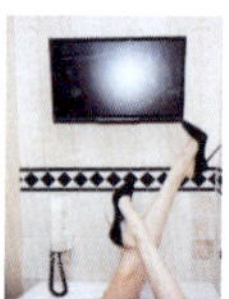

169. *mise en abîme*
Gstaad, 2014

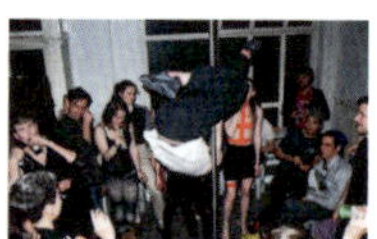

170. *south pole*
Berlin-Neukölln, 2012

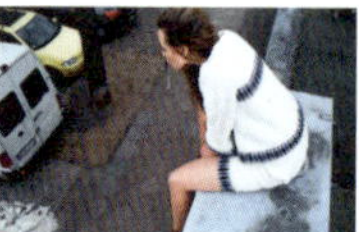

171. *Celyn*
Berlin-Wedding, 2013

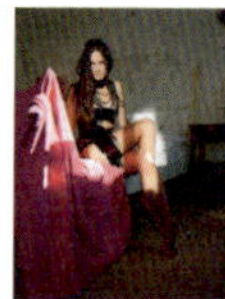

172. *Filppa on her bed*
Berlin, 2013

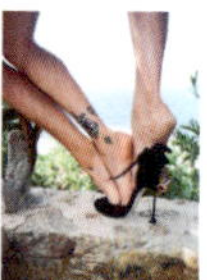

173. *Cinderellas*
Costa Paradiso, 2016

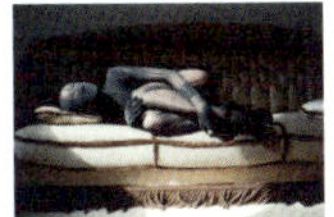
174. *twilight trap*
2012

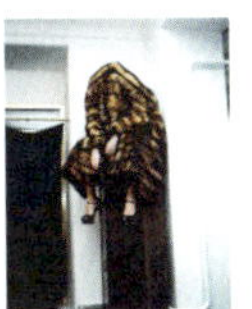
175. *Tracy and fur on the shelf*
Berlin, 2014

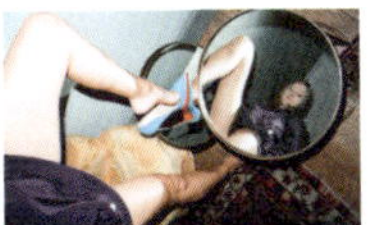
176. *Kim*
Berlin, 2016

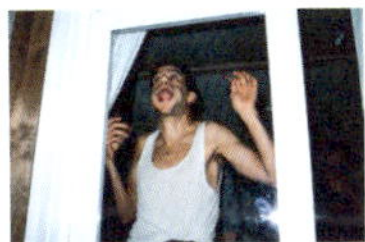
177. *aquarium*
Volonne, 2013

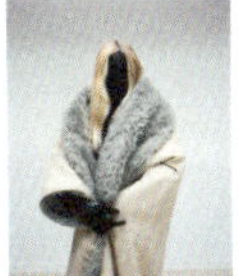
178. *the broken muse*
2012

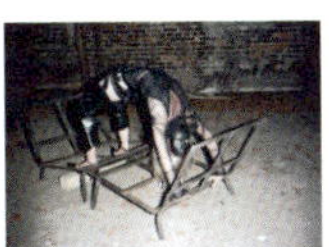
179. *unpractical chairs*
Berlin, 2016

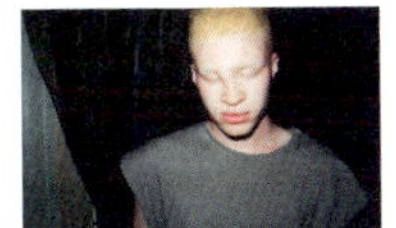
180. *Shaun*
Paris, 2016

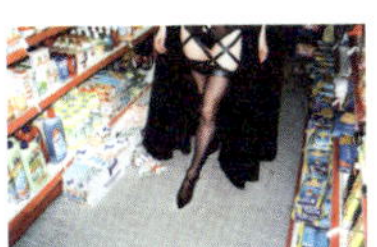
181. *night shopping*
Berlin, 2015

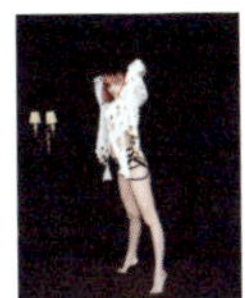
182. *Sita burning*
Paris, 2016

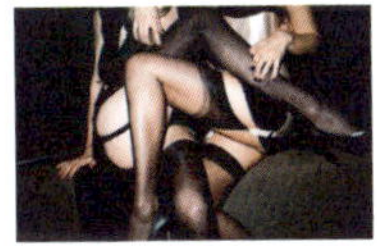
183. *nylon gradient*
Berlin, 2012

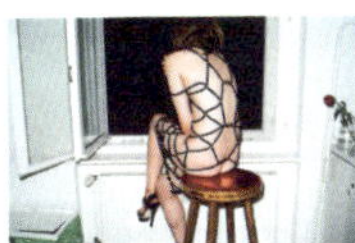
184. *roses*
Berlin, 2014

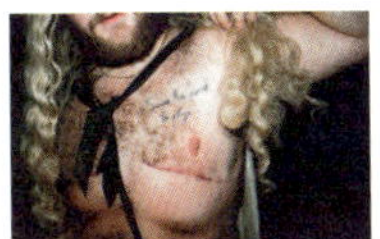
185. *sous les pavés*
Berlin, 2012

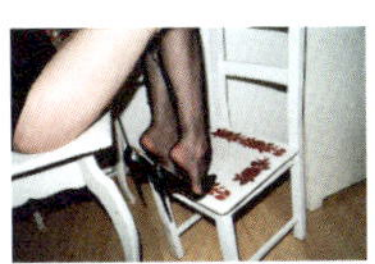
186. *demi-pointes*
Berlin, 2015

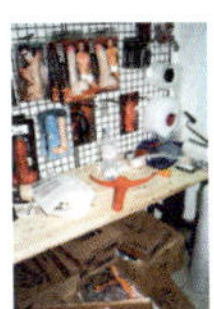
187. *packing*
Paris, 2015

189 — 220

Le sordide et le sublime

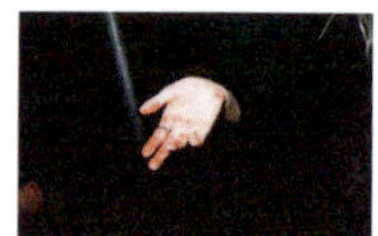
190. *sharp nights*
Berlin, 2017

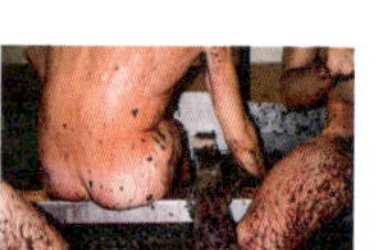
191. *le cul dans le raisin*
Condrieux, 2009

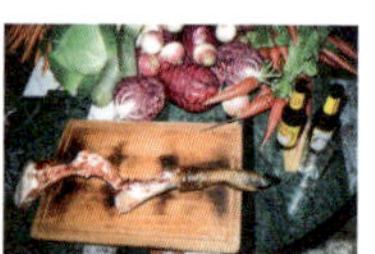
192. *marble palette*
Berlin, 2016

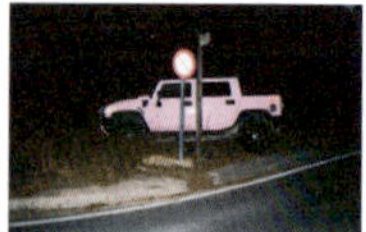
193. *anarchy*
Ibiza, 2013

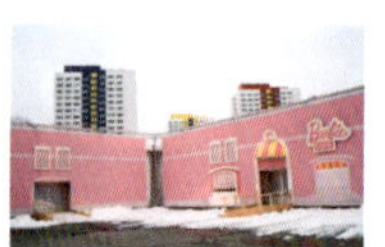
194. *"the dreamhouse experience"*
Berlin, 2013

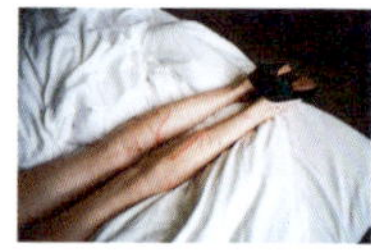
195. *nuit blanche*
Stockholm, 2015

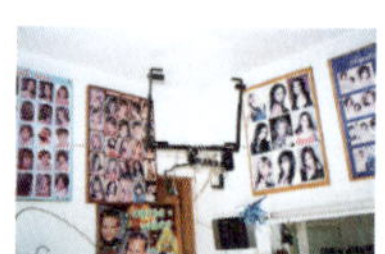
196. *concurrence*
Mexico, 2016

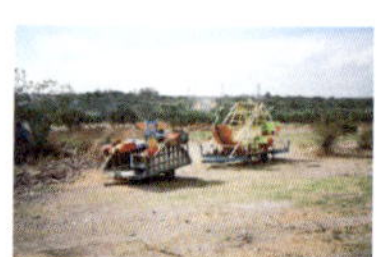
197. *retired dreams*
Mexico, 2016

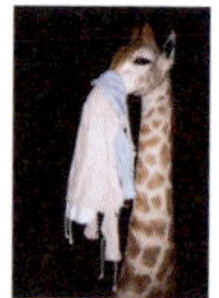
198. *sniffles*
Paris, 2015

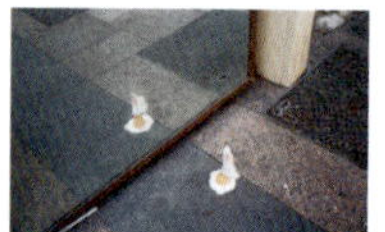
199. *cone dressing up*
Cannes, 2013

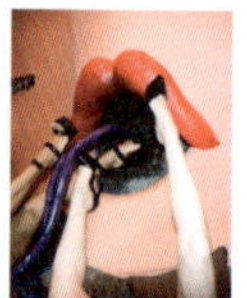
200. *gourmet ogress*
Mexico, 2016

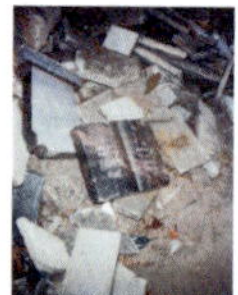
201. *unpaid rents*
Berlin, 2015

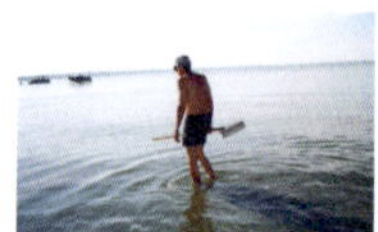
202. *infinite garden*
Ma-me-mo Beach, AB, 2012

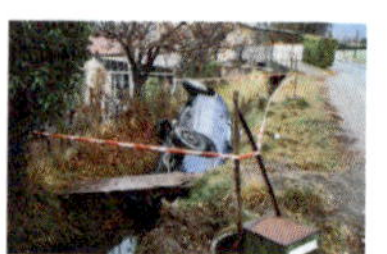
203. *untitled, one year later*
2014

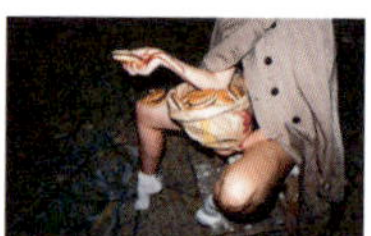
204. *aftertaste*
Berlin, 2016

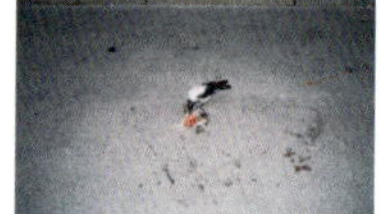
205. *raven's lunch*
Berlin, 2014

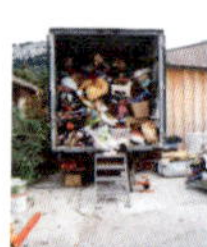
206. *broken dreams*
Marseille, 2015

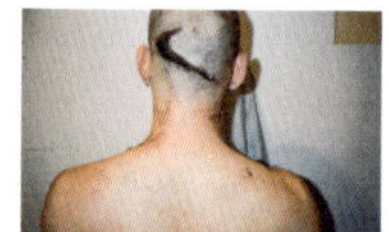
207. *Fred*
Berlin-Neukölln, 2008

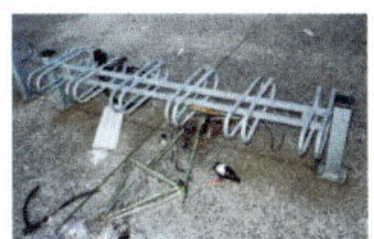

208. *skeleton*
Villeurbanne, 2013

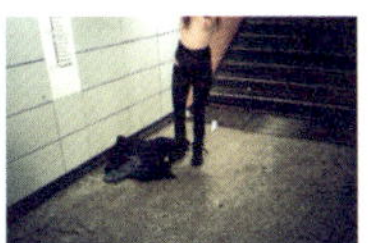

209. *Camille dans U-Bahn*
Berlin, 2008

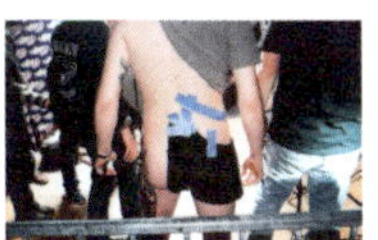

210. *universal tape*
Paris, 2015

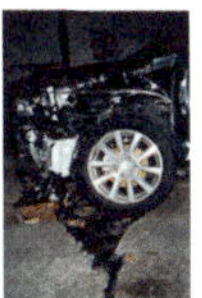

211. *slimy feeling*
Gowanus, 2014

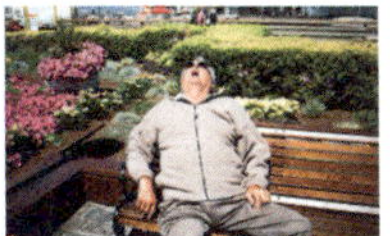

212. *gobeur de mouche*
San Fransisco, 2012

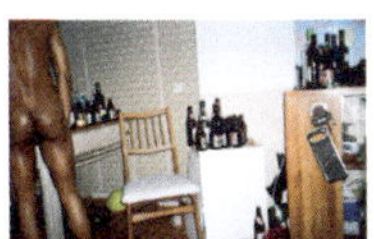

213. *Forsterstrasse*
Berlin, 2008

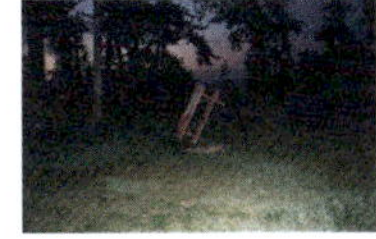

214. *sunset*
Ma-me-mo Beach, AB, 2012

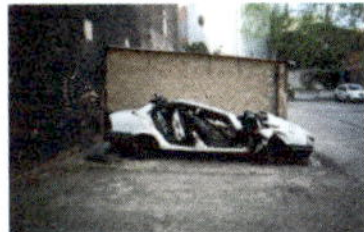

215. *around the corner*
Berlin, 2010

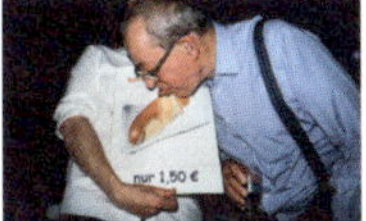

216. *Könige*
Berlin, 2017

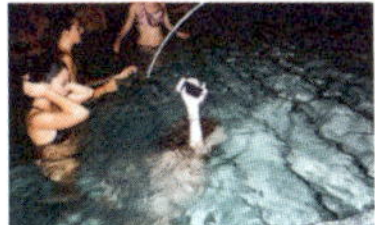

219. *shipwreck*
Miami, 2015

221 — 256

Blue tears

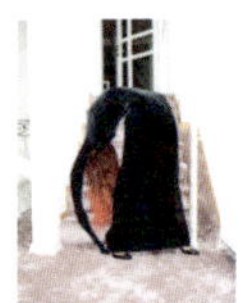

222. *velvet loop*
Berlin, 2017

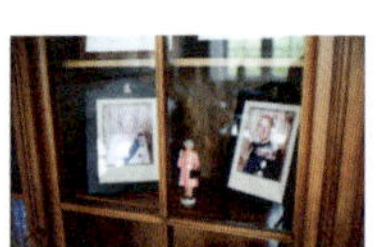

224. *Queen Elizabeth*
Berlin, 2016

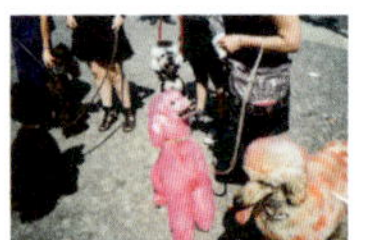

225. *a man's best friend*
Berlin, 2011

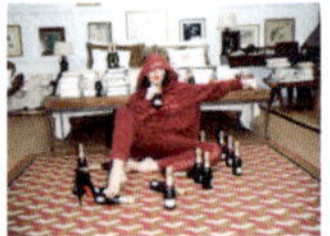

226. *homework*
Berlin, 2016

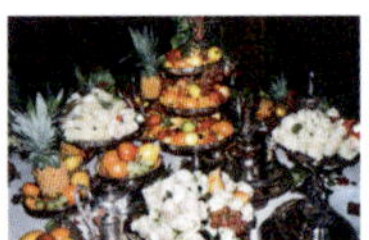

227. *left over*
Paris, 2012

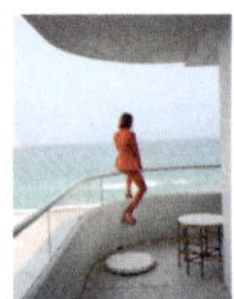

228. *Miranda*
Miami, 2015

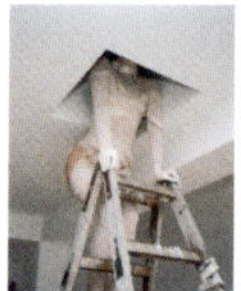

229. *glaring ascent,*
Berlin, 2013

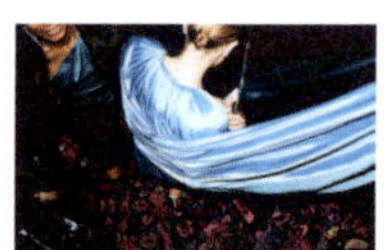

230. *anticyclone*
Paris, 2015

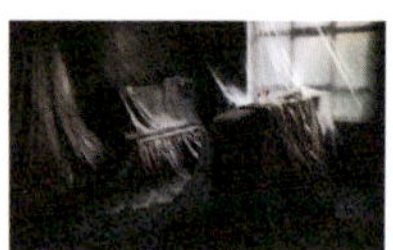

231. *ghosts toast*
Berlin, 2016

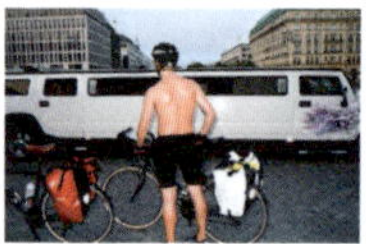

232. *tourists*
Berlin, 2014

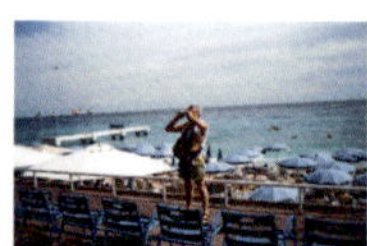

233. *cliché*
sur la Promenade des Anglais, 2011

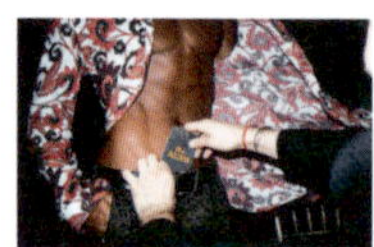

234. *secrets*
Miami, 2013

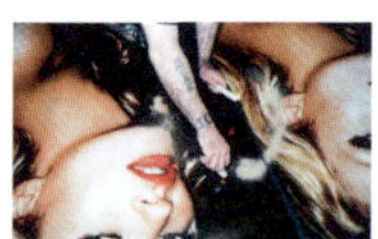

235. *Douglas and Kate*
Berlin, 2015

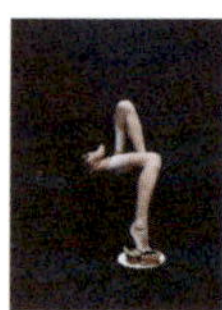

236. *nylon dressing*
Berlin, 2012

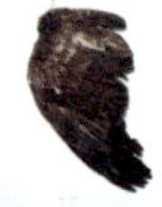

237. *forged Dürer*
Berlin, 2015

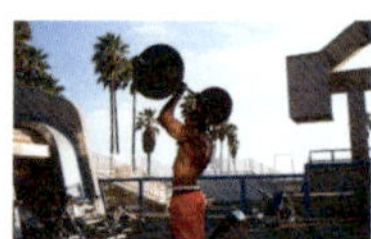

238. *playground*
Venice, 2014

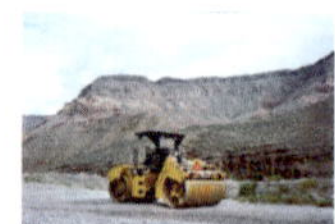

239. *platonic love*
Arizona, 2012

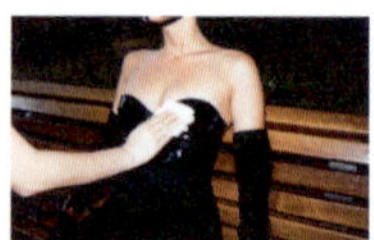

240. *at the cemetery*
Berlin, 2012

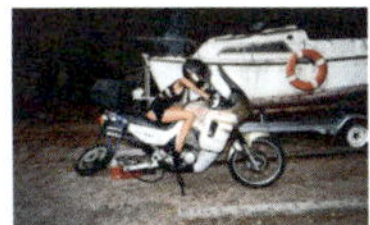

241. *full speed*
Los Masos, 2016

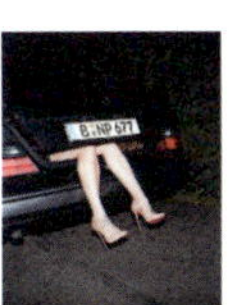

242. *Niki in her Benz*
Berlin, 2014

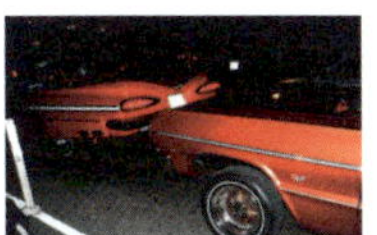

243. *sniff*
NYC, 2014

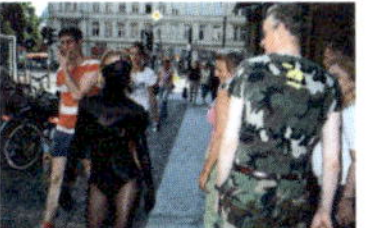

244. *Helga*
Berlin, 2012

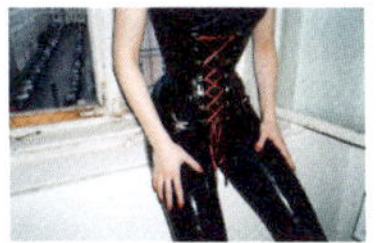

246. *Jana, à la fenêtre*
Berlin, 2009

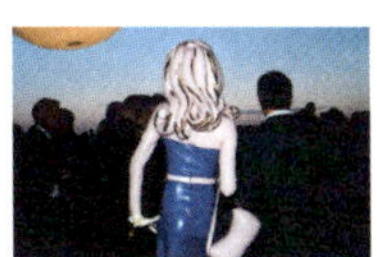

247. *Pandemonia*
Tempelhof, 2014

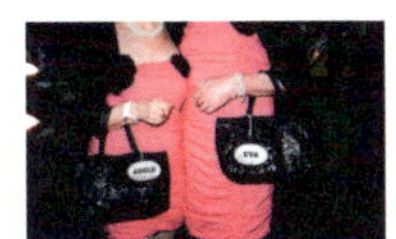

248. *Eva and Adele*
Berlin, 2014

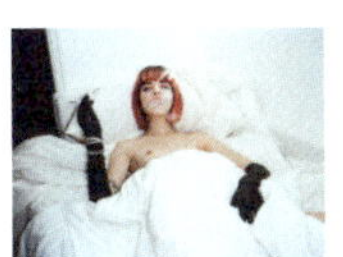

249. *Sita*
Paris, 2016

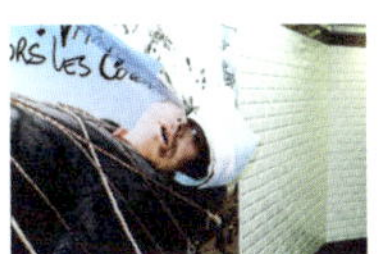

250. *poster, effrayé*
Paris, 2011

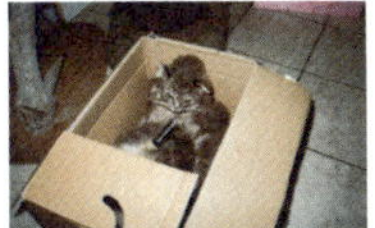

251. *cat in the box*
Berlin-Zehlendorf, 2012

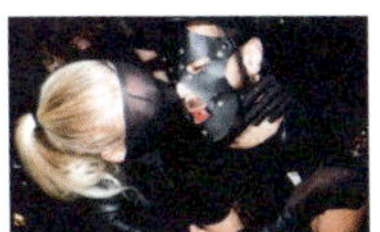

252. *silent romance*
Berlin, 2014

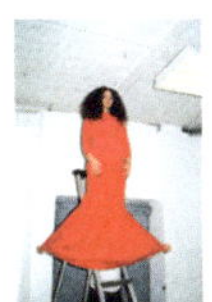

253. *Joy*
Berlin, 2017

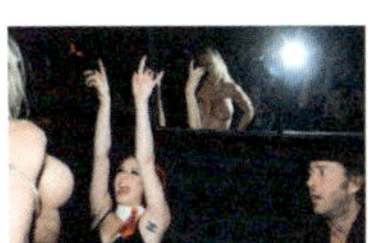

254. *Tracy and John*
Berlin, 2014

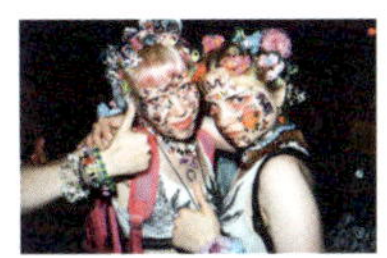

255. *camouflage*
Berlin, 2013